Descendants of Reuben Phillips

John Wesley Phillips

HERITAGE BOOKS
2008

HERITAGE BOOKS
AN IMPRINT OF HERITAGE BOOKS, INC.

Books, CDs, and more—Worldwide

For our listing of thousands of titles see our website
at
www.HeritageBooks.com

Published 2008 by
HERITAGE BOOKS, INC.
Publishing Division
100 Railroad Ave. #104
Westminster, Maryland 21157

Copyright © 1995 John Wesley Phillips

All rights reserved. No part of this book may be reproduced or transmitted in any form or by any means, electronic or mechanical, including photocopying, recording or by any information storage and retrieval system without written permission from the author, except for the inclusion of brief quotations in a review.

International Standard Book Numbers
Paperbound: 978-0-7884-0390-3
Clothbound: 978-0-7884-7120-9

TABLE OF CONTENTS

Introduction	v
Acknowledgements	vii
Chapter 1 – Maryland	1-14
Chapter 2 – Reuben Phillips Sr.	15-18
Chapter 3 – Thomas Phillips Sr.	19-20
Chapter 4 – William Phillips Sr.	21-36
Chapter 5 – Levi Phillips	37-38
Chapter 6 – Jonas Phillips	39-51
Chapter 7 – Jesse Phillips	52-53
Chapter 8 – Reuben Phillips Jr.	54-57
Chapter 9 – Adam Phillips	58-380
Adam Phiilps/Phillips	58-92
Eli A. Philips/Phillips	93-254
James O. Phillips	96-109
Reuben Frank Phillips	109-252
John R. Phillips Biography	120-168
Wes Phillips Biography	169-244
Christenberry Phillips	252-254
Elizabeth Phillips Wells	254-265
Eli K. Hutsell	254-258
Francis Marion Wells	259-265
Elisha Phillips	266-277
Archibald Russell	272-273
Sewell Phillips	273-275
Reverend Reuben Philips	278-370
Elisha Philips	338-366
Mary Ann Philips Pharr	371-373
Catherine Philips Bell	373-378
Hiram Philips	378-380
Bibliography	381-382

Index

1. Places and Things   383-392

2. People and Families   393-419

Maps

1. Yadkin River, Rowan County NC about 1790   15a
2. Phillips family in Rowan County N.C.   16a
3. Between Crane Creek and Dutch Second Creeks   17a
4. Mecklenburg County N.C. about 1790-1800   58a
5. Survey for Adam Phillips   59a
6. Peede, Texas about 1890   120a
7. Phillips Farm, Peede Texas   121a
8. Ballinger Texas about 1910   123a

INTRODUCTION

Adam Philips took his well worn hat from its peg near the door and stepped outside. It was a cool crisp fall morning with the leaves on the chestnuts a bright yellow and the sweetgums with a fiery scarlet red. It was harvest time, but first there were the daily chores to dispense with — milking the cows, feeding the chickens, and of coures catching up the mule.

Hannah busied herself in the kitchen fixing breakfast. Corn cakes, and bacon were already cooking, and now she stepped out to go to the spring house for milk, cream, and eggs. She had on a light-weight coat to protect her from the cold and she pulled her bonnet down to keep the morning sun out of her eyes.

It must have been much this way on the Phillips family farm in the early 1800s. It is really too bad we can't be more specific. Records now available show us much about the way of life on a Buncombe County North Carolina farm in the 1800s, but more will become available as time goes on.

What was it like to teach school in the mid-19th century? Reuben gives us some idea, and other sources supplement his rememberances. John R. Phillips well remembered the house where he grew up in Kaufman County, Texas. He could tell the size of the rooms, how far it was to the creek or the schoolhouse and what he did in his spare time.

There is no such thing as a complete family history. This is an ongoing project, and I hope to continue it for many years to come. It is currently at nearly 400 pages, but even more may be possible. Not everyone wants to know all about their ancestors. Maybe some of the things they did were not of the most noble sort. They were, however, my ancestors and in part they tell where I came from.

Acknowledgements

My Parents, John R. and Ada (Hall) Phillips began this project over 50 years ago, and to them I owe much of the material which appears in this volume. They in turn supplied their material to Gladys (Helms) Phillips who printed up the first short family history of the Descendants of Adam Phillips in 1968 from their notes.

In the 1970s, I published a work on the descendants of Adam Philips and the biography of the Reverend Reuben Philips. Shortly after the publication of this volume, my brother James R. Phillips found our Florida cousins and contacted Corinne and Russell Philips who supplied much information on their line and in turn gave me the name of Billie Philips of Ohio who filled in some blank spots in the story of the descendants of Reverend Reuben Philips.

My father had left us his memoirs before he died, and in the early 1980s I worked these up into the volume of his life story which is now included in the present volume.

In the late 1980s Margaret Coker of South Carolina filled me in on the descendants of Jonas Phillips, brother of Adam Philips. I had hired a researcher to find out about him and his descendants, but had not had much luck before she called me one night and soon thereafter sent me much of the material which appears in the chapter of his descendants.

I would like to thank Margery Phillips Gunn of Richardson Texas for giving me some advice on putting the family history together, and her brother Rupert Phillips Jr., who has supplied me with information on his line. Richard Phillips and Forrest Philips have also supplied information on their families, as have others too numerous to mention. I am especially indebted to Julian Philips for his history dealing with the Second World War.

James Wood of Oklahoma City supplied me with much material on William Phillips Sr. and his descendants.

I would like to thank Clio Phillips Jolly for information on Thomas Phillips of Tennessee. We cannot at this time connect him directly with William of Overton county, but when we make that connection, this information will appear in future volumes.

Lastly, but most important, I would like to thank the Coosa County, Alabama Historical Society for use of materials in "History of Coosa County, Alabama" by the Reverend George E. Brewer. This volume had long been out of print, but was reprinted by the society in 1990.

CHAPTER 1

Colonial Maryland in the mid 17th century was a shoreline economy, with houses built on or near the shoreline. Everyone had a small boat or shallop which they used for transportation and to take their produce which was usually tobacco, to the port for shipping across the Atlantic. The Eastern Shore, today known as the Delmarva Peninsula, was highly wooded and, away from the shoreline, still very much a wilderness. White oak, pine, tulip poplar, elm, horse chestnut, beech, birch, cypress, and cedar were the common trees. Blackberry, creeper, and poison ivy were all a tangle in the underbrush of dogwood, cherry, and spicebush.

The marshy areas predominated in the places the early settlers chose for dwelling spots, with cattail and marsh grass interspersed with the stands of bald cypress. Beavers and muskrats were common here, and great blue herons waded along the shore looking for such fish as spot, grunt, or croaker or perhaps a softshell crab in the shallows waiting for its shell to reharden after shedding. Redwing blackbirds were abundant everywhere, the dull colored females nesting among the cattails and marsh grass.

Back away from the tidal creeks, other animals were more common. Otter, mink, skunk, raccoon, opossum, rabbits and foxes as well as fisher cats and bobcats to prey on the small fry. Bears, mountain lions, locally called panthers, and wolves were also present and much too common to suit the early landowners.

From the Chesapeake Bay, inland for a good ways, the soil is a stiff white clay, while toward the Atlantic it tends toward sandy loam or even a nearly pure sand in places. The country ranges from nearly flat to slightly rolling in some, but is nowhere more than hilly. These soils with abundant rainfall made the growth of plant life a real jungle, especially to a people familiar with the well cropped lands of Great Britain. Deer and wild turkey were abundant and added much to the diet.

Farming came naturally in such a country, and tobacco soon became the most important economic crop, though corn often ran it a close second. Vegetable crops were planted as well as hay and small grains, especially wheat, rye, and oats. Linen and sometimes cotton were grown for clothing to add to the wool from the sheep. Fruit and nut trees including hickory and walnut were often cultivated, and livestock was raised including cattle, horses, pigs, sheep, goats, and a variety of poultry.

The waters of the Atlantic and Chesapeake Bay furnished fish, oysters, crabs, and other seafood in abundance. The woodlands produced trees for shipbuilding and furniture making as well as building. It was an age of wood - wooden tools, wooden trenchers to eat from, wooden spoons to eat with, and a wooden peg on which to hang your hat. It was a society regulated by the tides, and since the tides depend on the moon, so did the settlers, planning and planting by the phases of the moon and by the season.

Wild plants were abundant: White oak for pipestaves (barrels), red oak for wainscot, walnut, cedar, pine, cypress, chestnut, elm, ash, poplar were used for building. Mulberries, persimmons, plums, and grapes for fruit. Mast and chestnuts were food for swine and made the meat taste like that of Westphalia. Strawberries in April; mulberries in May, raspberries in June, maracocks in August. Cornsallat, violets, sorrel, purslane were spring herbs used for salads and in broth.

"There is a meal called omene (hominey) which is like furmenty which will malt and make good beer." Peas, beans, tobacco, muskmelons, watermelons, cucumbers, carrots, parsnips, turnips, cabbage, radish, wheat, barley, pears, apples, plums, peaches, pumpkins, apricots, figs, rapeseed, aniseseed, woad, madder, saffron, silkworms, pomegranates, oranges, lemon, hemp.

Into this society about March 1660 came John Taylor, with his children Arthur, John Jr., Robert, and Mary Taylor. With them came Thomas Phillips, Catherine Phillips, Dorothy Phillips, John Phillips, Thomas Phillips Jr., Elizabeth Phillips, and William Phillips.

The relationship between the Phillips and the Taylor families is unclear. Perhaps Thomas Phillips was the son-in-law or brother-in-law of John Taylor.

At any rate, Thomas Phillips was a farmer and a stock raiser as evidenced by the sale of cows to Mr. Brodaway in Talbot County Maryland on July 9, 1662 and in 1664 he bought one brown cow from Mr. Elonworth. In January 1665, "Phillips Range" was surveyed for Thomas Phillips on the Northeast branch of the Great Choptank. Before 1667, Thomas remarried to Mary Overton, widow of Francis Overton of Talbot County. Thomas had worked hard on his plantation by this time, only to see it destroyed in the hurricane of 1667 which tore through the Chesapeake region, destroying nearly everything in its path.

A big step in the history of the Eastern shore came in 1663 when Maryland made slavery legal. This blessing of cheap labor was to become in the next two hundred years one of the most controversial and devastating problems for the South.

Dorchester County was set aside from Talbot County in 1668. By 1669 John Taylor was dead. John Taylor's heirs assigned 50 acres called "Isaac's Field" to Thomas Phillips in July 1673.

In 1660, Parliament passed laws declaring that colonials could deal with other nations only through Great Britain and its ships. This caused a rise in shipping prices, and a drop in tobacco prices. Tobacco rotted at the dock, and all classes suffered, but small farmers like the Phillips family were hardest hit. Many families became tenants and in 1663, slavery was legalized to provide a working class.

Thomas Phillips soon had his "Plantation" even if it was only 50 acres or so. He would start with a house and perhaps a barn, and as his fortunes prospered he would add other outbuildings. Near his house or attached to it would be a cooking shed with its own chimney, with cooking utensils of iron and brass, pewter and wood. He might also store his gun and fishing tackle in this shed.

Inside the house, since there might not be a storage shed, many items might have been stored such as guns, swords, pistols, saddles, bridles, bedding, cookware, and clothes. The fireplace was large in most of these early houses, and might support half a beef, with a drip pan beneath to catch the drippings. It would be the job of one of the smaller children to turn the spit to cook the meat evenly (Hence the saying "done to a turn"). Cookware might include griddles, bakestones, and clay ovens, with a boiling pot hung from a crane which could be swung out from the fireplace for serving into wooden bowls called trenchers. Furniture was not fancy, and the table might be a board placed on trestles, and taken down when not in use to make more room, or a crude wooden table might be constructed for a work area and to support such utensils as mortar and pestle, brass skimmers, and rolling pins. Other furniture might consist of stools and benches, but often the children were expected to stand at table. Chests were often provided for clothing, but many homes simply hung the spare clothes around the walls or at the foot of the bed. Beds might be attached to the wall, and fixed with ropes underneath to support a mattress stuffed with straw. A bed wrench was supplied to tighten the cord supports for the mattress.

Though they lived on the frontier, these early settlers often brought some of the good life with them. Imported pottery was often found in the home, especially Spanish Majolica ware, but including English and Dutch Delftware, German blue on gray, Italian Subgraffito, and oriental china ware. The biggest variety was imported from England, and included brown stone ware, yellow slipware, Staffordshire blueware, coarse tempered ware from Devon, and polychrome. Indian pottery was sometimes used also. Some glass may have come from Jamestown, Virginia where there was a glass factory, but most glass was imported, and included bottles for wine and gin, goblets, vials, tumblers, beads, and some window glass.

Honey bees imported from England were beginning to become more widespread now, and Thomas might have a stand of bees in his yard or near the vegetable garden. If he had a cider press, it was probably near the orchard.

In 1672, Thomas Phillips, of Dorchester County Maryland sold his land grant "Phillips Range" on the Northeast Branch of the Choptank River, to Henry and Thomas Stevenson, his sons in law.

Isacks Field was surveyed in July 1673 for Thomas Phillips 50 acres.

In May 1674, Thomas Phillips acquired "Killom" 1,107 acres, in Talbot County on the North Side of the Choptank River.and in October he sold a tract of fifty acres called "Grovelling" to William Simpson. Cecil County Maryland was formed in 1674 and the first settlements were made in nearby New Jersey.

In June 1676 "Piney Point" of 250 acres was surveyed for Thomas Phillips on Hogg Creek in what is now Caroline County. The name Hog Creek may be significant, since hogs were allowed to roam everywhere and were identified through earmarks. Laws were passed in some colonies making it illegal to have a pig without ears, as it was presumed stolen.

Every plantation had a garden. Wheat, rye, barley, and oats were grown, also flax and occasionally hemp. The orchard might contain pears, apples, plums of several varieties, peaches, apricots, figs, grapes, and pomegranates. Wild fruits might be added including blackberries and maracocks(maypops). Oranges and lemons were imported.

In the nearby colony of Virginia, Bacon's rebellion had everything in turmoil. Maryland expansion rose as disgruntled colonists from Virginia moved into Maryland. Calico now began to be imported and later made in the colonies.

In 1677 "Cockiases Field" (Coquerricus Field) was patented for Thomas Phillips, It contained 600 acres, and was on Phillips Creek.(Later called Mill Creek.)

Wakefield was surveyed 8/4/1680 when it came from Thomas Phillips. Thomas Phillips Jr. in 1681 acquired 50 acres a part of "Rosses Range". Rosses Range to John Ross 12/22/1681 split to Edwin Ross, Thomas Phillips and John Harrington 50 acres each. In 1682, John Edmondson was the attorney for Mary Phillips when she sold 250 acres on Hogg Creek called Piney Point. This indicates that Thomas died about 1680.

Pennsylvania was founded in 1681 and in 1682 William Penn also acquired New Jersey and part of Delaware. Pennsylvania had some freedom of religion, and quakers in particular came into the area. New Jersey attracted French Huguenots. In 1688 William and Mary became the King and Queen of England.

Thomas Phillips Jr. now comes firmly into the record with 50 acres "William's Good Will" between Blackwater and Slaughter Creek. In 1690, John and Mabel Ross sold 58 acres between Hudson Creek and Arthur Wright's Creek on the north side of the Little Choptank River. The weather at this time was unusually mild. William and Mary College was founded in 1693.

The year 1697 began with a severe winter. Thomas Phillips Jr. was listed as a cooper when he and his wife Cornelia sold 'William's Good Will" in July 1698 to John Pollard. The wet cooper made barrels from white oak and also sap carriers, tubs, and piggins. The dry cooper or slack cooper used maple, oak, ash, hickory, and chestnut for containers which kept sugar, flour, and cakes. The white cooper used pine, birch, maple, ash for boxes, baskets, pails, bowls, and other containers. Maple sap buckets were made from maple wood with hickory for the hoops and birch pins.

Indian tribes of the Eastern Shore were of Algonquin stock, and in Dorchester County the Nanticokes, a branch or related tribe to the Delaware lived. Land was granted in Dorchester County to the Choptank Indians in 1699 and in 1704 to the Nanticokes. The land was surveyed in 1721 and confirmed in 1723.

In 1701 John and Elizabeth Barnes and William and Grace Lawyer sold "Phillips Range" to Henry King. The town of Nottingham was founded this year in Cecil County, Maryland. Delaware was separated from Pennsylvania in 1704.

In March 1704, Thomas Phillips made his will in which he names sons Thomas and Rubin. In 1707 brother John Phillips made his will which was proven the following February. In this will he names sons William, Thomas, and Benony and daughters Elizabeth Ferguson, Mary Robson, and Anne. In 1708, Christiana Presbyterian Church was founded in Cecil County.

John Taylor Jr. died about 1710. He appears to have married Dorothy Phillips and had sons Thomas and William.

In August 1711, the will of Thomas Phillips was proven, naming brother William and Sisters Ann Phillips and Mary Robson.

In 1715, the first stock act was established in Cecil County, Maryland. Rangers were required to impound stock found out of control.

In 1716 Thomas Phillips was granted land called Rachoon Range which he had occupied from at least 1714 in Cecil County Maryland. 1717 was the year of the Great Snow Storm.

In 1720, "The Rock" Presbyterian Church was founded in Cecil County and in 1723 Bethel Presbyterian.

In 1723, Cornelia Ross Mackeel was deceased. John Tregoe and William Phillips were listed as near kin. In 1724 Reuben Phillips was also listed.

October and November 1728 proved to be wet months.

The Phillips family settled near head of Elk, on land once owned by the Susquehannock Indians of Iroquoian stock, though by the time the Phillipses settled there the Indians had withdrawn to Pennsylvania. Still, they didn't relinquish their claim to the area for many years.

Smallpox broke out in Cecil County in 1730.

In 1731 Thomas Phillips was granted a tract of land known as Forrest in Cecil Co. Maryland.

September 1732 was a dry time. It had rained so little that many of the streams, especially in the mountians were nearly dry but on the 21st, a downpour came which soaked everything.

In 1732 Thomas Phillips was granted a tract of land known as Phillips Bottom in Cecil County on which he had farmed at least since 1730.

September 1733 was a wet month as was October. Catherine Phillips was born 28, April 1734 (daughter of John and Elizabeth?). Mary Phillips daughter of John and Elizabeth was born 29 May 1737. (St. Mary Anne's Parish Register 1709 - 1799 Cecil Co. MD)

In 1735, Thomas Phillips and wife Eliner of Cecil County Maryland sold a tract of land called Phillips Bottom to Samuel Houston.

George Whitefield the famous Methodist Minister visited Cecil County in 1739 and 1740. It was not a good year. Fear spread quickly among the settlers when a slave rebellion centered in Prince George's County Maryland this winter nearly succeeded.

In 1740 Thomas and John Phillips were Corporals in the Cecil County Militia and William, Rubin, and Samuel Phillips were privates.

By 1742, the Indians of the Eastern Shore, in conjunction with the Shawnee to the north plotted an uprising against the Colony of Maryland. Friendly Indians intervened and informed the settlers and war was averted. The petition to create Frederick County through Division of Prince George's County dated October 16, 1742 included the signature of John Philips.

In 1746 in Dorchester County Eliner Phillips was appointed Administrix for the estate of Thomas Phillips deceased. Inventory of the Estate of Thomas Phillips Dorchester Co. Md. April 10, 1746: Items included: Wearing Apparel, old broad cloth, Old Shalloon Cloth, 22 metal buttons, 2 hanks of mohair, old Simeon Wheel, a chest, 1 old mare and one yearling, 2 heifers, 2 sorry cows, 1 small bull, 1 small heifer, 6 sows, 12 sorry pigs, a parcel of old iron, one old bed wearing 63, old bed covering, old bedstead and cord, 1 raw hide, an old testament and a pocket book, 9 pence in money, 2 quart bottles, earthen ware, 1 broken pot and a pair of pothooks, a peck and pottle(4 pints) of salt, 98 pounds of dried pork, 2 barrels of corn, 10 lbs of new feathers, a pair of old wool cards, 16 pounds of hog fat, a parcel of old lumber, wheat growing in the ground, 2 ewes with their lambs, 500 pounds of tobacco. The total being worth 26 pounds, 17 shillings, and 2 pence. Taking this inventory were William Stanford and Isaac Partridge.

The account of Elinor Phillips of Dorchester of all the singular goodes and chattles of Thomas Phillips late of Dorchester.

Disbursements
To Peter Grimes 300
To Edward Mills 355
Betty Vaun 100
Grissel Norton 209
Dr Wm Murray 2187
Henry Hupper 1160

Disbursements 1961
Balance 7111
Total 27172
(26)
Creditors William Murray Rebecca Wall. Next of kin: only Children.
Administrix Elinor Philips
26.17.2 Apr 10 1746
June 12, 1746

St. Mary's Church was built in 1742 in North Elk Parish which had been laid out in 1706. The new church was built in 1742 and was a pretty brick building with a hipped roof and a barrel vaulted ceiling. Many of the congregation came to church by boat, since what few roads there were very bad. Queen Anne presented the congregation with a new bible.

[Hiatus]

There is a problem connecting the Phillips family of Dorchester County with Thomas Phillips of Cecil County Maryland. It is possible that he is connected with that family, but it is also possible that he is not. Here are the arguments:

For:
1. Thomas Phillips in his will of 1704 listed sons Rubin and Thomas. Rubin remained in Dorchester County, but Thomas disappears from the record.

2. Thomas Phillips of Cecil County Maryland had wife (listed on deed records) Elinor.

3. An Elinor Phillips was the administrix of the estate of Thomas Phillips of Dorchester County in 1746.

4. No other Thomas Phillips found in the records of Dorchester County matches this Thomas.

5. Thomas Phillips of Cecil County had a son Reuben perhaps named for his brother who remained in Dorchester County.

6. Thomas Phillips of Cecil County Maryland named one of his parcels of land "Rackoon Range".

7. Reuben Phillips of Frederick County who was born in Cecil County named his first parcel of land in Frederick County "Rachoon Range"

8. Reuben Phillips of Cecil County named his first son Thomas.

Against:
1. A Thomas Phillips appears on the records of Cecil County in 1753 as owing a debt in the county. (This could be an unpaid debt left by Thomas when he died, since his estate was proven in Dorchester County)

2. A Thomas Phillips appears on the Records of Frederick County Maryland in 1762. (Perhaps a brother of Reuben?) (see 1762 below)

In 1747 a tract of land known as Indian Quarter was resurveyed for William Thomas and Rubin Phillips into a new tract called Thomas Choice.

Frederick County Maryland was created by an act of the Maryland Assembly passed in 1748 from Prince Georges County. The bounds began at the lower side of Rock Creek from there by a straight line to the Patauxtant River and with that river to the line of Baltimore County and with those lines to the boundary of Maryland.

Much of the country is part of the Piedmont section of the east coastal plain, though in the beginning the western part of the county was traversed by parts of the Blue Ridge chain known locally as Catoctin Mountain and South Mountain. The Monocacy River formed the principal stream with numerous smaller streams often in deep valleys crossing the county in other parts. Early settlers simply moved onto uncleared land and girdled the trees as the Indians had taught them, planting corn, beans, and squash in hills among the stark skeletons of the departed forest. Stock was allowed to roam free in the forests eating acorns, nuts, and other natural products and being fed only in times of severe weather.

Tobacco was the main cash crop, supplemented by small grains and corn. Each farm would have its own vegetable garden and fruit orchard and very likely a plot of flax to make into linen for clothes and household linens. Farm animals often included one or more oxen, possibly a horse, a cow or two, several pigs and numerous barnyard fowl. Sheep were often kept for wool.

The Spring of 1748 was extremely wet. It rained continuously from March 20th through the 22nd, but cleared on the afternoon of Wednesday March 23rd. It rained again the sixth and seventh of April. All the streams were flooded.

The tide of settlement was moving westward. The German settlements, long centered at Philadelphia, now began to concentrate around Baltimore.

The estate of John Jones of Frederick County, Maryland, was proven early in 1750(Feb 27, 1749 on the records). Appraisers were Zebulon Hollingsworth and David Houston. Nearest kin were Elore Catherine Philips, and Catron Jones. Executor was Robert Jones.

On September 25, 1751 Levi Phillips was born to Reuben

and Catherine Phillips and the birth was recorded on the records of St. Mary Anne Parish in Cecil County Maryland.

In 1753, Thomas Phillips of Cecil Co. Maryland owed money to James Bayard.

On March 14, 1753 Reuben Phillips received a tract of Land in Frederick County Maryland called Rackoon Range at Cancyachuga Manor. The same year John Phillips received a tract of land called Resurvey on Walnut Bottom.

The move to Frederick County from Cecil County was not easily accomplished. During the 1750s the English colonies were involved in the French and Indian War, and Indian attacks forced Reuben to move back to Cecil County at least once during this period.

Though more mountainous than Cecil County, Frederick County had much the same plants and animals as found on the Eastern Shore. White tailed deer, bear, wolf, elk, cougar, flying squirrels, red and gray fox, beaver, muskrat, long tailed weasel, raccoons, possums, porcupines, gray squirrels, rabbits, and rodents were abundant. Birds included great blue herons sometimes called shitepokes, great horned owl, red-tailed hawk, bald eagles, mockingbirds, cat birds, oven birds, blackbirds, crows, kingfishers on the branches along the streams, and vireos and warblers in the bushes.

Plants were still the familiar ones, with virginia pine, white oak, mockernut hickory, yellow poplar or tulip tree, big tooth aspen, sassafras, beech, dogwood, red maple, southern red oak, chestnut oak, speckled alder, willow oak, black willow, bay berry, redbay, and red cedar all well represented. Herbaceous plants included broomsedge, asters, horseweed, crabgrass, pigweed, green brier, and poison ivy sometimes reaching huge proportions where it was moist.

The Rattlesnake was still to be feared, so too were the cottonmouth and copperhead, and a variety of harmless reptiles such as blacksnakes and garter snakes were abundant. Turtles, though they could bite much harder than the snakes, were not feared, but looked on as food. Though the common box turtles were not eaten, many of the larger turtles such as the snapping turtles were considered toothsome.

Frederick Maryland was a relatively new town, seven years old, with 200 houses and a German and English population with a church for each. There were livly times with balls, fish feasts, dancing schools, christenings, cock fights, horseraces, chariot races, and parties, which added to the atmosphere of the area. Nearly everyone attended church with the Episcopal being supported by the government. General Braddock and the troops camped nearby in April of 1755 and added some new entertainments for the local populace.

About 1756 Reuben Phillips owed a debt to Edward Beatty In Frederick County, Maryland.

On January 13, 1757 the following notice appeared: "Reuben Phillips living near John Digges Mill on Little Pipe Creek in Frederick County has a stray gelding in his possession." If no one claimed the stray, it became his property. (Digges Mill was evidently near Digges Works - a copper mine)

Reuben Philips name appears on a Frederick County Muster Roll under Captain John Middaugh about 1757.

On December 27, 1757 Reuben Phillips was born to Reuben and Catherine Phillips and the birth was recorded on the records of St. Mary Anne Parish in Cecil County Maryland.

On August 18, 1759 Reuben Phillips was granted a parcel of land known as Pleasant Valley in Frederick County Maryland.

On February 18, 1760 John Phillips received a tract of land in Frederick County Maryland called Laugh and be Fatt. It had been cold, but now thawing began, with a mist in the morning and sun and warm winds in the afternon. As the weather cleared, the nights became frigid. It was hog killing time.

June Court Frederick County Maryland 1761:
Sundry Inhabitants, unnamed, present a petition to the court "... your petitioners are in very great want of a road from Conococheague to cross the mountain to Baltimore Town to transport their wheat to market"...(Rice, Millard Milburn This Was the Life, Genealogical Publishing Co. Baltimore 1984.) Proposed road goes by John Digges Mill.

March 1762 Thomas Phillips of Frederick Co. Md. owed a debt to Lawrence Owen.

On December 27, 1762 Adam Phillips was born in Frederick County Maryland, the son of Reuben and Catherine Phillips.

In May 1763, the first blows fell on forts in the west in "Pontiac's Conspiracy". By July, Pontiac had seized all but the strongest western forts. Fort Pitt on the doorstep of Western Maryland was under attack which lasted until mid August.

In 1765, the dollar appeared in Western Maryland being worth 4 shillings six pence. Bennet Allen, a minister appointed by Lord Baltimore caused a scandal in Frederick County by his bad language and horrible acts of breaking into the church before the funeral of his predecessor the Reverend Thomas Bacon.

On October 17, 1765 Reuben Phillips assigned a tract of land called Hunting Lott to Samuel Chase all of Frederick Co. Maryland.

The Stamp Act took effect November 1, 1765, but was never implemented in Western Maryland. In late 1765 Captain Evan Shelby (Born 1720 Wales) of Frederick Co. Testified under oath that between three and four hundred westerners with guns and tomahawks had gathered at Fredericktown to march on Annapolis.

The tobacco crop didn't do as well in 1766 as it had in previous years on the Phillips farm. Tobacco required heavy care and continuous cultivation. Several small plots were chosen in moist ground. The tobacco was fertilized through the burning of brush on the field prior to plowing and planting. The tobacco itself was sowed in mid January during a thaw and raked into the rich soil to insure proper sprouting. More brush was brought in to keep the young plants warm as they began to grow. The soil was soon worn out from years of cultivation and even with careful weeding and cropping, the plants were chlorotic. This was discouraging and the Phillips family must have thought of moving to find better land.

Corn and small grains fared better. An area was selected and fenced each year which had laid fallow for a year or more. The area was plowed, the crops sown cultivated, and harvested. The fences were then taken down and the stock was allowed to forage off the stubble. If allowed to remain fallow too long, the sandy soil soon went to shrubs.

The temperatures in mid-March of 1767 warmed to near 70 by the 22nd. Daffodils, hyacinth, and violets began to bloom and almond and apricot trees also flowered. Highs cooled down to the fortys by the end of march and the first of April, but a gradual warm up occurred, so that by the end of april 70s were the rule. The asparagus and radish in Catherine's garden grew tremendously and the peas and beans did well.

The muster roll of Frederick County Maryland shows that Rubin Philips order was paid to Thomas Beatty Jr. on April 1, 1767 for service in the recent wars. A good soaking rain had fallen on the 3rd and 4th of April, and just after the first of May, the rains returned and continued through the middle of the month.

On July 4, 1768 Elizabeth Phillips was born to Reuben and Catherine Phillips and the birth was recorded on the records of St. Peter's Lutheran Church Woodsboro, Frederick County Maryland.

On August 16, 1768 Reuben Phillips of Frederick County Maryland sold a tract of land known as Hunting Lott to John Smouce.

In 1769, the will of John Phillips of Frederick County was proven, listing wife Elizabeth and children Sarah, Catherine, Rachel, Grace, and Ruth.

On December 11, 1769 Reuben Philips and wife Catherine sold a tract of land in Frederick County Maryland called Pleasant Valley to Henry Lantiss.

CHAPTER 2

Reuben Phillips Sr.

Compiled by John Wesley Phillips, P.O. Box 1073, Fritch, TX 79036

Reuben Phillips Sr. born ca. 1715/1720 in Cecil Co. MD. Son of Thomas Phillips of Cecil County whose wife was Eleanor _____
died after 1800 probably in Oglethorpe Co. Georgia.

1740 - In Cecil County Militia with his brother William
1747 Owned part of <u>Indian quarter</u> in Cecil County
1751 Son Levi born (birth recorded in Episcopal Church Cecil Co. MD) September 25.
1754 - Patented <u>Rackoon Range</u> in Fredrick Co. MD
1755 - Patented <u>Hunting Lott</u> in Fredrick Co. MD
1757 - Son Reuben born December 27 (Birth Recorded Episcopal Church Cecil County MD)
1759 - Patented <u>Pleasant Valley</u> in Fredrick Co. MD
1762 - Son Adam born December 27, 1762 in Fredrick Co. MD
1767 - Reuben was paid a bounty in Frederick Co. MD for military services
1768 - Daughter Elizabeth born (Birth recorded St. Peter's Lutheran Church Fredrick Co. MD)
1769 John Phillips (?Reuben's brother) died in Fredrick Co. MD
wife Elizabeth. Children Sarah, Catherine, Rachel, Grace, Ruth.
1769 - All land owned by Reuben Phillips and wife Catherine in Fredrick Co. MD was sold.

In 1770, St. John's Church was in operation in Salisbury, N. C. Guilford and Surry Counties were separated from Rowan County this year. The assembly passed an act regulating the town of Salisbury, providing for a town commons and fire control. There was no sheriff in Rowan County because of the movement of the Regulators.

Queen's College was chartered January 15, 1771 at Charlotte, North Carolina. Run by the Presbyterians, it offered a good classical education to those interested in things other than the three R's. The Union Lutheran Pine Church was formed eight miles Southeast of Salisbury. The Rowan House was in operation in Salisbury this year. The Battle of Alamance was in May. In 1773 the Zion or Organ Lutheran Church was founded.

1774 - Reuben witnessed a deed of land in Mecklenburg Co. NC to William Phillips (Probably his son William who would have been about 25). Even in the backwoods of North Carolina, there was unrest among the citizens because of the British policys. The closing of the port of Boston alarmed people all across the British Colonies. On June 1, 1774, everyone stopped all activities except the necessary ones for a day of mourning.

Rowan and Mecklenburg Counties were frontier counties. The men dressed in typical pioneer fashion with hunting shirts, mid calf length breeches, leggings and moccasins of deerskin while the women wore simple linen or woolen dresses and often went barefoot in the summertime. Bonnets were common headgear for the women, though some wore men's hats. Oxen were still in common use, and cabins often had a dirt floor and a sleeping loft above for the children.

Plant life in Western Carolina must have been similar to that of western Maryland, with large chestnut trees, oak, pine, walnut, black gum, black locust, cherry, beech, yellow poplar, and sassafras. Magnolias were more common here than in the old state, but many of the common herbaceous plants were similar and the flowers were well known.

Mammals included bear, deer, bobcat, mountain lion, groundhogs, squirrels, rodents, fox, otter, beaver, muskrat, possum, raccoon, moles, weasels, mink, and skunk. Game birds were turkey, quail (often called partridge by the early settlers), ducks, geese, and passenger pigeons by the thousands.

Fishing was continued, much as they were used to in Maryland. Fish traps had been placed in the rivers by the Indians, and now the settlers operated these traps and kept them in repair. Fish taken were shad, mullet, redhorse, rockfish, suckers, catfish, and bream. Shad were caught in the shoals just above Dutchman's creek.

The frontier atmosphere was tempered by the law. In 1775 Thomas Herd was whipped at the Whipping Post and Stephan Herring and Joseph Pettaway were hanged as criminals. The Revolution loomed near, and Griffith Rutherford was appointed Brigadier General for the Salisbury District. On March 4, 1775 Thomas Polk was granted 187 acres on Safford's Branch of Crooked Creek joining Robert Maxwell and William Black.

The people of the various counties in North Carolina came together for meetings of committees of safety and other groups designed to show union against British regulations. Many counties had meetings in 1775 in which a set of resolves were drawn up to show their displeasure against the British policies.

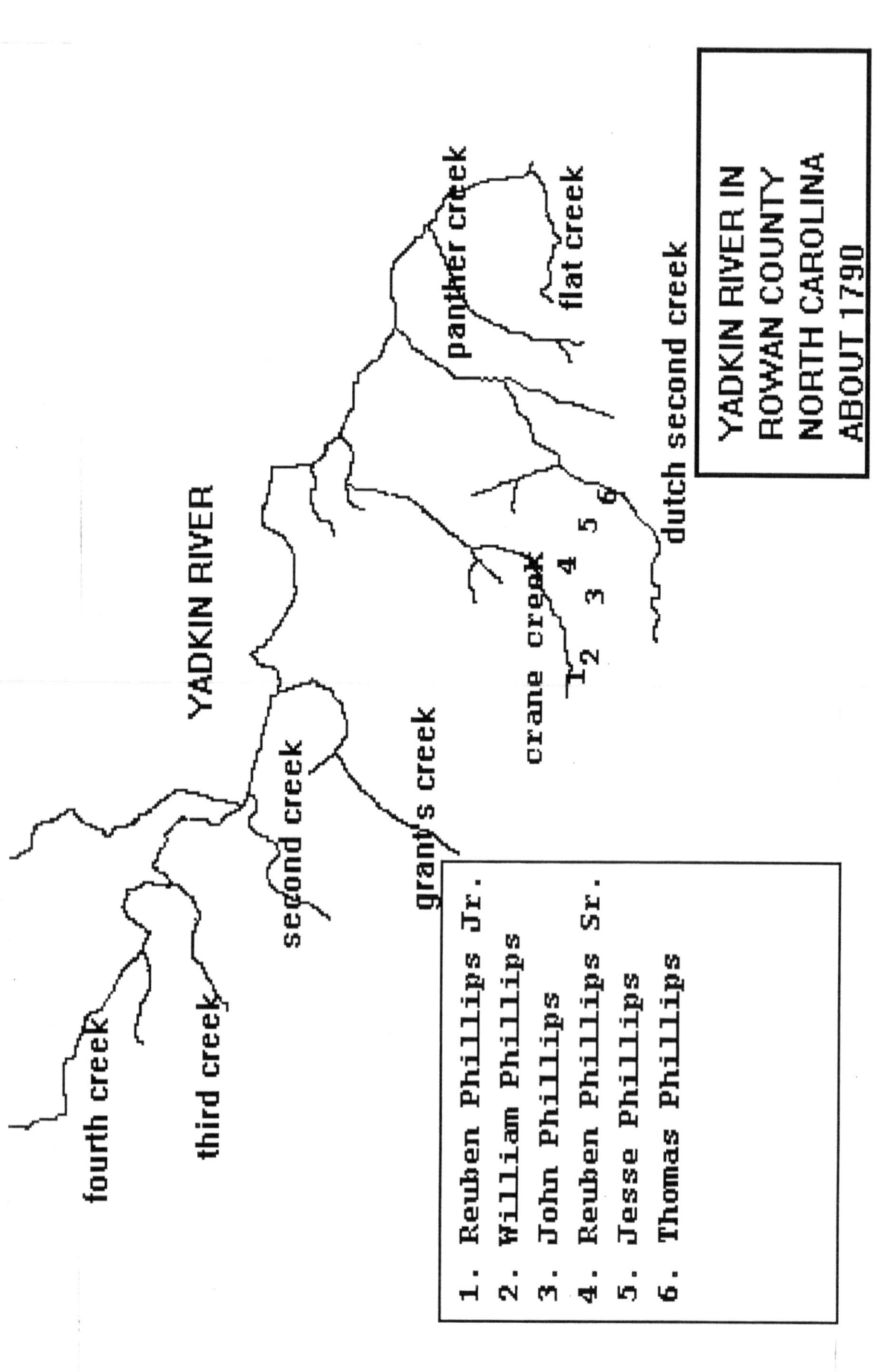

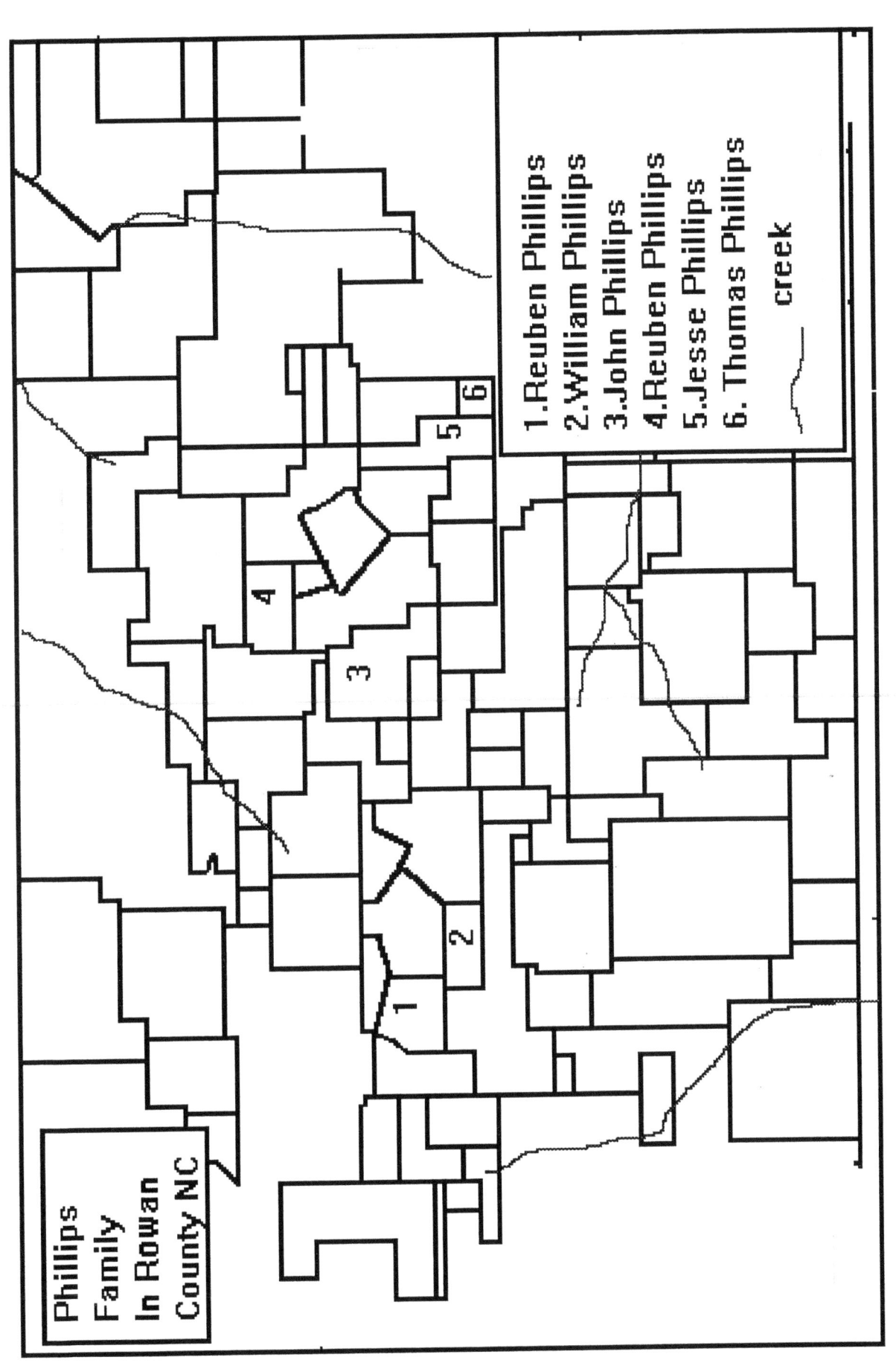

1778 - Reuben and Son Levi on Tax list in Rowan Co. NC
On November 5, 1778 Reuben Phillips was appointed Road Overseer in Rowan County.

1783 - Reuben with sons Reuben, William, Levi, Jesse, Reuben, and Thomas are on the Tax list in Rowan County.

name	acres	horses & mules	cattle	propty val.
Levy Fillips	10"10	20	6	36"10
Rubin Phillips	20	25	10	55
Wm. Phillips	14	15	4	33
John Fillips	12	18	6	36
Jessey Fillips	24	16	5	45
Rubion Phillips	14	12	4	36
Thos. Phillips	10	16	3	29

Horse racing was a common pastime in Rowan County, and though the Phillipses bred horses, few of them were probably race horses, but rather brood mares for the production of mules. Among them, the family owned 122 horses and mules, which would indicate that they were breeding them. The acres is the value per ten acres for tax purposes, so 10"10 is 101 acres.

On October 10, 1783 Reuben Phillips was granted 200 acres on Crane Creek. "10 Oct. 1783 State Grant @50 shilling the 100 A to Reuben Phillips 200 A on S Fork of Crane Creek at a Flat Rock marked RP & Crossing the Mirey Branch.

On February 8, 1785 Francis Ross was appointed overseer on the road instead of Reuben Phillips.

The war years now being over, a bit of prosperity showed its head in sections of the country, and the Phillips family determined to leave Rowan County. Reuben with his sons Thomas and Levi moved to Wilkes County Georgia, and in 1792 were in the section set off to become Oglethorpe County. William and perhaps Jesse moved to Tennessee. Jonas moved first to Montgomery County North Carolina, and then to Pickens District South Carolina. Reuben Jr. moved to Wilkes County North Carolina where he died in 1814, and Adam moved first to Mecklenburg County and then in 1803 to Buncombe County North Carolina.

1786 - Reuben and Levi move to Wilkes County Georgia
1787 - Son Adam moves to Mecklenburg Co. NC
1789 - Timothy Brown appointed road overseer in the place of Reuben Phillips. On August 3, 1789 Timothy Brown was appointed road overseer from John Graham's to a pond near Reuben Phillips.

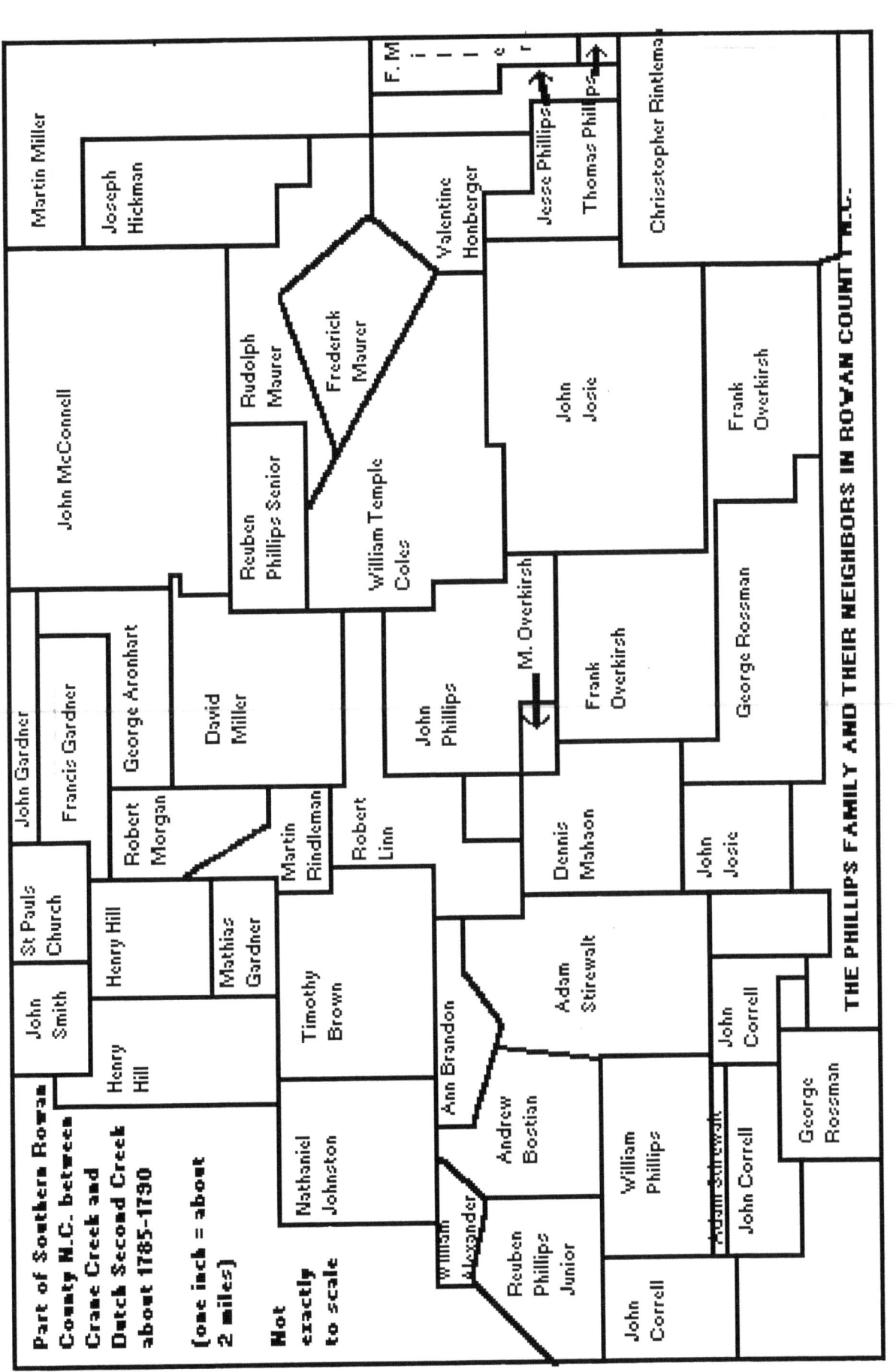

In 1789, Reuben Philips of Wilkes Co. GA. received 142 acres of land. On November 24, 1789 Reuben and Catherine Phillips of Wilkes County Georgia gave a title bond to land in Wilkes County to Adam Phillips of Mecklenburg County North Carolina.

1790 - Sons Levi and Thomas in Georgia. Sons William, Reuben, Jonas, Jesse, and Adam still in North Carolina. Tuesday August 3, 1790 - Overseer of roads: William Anderson instead of Reuben Phillips.

1792 - Reuben's land in Wilkes Co. GA becomes part of the new county of Oglethorpe.

Levi and Reuben Phillips were on the Tax List for Oglethorpe County Georgia in 1798.

In 1800, Reuben Phillips appeared on the census of Oglethorpe County Georgia with two males in his household, two females, and no slaves. Two Levi Phillipses appeared on the same census.

CHAPTER 3

1. Thomas Phillips Sr. born ca. 1745 Cecil Co. MD d. ca 1834 Jackson Co. GA wife Elizabeth

On June 30, 1781 Thomas Philips entered 150 Acres of land on the waters of Northwards Creek next to Nicholas Trosper and John Henderson and including Trosper's Improvements.

Thomas Phillips appeared on the 1783 tax list of Rowan County, NC.

Adam Phillips son of Thomas and Elizabeth Phillips was born in Rowan County in 1783. Henry Phillips son of Thomas and Elizabeth Phillips was born in Rowan County N.C. in 1784. On November 4, 1784 Thomas Phillips was granted 100 Acres on Dutch Second Creek.

On May 6, 1785 Thomas Phillips was appointed a Justice to take taxables in Rowan County.

Reuben with his sons Thomas and Levi moved to Wilkes County Georgia, and in 1792 were in the section set off to become Oglethorpe County.

John and Thomas Phillips appeared on the tax list for Jackson County Georgia in 1800.

Thomas Phillips was on the 1804 tax list for Jackson County, Georgia.

Thomas and Adam Phillips appear on the 1810 Tax list for Jackson County, Georgia.

In 1817 Thomas Phillips was granted land in Jackson County Georgia. He was on the Tax list in Jackson County this year, and was probably granted land on which he was already living. Adam, Levi, and two other Thomases were on this tax list.

On May 5, 1834, the will of Thomas Phillips son of Reuben and Catherine was proved in Jackson County Georgia, listing wife Elizabeth, and sons Adam, John, Thomas, Henry, and Levi.

Children:
    1-1. Thomas b. ca. 1775 - wife Elizabeth Bellough (married 08/07/1800)(or m. Thomas I)
    1-2. Adam born 1783 Rowan Co. NC married Temperance Pierce   Children - Martha, Tempy, William F., Elihu, John, Anne b. 1812 m. ___

_ Gordon.

1-3. Henry b. ca 1785 believed to have married Nicea Ward daughter of Benjamin and Rachel Ward children:

        1-3-1. John ca 1820 m. Nancy;
        1-3-2. Simeon b. 1822 m. Elizabeth_____;
        1-3-3. Levi b. 1823 m. Matilda _____
        1-3-4. James b. 1825 m. Martha _____
        1-3-5. John b. 1829
        1-3-6. Francis b. 1832
        1-3-7. Louisa b. 1836
        1-3-8. Martha b. 1838

1-4. Levi b ca. 1790 (It is believed that this is the Levi who married Julia Ann Booth on Nov. 14, 1828 Tuscaloosa Co. Alabama. If so children were: Amanda M. 1832, Julia Ann 1835, Mary Susannah   , James W. 1844 and John M. 1849)

CHAPTER 4

2. William Phillips Sr. b. 1749 Cecil Co. MD; d. 1843 Overton Co. TN wife unknown.

On June 9, 1774 Reuben Phillips, another Reuben Phillips and John Black witnessed the sale of a tract of land from Edward and Rebecca Black to William Phillips in Mecklenburg County, North Carolina. Mecklenburg County North Carolina was formed in 1762 from Anson County. It was named for Charlotte of Mecklenburg, the new queen. The population in 1790 was 11,393 and growth was slow. By 1850 the population was only 13,914. Union and Cabarrus counties were formed from Mecklenburg and by 1850 they had a combined population of around 20,000. In the early years, Mecklenburg County was involved in the Regulator movement which erupted in violence in 1771.

In 1776, William Phillips served under Colonel Locke and General Rutherford in a retaliatory strike against the Cherokees at Hiway in Tennessee. General Rutherford led 1900 men across the mountains. The casualties were buried at Third Creek Church.

On February 9, 1778 William Phillips filed for 100 acres of land on the headwaters of Dutch Second Creek next to Andrew Holtshouser, Wendle Miller, and Jesse Phillips in Rowan County North Carolina.

William appeared on the 1783 tax list of Rowan County.

Moses Phillips son of William Phillips was born in 1786 in Rowan County N.C. Levi Phillips signed the Revolutionary Warrant of William Phillips in 1786. On October 25, 1786 William Phillips was granted 200 acres on Dutch Second Creek.

When the Phillips family split up in the late 1780's, William appears either on the Mecklenburg County census or on the Wilkes County, North Carolina Census in 1790. William went west, settling first in Blount County, Tennessee and later in Overton Co. Tennessee.

Thomas Phillips son of William Phillips was born in 1788.

Adam Phillips son of William Phillips was born in 1794.

Beaty Phillips son of William Phillips was born in 1796.

Samuel Phillips son of William Phillips was born in 1798.

William Phillips appeared on the Census of Overton County

Tennessee in 1820.

Moved to Blount Co. TN ca. 1815 then to Overton Co. TN

William Phillips appeared on the Census of Overton County Tennessee in 1820.

William Phillips appeared on the 1830 census of Overton County, Tennessee aged 80 to 90.

On September 24, 1832 William Phillips of Overton County Tennessee applied for a pension for his service in the Revolutionary War in Rowan County North Carolina. He had served under Colonel Francis Locke and Captain Berringer.

Pension Record: [William Philips] states that in the fall of the year [1776] he entered the service of the United States as a volunteer rifleman for a tour of three months in the County of Rowan, North Carolina. Marched into a place now called Hiway in the State of Tennessee, then Cherokee Nation, against the Indians...They had a small engagement at the Valley Towns, but the Indians soon fled. They destroyed the town and took some prisoners [including] an Indian called Hicks and his wife with many other prisoners and some property. They found some torys with the Indians upon another occasion while he was with some other men cutting down corn. They were fired on by the Indians and some were killed. One man next to him was shot down.

Some time after this he was drafted for three months... He marched to a place called New Providence in the Same State and was there stationed and remained for the whole time of his service and was discharged without being in any engagement.

William Phillips appeared on the 1840 census of Overton County Tennessee aged 90 to 100.

William Phillips died in Overton County Tennessee about 1843.
Children Reuben ca. 1781, Moses 1786, Thomas 1788, Adam 1794, Beaty 1796, Samuel 1798
    2-1 Reuben Phillips b. ca. 1780 N.C. d. ca. 1855 Arkansas. Married Alfretta "Feriba" _____ (She born 1785 N.C. d. ca. 1855 Arkansas.)
        2-1-1 Reuben Phillips Jr. b. 15 May 1810 Overton Co. Tennessee d. 5 April 1883 m. Elizabeth Hammons.
            2-1-1-1 John Phillips b. 15 November 1837 Overton Co. Tenn. d. 23 April 1928

Whorton Creek Arkansas. m. Mary Francis (Molly) Elliot 25 December 1892

2-1-1-2 Reuben L. Phillips b. 1845 Tennessee

2-1-1-3 Elizabeth Phillips b. 1836 Tennessee

2-1-1-4 William Phillips b. 1852 Tennessee

2-1-1-5 Andrew Phillips b. 1858 Arkansas

2-1-2 Drury (Drewery) b. 18 November 1811 North Carolina m. Martha _____ b. 20 Dec. 1808 Tennessee

    2-1-2-1 Ferbia Phillips b. 22 Aug 1832/33 Tenn. d. 1915 Arkansas did not marry.

    2-1-2-2 Elizabeth Phillips b. 7 February 1836 Tenn. d. 1933

    2-1-2-3 Reuben L. Phillips b. 15 November 1840 Tennessee d. 1 October 1836 Arkansas. M. Melissa Emma Dotson

    2-1-2-4 Nancy Phillips b. 10 Nov. 1841 Tenn.

    2-1-2-5 Margaret Peggy Phillips b. 25 August 1844 Arkansas

    2-1-2-6 Amos Richardson Phillips b. 9 April 1849 Arkansas

    2-1-2-7 William Lee Phillips b. 22 January 1853 d. 21 August 1911. m. Melissa Dotson. 15 Aug. 1867

    2-1-2-8 Willis Phillips b. 15 December 1846 Arkansas. m. Matilda Catherine Dotson 15 August 1867. Methodist Minister.

        2-1-2-8-1 Martha Ellen Phillips b. 12 May 1868 died 29 Dec. 1925 m. Scott Yingst.

        2-1-2-8-2 Amanda E. Phillips b. 1 Oct. 1870 d. 1944 m. Lincoln Hallie Yingst

        2-1-2-8-3 Hannah Elizabeth Phillips b. 2 October 1872 d. 12 February 1958 m. John Henry Inman 17 March 1886

            2-1-2-8-3-1 Bert Inman b. 7 Sept 1889 m. 1)Ollie Hamilton 2) Bernice Snow

            2-1-2-8-3-2 Tilda Catherine Inman b. 27 April 1890 d. 14 May 1981 m. Densmore Jones

            2-1-2-8-3-3 Thursa Mae Inman b. 17 April 1892 d. 26 October 1944 m. Clarence Herbert Steele

2-1-2-8-3-4 Flora Ellen Inman b. 18 Oct. 1899 m. 1)Hosea Easterling 2) Mallie Burgess
2-1-2-8-3-5 Alonzo Berry Inman b. 9 March 1909 m. Ethel Ledbetter
2-1-2-8-3-6 Daisy Mollie Inman b. 9 March 1909 m. Clell Jones
2-1-2-8-3-7 Arlie Earnest Inman b. 7 February 1913 d. 12 April 1913

2-1-2-8-4 William Lee Phillips b. 22 Nov. 1875 d. 22 Oct. 1880
2-1-2-8-5 Rosa Belle Phillips b. 13 September 1879 d. 29 July 1942 m. M.I. Shuster.
2-1-2-8-6 Green Berry Phillips b. 24 August 1881 m. Lizzie Tucker.
2-1-2-8-7 Desta Louanna Phillips b. 6 August 1886 d. 9 Oct. 1915. m. Eli Jones.

2-4 Adam Phillips b. ca. 1795 Georgia m. Delilah Quarles
    2-4-1 Adam Phillips b. 27 March 1828 d. 1 Mar. 1910 m. Elizabeth Fisher
        <u>A.</u> Thomas Jefferson Phillips b. 28 May 1847 d. 21 Feb 1933 m. Sarah C. Tabor
1. Adam Wesley Phillips b. 29 Jan 1871 d. 12 Mar. 1879 (probably died in the Yellow Fever epidemic)
2. John Newton Phillips b. 27 Jan. 1873 m. Etta Burk
3. William Jasper (Jap) Phillips b. 18 June 1875 d. 10 Apr. 1904 m. Louisa J. Harris
4. Martha Elizabeth Phillips b. 19 Dec. 1877 d. 5 Apr 1879 (Probably died in the Yellow Fever Epidemic)
5. Manerva Elveda Phillips b. 2 June 1880 d. 15 Mar. 1947 m. James Jackson Evans
6. Josie Phillips b. 20 September 1882 d. 10 July 1943 m. 1. Logan Jones 2. Elisha Yarbrough
7. Anna Phillips b. 16 Oct. 1884 m. Boley Tiner
8. Minnie Phillips b. 11 Dec. 1886 m. William Meade
9. Elmer Jackson Phillips b. 10 Dec. 1888 d. 9 Sept. 1889
10. Allie May Phillips b. 5 Jan 1890

d. early 70's m. Jim Perry

B. Charles W. Phillips b. 15 Nov. 1850 d. 26 July 1936 m. Mary Jane Suttles

    1. Dovey Rosetta Phillips b. 15 June 1877 m. William K. Grimes
    2. Elvira Elizabeth Phillips b. 7 July 1879 m. George W. Wilcox
    3. Louisa Phillips b. 7 July 1879
    4. Edward Silvester Phillips b. 26 Mar 1882 m. Beulah Conway
    5. James Allen Phillips b. 19 May 1885 m. Clementine Yarbrough
    6. Walter E. Phillips b. 2 March 1887 m. 1. Maggie Yarbrough 2. Ruth Hogan
    7. Lillie Maud Phillips b. 22 Feb. 1890. m. Silas Harmon
    8. Oda Stella Phillips b. 23 April 1892 m. Claud Smith

C. Allen Newton Phillips b. 6 Dec. 1852 d. 10 March 1935 m. Sarah Johnson

    1. William Thomas Phillips b. ca. 1875 m. Martha Eliza Yates
    2. Charles Frank Phillips b. 29 May 1883 d. 19 May 1980 m. Amelia Holland.
    3. Elizabeth Ella Phillips b. Mar 1886 m. Robert H. Tassey
    4. Ada J. Phillips b. Oct. 1887 m. Joe Hammons
    5. Cora M. Phillips b. April 1890 m. Abraham Hammons

D. McKane Phillips b. 26 Mar. 1855 d. 18 July 1929 m. 1. Susan Wilcox 2. Dorthula Kincannon

    1. Ada Phillips b. ca. 1875 d. ca. 1950 m. Eldon Qualls
    2. William Henry Phillips b. 1 Sept 1875 d. 14 Mar 1976 m. Effie Mae Qualls
    3. James Ervin Phillips b. 19 Dec. 1885 d. 7 Mar 1972 m. Maggie Mae Martin.
    4. Harve E. Phillips b. 13 Dec. 1886 m. Ora B. Holt
    5. Burl M. Phillips b. 3 Aug. 1891 d. 19 Dec. 1979 m. Jennie Nelson
    6. Artie J. Phillips b. 29 April 1907 d. 12 Mar. 1964
    7. Archie Phillips b. 29 Apr 1907

E. Reuben Matthew Phillips b. 10 Feb. 1857 d. 5 Nov. 1916

> F. Henry Phillips b. 1861 m. Polly Burkes
> G. Cynthia Louisa Jane Phillips b. 4 April 1865 d. 13 Mar 1943 m. Jefferson Sylvester Blackford
>> 1. Mallie A. Blackford b. 9 Aug. 1893 d. 14 Apr. 1969 m. Mazie Marie Gyer
>> 2. Ozzie Blackford b. 23 Mar. 1895 d. 18 Oct. 1976 m. May Brown.
>> 3. Lonnie F. Blackford b. 19 Apr 1902 d. 8 May 1977 m. Blanch Honiker
>> 4. Allen Herklee Blackford b. 4 Nov. 1904 d. 22 Sept 1922 m. Mary Smith

A narrative story of the descendants of William Phillips by Forrest F. Phillips of Portland, Oregon:

Reuben Phillips, Sr. and his wife Catherine C. (Howard) moved from Cecil County Maryland to Fredrick County, Maryland, where they appear in 1754. With them is their son William Phillips b. 1749 in Cecil County, Maryland.

Reuben and his family lived in Maryland until 1769 when he sold all his land and moved to Rowan County, North Carolina and was still living there until 1783. In 1786 Reuben moved to Wilkes County, Georgia an area that later became Oglethorpe, Georgia. The last known record of Reuben was the 1800 census. He apparently died shortly thereafter. He would have been 80 - 85 years old at that time.

William, from whom my branch of the family descended, did not move to Georgia with his father Reuben. Rather, he moved to Mecklenburg County, North Carolina where his father witnessed the purchase of land by William Phillips in 1774.

In the fall of 1776 William entered the service of the United States as a volunteer rifleman in the Revolutionary War for the County of Rowan, North Carolina. He served for two separate periods of three months each.

Around 1815 he moved to Blount County, Tennessee and then to Overton County, Tennessee, where he appears in the 1820, 1830, and 1840 census.

On September 24, 1832 William Phillips of Overton County, Tennessee applied for a pension for his service in the Revolutionary War in Rowan County, North Carolina. He had served under Colonel Francis Locke and Captain Berringer.

Pension Record

[William Philips] states that in the fall of the year [1776] he entered the service of the United States as a volunteer rifleman for a tour of three months in the County of Rowan, North Carolina. Marched into a place now called Hiway in the State of Tennessee, then Cherokee Nation, against the Indians...They had a small engagement at the Valley Towns, but the Indians soon fled. They destroyed the town and took some prisoners [including] an Indian called Hicks and his wife with many other prisoners and some property. They found some torys with the Indians upon another occasion while he was with some other men cutting down corn. They were fired on by the Indians and some were killed. One man next to him was shot down.

Some time after this he was drafted for three months... He marched to a place called New Providence in the Same State and was there stationed and remained for the whole time of his service and was discharged without being in any engagement.

Overton County, named after Judge John Overton, was formed out of a large area of North Central Tennessee, more commonly known as Upper Cumberland Country. After Statehood by Tennessee in 1796, this area eventually was divided into Sumner County in 1796, Smith County in 1799, Jackson County in 1801 and Overton and White County in 1806. By an act of the General Assembly on June 1, 1810 Monroe with a population of 200 was designated as the county seat of Overton County. The County's main waterways are the Obed and the Roaring Rivers, tributaries of the Cumberland River. The area is hilly and the soil very fertile. It was a prime sheep and cattle grazing area with stands of excellent timber. In 1802 the total population of Overton County was approximately 1030 families.

In this area David Crockett was born in 1786. His grandfather was killed by Cherokee Indians in 1777, led by one of their more ruthless warriors, Dragging Canoe. In 1827 John M. Clemens the father of Samuel Clemens (Mark Twain) was residing in this area (Jamestown)

In 1805, in Clay County, (Northwest of and adjoining present day Overton County) is the Rock Springs Church of Christ at the little town of Rock Springs, Tennessee. The Church was organized in January, 1805 and is probably one if not the oldest Church of Christ in the Country.

The initial service took place in the little log home of John McAdams. Alexander Campbell, founder of the Church of Christ, "Racoon" John Smith, Isaac T. Denton, John Newton Mulkey, and many others of bygone days preached here. In 1820 a church was built which was eventually replaced about forty five years later. Church services are still held to the present day. (Nashville Tennessee, January 1, 1949, Gordon Turner)

The Church of Christ has played an important part in the lives of my family as my father, William Francis "Frank" Phillips was an Elder in the Church of Christ in Brawley, California where I was baptized, ca. 1947.

Reuben, William's eldest son was born in 1780 in North Carolina and moved to Georgia, ca. 1800, where his first son Adam was born before 1800. By 1810 he had returned to North Carolina where his second son Reubin Jr. was born in 1810. Reuben Sr.'s wife was Frieba which was probably a derivative of Alfretta.

Sometime after 1840 and before 1850 (probably ca 1844 after his father's death) Reuben (Sr.) moved most likely by wagon train, along with other family members to Madison County Arkansas where he appears in the 1850 census.

The trip to Arkansas would have taken one of two routes used by the early settlers of Northwestern Arkansas. One would have followed the Arkansas River to Fort Smith and then overland through Fayetteville to War Eagle. The other was to cross the Mississippi into Missouri and travel across that State Southwesterly to Springfield and then to Northwestern Arkansas.

Reuben Sr. and his family members would have arrived in a sparsely populated relatively primitive area of Arkansas, which only recently was inhabited primarily by Indians.

Arkansas became a territory in 1819, and was admitted to the Union in June of 1836. In 1830 Washington County, Arkansas located in the Northwest corner of Arkansas, encompassed the later Counties of Benton, Washington, Eastern Carroll and Eastern Madison Counties.

The 1830 census of this area listed 217 heads of households. There were no recorded Phillipses in this area at that time. In nearby Izard County there was one Phillips family headed by Francis Phillips.

Madison County was formed out of Southeastern Washington

and Eastern Izard County by the Arkansas State Legislature in its first session on September 30, 1836.

The 1840 census of Madison County Arkansas indicated the following Phillipses.

1840 Census Madison County, Arkansas, War Eagle Area

James Phillips	2/1/1/0/0/1	0/1/2/0/1
John Phillips	0/0/0/2/2/0/0/1	0/0/0/1/1/0/0/1
Charles Phillips	2/0/0/2	0/1/0/0/1

According to Goodspeeds History, written in 1889, some of the earliest settlers of War Eagle were William Hawkins who settled there in 1830, David Phillips from Jackson County, Alabama who moved to the vicinity of Huntsville in 1831 and John Phillips in the same year. Richard Withrow settled three miles south of Huntsville in 1831.

1840 Census Madison County, Arkansas, Kings River Area

James Phillips	1/1/0/0/0/1	0/1/0/0/1

Kings River was named after Henry King who with Thomas Cunningham, and John J. Coulter made a prospecting expedition in the valley of the Kings river in 1827. Henry King died on that expedition and was buried on the banks of the stream that bears his name. Thomas and John returned to Alabama shortly thereafter.

I have not found a link of these Phillipses to the William Phillips' line whose descendants Reuben and his family moved to the same locale of Arkansas ca 1844.

According to the 1850 census of Madison County, Arkansas, Reuben and his sons Drury and Adam along with their families were living in the War Eagle area.

Reuben is now 70 years old and the patriarch of the family in Arkansas. He was born in North Carolina in 1781. He has lived in Georgia, and afterwards Tennessee where he lived most of his life. His wife Feriba, was also born in North Carolina and is now 65 years old. Reuben cannot read or write. They are living on land in the War Eagle area of Madison County, valued at $200. They apparently died prior to 1860 as neither of them appear in the 1860 Madison County Arkansas Census.

Living in the same area is Adam born in 1800 in Georgia and Drury born 1811 in NC. They are definitely two of Reuben's sons as evidenced by a transfer of deed after Reuben's death.

Reference Madison County Arkansas Deed Record Volume "E" 1853 to 1874 page 400 micro film roll #1035197.

"L Phillips Et al
To Deed
James Stroud

Known all men by these presents that we (Levi Phillips, William Phillips, William Montgomery and Wife Elizabeth Montgomery and Drewry Phillips and Adam Phillips and his wife Delia Phillips have conveyed our right and title to J.W. Rogers the real estate of our father Rubin Phillips deceased. Known by all men present that I (J. W. Rogers) do hereby sell transfer and convey unto James Stroud and unto his heirs and assign forever for the sum of (One hundred and twenty dollars......[dated] 7 day of September 1861"

Apparently Reubin and Feriba died prior to this time, leaving their property to their sons and daughter, who had sold the property to J. W. Rogers, who in turn sold the property to James Stroud. This entire transaction probably occurred over a period of time, but was officially recorded in this deed on September 7, 1861.

Adam and Delilah (Qualls) Phillips had 11 children.

1840 Census Overton County Tennessee

Adam   2/0/2/1/0/0/1   1/2/1/0/0/1

The 1850 census indicates that living on adjoining property to Reubin is the aforementioned Adam N. Phillips, 22 years old, and born in Tennessee. The value of his land is blank, which could indicate that he may be living on part of the land Reubin owns. Adam cannot read or write. His wife's name is Betsy. She is 20 years old and was also born in Tennessee. At this time they have two children Adam, three years old and Charles, four months old. (The son named Adam is listed as T.J. in the 1860 census.)

The relationship of this Adam Phillips to the descendants of William Phillips in unclear at this time. However the following facts seem to indicate that he was part of the family of the descendants of William Phillips who moved to Arkansas with Reuben and his parents were Adam and Delilah..

1. Adam was born in Tennessee

2. Based on the birth dates of the children of Reuben's sons, Adam (m. to Delilah) and Drury (m. to Martha), the move of the Phillipses to Arkansas from Tennessee would have occurred about 1844. Adam (Jr.?) would have been about 15 years old at that time and most likely would have traveled from Tennessee to Arkansas with

his parents.

    3. The Phillipses born in Tennessee (Adam in Ga.) and living in the War Eagle area in the 1850 census of War Eagle, Madison County Arkansas were as follows:

    #628 George W. Phillips 22 b. Tn. Property value $-0-
    #633 Reuben Phillips, 21, b. Tn Property value $100
    #671 Adam Phillips 50, b. Ga. Property value $200
    #725 Willis Phillips 34 b. Tn, Property value $200
    #727 Adam Phillips 22, b. Tn. Property value $-0-
    #728 Reuben Phillips 70, b. NC Property value $200
    #744 Drury Phillips 35, b. NC. Property value $150

Based on the ages indicated (after eliminating Reuben), the only person in the family who could have been Adam's father, assuming that Adam moved from Tennessee with other family members, was Adam Phillips b. Ga.

    Adam (Jr.) fits the age category of a son of Adam (Sr?) in the 1840 census of Overton County, Tennessee.

    5. Some research on the family by James Wood in 1979 concluded that his Great Grandfather, Reuben C. Phillips and Adam N. Phillips were both sons of Adam Phillips b. 1800 Ga. and married to Delilah.

Further research is necessary to prove this relationship as, at this time, my conclusion is based only on a logical deduction.

This Adam Phillips (1850 census Arkansas, Madison County, War Eagle #727) was my Great, Great, Grandfather. This conclusion is based on the following.
    1. The death certificate of Allen Nute Phillips, my known (from the memory of my Mother, Maxine Phillips) Great Grandfather, indicates that he was born in 1851 (52?) in Kingston Arkansas. His father was Adam Phillips b. Tennessee and his mother was Elizabeth Fisher also born in Tennessee.

2. (Allen) Newton is shown as a son of Adam in the 1860 census and is eight years old, which would tie into his birth date of 1852. Also his brothers shown on the 1850 and 1860 census are the same names as recalled by my mother Maxine Phillips.

Adam and his wife Elizabeth (Fisher) continued to live in the War Eagle, Kingston area of Madison County, Arkansas for several years.

Adam Newton and Elizabeth Phillips had eight children.

Thomas "Jeff" Phillips (Adam in 1850 cen), b. May 28, 1847 m. Sarah C. Tabor
Charles Wesley Phillips b. November 15, 1850 m. Mary J. Suttles
Allen Newton Phillips b. December 6, 1852 (1851?) m. Sarah J.

Johnson
McKane "Babe" Phillips b. 1855, m. Mary Wilcox/ Dorthula Kincannon
King Phillips b. 1857
Reuben Matthew Phillips b. February 10, 1859, Murdered November, 1916.
William Henry Phillips b. 1861 m. Polly Burkes
Cinthia Phillips b. April 4, 1865 m. Jefferson S. Blackford.

All children were born in Arkansas.

Reuben "Matt" Phillips was murdered November, 1916. As per the Obituary column of the November 16, 1916 Madison County Democrat:

> Phillips, Reuben Matthew of nr Purdy 57 y b Feb 1859 Huntsville, Mad, Ark d Nov 1916 (murdered in his sleep for his hidden money, body found the 10th badly decomposed, last seen alive on the 5th) unmd s/o Adam & Elizabeth

Several stories are told of another killing of a Phillips family member. William Jasper "Jap" Phillips, the third child of Thomas Jefferson Phillips & Sarah Tabor Phillips. He was shot by a neighbor over a disputed property line & died on April 8, 1908.

Upon learning of who allegedly shot and killed Jasper Phillips, Allen "Nute" Phillips, who was a deputy sheriff at the time, went to the neighbor's home to arrest him. Since the home was located outside of the county, he took the sheriff or deputy sheriff of that county with him. The sheriff knocked on the front door & Allen positioned himself at the back door hoping he would try to escape so he could shoot him. However he heard Allen "cock" his pistol & gave up to the sheriff at the front door.

Adam and Elizabeth's third child Allen "Nute" Phillips, my Great Grandfather, was married to Sarah J. Johnson. They lived in Southern Madison & Northern Johnson County, Arkansas their entire lives. Sarah died in Hill Township, Johnson County, Arkansas on January 26, 1928 and Nute died in the same township on March 10, 1933. They are both buried in Evans Cemetery in Johnson County just south of the border of Madison County. This cemetery is located on Evans Mountain, named after the Evans family, a pioneer family of the area. "Uncle" Bill Evans was a gospel preacher, for many years, in this area in the early 1900's.
Allen and Sarah Phillips had five children:

William "Tommy" Phillips b. September 11, 1872 m Martha Eliza Louisa Yates

Charlie "Frank" Phillips b. May 29, 1883 m. Amelia "Mealie" Holland.
Lizzie "Ali" Phillips b. 1886 m. Robert H. Tassey
Ada Phillips b. 1887 m. Joe Hammons son of Abe Hammons
Cora Phillips b. 1890 m. Abe Hammons, father of Joe Hammons

All children were born in Arkansas.

Allen "Nute" Phillips owned a small farm on Friley Creek which flowed into the Little Mulberry Creek in Johnson County, Arkansas. Charlie his eldest son continued to live on the farm into adulthood. After his fathers death Charlie "Frank" Phillips inherited the farm and lived there with his wife "Mealie" until old age. They did not have any children, however Wesley Phillips their nephew and eldest son of William "Tommy" Phillips, lived with them and eventually cared for them in their old age.

As a young boy of around 12 years old (ca 1946) I spent a month on this farm with my mother and father who were visiting the family in Arkansas. The farm had a creek in front of the property which you had to ford to enter the property.

I recall with fondness helping my Uncle Wesley "slop" the hogs. They ran loose on the hillsides eating acorns and as he would walk up to the area where he fed them he would call them, suey, suuuey, suuuuuuey and down from the sides of the hills they would come! Fishing was a few feet away from the front door and squirrel hunting was a favorite past time. And of course, a saddle horse was available any time, if you could catch him in the pasture!

My Grandfather William "Tommy" Phillips the second child of Allen "Nute" Phillips married Eliza Yates on August 24, 1904. He was 28 and she was 18. He had homesteaded 240 acres on the Miller Mountain in Northern Johnson County, Arkansas and raised nine children there.

In 1937 they moved to Brawley, California. Tommy Phillips died in Pomona Ca on August 21, 1951 and Eliza Phillips died in Brawley on August 7, 1972. They are both buried in the Riverview Cemetery in Brawley, California.

William "Tommy" and Eliza Phillips had nine children.

Wesley Allen Phillips b. August 17, 1905 Never married.
William Francis "Frank" Phillips b. March 12, 1907 m. Maxine Clark
John David Phillips b. March 3, 1909 m. Anna Stamps
Elsie Gertrud Phillips b. February 11, 1911 m. Sherman Denzer
Henry Bryant Phillips b. February 13, 1913 (died Sept 14, 1914)
Omer Green Phillips b. April 5, 1915 never married
Verlin Thomas Phillips b. October 14, 1917 m. Donna M. Rhodes
Alvin Lloyd Phillips b. March 13, 1920 m. Jean E. Holland
James Wayne Phillips b. August 28, 1922 (Died WWII Germany)

My father William F. "Frank" Phillips the second son of Tommy Phillips grew up on the Miller Mountain homestead and was acquainted with his future wife Maxine Clark from early childhood.

When Frank was about 20 years old his father Tommy decided the farm was too difficult to maintain and moved off his property on the Miller Mountain and moved to the Little Mulberry Creek area. He retained title to the land and eventually sold it to the Government shortly before he left for California ca. 1937.

In 1929, Frank was working in the timber for his Uncle Fonzo Yates when he heard of an advertisement in the paper (probably the Kansas City Star) for field workers in California. Frank asked Uncle Fonzo what he thought about the idea of going to California. He told Frank to go and if he were younger he would go with him. Without telling his parents, Frank left for California in a truck with a group of people from the area. They traveled to Holtville, Imperial County, a small town in Southern California just a few miles north of the Mexican Border. Here they found work as field hands. Imperial Valley, a dry desert area, had been transformed into a fertile agricultural area by irrigation water from the Colorado River. It must have been quite a change from the green, lush hills of the Ozarks in Arkansas.

While in California Frank wrote to Maxine Clark and asked her to marry him. She agreed, and in 1930, he returned to Arkansas to marry Maxine. Maxine said that when he arrived he realized what a big step this was in his life. However, she reassured him that every thing would be alright and they were married on September 12, 1930 by a Justice of the Peace for Johnson County, J. B. Laster.

Immediately afterwards they left for California by automobile along with Johnny Phillips, Frank's brother and O. A. "Dude" Clark, Maxine's brother.

They arrived in Holtville in October, 1931 to begin a new life in California.

Frank and Maxine Phillips had three children.

Forrest Franklin Phillips b. June 8, 1934 Ca. m. Diane Rosalie Wadsworth
    m. Norine F. Smith
    m. Helen (Geiger) Bucar
Linda Francis Phillips b. July 3, 1943 Ca. m. Hall Ross
Virginia Elaine Phillips b. June 13, 1947 m. Randy Wood
    m. Bill Suits

All children were born in Brawley, Imperial County, California.

For a few years Frank worked on a farm for Frank Marlow a foreman on the John Zenith Ranch. He tells that at one time they had 150 mules working the various lands under cultivation.

Over a period of time several families including the Stamps and the Acords who lived in the same area of Arkansas as my family moved to Imperial Valley.

Around 1937 Frank's father and mother Tommy and Eliza moved to Brawley. By this time all members of my father's immediate family had moved to Imperial Valley with the exception of Frank's brother Wesley Phillips who continued to live on the Friley creek farm in Arkansas, with his Uncle Frank & Aunt Mealie Phillips

In 1943, Maxine's father and mother, Rufus and Peggy Clark also moved to Brawley.

In ca. 1937, "Dude" Clark, Frank's brother-in-law decided to open a grocery store in Brawley. Dude purchased some land on "A" Street from a Mr. Jacobson and he and my Dad built the store and named it College View Grocery (it was at the same intersection as the Junior College) My Dad leased the store from Dude and operated it until ca 1942. The store is still in existence although remodeled several times.

One of my earliest recollections was a Saturday night during a summer evening in ca. 1940. I was perched on a stool behind the counter of the grocery store when a very strong earthquake occurred. Brawley is located very near the infamous San Andreas Fault and is prone to earthquakes. My father grabbed me and ran out of the grocery store. I was quite frightened and asked Dad if there was a fire. He responded, "no it was an earthquake!" After we were outside I recall him trying to close the store. The front of the store consisted of accordion doors and the entire front was open. Dad would run in and begin to close the doors, an after shock would occur and he would run out. This happened two or three times before he finally secured the building. We had planned to spend the next day in Julian, a mountain community about 80 miles from Brawley. The earthquake hastened our departure. When we returned, many buildings in Brawley were damaged especially the Dunlap Hotel located in the center of Brawley. There was not much damage to the grocery store, but the mess inside was substantial, with canned goods spilled into the aisles. One area consisted of ketchup, mayonnaise, pickles, mustard and I can to this day remember the sight of all the broken bottles and especially the smell.

After leaving the grocery store business my father purchased some land outside of Brawley and began to farm. He owned two parcels near Weise Lake, one of 360 acres and the other 80 acres. The primary crops were alfalfa, flax, and cotton.

He eventually leased another 1000 acres and farmed in the area for a number of years. He finally sold his property and raised cattle and started a hay baling business. Eventually he purchased several pieces of rental property in Brawley.

During this time my two sisters and I graduated from high school in Brawley. I graduated from the University of Southern California, in Los Angeles in 1955. Linda and Virginia graduated from Whittier College in Whittier, California.

About 1971, Frank Phillips sold some of his rental property in Brawley and purchased a mobile home park in Hemet, California. He sold the park in 1975 and retired to Beaumont, California where he died in 1981.

Maxine has since remarried to Bill Zachary and is now living in Upland, California.

Linda is a teacher and lives in Long Beach, California with her husband Hall Ross. Virginia is also a teacher and lives in Brawley California, with her second husband Bill Suits.

After graduating from the University of Southern California in 1955, I married Rosalie Wadsworth, whom I had met in College. I went to work for Fruehauf Trailer Corporation the same year and we eventually purchased a home in Whittier, California.

Forrest and Rosalie Phillips had two children.

Gregory Dean Phillips b. January 21, 1959, Unmarried
David Michael Phillips b. February 26, 1957, Unmarried

Both children were born in Pasadena, California while we were living in Whittier, California.

I am still working for Fruehauf, having worked in various positions for them in Los Angeles, Fresno, Oakland and back to Los Angeles California in 1972. In 1975 as I divorced from Rosalie and in 1978 moved with my two boys from Los Angeles California to Portland, Oregon.

In 1980 I married Norine (Newell) Smith. She died in 1985. In 1987 I married Helen (Geiger) Bucar. We now live in Portland, along with a rather extended family which includes my two sons, along with four step children from my second marriage, and four step children from my third marriage. These three marriages have resulted in several step grandchildren (currently 20), all living in the Portland area. Helen has the lion's share of these grandchildren, as her four daughters have 14 children among them. The step children from my second marriage have contributed the other six.

CHAPTER 5

3. Levi Phillips b. 9/25/1751 Cecil Co. MD d. 1/14/1840 Carroll Co. Georgia.
On September 25, 1751 Levi Phillips was born to Reuben and Catherine Phillips and the birth was recorded on the records of St. Mary Anne Parish in Cecil County Maryland.

1778 Tax list Rowan Co. NC. Capt. Brannons District.
On February 10, 1778 Levi Philips filed for 150 acres on a branch of Buffalo Creek next to William Anderson, Joseph Hayes, Rubin Philips, and Timothy Brown in Rowan County. Levi had improvements already in place on this property.

1783 - Tax List Rowan Co. NC shows Levi with 20 horses and six cows.

Levi Phillips signed the Revolutionary Warrant of William Phillips in 1786.

Nathan Phillips son of Levi Phillips was born in 1788.

1789 - Purchased 200 acres on Little Troublesome Creek in Oglethorpe(Wilkes) Co. GA.

1792 - Received a Bounty Land Grant for 200 acres in Wilkes Co. GA.

On June 12, 1794, Court was held at Charles Lane's in Oglethorpe County, Georgia. Levi Phillips appeared on the jury list.

Levi Phillips appeared on the 1796 tax list for Oglethorpe County, Georgia.

1798 - On Tax List Oglethorpe Co. GA.

1800 Tax List Oglethorpe Co. GA.

In 1800, Reuben Phillips appeared on the census of Oglethorpe County Georgia with two males in his household, two females, and no slaves. Two Levi Phillipses appeared on the same census.

1805 - Tax List Oglethorpe Co. GA.

In 1807, Levi Phillips received a land grant in Oglethorpe County, Georgia for 300 acres.

1810 - Tax List Oglethorpe Co. GA.

On March 28, 1828 Levi Phillips of Carroll County, Georgia witnessed a deed.

On November 30, 1830 Sanders W. Ray sold 202 and 1/2 acres of land in Carroll County Georgia to Levi Phillips Sr. for $247.50.

On January 7, 1833 Levi Phillips applied for a pension on his revolutionary war service in Carroll County Georgia. He had served under Colonel Locke and Captain Brannon.

Pension Record: [Levi Phillips] states that he is eighty one ... years old and that he entered the service of the United States on the 25th day of December 1781 and served a tour of duty of three months...[they] were marched from [Fifer's Mill in Rowan County] through Mecklenburg County to Hanging Rock where .. he was discharged in the spring of 1782. He was again drafted for three months and rendezvoused at Fifers Mill. He served three other tours.

Children Catherine ca. 1785, Levi ca. 1788, Nathan, Sarah, Thomas, ?Reuben, ?Frances b. ca. 1797 m. Colemore Harrison

Levi Phillips witnessed a deed in Carroll Co. GA on April 14, 1835.

Levi Phillips died in Carroll County, Georgia on January 14, 1840.

CHAPTER 6

(contributed by Margaret Coker)

4. Jonas Phillips b. Cecil or Fredrick Co. MD. d. ca. 1835 Pickens Dist. SC. Married Faraby Gurly 1778 Rowan County, N.C.

September 3, 1778 Jonas Phillips 100 acres on the waters of Crane Creek and Eddleman's Sawmill Branch adjoining Moses Bellah below on said branch. (Rowan Co. Vacant Land Entries #1475)

Edward Williams sold 10 acres in Rowan County, NC to John Liddon on August 13, 1787. The deed was proved by Jonus Felps(Jonas Philips).

Thomas Sanford of Pickens District for $100 sold to Seaborn Shedd, 122 acres a part of a tract of land granted to Jonas Phillips by his Excellancy John Giddes. The same being a part of said land beginning on a hickory, SE 32 chains to a spanish oak thence 20 E 10 conditional corner, then the course continuous through the survey. 30 July 1857.

1800 census Montgomery Co. NC
1810 Census York Co. SC
1820 Census Pendleton District SC
1830 Census Pickens Co. SC
Jonas Phillips died about 1835 in Pickens County, S.C.
Children
    4-1 Reuben born ca. 1785 Rowan Co. NC m. Charlotta

Reuben Phillips from David Quarles both of Pickens District, on Whetson or Whetstone Creek being a part of land originally granted to sd Quarles on the southside of creek, beginning at the creek below Earle's Mill opposite the Dogwood Station, 110 acres, 14 January 1833.
Abel Williams and wife Feriba
Presley Mosley and wife Sallie
Abel Williams
by virtue of a power in me vested by Jonas Phillips Jr. Nathaniel Phillips, Henry Phillips, Evan Phillips, Peter Phillips, Presley Mosley and Charlotte Phillips and Anderson Phillips in consideration that the said Abel Williams did on the 23 april 1858 contract to sell the premises hereinafter described to Kennon Breazeale for $1300.00 to us in hand paid by the said Kennon Breazeale in the State aforesaid and District of Anderson. All that tract of land lying in the State and District aforesaid adjoining lands of Hubbard Quarles and others containing 490 acres... and also a deed made by David Quarles to Rheubin Phillips. This March 1861.
Signed: Abel Williams   Witnessed by: Gambrell Brazeale
        Presley (X) Mosley   William H. Thrift
        Jonas Phillips
        Henry (X) Phillips

Evan Phillips
Peter Phillips
Nathaniel Phillips

Before Abel Robins one of the magistrates in the State and District aforesaid appeared the wifes of Jonas, Nathaniel, Henry, Evan & Peter Phillips, signed:
Anor (X) Phillips
Mahala (X) Phillips
Vianna (X) Phillips
Margaret (X) Phillips
Mary C (X) Phillips
Nelly (X) Phillips

Aslo came Feriba Williams, Sallie Mosley the wives of the within named Abel Williams and Prseley Mosley. Signed:
Feriba (X) Williams
Sallie (X) Mosley

Connected with this are the following items:
Georgia, Raburn County: To bind my heirs, ets and administrators to be paid to Captain N. Phillips of the State aforesaid all monies, that I have or may collect for the estate of R. A. Phillips deceased, etc. 20 April 1857. Signed: Abel Williams. Recorded 1 July 1861

20 April 1859 State of Georgia, Raburn County: I do appoint Captain Nathaniel Phillips of the State and County aforesaid my lawful attourney to collect all debts which is now or may become due the estate of R. A. Phillips, deceased late of the state and county aforesaid. Signed Viannah (X) Phillips

    4-1-1 Faraby b. 1816 d. after 1880 m. Abel Williams. Lived in Rabun County Georgia from 1840-1880
        4-1-1-1 Elizabeth Nancy Williams 1840
        4-1-1-2 Charlotta Williams b. 1842
        4-1-1-3 Henry James Williams b. 1845 m. Thrusey L.
            Mary G. 1867
            Surreptha 1871
            Fanny S. 1874
        4-1-1-4 Sarah Williams b. 1846
        4-1-1-5 Elisha Berryman(Barnabus) Williams b. 1847
        4-1-1-6 Melissa Jane Williams b. 1848 m. Henry A. Cannon
            Ida A. Cannon 1870
            Julia A. Cannon 1872
            Elizabeth(Lizzie) Cannon 1874)
            Russell H. Cannon 1876
            Abel B. Cannon 1878
        4-1-1-7 Mary Williams b. 1849
        4-1-1-8 William (Wilbern) Williams b. 1850
        4-1-1-9 Allen Williams b. 1854 m. Samantha M.
            Garnet M. 1878
        4-1-1-10 Martha A. Williams b. 1856
        4-1-1-11 John Williams b. 1857

4-1-1-12 Clarissa(Clarinda) Williams b. 1861
    4-1-1-12-1 Luanah b. 1877
    4-1-1-12-2 (unnamed daughter)

4-1-2 Nathaniel Phillips b. 1814 m. Mahala P. Gasaway. Nathaniel Phillips and Family were living in South Carolina near Charlotta Phillips in 1850. They were in Rabun County Georgia in 1860, but soon returned to South Carolina where Nathaniel bought land from his first cousin Jonas Phillips Jr. on Long Creek.

    4-1-2-1 Mary Ann Dec. 15, 1848 d. Jan 16, 1939 did not marry
    4-1-2-2 Nancy Ann Manerva Aug. 7, 1851 - d. Oct. 29, 1916 did not marry
    4-1-2-3 Patton K. b. 1855 d. 1938 m. Malissa C.
        4-1-2-3-1 Luther F. b. Feb. 1885 m. Eva
        4-1-2-3-2 Ira N. b. August 1887 m. Lillie
            Roy 1911
            Jessie 1914
            Gus 1916
            Lawrence 1919
        4-1-2-3-3 John M. b. June 1886 d. July 1886
        4-1-2-3-4 Rance E. b. Dec. 1889 m. Essie
            Myra 1915
            Louise 1918
        4-1-2-3-5 Allie(Ollie?) E. b. Sept 1894
        4-1-2-3-6 Henry P. b. 1897 d. 1920
    4-1-2-4 Rachel Canada b. June 14, 1858 d. Sept 29, 1922 m. Guss Arve
        4-1-2-4-1 Roxie Arve b. Oct. 30, 1889 d. Dec. 6, 1971 m. Andrew Ramsey Pitts
            4-1-2-4-1-1 Beunice Pitts b. Dec. 25, 1915 d. Feb. 14, 1990 m. Phillips J. Phillips
                Greta
                Carlton
            4-1-2-4-1-2 Edwin Grant Pitts
        4-1-2-4-2 unknown child
    4-1-2-5 Clayton J. b. Feb. 1861 m. Jennie C.
        4-1-2-5-1 Fleta C. b. Oct. 1899 m. Mr. McClellan
    4-1-2-6 Jones N. b. Oct. 1863 d. ca. 1930 m. Martha A. Holmes March 3, 1889
        4-1-2-6-1 Dover L. b. July 1885 d. 1941 m. Drucie M.
        4-1-2-6-2 Wymer K. b. 1888 m. Berdie E.
        4-1-2-6-3 May b. Sept 1885(1895?)
        4-1-2-6-4 Fred D. b. 1903

4-1-3 Elijah Phillips b. ca. 1817 m. Nancy _____ Elijah died in 1850 of Typhoid Fever after a sickness of 29 days.
    4-1-3-1 Charlotte
    4-1-3-2 Anderson

4-1-4 Jonas Phillips b. ca. 1818 m. Ana Williams m. Feb

24, 1842. Jonas and family lived near Peter's widow Margaret(Peggy) Phillips in Rabun Co. Georgia. Jonas and Ana were still living in Georgia in 1900. Jonas and his son Evan were in the Civil War from Rabun Co. GA and Evan died in the war.

    4-1-4-1 Rachel b. 1843
    4-1-4-2 Evan b. 1844 d. in Civil War.
    4-1-4-3 Ary b. 1846
    4-1-4-4 Sarah b. 1848 did not marry.
    4-1-4-5 Lucinda b. 1849
    4-1-4-6 Mahala b. 1853
    4-1-4-7 Charlotta b. 1855
    4-1-4-8 Bry F. b. 1860 m. Sarah M. _____ in 1883.
        4-1-4-8-1 John B. b. 1899
        4-1-4-8-2 Logan S. b. 1905
    4-1-4-9 William b. 1864
    4-1-4-10 Hannah E. b. 1864

4-1-5 Robert Asbury Phillips b. ca. 1821 d. before 1860 m. Vianna_____. They lived in Pickens Co. S.C. for many years. He is buried at the Baptist Church Cemetery, Dillard, Rabun Co. GA.

Georgia, Raburn County: To bind my heirs, ets and administrators to be paid to Captain N. Phillips of the State aforesaid all monies, that I have or may collect for the estate of R. A. Phillips deceased, etc. 20 April 1857. Signed: Abel Williams. Recorded 1 July 1861

20 April 1859 State of Georgia, Raburn County: I do appoint Captain Nathaniel Phillips of the State and County aforesaid my lawful attorney to collect all debts which is now or may become due the estate of R. A. Phillips, deceased late of the state and county aforesaid. Signed Viannah (X) Phillips

    4-1-5-1 Thomas R. b. 1847
    4-1-5-2 James b. 1850
    4-1-5-3 Isaac b. 1851
    4-1-5-4 Mary A. b. 1853 m. Mr.Ramey
    4-1-5-? David
    4-1-5-5 Robert Asbury b. 1859 m. Martha S.

4-1-6 Henry Phillips b. ca. 1825 m. Nelly(Nellie) Henry served in the Civil War from Pickens District, S.C.

    4-1-6-1 Faraby Adeline Phillips b. ca. 1848. m. Mr. Jones
    4-1-6-2 Martin L. b. April 1,1852 d. May 12, 1925 m. Marthena ("Mattie") Harden b. Jan. 23, 1853 d. May 27,1926
        4-1-6-2-1 Dora B. b. Feb. 1875
        4-1-6-2-2 Alexander P. b. Jan 1878 m. 1.)Roda Essie Duncan and 2.) Essie Hamby
            4-1-6-2-2-1 Martin
            4-1-6-2-2-2 Charlie

    4-1-6-2-2-3 Thomas
    4-1-6-2-2-4 Raymond
    4-1-6-2-2-5 Pearl m. Mr. Farr
    4-1-6-2-2-6 Minnie m. H.C. Reynolds
    4-1-6-2-2-7 Faye m. Mr. Gordon
    4-1-6-2-2-8 Ray Ezekiel ("Zeke") d. Oct. 25, 1987 m. Eloise Matheson
      4-1-6-2-2-8-1 Donald Ray
      4-1-6-2-2-8-2 Karen m. Mr. Harden
  4-1-6-2-3 Clinton b. Feb. 1875
  4-1-6-2-4 Lilly b. Feb. 1883
  4-1-6-2-5 Addie b. Apr. 1885
  4-1-6-2-6 Ezkiel b. Apr. 16, 1885 d. June 3, 1925
  4-1-6-2-7 Charley b. Dec. 1889
  4-1-6-2-8 Danie Frances b. Nov. 22, 1891 d. Oct. 13, 1917
  4-1-6-2-9 Lucy b. May 1896
  4-1-6-2-10 Clem b. March 1900
  4-1-6-2-11 Beatrice b. 1910
4-1-6-3 Amanda b. Feb. 19, 1854 d. Jan 17, 1941 m. John T. Ramey
  4-1-6-3-1 J. Nelson Ramey b. May 18, 1878 d. May 23, 1964
  4-1-6-3-2 Simon A. Ramey b. Dec. 1879
  4-1-6-3-3 Savannah Ramey b. Apr. 1882 d. 1967 m. Frank Ramey
  4-1-6-3-4 Logan Ramey b. July 1864
  4-1-6-3-5 Thomas Julian Ramey b. July 7, 1886 d. March 7, 1963
  4-1-6-3-6 Ella V. Ramey b. Sept. 1889 m. Evan A. Nicholson
  4-1-6-3-7 Henry Lipscomb Ramey b. Apr. 1892 did not marry.
  4-1-6-3-8 Sibbie b. Dec. 1894 d. 1971 did not marry
4-1-6-4 Reuben J. b. ca. 1855 m. 2 Mary
  4-1-6-4-1 Lila b. 1896
  4-1-6-4-2 Minnie b. 1899
  4-1-6-4-3 George b. 1903
  4-1-6-4-4 Claud b. 1905
  4-1-6-4-5 Leasy b. 1907
  4-1-6-4-6 Melissa b. 1909
4-1-6-5 John P. b. March 1862 m. Amanda
  4-1-6-5-1 Logan b. Aug. 1885
  4-1-6-5-2 Ira b. June 1888
  4-1-6-5-3 Etta b. June 1891
  4-1-6-5-4 Glenn Edward b. March 1895
  4-1-6-5-5 William Lafayette b. Aug. 1899
  4-1-6-5-6 Henry b. 1903
4-1-7 Sarah (Sallie) b. ca. 1827 m. Presley Mosley
  4-1-7-1 John b. 1842

4-1-7-2 Frances b. 1843
4-1-7-3 Margaret Mahala Mosley b. 1854 m. Ephraim Williams
    Julius H. Williams 1880
    Warren R. Williams 1884
    Mary S. Williiams 1885
    Albert S. Williams 1886
    Amanda E. Williams 1890
    Charley M. Williams 1892
    Martha D. Williams b. 1894
    Margaret E. Williams b. 1897
4-1-7-4 Martha b. 1855
4-1-7-5 Sarah J. Mosley b. 1856
4-1-7-6 Celia A. Mosley b. 1858
4-1-7-7 James Mosley b. 1863
4-1-8 Evan Phillips b. ca. 1830 m. Mary C. _____
    4-1-8-1 Susannah A. b. 18 Oct. 1855
    4-1-8-2 Martha J. b. ca. 1858
    4-1-8-3 Arah Adeline b. 5 May 1860 did not marry
    4-1-8-4 George W. b. ca. 1862 m. Lavina Snider
        4-1-8-4-1 John E. b. June 1885
        4-1-8-4-2 Ruth C. b, Sept 1887
        4-1-8-4-3 Ella (Twin) b. March 1894
        4-1-8-4-4 Della (Twin) b. March 1894
        4-1-8-4-5 Stella b. Dec. 1896 d. Jan. 25, 1992 m. Walter Leopard
        Dora m. Mr. Ledford
    4-1-8-5 Nancy b. ca. 1866
    4-1-8-6 Nellie F. b. 15 Oct. 1867 d. 23 Feb. 1968 m,. Henry Edward Snider
        4-1-8-6-1 Novie Snider b. 1900 d. 1984
            4-1-8-6-1-1 Grover Snider
            4-1-8-6-1-2 James "Roy" Snider d. Dec. 11, 1991 m. Sarah _____
            Ronnie
            Roy
            Reta m. Mr. Radford
            Rochelle m. Mr. Anderson
            4-1-8-6-1-3 Maude
            4-1-8-6-1-4 Eula m. Mr. Hughes
            4-1-8-6-1-5 Hazel m. Mr. Webb
            4-1-8-6-1-6 Mattie m. Mr. Hooper
            4-1-8-6-1-7 Rosie Lee m. Mr. Woods
            4-1-8-6-1-8 Ruby m. Mr. Webb
        4-1-8-6-2 Mattie "Marie" Snider b. 1903 d. Dec. 20, 1991 m. Oscar King 1931
        4-1-8-6-3 Mamie Snider b. 1906 m. James Owens
        4-1-8-6-4 Samuel ("Frank") Snider b. 1908
    4-1-8-7 John Franklin b. ca. 1870 m. Catherine Elizabeth Ramsey

> 4-1-8-8 Leander J. b. ca. 1876 m. Jane Snider
> 4-1-8-9 Mary (Mollie) b. 10 April 1877 d. 1 Oct. 1955
>
> 4-1-9 Peter Phillips b. ca. 1833 m. Margaret Jones 1 Feb. 1864 Point Lookout Maryland
>> 4-1-9-1 Malissa b. ca. 1853 m. Mr. Rochester
>> 4-1-9-2 Harbin Portman b. 14 Oct. 1855 S.C.d. 17 May 1935 m. Sarah E. Williams (aka) Elizabeth Mize
>>> 4-1-9-2-1 Lillie b. May 17, 1878 d. May 14, 1940 m. Newton Commodore Oliver
>>> 4-1-9-2-2 William Jonah b. May 30, 1882
>>> 4-1-9-2-3 George Paul b. Jan 9, 1883 d. Aug. 18, 1976
>>> 4-1-9-2-4 Lula Belle b. May 30, 1886 d. ca. 1948 m. James Daniel Moore
>>>> 4-1-9-2-4-1 George Daniel Moore b. Oct. 8,1905 d. Aug. 3, 1979 m. Ida Melissa Chapell Dec. 27,1925
>>>>> Alvin Henry Moore 1927
>>>>> Melvin Moore 1929
>>>>> Evertie Edward Moore 1931
>>>>> James Moore 1933
>>>>
>>>> 4-1-9-2-4-2 Eva Leola Moore b. July 26, 1907 m. Luther Columbus Bryson
>>>>> Bernice Bryson 1923
>>>>> Doyle Columbus Bryson 1925
>>>>> Eva Belle Bryson 1926
>>>>> Lois Bryson 1936
>>>>
>>>> 4-1-9-2-4-3 Annie Elizabeth Moore b. July 21, 1909 m. Julian Ramey Snider April 6, 1929
>>>>> Margaret Marie Snider b. 1930

Newspaper Clipping - Thursday January 20, 1994. The Greenville News, Greenville S.C.

THE BOYS STOOD UP AND CLAPPED

Margaret Snider Coker of Anderson, one of the first 11 women to attend Clemson 39 years ago, says her advice to Shannon Faulkner would be "to not go" to the Citadel.
By Ron Barnett

Clemson — It was a joyous day for Clemson College cadets when the wall barring women came down in 1955. Unlike The Citadel, which almost 40 years later is fighting the admittance of a woman into its ranks, Clemson raised banners and opened its arms when its all-male military establishment was invaded by the opposite sex, the first Clemson graduate recalls.

When we got there, they had a big sign out front. They had cut out big letters, and it said, 'Welcome Co-eds'" said Margaret Snider

Coker of Anderson, one of 11 women who made history one cold day in February 1955.

"When I went into class, the boys all stood up and clapped." she said Wednesday.

Despite her pioneering role, Mrs Coker, 63 says she doesn't see any need for gender restrictions at state supported schools to be done away with entirely. But she says she favors "women getting ahead (having) equal rights and having better jobs."

"I needed a state-supported school, so I was really glad when they opened up Clemson to women," Mrs Coker said. "But I didn't force them to. I didn't have any trouble. Everybody seemed to welcome the girls."

She said her advice to Shannon Faulkner, the Powdersville teenager who is fighting a legal battle to enter The Citadel's cadet corps, would be "to not go." "Really, I feel that Shannon should let one college be a military college and all boys if that's the way they want it to be." she said. "I don't feel that every college has to be co-ed, as long as they have some good colleges (open to women)."

Mrs Coker, who had attended Anderson College for two years before arriving at Clemson, earned her degree in Chemistry in May 1957 — making her the first woman to graduate. She went on to land "a man's job" in Owens Corning Fiberglass in Anderson where she worked 29 years before retiring and was a supervisor.

"The only way I became accepted at work was that I did an excellent job and did prove to them that I could do it.," she said. "I would be in meetings with all men almost all the time I worked down there."

Breaking new ground requires an extra effort and exceptional ability, said Mrs Coker, who is the mother of two children and the grandmother of two. She said that's something she would advise Miss Faulkner to be prepared for if she wins her battle with The Citadel.

"To go somewhere for four years where you're not welcome would be an awfully hard row to hoe because college is hard enough." Mrs. Coker said. "But if she does go ahead and go, the only way she's going to be successful is if she's exceptionally smart and makes good grades"....

    James Leroy Snider 1932
    Barbara Louise Snider 1934
4-1-9-2-4-4 Edward David Moore born June 20, 1911
4-1-9-2-4-5 Fred William Moore b. Sept 9, 1915
    Dorothy Christian Moore b. 1935

       Shirley Sue Moore b. 1937
       Gerald Fred Moore b. 1940
       Genevive Moore b. 1942
       Sandra Lee Moore b. 1946
       Linda Gayle Moore b. 1949
4-1-9-2-4-6 Levine Henry Moore b. Sept 24, 1917 m. Intha Mary Reynolds
       Elnora Christine Moore 1938
       Betty Caroline Moore 1934
4-1-9-2-4-7 Mary Ruth Moore b. June 23, 1922 m. (1) Heyward Cleveland Moore (2) James Whitlock
       Francis Olivia Moore 1940
       Harold Cleveland Moore 1942
       Rachel Esterline Whitlock 1954
       Edward Lee Whitlock
4-1-9-2-4-8 Lula Geneva Moore b. 1926 d. 1927
4-1-9-2-5 Nancy Addie b. Sept 18, 1888 d. ca. 1917 m. _____ Quarles
4-1-9-2-6 James Virgil b. ca. 1890
4-1-9-2-7 Edward b. ca. 1893 d. ca. 1917
4-1-9-2-8 Lassie b. Mar. 1896 d. ca. 1918
4-1-9-2-9 John L. b. Dec. 1898 d. 1960
4-1-9-3 Perry L. Phillips b. Jan. 1858 m. Martha E. Mize
   4-1-9-3-1 Clerinda Jane b. July 28, 1882 m. Edd Dryman
   4-1-9-3-2 Rose b. Oct. 1883
   4-1-9-3-3 Margaret Louvenia b. Oct. 1887 d. 1956 m. Joseph Daniel Winchester
      4-1-9-3-3-1 Leona
      4-1-9-3-3-2 Marvin
      4-1-9-3-3-3 Lawrence Winchester
      4-1-9-3-3-4 Joseph Winchester
      4-1-9-3-3-5 Stella Winchester
      4-1-9-3-3-6 Evangeline Winchester
      4-1-9-3-3-7 Vinela Winchester
      4-1-9-3-3-8 Geneva Winchester
      4-1-9-3-3-9 Louise Winchester b. 1925 d. Mar. 27, 1988 m. Robert Wilder
        Tony Wilder
   4-1-9-3-4 Nancy Alice Phillips b. Sept. 1892
   4-1-9-3-5 Lala Genova Phillips b. Nov. 10, 1895 d. May 21, 1934 m. Charles Quinton Deaton
   4-1-9-3-6 William H. b. Aug. 1898
   4-1-9-3-7 Jesse A. Phillips b. July 16, 1894 d. June 20, 1947 m. Maude C. _____
      Christine b. 1915
      Grover b. 1917
      Milton b. 1919

        4-1-9-4 Sarah Nancy Phillips b. ca. 1860 m. _____ Stansell
        4-1-9-5 Margaret A.B. Phillips b. ca. 1863
    4-2 Jonas Jr. b. 1791 m. Charlotta _____

Jonas Philips to James Cole, both of Pickens District, SC, for the sum of $700. That plantation or tract of Land granted to the said James Cole on the 6 December 1824 containing 314 acres being in the District of Pendleton on both sides of Long Creek waters of Chatooga River known as tract No. 5 in the territory acquired by treaty in the Cherokee nation Indians, bounded by lines running SW by No. 1, SE by No. 8, NE by No. 6, and NW by NO. 17 FEbruary 1830.

Jonas Phillips Jr. was fined $10 each for two counts of Assault and Battery in the 1853 term of court Pickens District, SC

        4-2-1 Nathaniel(Nathan) W. Phillips b. ca. 1815 m. 1836 Rabun Co. GA. Jane Williams
            4-2-1-1 Reuben W. b. ca. 1838
            4-2-1-2 Charlotte b. ca. 1840
            4-2-1-3 Mahala b. ca. 1842 m. 1. William Gault Ellis 2. Joseph Phillips 3. John Black
            4-2-1-4 Elizabeth b. ca. 1845
            4-2-1-5 Phebe b. ca. 1848
            4-2-1-6 Margaret Mary b. ca. 1850
            4-2-1-7 Nancy A.M. b. ca. 1852
            4-2-1-8 Patton A. b. ca. 1855
            4-2-1-9 Rachel C. b. ca. 1858
    4-2-2 son (no further information)
    4-2-3 Joel L. b. 1817 m 1.Sarah Williams 2.Zilly
        4-2-3-1 Elizabeth 1841
        4-2-3-2 Charlotte 1842
        4-2-3-3 Jane ("Jennie") b. 1843
        4-2-3-4 Nathaniel b. May 21, 1845 d. June 17,1920 m. Tabitha Wilbanks. They lived at Long Creek SC.
            4-2-3-4-1 Amanda Isabella
            4-2-3-4-2 Canzada Jane Phillips b, Oct. 17, 1869 d. Dec. 16, 1899 m. Joel Barker
                Nellie M. Barker 1899-1907
                Minnie Belle Barker (living 1920)
            4-2-3-4-3 Jonathan Ledbetter Phillips b. Oct. 1869 m. Emma E. _____
                Ida L. b. Oct. 1896
                Basil Phillips b. April 1898
                Lewis Phillips b. Feb. 1900
                Claudelle Phillips b. 1905
                William L. Phillips b. 1906
                Furman Phillips b. 1908 (Twin)
                Nellie M. Phillips b. 1908 (Twin)
            4-2-3-4-4 Miles Leroy Phillips b. Sept. 7, 1871 d. Jan. 28, 1944 m. Mary Ella Grahl
                Arthur Phillips b. Aug. 5, 1891 d. June 28, 1952 m. Eulah Grant

      Effie C. Phillips b. 1894
      Harlie W. Phillips b. 1896
      Annie Phillips b. 1898
      Harold N. Phillips b. June 20, 1903 d. Jan 9, 1979
      Hallie (Hattie) Phillips b. 1906
      Pearl Phillips b. 1908 m. Mr. Ramsey
      Martin Phillips b. 1911
  4-2-3-4-5 Celia Ann Dovilla Phillips m. Mr. Cannon
  4-2-3-4-6 Roseanna Savada Phillips m. Mr. Ivester
  4-2-3-4-7 Sarah Etta Phillips m. Mr. Fochs
4-2-3-5 Anah ("Annie") Phillips b. 1847
4-2-3-6 Miles Phillips b. 1849
4-2-3-7 Rachel Phillips b. 1850
4-2-3-8 Lijah Phillips b. 1855
4-2-3-9 Norman (?Harmon) Phillips b. 1857
4-2-3-10 Bieman Phillips b. Sept. 4, 1860 d. April 15, 1932 Married Charlotte ("Lottie") Stubblefield
    Frances J. Phillips b. June 1886
    Reecie Phillips b. September 1888
    Henry Phillips b. Nov. 9, 1891 d. Nov. 13, 1955 m. Leona W. _____
    Clifton Phillips b. Feb. 1897
4-2-3-11 Sarah ("Sally") Phillips b. Oct. 1867
4-2-3-12 Newton Phillips b. Oct. 1867
4-2-3-13 Jonas J. Phillips b. Oct. 25, 1869 d. Dec. 10, 1936 m. Dora Ivolee Grahl
  4-2-3-13-1 Lula Mae Phillips b. March 12, 1892 d. July 25, 1912
  4-2-3-13-2 Edward Phillips b. 1895
  4-2-3-13-3 Clifton B. Phillips b. 1897
  4-2-3-13-4 Essie L. Phillips b. 1902
  4-2-3-13-5 Hettie Phillips b. 1905
  4-2-3-13-6 Ila Phillips b. 1906 m. R. Lake McClellan
      Joyce McClellan m. Clafer Honea
      Virginia McClellan m. Mendel Morris
  4-2-3-13-7 Gena Phillips b. 1909
4-2-3-14 Ledbetter Phillips b. Sept 1871 d. after 1920 m. Hannah Malois
    Corrie Phillips b. 1901
    George J. Phillips b. 1903
    Jonas B. Phillips b. 1907
    Fleeta Phillips b. 1910
4-2-3-15 Ara Phillips b. Oct. 1883(1873?)
4-2-3-16 Lewis Phillips b. June 26, 1876 d. May 12, 1942 m. Lela Taylor
    Joel Phillips b. 1907
    Newton Phillips b. 1909
4-2-3-17 Olive Phillips b. Feb. 1884

4-2-4 William H. b. 1820 m Arene Chambers
    4-2-4-1 James B. Phillips b. March 1846 served in CSA m. Rity J. _____
        4-2-4-1-1 William H. Phillips b. Jan 1876 m. Lula _____.
            R. J. Phillips b.1908
        4-2-4-1-2 John Walter Phillips b. Feb. 20, 1878 d. Jan 16, 1942 m. Lillie F. S.
        4-2-4-1-3 Carrie J. Phillips b. Nov. 1884
        4-2-4-1-4 Charley R. Phillips b. Feb. 10, 1886 d. July 14, 1947 m. Nancy Butts
        4-2-4-1-5 Marshal A. Philips b. July 23, 1889 d. Aug. 31, 1964 m. Fanny A. _____
        4-2-4-1-6 James C. Phillips b. May 1892 m. Cora _____
    4-2-4-2 Jenett Phillips b. 1847 d.y.
    4-2-4-3 Mary M. Phillips b. 1849
    4-2-4-4 Jonas E. Phillips b. Dec. 3, 1850 d. May 16, 1923 m. Rachel A. Lee
    4-2-4-5 Prudence Elizabeth Phillips b. July 1852
    4-2-4-6 Rachel A. Phillips b. 1862
4-2-5 daughter (no information)
4-2-6 daughter Nancy H. b. sept 13, 1824 m. James C. Lee died May 20, 1907
4-2-7 Jonas Phillips b. 1826 m. Elizabeth Minerva Gassaway 2. Catherine
    4-2-7-1 James J. Phillips b. October 1852 d. after 1910 m. Mary Ann _____
        4-2-7-1-1 John M. Phillips b.
        4-2-7-1-2 William S. Phillips b. 1881
        4-2-7-1-3 Moses J. Phillips b. April 1882
        4-2-7-1-4 Sarah M. Phillips b. 1899 m. Jabe B Wilbanks
    4-2-7-2 Rachel Philips b. 1855
    4-2-7-3 John Sloan Phillips b. March 4,1857 d. September 21, 1923 m. Angeline Ada _____
        4-2-7-3-1 Julius S. Phillips b. 1883 d. 1952 m. Martha Lula S. _____
            4-2-7-3-1-1 Retha A. Phillips b. 1905 m. M.B. Smith
                Leroy Smith b. 1925 d. 1940
                Eleanor Smith b. 1930 d. 1948 m. Mr. Murphy
            4-2-7-3-2 Gussie M. Phillips b. 1907
            4-2-7-3-3 Beatrice Smith Phillips b. 1915 d. 1917
            4-2-7-3-4 Clarence B. Phillips b. 1913
            4-2-7-3-4 Ruby B. Phillips b.1918
        4-2-7-3-2 Jonas Cleve Phillips b. Feb. 16, 1885 d. Apr. 19, 1954 Married Delphia Lee and 2.) Catherine C. _____
            Nell I. b. 1905

Wade P. Phillips b. 1906
Mahala B. Phillips b. 1908
Ader Phillips b. 1911 d. 1914
Ralph Phillips b. 1913 d. 1915
Clara Phillips b. 1915 d. 1917
Nora Phillips b. 1918
A.R. Phillips b. 1920 d. 1966 m. Edith _____

Jake O. L. Phillips b. Jan. 3, 1925 d. Jan 14, 1945

4-2-7-3-3 Matty P. Phillips b. August 10, 1887 d. March 20, 1907
4-2-7-3-4 John Gus Phillips b. 1889 d. 1965 m. Nora _____
4-2-7-3-5 Lex Vance Phillips b. 1881 d. 1964 m. Zelia L. _____
    J.V. Phillips
    Emma Phillips
    Icie Phillips
4-2-7-3-6 Clarence B. Phillips b. Feb. 1884 m. Ollie B. _____
    Cleo N. Phillips b. 1918
    Edwin Phillips b. 1919
4-2-7-3-7 Ida M. Phillips b. Feb. 1896 m. Mr. Moore
4-2-7-3-8 Ethel B. Phillips b. August 1898
4-2-7-3-9 Coates L. Phillips b. August 29, 1900 m. Zelia T. _____
4-2-7-3-10 Sally B. Phillips b. 1908
4-2-7-3-11 James Crate Phillips b. 1910 m. Grace Pauline Thrift
    4-2-7-3-11-1 Doris Kay Phillips b. d. Feb. 19, 1990 m. Clifford Canupp
    4-2-7-3-11-2 Horace Phillips
    4-2-7-3-11-3 Pete Phillips
4-2-8 Prudence Elizabeth b. 1828 did not marry
4-2-9 Charlotta b. 1831

CHAPTER 7

5. Jesse Phillips b. Cecil or Fredrick Co. MD
   Wife Elizabeth No Known children.

On February 9, 1778 William Phillips filed for 100 acres of land on the headwaters of Dutch Second Creek next to Andrew Holtshouser, Wendle Miller, and Jesse Phillips in Rowan County North Carolina.

On March 7, 1778 Jesse Phillips filed for 250 acres in Rowan County, on Dutch Second Creek next to Andrew Holtshouser, Windle Miller, Peter Call, and Valentine Hornbager and including his own buildings.

On the 1778 Tax list, Jesse Philips (listed as Jesse Philipson) had 105.9 £ worth of land.

On April 22, 1780 Jesse Philips filed for 250 acres on Mirey Branch of Dutch Second Creek adjacent Rubin Philips, Frederick Mowrer and William Temple Coles. (This entry was later made over to Henry Walker.)

On May 4, 1780 Jesse Phillips was appointed constable in Captain Miller's company, of Rowan County.

May 9, 1782- Ordered that George Finson an orphan formerly bound to Benjn Robinson be taken from him and bound to Jesse Phillips 'till he attain the age of 21 years being now 11 1/2 yearsold, to be a farmer; said master to comply with the law.

The 1783 Tax List of Rowan County showed Reuben Phillips and his sons Levi, William, John, Jessee, Reuben, and Thomas. They were engaged in farming and were raising horses and cattle.

Jesse Phillips was on the Jury in Rowan County for the May session 1784. Tuesday May 4, 1784 - Alex Dobbins VS Robert K. Jury David Pool, Jesse Phillips, Fredk Griminger, Fredk Mower, Jacob Correll, Phillip Yost, John Correll, Abm Hill, Malcham Blew, Hugh Corson, Thos Plinxton, Har. Burcher (judgement 2 pounds)

On February 6, 1787 Jesse Phillips gave his apprentice George Vincent to Adam Phillips to learn the trade of shoemaker.

The 1790 Census of Rowan County showed Jesse Phillips with a wife but no children.

On December 20, 1791 Jesse Phillips was granted 200 acres on Dutch Second Creek.

Friday August 10, 1792 - Venire for November Court included Jesse Philipz.

On November 12, 1793 Jesse Phillips and wife Elizabeth sold 230 acres on Dutch Second Creek.

In 1796, there was a judgement against Jesse Phillips in Iredell County, N.C. There was an order to sell Jesse Phillips land on head branch of Houston's creek on February 17, 1796 in Iredell Co. N.C. About this time, he is believed to have moved to Carter County Tennessee.

CHAPTER 8

6. Reuben Phillips b. Dec. 27 1757 ?Cecil Co. MD d. 1814 Wilkes Co. NC. Wife Judith

Reuben Phillips Jr. appeared on the 1778 Tax list as Reuben Phillipson.

The 1783 Tax List of Rowan County showed Reuben Phillips and his sons Levi, William, John, Jessee, Reuben, and Thomas. They were engaged in farming and were raising horses and cattle.

Horse racing was a common pastime in Rowan County, and though the Phillipses bred horses, few of them were probably race horses, but rather brood mares for the production of mules.

The 1790 Census of Rowan County showed Jesse Phillips with a wife and Reuben Phillips with a wife, two sons and six girls.

On August 2, 1793 Reuben Phillips and wife Judith sold 200 acres on Crane Creek and Dutch Buffalo to George Gents. This was land granted December 20, 1791. Saturday February 8, 1794 - Reuben Philips and wife Judith to George Gents 200 acres on Crane Creek and Dutch Buffalo: August 2, 1794 (1793).

31 August 1796 Reuben Philips was a witness between Henry Hereford and James Campbell in Iredell Co. NC.

Reuben Jr. moved to Wilkes County North Carolina where he died in 1814. Reuben Phillips land bounded that of Charles Forester, William Shamlen, and John Scott on February 6, 1798 in Wilkes County, NC.

Reuben Phillips Jr. appeared in the 1800 census of Wilkes County, N.C.

In Wilkes County, N.C. on February 1, 1803 an apprentice bond was made out in which Polly Philips was bound to Reuben Philips to learn the occupation of spinster until her eighteenth birthday.

On December 17, 1803 Reuben Phillips received 100 acres on Grassy Creek, Waters of Little River next Solomon Barnes in Wilkes Co. NC.

On December 9, 1809 Reuben Phillips acquired 70 acres on Grassy Fork, Little River, Wilkes Co. NC on his own line and 60 acres adjacent Solomon Barnes.

1810 Census Wilkes Co. NC: The 1810 census of Wilkes County North Carolina showed Reuben Phillips with two sons.

On December 20, 1813 Reuben Phillips Jr. of Wilkes County North Carolina wrote his will which was proven in the Spring term 1815.

It lists wife Judith, daughters Elizabeth, Catherine, Hannah, and Sarah and sons Nathaniel, John, Jacob, and Jesse.

Children:
6-1 Elizabeth Phillips
6-2 Catherine(Caty) Phillips
6-3 Hannah Phillips
6-4 Sarah Phillips   m. John Hall
6-5 Nathaniel Phillips b. 1779

Biography of Noah J. Phillips of Blountsville, Tennessee.

I was born just sixty nine years ago in Wilkes County, North Carolina, only a few miles from Taylorsville, in what is now Alexander County. My Parents were Elijah and Micheal Phillips, both [now] dead. He was born in 1814 and she in 1816. His father was Nathaniel Phillips, perhaps of Rowan County, N.C. Her father was Amon Bumgardner, who removed from Lincoln County, N.C. to Wilkes County N.C.

I knew my grandparents on both sides in Wilkes County North Carolina when they were old, and I was but a boy. When I was about seven years of age, my father removed to Burke County and I saw but little of my grandparents, uncles, and aunts afterward.

From my youth I desired an education. My parents were poor and unlearned, but gave me the best advantages they could in the common schools. When in my teens I had to work most of the time. I left home at the age of seventeen with little clothing and no money, and soon made my way to Tennessee.

After working on a farm for William Pierce, I started to school in the fall of 1854 to James G. Bruner, who was one of the best and most painstaking teachers I ever saw. I had not been with him long until he said "If you will live with me until you are twenty one, I will give you as good education as I have, and a good horse, saddle, and bridle." I accepted his proposition. I was then in my eighteenth year. I remained with him and he treated me the best he could. He was in ordinary circumstances. He owned no land and no home. He rented land, farmed in summer and taught school in winter.

When my time was nearly out with him, and he had not fulfilled his part of the contract, he agreed that I might go to Fall Branch Seminary. Mr. Bruner paid a little tuition for me instead of giving me a saddle. He then gave me a young horse and a cheap bridle which I sold to Jonathan Crouch at Fall Branch for $75.00, and took it up mostly in board. This was in 1857.

I had no money, and but little else, except character. I performed the duties of janitor of the Seminary, which paid part of my tuition, and I went in debt for the balance. I bought some books, and borrowed others, and did the best I could. I studied almost day and night.

In 1859, finding myself getting in debt, I told Professor Bennett that I had decided to teach a school. Without my solicitation he gave me a splendid recommendation. I taught and studied more assiduously, if possible, than my students did, and went back to school to the same teacher.

In October 1860. I married Miss Ellen Hall Mullenix, and taught school, mostly in Greene County, but partly in Sullivan, during most of the Civil War. I was exempt from military service in the Confederate Army by two acts of the Confederate Congress; first, exempting teachers who had twenty pupils; and second, those who had been teaching three years.

In May 1864, I went with my family to Kentucky, and taught one year, or until the war closed in 1865, and then came back to Fall Branch. I again taught a while, then sold goods as a clerk for Reeves and Riper at Fall Branch. I was postmaster there in 1866-7-8 and until I came to Blountsville in September 1868.

I was register of Sullivan County for a time; was clerk of the county court about eighteen months, filling out the unexpired term of David Pence, deceased.

In November 1870, I became clerk and master of the chancery court at Blountsville, and have occupied that position most of the time since.

My first wife died in 1886, and two years later I married Rebecca C. Millard.

I have been a newspaper correspondent for nearly forty years; and edited a paper about five years. I have written up the lives and deaths of many persons - younger and older than myself. I am on the down-hill of life. If I may live another year, I shall have rounded out the "three score and ten" mentioned in the Bible. I have one brother and one sister [living] and five children...

I cannot see that I have accomplished much good: I have made many failures; but while I live I hope to be found on the side of right and against the wrong as I see it; and may the Divine Hand Guide me. And I ask His blessings upon all. N.J. Phillips May 13, 1906
6-6 John Phillips
6-7 Jesse Phillips b. 1795
6-8 Jacob Phillips b. 1796 m Elizabeth Cope 12 February 1820 Wilkes Co. NC 2, Elizabeth Brown Ball.
    6-8-1 Jesse Phillips b. Aug. 1829 m. 1.) Sarah Williams 2.) Margaret L. Dykes
    6-8-2 John b. 25 Sept 1834 m. Sarah Woodruff d. 27 Apr. 1918
    6-8-3 Mary Phillips b. 1836

6-8-4 George Phillips b. 1839 m. Manerva J. _____
6-8-5 Ruben Edward Phillips b. 1842 m. Martha W. _____
6-8-6 Aaron Phillips b. 1845 m. Nancy Ann Spencer
6-8-7 Jacob Phillips b. 1847
6-8-8 Andrew J. Phillips b. 1855 Bradley TN m. Sarah A._____

CHAPTER 9

7. Adam Phillips b. Dec. 27, 1762 Fredrick Co. MD d. Dec. 27, 1858
   Married (2?) Hannah Bailey ca. 1787 Rowan Co. NC

1781 - In Battle of Cowan's Ford under Colonel Locke, Major Simmons, and Captain Smith. In February 1781, Adam Phillips was in the Revolutionary War at the Battle of Cowan's ford. The troops first assembled at Beatties Ford on the Catawba River, many of them coming straight from church. The Reverend James Hall had called them from Fourth Creek Church, while Reverend Thomas Mc Caule called them at Centre Church. The troops were divided, half of them assigned to Beatties Ford, and Half of them to Cowan's Ford. Adam was with the 300 assigned to Cowan's Ford, and was in the thick of battle during the morning of February 1, 1781. The guide was not entirely familiar with the ford, and took the troops straight across, which actually helped the british since it put them out of reach of most of the bullets for a while. Perhaps as many as 100 men were killed on the British side, with that many being found in Thompson's fish dam down the river. On the American side, the greatest casualty was General William Davidson, who had just been talking with Adam Phillips shortly before his death.

State of North Carolina
Salisbury District N2420} Agreeable to an act of the Governing assembly papers in Wake County the 11 July 1782 Adam Philips was allowed nine pounds four shillings specie for Militia Service by the board of _____ February 9, 1783.
By Order
                              David Wilson}
                              Will Cathey }Aud
Richard Trotter C.B.

1787 - Living in Rowan Co. NC where he takes an apprentice to learn the trade of Shoemaker. On February 6, 1787 Jesse Phillips gave his apprentice George Vincent to Adam Phillips to learn the trade of shoemaker. As a journeyman shoemaker, Adam raised cows for leather and meat. He often tanned the hides too, using mountain oak and white oak for tanbark and ground it up in a vat with water. If he also had the trade of saddler he might make saddles, harnesses and bridles as well as boots and shoes.

In 1787 John Phillips was granted 384 acres on Dutch Second Creek. Adam Phillips and Hannah Bailey were married about this time, and moved to Crooked Creek in Mecklenburg County(now Union County) North Carolina. They located twelve miles southeast of Charlotte. Charlotte was a village with 276 people, 153 of which were whites, and 123 negro slaves. Businesses included a saw mill, a flour mill, a blacksmith shop, and three stores. For a frontier county, this was a large town, partially because it had become the county seat in 1774, and partially because of Liberty Academy which had been established in 1777. Charlotte was around 37 years old, and

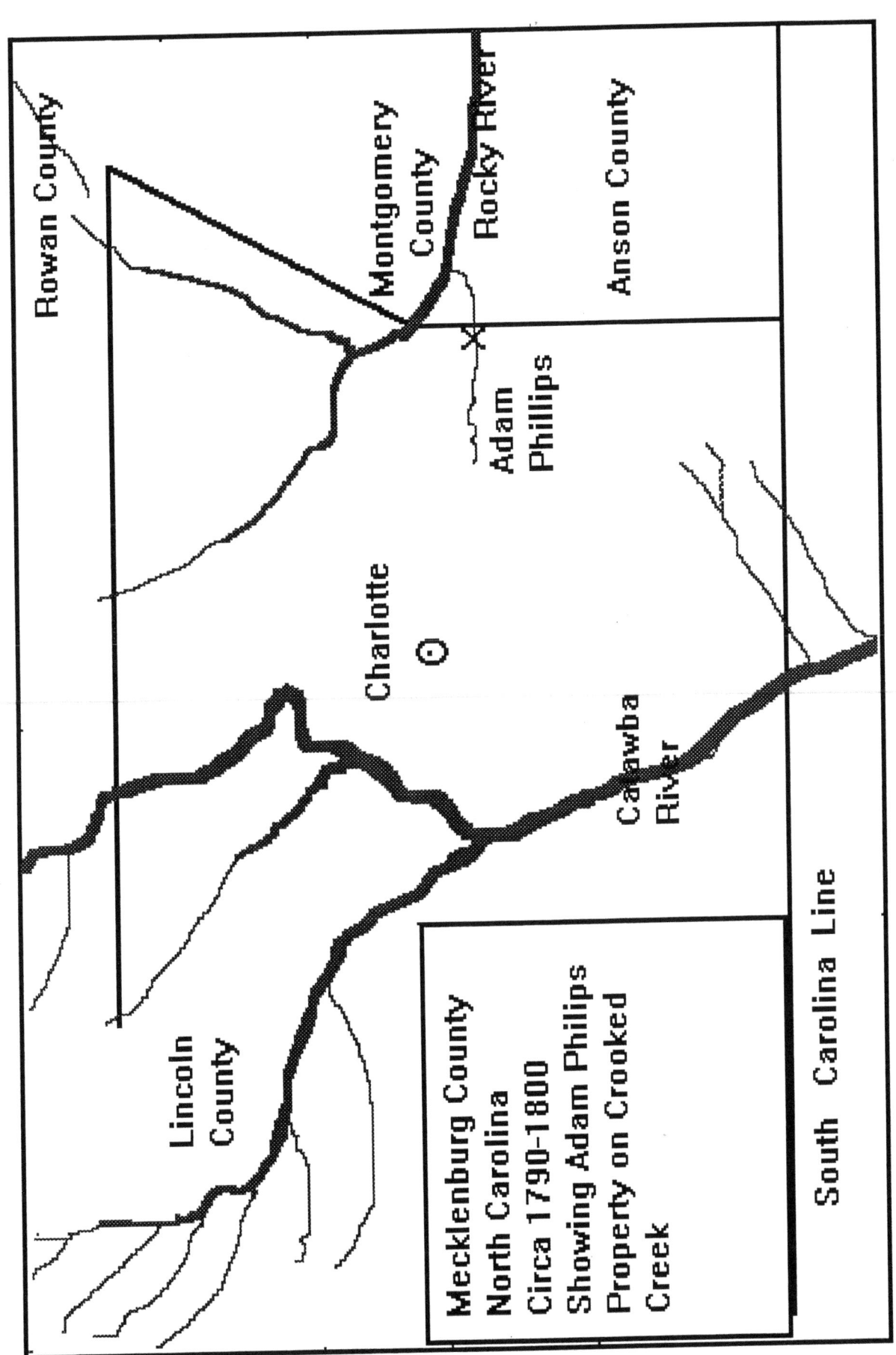

a thriving town. The lands between Charlotte and Salisbury were very fine, of a reddish cast and well timbered, with but very little underwood. Between these two places the first meadows were seen on the road and here also was a fine Wheat Country.

Adam's farm would have been like many of his neighbor's places. Buildings might include the plantation house, barn, garden, privy, smokehouse, woodshed, chicken house, spring house, corn crib, bee gums, wash house with a clothes boiler, cellar(apple house), horse lot, wagon shed, pig pen, cow pen (barn yard), blacksmith shop, store house, granary, school or chapel, sorghum mill or grist mill, butchering shed, corn field, tobacco patch, flax field, pasture, woodlot, carpenter shop, cobbler shop, slave quarters, brick kiln and others.

The Phillips family was not among the wealthiest, so many of these buildings would be missing. It was however a satisfying life. Items in a pioneers life might include a mint still, sorghum mill, evaporating pan, soap making kettle, gristmill. Crops were harvested by hand scythe, or reaphook. Grain was threshed by flailing it with a hickory pole. Sheep were kept for wool. White snakeroot was called milk sick and could kill a cow.

Roots gathered and sold were puccoon, may apple, black cohosh, alumroot bark, wild cherry, withe rod viburnum, white pine (for coughs).

Granny sat by the fire telling stories to the younguns. Bees swarm in May and June. Coursing bees for the honey wes done in late summer. There may have been only three months of school per year. Hoeing corn. A slop bucket was kept in the kitchen for scraps and dishwater. The season for camp meetings was from August through October. Talkin' religion may have been arguing a point with the aid of scripture. Backwoodsman bragged about building the best fire or having the best gun or dog or knife.

1788 - Living in Mecklenburg Co. NC on Crooked Creek with wife Hannah

On August 12, 1788 Adam Philips acquired 50 acres on Crooked Creek bordering the land he lived on.

On March 2, 1789 John Donaldson and Wife Elizabeth deeded 62 acres on both sides of Crooked Creek to Andrew Moor. The witnesses were Adam Philips and Elijah Stilwell.

On November 24, 1789 Reuben and Catherine Phillips of Wilkes County Georgia gave a title bond to land in Wilkes County to Adam Phillips of Mecklenburg County North Carolina. On December 22, 1789 North Carolina gave its western lands to the United States.

1790 - On Census in Mecklenburg Co. NC. On the 1790 census of

W1243

State of N. Carolina Mecklenburg County by survey for Adam Phillips fifty acres of Land in said county lying on the waters of Crooked Creek Beginning at a pine near a road and runs south fifty seven East Eighty four poles to a Black oak on or near the Governors Line then with the said line north one hundred poles to a small water oak his own old corner then with his Line North fifty five west one hundred and sixteen poles to a stake thence to the Beginning
July 20 Day 1790
Saml Black D.S.

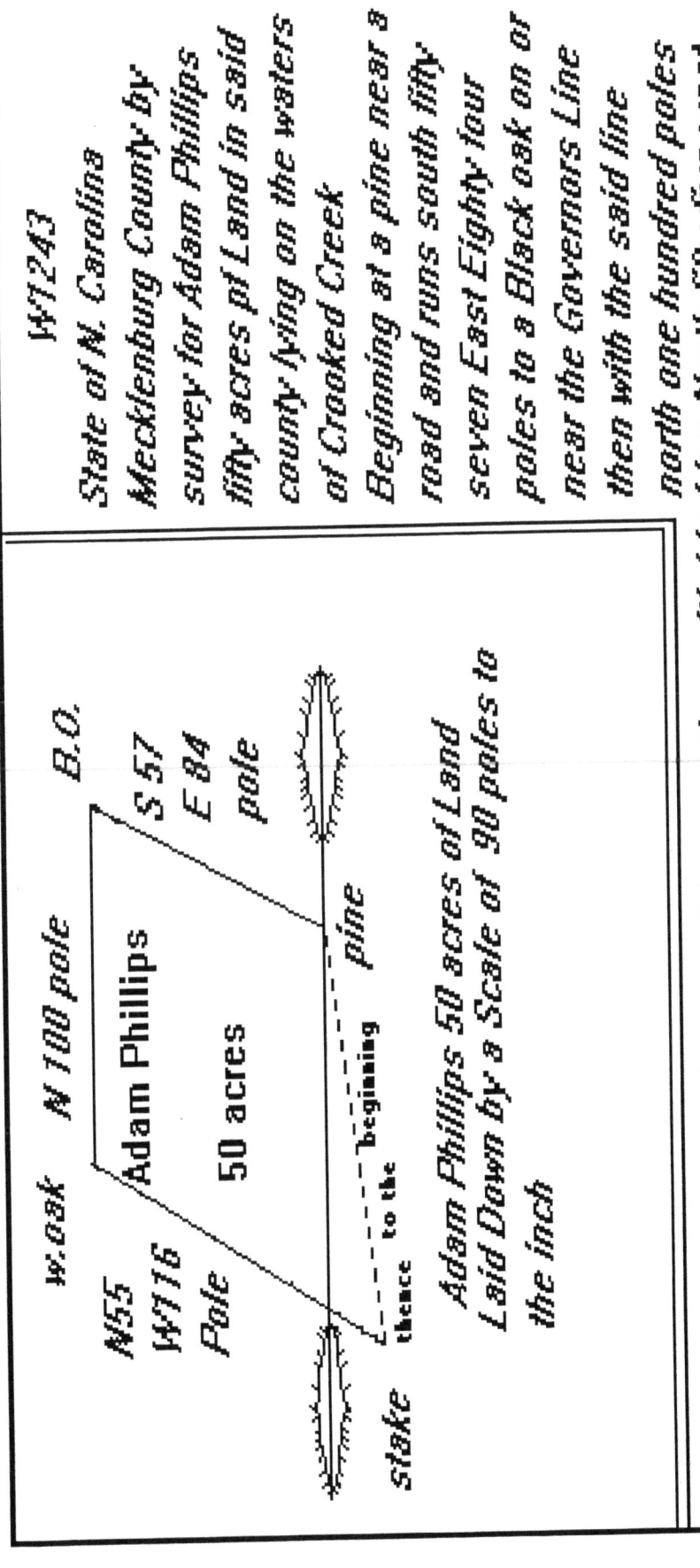

w. oak   N 100 pole   B.O.

N55 W116 Pole   Adam Phillips   S 57 E 84 pole
                 50 acres

stake ----- Beginning pine
       to the
       thence

Adam Phillips 50 acres of Land Laid Down By a Scale of 90 poles to the inch

John Donaldson
   and   C.B.
George Phinson

Mecklenburg County North Carolina Adam Phillips was shown with a wife and child. Mecklenburg County North Carolina was formed in 1762 from Anson County. It was named for Charlotte of Mecklenburg, the new queen. The population in 1790 was 11,393 and growth was slow. By 1850 the population was only 13,914. Union and Cabarrus counties were formed from Mecklenburg and by 1850 they had a combined population of around 20,000. In the early years, Mecklenburg County was involved in the Regulator movement which erupted in violence in 1771.

State of North Carolina
Mecklenburg County   Surveyed for Adam Phillips 50 acres of land lying on the waters of Crooked Creek Beginning at a Pine near a road and runs South <u>57</u> East <u>84</u> Pole to a Black Oak on or near the Governor's Line then with said line North <u>one hundred</u> Pole to a small Water Oak his own old corner then with his line North <u>54</u> west one <u>hundred 16</u> Pole to a stake thence to the Beginning
July 20 1790

John Donaldson}C.B.   Saml Black
George Phinson

Adam and Hannah had a daughter Elizabeth born March 27, 1791. George Washington made a tour of the country this year, and passed through Salisbury. Cathey's Meeting House changed its name to Thyateria Church. On November 26, 1791 James Roberts sold 200 acres on Cedar Creek to John Phillips. On December 20, 1791 Jesse Phillips was granted 200 acres on Dutch Second Creek. On the same date, State Grant 969 was granted to Adam Philips by J. Glasgow. It was for fifty acres on Crooked Creek adjacent to a road and his old land.

Adam and Hannah's son Elisha was born in 1793.

On February 1, 1794 Squire Stephens acquired 50 acres on the middle fork of Crooked Creek at the mouth of Scaffold Branch bordering Adam Philips, James Maxwell, and John Black. By 1794, Salisbury had a printing press. There was a spring flood which uncovered a natural rock wall. This raised considerable speculation in the community, with the most favoring the theory that the rock wall was built by an earlier race of superior intelligence. A description of Salisbury at this time states that the houses were of frame construction and weatherbeaten. Negroes worked on the sabbath. People gambled, drank, played billards and all fours.

In the October session of the County Court, 1795, Adam Phillips was listed as one of the hands on the road crew which worked the road from the South Fork of Crooked Creek to Matthew Stewart's plantation. On December 4, 1795 Reuben Phillips was born to Adam and Hannah.

In the October session 1796, Adam Phillips was one of a jury appointed to lay off a new road from the Cabarrus County line to Blairs Mill on Goose Creek.

The 1798 Tax list for Mecklenburg County shows Adam Phillips in Captain John Hood's company with 87 acres of land. On April 21, 1798 Mary Ann Phillips was born to Adam and Hannah. In the October term 1798, Adam Phillips was appointed overseer of the road from Blairs Mill to John Cockrans.

In 1799, Adam Phillips and his family attended the Presbyterian Church. The pastor was Reverend Barr. Adam was on a tax list this year in Mecklenburg County with 153 acres of land and is listed as "one white poll".
On March 19, 1799 State Grant 1462 was granted to Squire Stevens for 50 acres on Crooked Creek including the mouth of Scaffold Branch adjacent to Adam Phillips, Thomas Gribble, and a path.

Catherine was born November 15, 1800 to Adam and Hannah Phillips.

The 1800 census of Mecklenburg County Showed Adam Phillips with a wife, three sons and two daughters. He was engaged in farming, and at times in teaching school, and attended the Presbyterian Church under the Reverend David Barr, pastor.

Reverend Reuben Philips writes: When I was four years old, my father taught a small neighborhood school and when the weather was pleasant he took me with him. On seeing the other children learning, I became anxious to try. My father made me letters on paper and pasted them to a paddle and I soon learned them all...

In 1803 Adam Phillips moved to Buncombe County North Carolina, where he rented land for a year on the beaver dams of Hominey Creek. He raised stock, probably including cattle, sheep, pigs, horses and mules. He had a flax field in Mecklenburg County, and probably continued this here to provide clothes for the family.

Reverend Reuben Philips writes: In the year 1803 my father moved to the mountains and settled in the western part of Buncombe County and lived one year in the neighborhood of Turkey Creek and as he rented land we had a hard year. In the fall of 1803 he purchased a piece of land unimproved on the beaverdams of Hominey Creek and we moved to it on the 10th of March 1804.

Fat pure-bred cows were still in the future. Pigs and cattle were turned out in the woods. A good milch cow could only produce about a gallon of milk per day. Cut worms soon became pests, and their parent moths were called "millers" since they went round and round the whale oil lamps of the period.

On May 7, 1803 Adam and Hannah had a son Hiram B. Phillips born.

Reverend Reuben: There being but few inhabitants we had no church, no school, and no Sabbath except at my fathers. He still kept up religious exercises in his family and was able to govern his family on the Sabbath. Gradually the older children formed association with the youth in the county... and began to retrograde in morals.

This was a land as close to primitive wilderness as any the Phillips family had lived in up to this time. If anywhere in his travels, Adam could be considered a pioneer, then the Beaverdams of Hominey Creek is that spot. It must have been a beautiful quiet spot, nestled in the hills of Western North Carolina, probably in modern Haywood County.

Wildlife must have been abundant, and hunting must have been good. Deer, bear, turkey, and other wild animals would have been easy to shoot or even trap. Deadfall traps and snares could easily have been set to trap any animals in the area.

Crops in this newly settled land may have been a problem. If the land had not been cleared, it would have been necessary to chop down the trees, or girdle them and leave them as deadenings.

On July 23, 1806, Adam Phillips bought 100 Acres of land in Buncombe County on Grassy Branch from Humphrey Cunningham. The Reverend Daniel Asbury came as a Missionary and stayed with the Phillips family.

In 1807, Jesse Richardson came to Buncombe County as a Methodist preacher. Adam Phillips became Class leader in the Methodist Society in Buncombe County.

Reverend Reuben: ...my mother became greatly stirred up in religion. She had a regular hour for secret prayer and kept her testament all the time where she went morning and evening for prayer and meditation. She often came home shouting from her place of secret prayer which was a large hollow chestnut tree where she resorted every day. On one occasion she took me with her and told me she wished me to assist her in putting some bushes around the tree to make it more secret and to turn off the evening sun.

On January 1, 1809 Adam Phillips bought land on Beaverdam Creek from William Davidson and at the same time he was granted 50 acres on South Turkey Creek by the State of North Carolina. The number of acres in his purchase are not stated. Later in 1809, Adam moved to Whitson's Creek (now Haw Creek near Bell Road and Bethesda Methodist Church in Asheville) near Asheville and left his son Reuben at home to go to school to a neighbor.

1810 Census Buncombe County showed Adam Phillips with a wife, three sons, and three daughters. On April 25, 1810 Eli and Sarah were the parents of their first son James Osborne Phillips who was born in South Carolina.

In 1811 there was a flood on the Swannanoa River near Asheville. We do not have a description of the Philips home, but contemporary descriptions may give a hint of the conditions:(Olmstead) The plantation often had an open work stable; a frame house with 2 rooms and a kitchen and a long porch in front, a loft was sometimes placed above the rooms. This might be a sleeping spot for the children or just for storage. A springhouse or a wellhouse might be placed behind the main house. Chickens and other animals would have free range of the premises. Behind or beside the other outbuildings a pig-sty and poultry coop, a ley-tub and quantities of home-carded cotton might be placed upon boards to bleach. Some fishing poles may hang in the porch and hunter's trappings on hooks in the passageway to the kitchen. In one room were perhaps three beds and in the other two, with only one in the kitchen. On the porch was often a loom with a piece of cloth in process. In larger houses the room would have two mighty feather beds and be hung about with all manner of family clothes and in one end a vast cavern for a fire. The floor was uneven and the hearthstones billowy. When the fire was lighted, the effect of the bright light in the cavern and the heavy shadows in the room was Rembrantish. The room was garnished with pistols and other arms and ammunition, rolls of negro-cloth, shoes and hats, handcuffs, a large medicine chest and several books on medical and surgical subjects and farriery(horse shoeing); while articles of both men's and women's wearing apparel hung against the walls which were also decorated with some patent-medicine posters. A woman might be spinning with the old-fashioned great wheel, and in the kitchen another woman weaving coarse cotton shirtings with the ancient rude hand loom. The mistress herself was spinning in the living-room. She made the common everyday clothing for all her family. All the bed-clothing, the towels, curtains, etc., in the house were of homespun. They only bought a few "store-goods" for their "dress-up" clothes. In the northern parts of Western North Carolina, it was common to see a square frame in which were piled a dozen bedquilts. The books were generally religious holiday books, such as Fox's Martyrs, the "Biography of Distinguished Divines," with others such as "The Alarm to the Unconverted" and "The Cause and Cure of Infidelity."

John Reynolds: [Adam Phillips] was our class leader when we were a boy, and perhaps no father was ever more solicitous about the temporal welfare of his own children than he was about the spiritual improvement of the members of his various classes. We say classes, for verily he often had charge of four or five different ones at the same time, frequently meeting two of them in one day, after holding prayer meeting with some of the others the previous night.

His congregations were nearly always large, not of his members alone but of other denominations as well as the world. His quick discriminating eye seemed ever on the alert for opportunities of doing good; and when an unusually large audience convened, he would sometimes hold a kind of general prayer meeting which resulted happily. So very punctual was he that he made it a fixed rule to begin his services at precisely the time appointed, causing some of the more tardy to style him the "minute man".

He never read long chapters or lessons, never prayed long prayers or at least they never seemed long. He addressed the Lord as friend talks to friend, and yet with the most profound humility; and so importunately did he plead for desired blessings, that his emotions would often choke for a time the utterance of his words.

Again he was one of Israels sweet singers, oft melting his hearers to tears while reading and singing his opening hymn. Though his meetings were generally short, still they were deeply impressive.

Perfectly satisfied with being a class leader, he said he desired no higher office in the church, nor would he accept ... a higher one. He maintained his religious character wherever found. Not only in the class, the Sabbath School, or the common school room, did he urge the necessity of practical heartfelt religion; but wherever he mingled with the world, even on the highway was this the absorbing topic with him.

He was punctual in his attendance on quarterly meetings, and always brought full reports from his classes. Loving and obedient to those who ruled over him in Church and State, he cheerfully "rendered unto Caesar the things which were Caesars and unto God the things which were Gods." Literally reducing to practice the divine injunction, to " owe no man, but to love one another". Few indeed had a more ready ear to hear the cry of the suffering, or a more willing hand to administer to their wants.

In his business relations he was a thrifty farmer, doing everything systematically, believing that whatever was worth doing at all was worth doing well.

On October 30, 1812 Adam Phillips sold 265 Acres on Grassy Branch to Eli A. Phillips. On November 17, 1812 Adam Phillips bought 200 acres on Beaverdam Creek from John Strother and others.

On January 5, 1813 Adam Phillips bought 200 acres on Whitson Creek from William Brittain. 1813 was a year with a cold winter. In March 1813, Eli Philips was ordered to serve on the road crew under Overseer Shoap.
On December 20, 1813 Reuben Phillips Jr. of Wilkes County North Carolina wrote his will which was proven in the Spring term 1815. It lists wife Judith, daughters Elizabeth, Catherine, Hannah, and Sarah and sons Nathaniel, John, Jacob, and Jesse.

State of N. Carolina   January Session 1814
Buncombe County   The following Deed was proven in open court

by the oath of Robert Hamilton the subscribing witness...
"This indenture was made this 30th day one thousand eight hundred and twelve between Adam Philips of the County of Buncombe & State of No. Carolina of one part & Eli A. Philips of the same county and state aforesaid of the other part. Witnesseth that for the consideration of the sum of one hundred dollars to me in hand paid by the said Eli A. Philips the receipt and payment thereof he the said Adam Philips doth hereby acknowledge hath granted, bargained, sold, aliened, conveyed and confirmed & doth by these presents grant, bargain, sell, alien, convey & confirm unto the said Eli A. Philips a certain piece or parcel of land situate lying and being in the county and state above written on both sides of a large branch passing into Swannanoa River on the north side known by the name of Grassy Branch including a cabbin Beginning upon a 2... Postoak ... on a ridge the original corner and runs with a line of the same North one hundred and eight poles to a post oak saplin near the north corner of a small glade or chasm thence west one hundred & forty eight poles ... to its corner stake then with the other old original line East one hundred and forty eight poles crossing said branch to the beginning containing by estimation one hundred acres ot the same more or less being part of a Tract of Land granted by the state to George Cunningham for two hundred & sixty five acres as per patent bearing the date Jan'y 19th 1796 together with all ways, woods, waters, watercourses, hereditaments & Appurtances thereunto belonging or appurtaining thereunto to have and to hold unto the said Eli A. Philips & his heirs and assigns at all times to warrant & forever defend the beforementioned premises with all its rights and appurtances... belonging or in anywise appearing to Eli A. Phillips his heirs and assigns forever free & clear of any encumbrance or any lawful claim of any person or persons whatsoever.

In Witness thereof I do hereunto set my hand & seal the day and date above written
Signed sealed and delivered in the presence of
Samuel Lusk   Adam Philips

(Certified by John Miller, Clerk the 8th day of February 1814)

On November 21, 1817 Adam Phillips was granted 100 acres on Beaverdam Creek by the State of North Carolina.

On January 4, 1819 Reuben Phillips bought 100 Acres on Laurel Branch from Adam Phillips.

On June 12, 1819 Adam Phillips bought 100 acres on Whitson's Creek from Thomas Westall.

The 1820 census of Buncombe County North Carolina showed Adam Phillips with a wife, two daughters and a son remaining at home.

On October 20, 1820 Reuben Philips married Elizabeth King. They took a trip to Virginia where they visited Elizabeth's mother Amy King, and then came back to Buncombe County where they took a room in Adam's house.

1830 - On Census Buncombe Co. NC
1840 - On Census Buncombe Co. NC

In the July court 1842, Adam Phillips presented the last will and testament of Bradley Powers to the Buncombe County court, he being one of the subscribing witnesses.

In the western North Carolina mountains in the summer the livestock such as cows, sheep, goats, and pigs were in pasture about six months. The hills were excellent range, and the mast was usually good, much being provided by chestnut, as well as oak, and smaller nut-bearing trees. The soil of the hills was a rich dark vegetable loam, and they were sometimes cultivated upon very steep slopes. It washed and gullied very little and was very absorptive. The valleys, and gaps across the mountain ranges were closely settled and all the level ground was fenced to keep the livestock out and either under tillage or producing grass for hay. The agricultural management was not as good as possible. Corn, planted without any manure, even by farmers who had large stocks of cattle, was cultivated for a long series of years on the same ground; the usual crop being from 20 to 30 bushels to the acre. Where corn failed, it was thought to be a good plan to shift to rye. Rye was sown in July, broadcast, among the growing corn, and incidentally covered with a plow and hoes at the "lay by" cultivation of the corn. It was reaped early in July the following year with cradles, an acre yielding from five to fifteen bushels. The following crop of corn was said to be much the better for the rotation. Oats, and in the eastern parts, buckwheat, were sowed in fallow land, and the crops were excellent. Herds-grass (<u>Agrostis vulgaris</u>), was sown on the valley lands, (rarely on the steep slopes of the mountains) with oats, and the crop, without any labor, paid for mowing and making into hay for from four to eight years afterward. Where it became mossy, weedy, and thin, it was often improved by harrowing or scarifying with a small "bull-tongue," or coulter-plow, and meadows thus made and occasionally assisted, were considered "permanent." The hay from them soon became in large part coarse, weedy, and bushy though if burned seemed to improve.

Natural meadows were formed on level land in the valleys, which was too wet for cultivation, by felling the timber and cutting up the bushes as close to the ground as possible, in August. The grass was cut the following year in June, and again in August or September, at which time the new growth of bushes yielded to the scythe. The bushesceased to flourish after the second or third year. Clover was a rare crop, but did well, and in some localities was perennial. Hay was stored on site with the larger part being stacked in fields. The hay fields were pastured closely in the spring and autumn.

Horses, mules, cattle, and swine were raised extensively, and sheep and goats in small numbers, throughout the mountains and afforded almost the only articles of agricultural export. Although the mountains were covered during three months of the winter with snow several inches in depth, and the nights, at least were nearly always freezing, there was never any shelter prepared for cattle. In the severest weather they were only fed occasionally, hay or corn being served out upon the ground, but this was not done daily, or as a regular thing, even by the better class of farmers. Some of the farmers had as many as four hundred head that were never fed at all, and never came off the mountain, in consequence of which many were starved and frozen to death every year. The cattle were of course small, coarse, and "raw-boned." They were usually sold to drovers from Tennessee when three years old, and were driven by them to better lowland pastures, and more provident farmers, by whom they were fattened for the New York market.

No dairy products were sold. There was little cheese, but butter of better quality than found elsewhere in the South, was made by all farmers for their own tables. Mules were raised by many people. The mares with foals were usually provided with a pen and shed, and fed with corn, cut oats(the grain and straw chopped together), and hay, daily during the winter. This was done by no means universally, however. In few cases was there stabling and really comfortable shelter prepared for a stock of mules; as a consequence, the mules were inferior in size and constitution to those of Kentucky, Tennessee, and Missouri, and commanded lower prices when driven to the plantations of South Carolina and Georgia — the market for which they were raised.

The business of raising hogs for the same market, which had formerly been a chief source of revenue to the mountain region, had greatly decreased under the competition it had latterly met with from Tennessee and Kentucky. It was now a matter of little concern except in certain places where the chestnut mast was remarkably fine. The swine at large in the mountains, looked good. It was said that they would fatten on the mast alone, and the pork thus made was of superior taste to that made with corn, but lacked firmness. It was the custom to pen the swine and feed them with corn for from three to six weeks before killing them. In some parts of the mountains the young swine were killed a great deal by bears. Twenty neighbors, residing within a distance of three miles, being met at a corn-shucking, one winter, in western North Carolina, account was taken of the number of swine each supposed himself to have lost by this enemy, during the previous two months, and it amounted to three hundred.

Bears, wolves, panthers, and wild-cats were numerous, and all killed young stock of every description. Domestic dogs should also be mentioned among the beasts of prey, as it was the general opinion of the farmers that more sheep were killed by dogs than by all other animals. Sheep raising and wool growing could have been the chief business of the mountains. If provided with food in deep snows, a hardy race of sheep could be wintered on the mountains with comfort. In spite of this, no sheep were kept with profit. No doubt they might have been if shepherds and dogs were kept with them constantly, and were they always folded at night. Eagles were numerous, and preyed upon very young lambs and pigs.

Many farmers kept small stocks of goats for the quantity of excellent fresh meat the kids afford when killed in summer. Their milk was seldom made use of. They required some feeding in winter, and the new-born kids, no adequate shelter ever being provided for them, were often frozen to death. Goats, in all parts of the South, were more generally kept by farmers than in the North.

The agricultural implements employed were rude and inconvenient. A low sled was used in drawing home the crops of small grain. Large loads may be moved with a sled across gullies where it would be difficult to use a cart or wagon.

In 1850 Adam appears on the Census in Buncombe Co. NC; He applied for a pension for his Revolutionary War service.

Pension Record: [Adam Phillips] entered the service of the United States [by being] drafted and served six months. Joined headquarters at Beaties Ford on the Catawba River [in] North Carolina. After marching through the country some time he marched to Salisbury and there guarded the prisoners some time... was then marched to Yadkin River. He was in an engagement with the British on Cowan's Ford where General Davidson was killed. He returned to Salisbury and [thence] to the Yadkin River where he [was discharged]. [His papers] remained in his possession up to the date of 1844 [when they were burned in a fire with other valuable papers, when his house caught fire].

On December 11, 1848 Hannah Phillips died in Buncombe County N.C.

Adam Phillips Pension Papers

Benjamin Green	37998
Washington City, D.C.	Adam Philips
(Address Side)	North Carolina

(Message)
N. B. Sec. so much as relates Adam Philips case

Asheville May 18th 1849

My Dr Sir
     I have received your welcome Letter with the Instructions enclosed but not the privates (   )
of which you spoke. I have the original declaration of Tho. Little & will forward them to the Department (where) you will please take charge of the case. The Ladies (   ) you may look

for soon. She lives some distance from me. Thos Little ( ) to it soon.

The Case of Adam Philips is this: in the first place I Can produce the Controllers Certificate for Eleven Pounds & 10 shillings as having bin paid him_ I can also prove by a living witness that he Saw Phillips discharge and will remember that it was for a six month tour and that the discharge as well as all the Olde Mans papers was Burnt in his house some years ago. Philips Says that his tour was six months But that he did not serve it out for the following reason. There was a young man took the Smallpox in the army and the officer in charge said he would release any man that would take the Man home and attend to him and that he Philips was the only Man in the Camp that had had the Small Pox and that he agreed to take him home with him and that the officer paid him up to the time & then gave him a full discharge & that it was Burnt as before stated.

You will please think of this Case and if you think we can succeed I will forward the Evidence. If we can get this case through it will pay as wills do your Buss and I will pay you liberally.

Write me soon on this particular case. That old <u>Man</u> is one of our Most Worthy Citizens.

(   )
Your Most Obdt

I. B. Sawyer

State of N. Carolina
Buncombe County   I Robert B. Vance, Clerk of the Court of Pleas & Quarter Sessions for the Said County do hereby Certify that the foregoing contains the original proceedings of Said Court in the matter of the Application of Adam Phillips for a Pension.
    In Testimony whereof I have hereunto set my hand and Seal of Office this the 11th day of April A D 1850
            R. B. Vance Clk

State of North Carolina   I Robert B. Vance, Clerk
Buncombe County   of the Court of Please & quarter Sessions for said county do hereby certify that I. B. Sawyer is and was at the time of signing the foregoing a Justice of The Peace for said county duly qualified to administer Oaths & that his Signature is Genuine.
    In (witness) whereof I have hereunto set my hand and office viz seal of office
    This 11 April 1850 RBVance clk

State of North Carolina
Buncombe County

County Court April Term 1850
Personally appeared before me James W. Patton Chairman qtr County Court of Buncombe North Carolina Henry Wells whom I am personally acquainted and who I certify to be a man worthy of credit and made oath in (   ) form of law. that he has seen in the possession of Adam Philips a discharge from the service of the United States as a private in the War of the Revolution in which the said Adam Philips was discharged regularly from the service, which discharge was signed by Major Smith of the U S Army and that in the year 1844 the said Adam Philips house was burned (with) all his papers together as to the discharge was consumed.

Sworn to in this court

attest
J.W. Patton J.P.
& C.C.B Buncombe

Henry Wells

State of North Carolina
Buncombe County

I Robert B. Vance Clerk of the county Court of said County hereby certify that James W. Patton Esq. is Chairman of said Court and that the signature to the forgoing statement purported to be his is genuine.

Given under my hand and seal of office at (office under register) the 11th day of april 1850
R.B. Vance Clk

State of North Carolina   Personally appears John Reynolds
Buncombe County   a Clergyman before the Court of
Pleas and Quarter Sessions at April Term 1850 and doth upon his oath state that he has been personally acquainted with the applicant Adam Phillips some forty years and that he is reputed and believed in the neighborhood, and further that he believed that the Said Claimant was in the War of The Revolution as set forth in his declaration.

Sworn and Subscribed Before   JohnReynolds
me 11th April 1850
    I.B. Sawyer JP

And the Court do hereby declare Their opinion after the investigation of the matter, and after putting the interrogations prescribed by the War Department that the above named applicant was a Revolutionary Soldier as he states, and the Court further certifies That it appears to Them that John Reynolds who has signed the preceding certificate is a Clergyman resident in the County of Buncombe and that Henry Wells is a creditable person and that their statements is entitled to credit.
                      John W. Patton JP
                      &CC.C Buncombe
                      John Hawkins JP

d
Washington April 22 1850

Hon. J.L. Edwards
    Commissioner of Pensions

Sir: I ask leave to present the application for Pension of Adam Philips a venerable Revolutionary Soldier of the age of eighty - seven years now residing in North Carolina. Some papers were filed in this case during last summer but they were not (decreed) satisfactory. When I call your attention to the extreme old age of this claimant, the circumstances of his not being likely to live long enough to enjoy his pension even when assigned I hope I suggest sufficient reason for a speedy action in his case.
                    I have the honor to be . Sir,
                        Your Obt. Svt
                            Richard H. Clarke
                                Atty. at Law..

Washington May 14th 1850

Attn: J. L. Edwards
    Commissioner of Pensions

Sir:

In the application of Adam Philips for Revolutionary Pension which I had the honor of sending to you about two weeks ago, I beg leave very respectfully to suggest in behalf of those whom I represent that as in case a pension is allowed a large proportion will be due immediately for back years & as the pensioner is extremely old & may not be able to go to the place where it may be made payable, the delay being great & inconvenient in sending a person to the place of payment to draw the money which is frequently a considerable distance off; to make the pension under this state of circumstances payable at Washington D.C.

    Very respectfully
      Your obt. Servant
        Richard H. Clarke

Washington June 7th 1850

Hon. J.L, Edwards
    Commissioner of Pensions

Sir: About two months or more ago I had the honor of filing for pension of Adam Philips an old Revolutionary Soldier now 87 years of age & subsequently of requesting that the pension might be made payable at Washington D.C. provided there were no indispensable rule of usage to the contrary. I have never heard from the Department on the subject of the application & respectfully ask leave to call your attention again to the case. The remaining days of this applicant are now numbered and unless he receives his pension soon (Provided he should be entitled to one) he may not live to receive and enjoy it at all.

    I have the honor to be Sir,
      Your most obt. Servant
        Richard H. Clark
    For Duff Green &Co.

Pension Office
June 11, 1850

Sir:

The declaration of Adam Philips of North Carolina under Act 7 June 1832 has been examined and filed. It would appear from a letter of I.B. Sawyer on file in the case of the applicant that a certificate of pay for his service, amounting to £ 11.10 was issued by the State of North Carolina as shown by the records in the office of the Comptroller of that state. This would not pay for six months service. The applicant alleges to have served a term of six months in the North Carolina Militia. There were no terms for so long a term as six months in the militia and the payment made shows his service to have been less than that time. The Act of 7 June 1832 provides for none who did not serve six months. The claim has consequently been rejected.

I am very respectfully
your obt. Servt
(Signed) J. S. Edwards

Richard H. Clark
    present

Washington June 14th 1850

Hon. J.L. Edwards
    Commissioner of Pensions

Sir; I am attorney in the case of Adam Phillips an applicant for Revolutionary Pension of N.C. I wish to see the papers filed by me in this case for the purposing of suggesting the procuring of additional evidence by the applicant. I cannot do so without examining the papers. I wish particularly to see the transcript of the proceedings in Court filed by me about 3 months ago. I am requested to suggest what new evidence I may judge expedient to file. The case has been a long time in the Department & I am not possessed of all the facts of the case, many of which I have forgotten & cannot move further in the case without looking a little into it.

    Very respectfully
    Your obt. Svt.
    Richard H. Clarke

State of North Carolina
Buncombe County

    I Robert B. Vance, Clerk of the Court of Common Pleas and quarter sessions for Buncombe County do hereby certify that I. B. Sawyer is a Justice of the Peace in & for said county duly commissioned and qualified according to Law & that the signature to the forgoing certificate of affidavit proposed to be his is genuine.

    Given under my hand & seal of said Court
This 24th day of June 1850   R.B.Vance.clk

State of NCarolina
Buncombe County

Supplement & additional account for Adam Philips in order to obtain the benefit of the act of June 7th 1832 which makes provisions for the surviving soldiers of the Revolution.

Came before Me I B Sawyer ( ) for the acting Justice of the Peace of this place in & for the County of Buncombe, Adam Philips who after being duly sworn according to Law makes the following additional statement to support his claim to a pension.

That he entered the service of the United States at Baties Ford (Mecklenburg) County ( ) under General Green at which place he remained a short time from which place he was marched to Cowan's Ford under the command of General Davidson at which place he was in an action in which General Davidson was killed, after which (he was marched) to Salisbury which place he remained some time guarding the British Prisoners of that place & from Salisbury he was marched to the Yadkin River at which place he remained some time but he does not now remember how long and that he received his discharge at that place from Major Smith.

Due to ( ) of olde age & loss of memory he is unable to state whether this service was (made) in two three months terms or in one six month term, But that he (swore) that he did rinder service to the United States in service as a Soldier & taking care of a youth who had the Small Pox under the directions & command of said Major Smith. Six Months and that he secured an Honorable and final discharge for two three months terms or one six month term & that the discharge was signed by Major Smith & Burned in his house with all his other papers as heretofore stated.

Adam Philip

Sworn to & subscribed to
before me this 24th day of June 1850
I.B. Sawyer JP

(House of Rep) July 9th 1850

Sir

(   ) desired to make a statement to you with reference to some pension cases forwarded by I.B. Sawyer Esq. I presume it will be (difficult) for me to state that I know Mr. Sawyer very well. He resides in the village of Buncombe County, and is a man of good character. I should regard any statement he has made of may make as entitled to full credit.

                                        Very Respectfully
                                        T.L. Clingman

(   ) J.L. Edwards

July 9th 50

I take pleasure in Stating to the Commissioner of Pensions that Adam Phillips & John Penland are known to me & are men of good character residents of North Carolina. I should have no hesitancy in placing full reliance of any statements made by them. Thomas Lytle Deceased was a highly respectable man & of a higher respectable connection leaving a family who would not improperly (present) and claim not founded in (Instill Burd) (decease) ( ) character is good and her husband a highly respectable citizen filed in the foregoing cases are correctly set forth as containing the facts in each case & are each of them entitled to full credit. Their attorneys and agents prosecuting in these cases are men of as high character & strict integrity as are in our state & I Trust therefore this together with Mr Clingmans statement will satisfy the deportment of the Justice of the claim.

Respectfully   B.M. Edney

Washington July 15, 1850

My Dear Sir-

Your Prompt attention is asked in the cases of <u>Lytles Heirs</u>, ( ), John Penland & Adaam Phillips. They have long on file & often amended. Allow me to say (this) as a <u>friend of yours</u>. That there is much feeling on these different cases in the community where they reside & Clingman has been written to in <u>loude complaints</u> by Gentlemen of the highest standing to have these cases allowed. They do not believe that your clerks are <u>confident</u> & that there is proof sufficient on file to have satisfied your mind long ago of the justice of the claims. The persons claiming are of good standing and the Agents & Attorneys engaged are of the best <u>character</u>. They are from Buncombe N.C.

I am going this Evening to Philadelphia. I will be back by third night & I do hope for your sake that these Cases will be examined and allowed for think all will certainly be Cerious difficulties growing out of them if they are <u>rejected</u>.

I make these suggestions as one of your best friends & I hope they will be appreciated as such - I have not brought all to your knowledge yet, which is in existence on this subject. I hope however I have said enough to <u>accomplish</u> the <u>purpose</u>. I have no earthly interest in the cases & have only interfered on account of the friendly relations subsisting between you and myself. I beg of you therefore not to neglect the material herein set forth.

Very Respectfully Your Obedient Servant.

B.M. Edney

J.L. Edwards Esq.

Undated
before 1852

To the Commissioner of Pensions

I simply wish to call your attention to the further fact that Adam Philips discharge as sworn to by him for a six month service was seen by (   ) <u>Henry Wells</u> Who swears Phillips had such a discharge & that it was consumed among his other papers & property by <u>fire</u>. The payment of £8 5 pence was made on indent on Army certificate (   ) by he (   ) of Salisbury & possibly may have been made to <u>some one else</u>. You stated in your letter to me the other day that, Philips stated, that he received his paper for the six months or for his <u>service</u> at the time of his discharge which is a mistake he has not made <u>any statement</u> in his original or, amended declaration, <u>about his pay</u> one <u>way or the other</u>. That the payments were made at different times <u>does not at all effect the validity</u> of his <u>claim</u>. Allow me to especially <u>suggest</u> that it is not at all <u>absolutely necessary</u> that <u>any payment</u> should have <u>been made</u> to render <u>his</u> or <u>any other claim valid</u>. This record (   ) is only sought as <u>corroborative</u>. Many claims have {been} paid <u>without any proof</u> of <u>payment by the State</u> for the reason that in many instances they were not made & in many they could not be made, for the records <u>were lost</u> or <u>destroyed</u>. Some of these payments may have possibly have been made to some other Man of his own name as you will see from the letter of the Comptroller which I herewith file, that he served the <u>six months</u> & that he was <u>honourably discharged</u>, is <u>fully shown</u> & <u>fully established</u> by his own <u>oath</u> & sustained by the <u>oath</u> of <u>Wells</u> both of whose characters are proven to be <u>first rate</u> & can't be <u>questioned</u>. If his house had not been <u>burned</u> & his discharge lost but filed here. I ask you if there could have been any <u>hesitancy</u> in allowing his pension, <u>independent</u> of any <u>payment made</u> by the <u>state</u>. Well the <u>loss</u> of sd paper & its <u>Identity</u> have been fully complied with & cannot now see, why there should be any longer delay & I think upon Mature reflection you will concur with me. <u>to do otherwise</u> is to convict <u>Philips</u> the <u>applicant</u> & <u>Wells</u> the <u>Witness</u> of wilful and corrupt perjury. I earnestly (ask) this <u>pension</u> will be <u>allowed</u>, without further <u>trouble</u>.

All of which respectfully submitted.

B.M. Edney

Know all men by these presents that I Adam Philips of the County of Buncombe and State of North Carolina a Revolutionary Soldier do hereby irrevocably constitute and appoint John (I) Neely Esq. of Washington City D.C. my true and lawful attorney for me in my name to examine into and present my claim for a pension against the General Government which may be now due me by virtue of my services in the War of the Revolution and the several acts of congress in relation thereto I hereby confirm whatsoever my said attorney may do or cause to be legally done in the prosecution of said claim, revoking any other attorney I may have given any other person in the premises whatever.

    Given under my hand and seal this 7th day of February 1852.

    Adam Philips {seal}

State of North Carolina
Buncombe County   On this 7th day of February 1852 Personally appeared before me Isaac B. Sawyer an acting Justice of the Peace for said County Adam Philips who acknowledged the forgoing Power of Attorney to be his act and deed and I certify that I well know the said Adam Philips and that he is the person present who executes the above power of Attorney.

    Given under my hand & seal this the 7th day of February 1852.

I Robert B. Vance, Clerk of the County of Buncombe County in the State of North Carolina certify that I.B. Sawyer Esqr, whose genuine signature appears to the within is an acting Justice of the Peace in & for said County, duly commissioned & sworn according to law.

    Given under my hand and seal of Office in Asheville, the 7th February 1852.

    R.B. Vance clk.

8955
INVALID

File no. _____8955_____
_____Adam Phillips_____
_____Priv.   Rev.   War_____

Act _____June 7th 1832_____

Index ----Vol. (702) Page 295

No 37998
Adam Philips
    NC
 Rejected
Sent to Duff Green 2 Aug 49
Sent to Duff Green 9 Aug 49
Sent to R.H. Clarke 11 June 50
Sent to Duff Green 8 July 1850
Gen B. M. Edney 6th August 1850
I.B. Sawyer 24 October 1850
Act 7 June 32

Let B.M. Edney July 27 52

Admit for 6 months
FFW
Sent to E.M. Edney
    Present

{Comptroller's Office N.C.
{July 15, 1852

Sir
    I and my clerk have spent a good portion of this day searching the records of payments to revolutionary soldiers, deposited in this office, for evidence of the services of Adam Phillips. We find payments amounting to £11.4.6 specie made to Adam Phillips and an additional payment of £8.8 specie to A. Phillips. Supposing the latter to be made to Adam, the whole would cover nearly eight months service__
    If you desire a certificate please inform me and enclose the usual for J5 on receiving which I shall immediately forward one.
                      Very Respectfully
                          Your obt. servt.
                        Wm. J. Clarke Compt'r

```
   11.4.6
    8.8
    2.  6
   21.13
    29
   ----
   42
   10.50
    1.62
   ----
  154  1  6
   40     4
   ----
   54    10          8 ms 7 days
```

Washington City
July 19 1852

Commissioner Pensions
Sir
I have on file in your office authority to examine &prosecute the claim of Adam Phillips a Rev Soldier of the N Carolina Service during the Rev war for a Pension under Act of Congress 7 June 1832 and I hereby give (   ) to (   ) Edney to take the claims in hand and attend to the (   ) & prosecution of said claim for a pension.

Yours Respectfully
(   )
Jno I Neely

Pension Office
July 27, 1852

Sir:
I have examined the claim of Adam Phillips of N.C. of 7 June 1832 in connexion with the certificate of the comptroller of that State recently filed by you. It is evident from the papers that the payments there shown could not have been made to claimant for the reason that they were made at three different times and indicate a service of nearly eight months whereas the applicant only claims six months and admitted to his attorney that he did not serve out his term but was paid for the time and discharged upon agreeing to take home one of his comrades who had been taken with the Small Pox.

Genl R.M. Edney
    Present,

Washington. July 28th 1852

Sir:

The decision of the department in the case of Adam Philips is <u>utterly</u> at variance with the former decision & wholly <u>inconsistent</u> with the declaration on file & not sustained in any particular by the facts contained in the comptrollers certificate but flatly contradicted by sd certificate for <u>offering a fact</u> & act upon it which nowhere appears in the record (Namely) That the third payment could not have been made to the applicant. It <u>was made</u> to <u>him.</u> Your department has no authority to decide otherwise. Any other conclusion or inference is not <u>warranted</u> by any fact appearing upon the face of the proceedings. You first reject the claim upon the ground the Comptroller said not paid enough. You now reject upon the opposit ground, that he had been paid a little too much. There are ... few cases on file in the pension office where the amt. paid & the <u>precise time record</u> on the pensioners <u>declaration</u> <u>exactly</u> <u>tally</u> for the cogent reason that the service was rendered <u>long ago</u>. The memorys of the applicants in many instances fail & the records of payments in North Carolina <u>Mutilated</u>, <u>Confused</u>, & <u>destroyed</u>. Adam Philips declaration simply states that he served in the war six months. His ... declaration states he does not well recollect whether the service one or two terms. There were in North Carolina <u>three</u> months service, <u>six</u> months<u> service</u> & <u>Nine</u> months service. <u>His may have been</u> a six and <u>three</u> months service. He (has) stated that he was detailed to attend a sick soldier with the smallpox which circumstances undoubtedly curtailed his service within the range of six months. He was a man of "<u>integrity</u>" & high standing & did not wish to overstate the time. <u>Base men</u> often do, but <u>correct</u> men <u>never</u>. The state of North Carolina may have paid him for the free service according to the payments contained in the comptrollers certificates at the time when his services were <u>fresh</u> in his <u>mind</u>. As he may have served only the six months as stated and the extra pay may have been given by the state for his attention to the Invalid soldier. What he received and the exact time so served he could not state having relied altogether upon his discharge which was consumed in his house by fire. His (   ) to six months service you reject said claim because he does not state <u>precisely</u> the number of <u>months</u> & days necessary to meet the amt paid by the comptroller. His statement is under the time you say it would be & (   ) to say that the <u>third</u> payment <u>does</u> <u>not </u>belong to <u>him</u> which if deducted might possibly reduce the other two <u>under</u> six months & therefore neither of them belongs to him. The latter conclusion would be quite as well founded as the former. Thus it is apparent that by drawing false conclusions, the best claim on file in your office might be mistified and ultimately lost. This (declaration) & those of the witnesses are before you & above suspicion! Maintain the (<u>leading proofs</u>) in the (   ) are as clear & satisfactory as the <u>Law</u> <u>requires</u> in cases so long ago audited and adjusted.

It is possible you might deduct the payment you say does not belong to him & find your <u>calculations</u>. The remainder to be just sufficient to entitle him to six months or if not that <u>particular one</u> then one of the others might be deducted producing the wanted result. The other ones & above six months may have been allowed him for other services than <u>those performed in the ranks</u>. I think it most likely it was as he says he performed other duties other than those of (   ) (   ) or he may have served over six months and not quite nine. One <u>important</u> fact is however <u>certain</u>, & <u>well</u> <u>established</u> & that too by proofs above <u>suspicion</u>. That he did serve six months in the public service of his country & that he has <u>never received a pension from the government</u> of the United States for said services & if the services of our gallant old soldiers are to go unpaid upon quibbles & technicalities, this relief <u>intended</u> to be <u>given</u> has <u>totally failed</u> & the soldiers in their declining years deprived of their legitimate rights. I respectfully ask a reexamination of this case & its immediate allowance. Otherwise, perhaps an appeal to the Secretary of the Interior where I hope to be fully able to expose the errors which have so long and mystically embarrassed the rights of this long delayed claimant, Very respectfully your obedient Servant.

              B.M. Edney
              Att. for A. Philips_

<u>33,049</u>
<u>North Carolina</u>
Adam Phillips

of   in the State of
who was a Private in the   commanded
by   in the   **NC**
line for **REVOLUTION**

Inscribed on the rolls of Asheville
at the rate of 20 Dollars - cents per annum
to commence on the fourth day of March 1831

Certificate of pension issued the 20 day of
Augt 1852 Gen. B.M. Edney
                Present
Arrears to the 4thof

Semi-annual ending

                            Revolutionary Claim
                            Act June 7, 1832

Recorded by R.M. McRae Clerk
Book F   Vol 6 1/2 page 69
Adam Phillips
Records corrected Nov. 22, 1904

Laborer's wages in North Carolina near Asheville were 50 cents to one dollar per day, or around eight dollars a month for steady work. Corn for bread was 50 cents a bushel and butter was eight cents a pound, since nearly everyone made their own butter. Many people around Asheville believed slavery to be a curse, but were used to the system.

Snow fell in April in Western North Carolina in 1854 and there had been a killing frost. A corn crop might make 20 to 30 bushels per acre.

Horses, mules, and cattle not only for meat and milk, but also for oxen were raised. The cattle were sold to drovers from Tennessee when three years old. Mares with a foal were provided with a pen and shed, where they were fed corn, cut oats, and hay during the winter. Hogs were raised extensively, running loose in the woods until several weeks before sale when they were penned and fed. The hills provided an excellent range for the stock, especially cattle and hogs. They fed on chestnut, oak acorns, and smaller nut bearing trees or "mast" producers. The soil of the hills was a rich loamy deposit and was cultivated even on steep slopes. Sheep and goats in small numbers were raised for meat, goat milk, and more commonly for wool.

Flax was raised for home-made clothing. Rye was grown, ground at the mill and made into bread with baking soda leavening (saleratus) which proved very tasty. A low sled was used to draw crops of small grain from the harvest. Common foods to be found on a breakfast table in the south were fried ham and eggs, sweet potatoes, corn bread, and boiled eggs. Molasses was often used as a sweetening.

Bears, wolves, panthers, and bobcats were numerous, and would take young stock when available, so often bounties were offered for the removal of these creatures. Eagles would take lambs and pigs and hawks would take chickens, so these too were despised. Crows and blackbirds were looked on as pests and shot on sight. Domestic dogs raided the stock as well, often killing more sheep than native predators.

Slaves were not commonly kept in the mountain country and were generally unwanted, the family and neighbors banding together to do the harvest and other farm chores. Common farm houses were of log, and often in the form of two pens with a porch between known as a dogtrot house. Fields were plowed with a turning plow, and clods broken up with a harrow, then the rows were laid out for crops. The corn planter was a long horn-like object made of tin with a funnel on one end. Often the children would carry buckets of seed corn and drop one grain on each step and one in between. Plowing in a garden plot was a difficult job. The plot was so small that the mule would have trouble turning without stepping on the crops. After the garden was planted, such plants as sage, rhubarb, catnip, or even castor beans might be planted at the end of the rows. To keep the horses from eating the crops while they were cultivating, wire muzzles were used. To improve a plot of land, it was let go fallow for a year, or was "clovered" to improve the growing conditions. After a field had laid out for a year, there was a danger of snakes. The most troublesome were copperheads, but there were also rattlesnakes, puff adders, coachwhips, and blacksnakes.

The mail was carried from Asheville to Murphy a distance of 140 miles by a boy on a mule, and was delivered once a week. The boy was paid five dollars per week for this service.

1855 - Adam received his Pension; Applied for Bounty Land Warrant.
BOUNTY LAND CLAIM

Form of Declaration for Surviving Officer or Soldier

State of North Carolina
County of Buncombe
On this 22 day of March A D one thousand eight hundred and fifty five, personally appeared before me I.B. Sawyer a Justice of the Peace duly authorized to administer oaths within and for the County and State aforesaid Adam Phillips who was a Private in the company in the Company commanded by Captain Name forgotten - in the ____ ____ Regiment of North Carolina Militia commanded by Francis Locke in the Revolutionary War with Great Britain that he was drafted at Rowan County at State of North Carolina - on or about the _____ day of _____ AD for the term of six months and continued in actual service in said war for the term of six months and was honorably discharged at Rowan County N.C. on the _____ day of _____ AD on account of _____ as will appear on the Muster Rolls of said Company that he was Honorably discharged in service which discharge was burnt in his home with many valuable papers...

He makes this declaration for the purpose of obtaining the bounty land to which he may be entitled under the "acts granting bounty land to certain officers and soldiers who have been engaged in the military service of the United States" of March 1855. That this is the only application he has made for bounty land under any county of the United States. That he is the identical Adam Philips who is now placed on the Pension list...
    (signed) Adam Philip
xxxxxxxxxxxxxxxxxxxxxxxxxxxxxxxxxxxxxxxxxxxxxxxxxxxxxxxxx

Sworn to and subscribed before me the day and year above written, And I hereby certify that I believe the said Adam Philips to be the identical man who served as aforesaid, and that he is of the age above stated, and that he signed the same before me after it had been correctly read to him.
    (signed) I. B. Sawyer J.P.

1858 - Adam died on his place on Haw Creek three miles east of Asheville and is buried in Haw Creek Cemetery.

(Asheville News)Death of the Oldest Citizen. Mr. Adam Phillips, the oldest citizen perhaps of Buncombe County, being in his 98th year, died Sunday night last, at the residence of his daughter, Mrs Catherine Bell, four miles east of this place. Mr. Phillips had been for sixty years a member of the Methodist Church - forty years of that time a class leader. He was a most excellent man and through his long life enjoyed the confidence and esteem of all who knew him. Green be the memory of his many virtues.

(Reverend John Reynolds) His Youngest daughter Mrs. C. Bell who so tenderly cared for him during his last years, often said she hoped the lord would let him stay just as long as possible, that she might enjoy the benefit of his prayers, and that her house, like that of Obededum, might continue to be blessed.
    Children

7-1 Eli A. March 11, 1784 d. after 1875 m. 1. Sarah (Gill?) b 1790 d. July 30, 1855. m. 2) Lucinda Smith Nov. 1855 Cherokee Co. GA.

In 1809 Eli A. Phillips married Sarah Gill in Buncombe Co. N.C.

On April 25, 1810 Eli and Sarah were the parents of their first son James Osborne Phillips who was born in South Carolina.

Eli A. Phillips served in the Buncombe County Militia during the war of 1812.

On October 30, 1812 Adam Phillips sold 265 Acres on Grassy Branch to Eli A. Phillips.

In March 1813, Eli Philips was ordered to serve on the road crew under Overseer Shoap.

On October 3, 1820 Reuben Frank Phillips was born to Eli and Sarah in Buncombe County N.C. On September 12th, Eli sold 150 acres on Bull Creek to Thomas Foster.

Christenberry Phillips was born November 21, 1821 to Eli and Sarah Phillips.

Reverend Reuben: I arrived at home and found my brother (Eli A.) anxious to look for a better country. He persuaded me to accompany him to the new part of Georgia. We set out and travelled as far as the Nachoocha Valley on the Chatahoochi River in Habersham County. Here we found a man by the name of Samuel Farris ...[who] informed us that he owned a quarter of a section of land on the head of Soquee some twelve miles back that would suit our notions being in the mountains and fine range...Next morning he came ... and we road over the land; it being all in the woods except an Indian Hut and patch. We were much pleased with the land and the price.

On October 22, 1826 Reuben and Eli moved to Habersham County Georgia.

In the 1830 census, Reuben and Eli Philips were living in Habersham County Georgia.

Hannah Phillips visited Reuben, Hiram, and Eli in Habersham County Georgia in 1833 where she remained until sometime in 1834.

The 1850 census of Cherokee County Georgia showed Eli A. Philips and wife Sarah, in the home of James and Matilda Pendry and family. Joseph W. Pharr and Eli's sister Mary Ann lived in Cherokee County also, as did James O. Phillips and family.

<u>Deed</u>
Eli A Philips   Georgia Cherokee County

            To   This Indenture Made the Thirtieth day
R. F. Philips   of December in the year of our Lord
No.348 15 2   Eighteen Hundred and Fifty Four
between Eli A. Philips of the State of Georgia and County of Cherokee of the one part and Reuben F. Philips of the State aforesaid & County of Cherokee of the other part, Witnesseth that the Said Eli A. Philips for and in consideration of the Sum of Two Hundred dollars, to him in hand paid at and before the sealing and delivery of these presents, the receipt whereof is hereby acknowledged, hath granted, bargained, sold, & conveyed, and doth by these presents grant, bargain, sell, & convey unto the said Reuben F. Philips, his heirs and assigns, all that tract or parcel of land, Situate, lying and being in the fifteenth district of the second section of said County of Cherokee known and distinguished in the plan of said district by the number three Hundred and Forty Eight - Containing forty acres, more or less, To Have and to Hold said tract or parcel of land unto him the Said Reubin F. Philips his heirs and assigns together with all singular the rights, members and appurtenances thereof to the same in amy manner belonging to his and their own proper use, benefit and behoof forever in fee Simple. And the said Eli A. Philips for himself his heirs, Executors and administrators the said bargained premises unto the said Reubin F. Philips his heirs and assigns will warrant and forever defend the right and title thereof against themselves and against the claim of all other persons whatever - In witness whereof the said Eli A. Philips hath hereunto set his hand and affixed his seal, this day and year first above written.
Signed, Sealed & Delivered}   Eli A Philips
in presence of   }
J. J. Hardin   }
James Jordan, Ordinary
Recorded January 4th 1855   J.L. Keith CC

From the <u>Southern Christian Advocate</u> issue of August 16, 1855: Died in Cherokee County Georgia, July 30, Sister Sarah Philips wife of Eli Philips aged about 70 years. Left husband and nine children.

Eli A. Phillips was still in Cherokee County, Georgia in 1870, living with daughter Martha, and children Lorenzo, Susan, and Cicero who he had had by his second wife Lucinda Smith. He may have grown his own cotton, but he was listed as a laborer, and probably worked for wages with some of the neighbors. He was 85 years old. The air was filled with the unforgettable fragrance of freshly turned earth. A second or cultivator plowing followed the first to kill weeds. A check row allowed for a second plowing the other way called cross plowing. Corn planted after May 20 had a chance of being damaged by an early September frost. For the garden there was a one horse shovel plow. When the potatoes started to sprout in the cellar in the spring, the sprouts had to be rubbed off, usually by a small boy, before the potatoes started to soften.

To make a cotton field, around two hundred pounds of fertilizer was applied per acre. A man could make about two bales of cotton per acre when he first married, but as his children grew up and could help with cultivating he might eventually make six or even eight bales per acre.

Crows were hated by the farmers as they suspected them of pulling the tender sprouts, so in the spring, when the crows were busy feeding their young, they were hunted and the young killed in the nest.

DECLARATION OF SOLDIER FOR PENSION

State of Georgia
County of Cobb

On this second day of May one thousand eight hundred and seventy one personally appeared before me Robert M. Mitchell a Justice of the Peace within and for the county and State aforesaid, Eli A. Phillips aged eighty six years, a resident of the county of Cherokee, State of Georgia, who being duly sworn according to law, declares that he is married; that his wife's name was Sarah Gills to whom he was married in Buncombe County N.C. in 1809; That he served a full sixty days in the Military service of the United States in the War of 1812; that he is the identical person who volunteered in Buncombe in 1812; that he was mustered at Buncombe North Carolina in the Infantry service of the United States in one of the companies of the Garrison & served for about five months. Discharge and all papers lost.

That he at no time during the late rebellion against the authority of the United States, adhered to the cause of the enemies of the Government, giving them aid or comfort, or exercised the functions of any office whatever under any authority or pretended authority, in hostility to the United States; that he will support the Constitution of the United States; that he is not in receipt of a pension under any previous act; that he makes this declaration for the purpose of being placed on the pension roll of the United States, under provision of the act approved February 14, 1871, and he hereby constitutes and appoints Samuel B. Niles of Washington City his true and lawful attourney to prosecute his claim and obtain the pension certificate that may be issued; That his post office is Akworth County of Cobb State of Georgia; That his domicile or place of abode is Cherokee County Georgia.
                                        Eli A. Philips

W.M. Putnam
N.J. Garrison

7-1-1 James Osborne Phillips born April 25, 1810

Seminole War
James O. Philips pvt. Capt. Cody's Co., 1 Regt Georgia Mounted Vols. Florida War. Appears on Company Muster Rolls:
Ft. Gilliland Dec 22, 1837 muster in date Oct. 5, 1837 Hall Co. Ga. for 6 months.

Camp Call, Hall Co. May 7, 1838 - due for clothing and arms $5.56. Horse failed and abandoned Mch 21 by order Gen. Nelson. Remounted himself Apr. 21 1c. shirt 1 blanket

Mexican War
James O. Philips, Pvt. Capt. Bird's Co. (K), 1 reg't Ga. Inf. (Mexican War) appears on Company Muster Rolls for:

June 15 to December 31, 1846. Discharged Nov 21" 46 by reason of Surgeons certificate of Disability. Joined for duty and enrolled May 28, 1846 Canton, GA. Period 12 months. In hospital at Camargo 3 Oct. 46

Pvt. Capt. Gramling's Co., Ga. Inf.(Canton Vols). Joined for duty June 15, 1846 Columbus

Nov. 46 - Loss Nov. 47 Discharged.

Co. Muster-out roll New Orleans May 28, 1847. Discharged by reason of Surgeons Certificate.

1850 Agricultural Census Cherokee County, Georgia:
p. 385 Line 10
James O. Philips
Improved land 30
Unimproved land 10
Cash Value of farm $300
Horses 0
Asses & mules 0
Milch Cow 1
Working Cattle 2
other cattle 1
Sheep 0
Swine 19
Value of livestock 65
Wheat 30
Rye 0
Indian Corn 150
other 73

DECLARATION FOR RESTORATION TO THE PENSION ROLLS OF A PERSON WHOSE NAME HAS BEEN DROPPED UNDER THE ACT OF FEBRUARY 4, 1862

State of Tennessee, County of Giles

On this 15 day of December, A.D. one thousand eight hundred and Seventy-four, personally appeared before me Clerk of a court of Record, the same being a court of record within and for the county and state aforesaid, James Osborne Phillips aged 64 years, who being duly sworn according to law, makes the following declaration, asking to be restored to the pension roll: That he is the identical James O. Phillips who was pensioned on the rolls of the agency at Canton Cherokee cty ALA[sic] and whose pension certificate No. _____ is lost, that he has resided since the first day of January 1861 as follows: He resided in Blount County Alabama from 1860 until 1864 when he moved to Lawrence City Alabama & Resided there one year and moved to Limestone Co. Alabama & lived there five years and then moved to Giles Co. Tennessee and has resided here ever since.

That he has not borne arms against the Government of the United States, or in any manner aided or abetted the rebellion, or those prosecuting the rebellion, or manifested a sympathy with their cause, but on the contrary, did, during the said rebellion earnestly desire its suppression by force of arms; that he was paid a pension to the 4th day of March 1859; that he was pensioned on account of losing sight of right eye in Mexican War which cause still exists.

That his residence is county of Giles, State of Tennessee and that his post office address is Prospect Giles County Tennessee.
                                                James O. Philips
J. P. Kelly
Jos E. Smith

Date of Sale - 16 August 1880. Sold to James O. Phillips 40.15 acres and same date 80.03 Acres. Lmestone County, Alabama. (James O. Phillips moved to Texas about 1882.)

Athens Post (Limestone County, Alabama) September 28, 1881. Mrs Susannah Phillips was born in Rutherford County North Carolina; at the age of 17 married J.O. Phillips; died on August 4, aged 65 years. Survived by her husband and children.

7-1-1-1 Sarah Phillips b. June 28, 1835 m. 1) J.M. Phillips 2) James Napolean Marshall 1858. d. 27 February 1922 Crandall, Kaufman County, Texas

    7-1-1-1-1 Norman Sylvester Phillips born 1855 Macon Georgia died 15 July 1913 Gray's Prairie, Kaufman County, Texas of Tubercular Mengitis. Married Zoe Isabella McKinzie

        7-1-1-1-1-1 John William Phillips b. 1882 Alabama

        7-1-1-1-1-2 Nora Bell b. 1884 ALA

        7-1-1-1-1-3 Ida Mae Phillips b. Ala

        7-1-1-1-1-4 Sue Rivers Phillips

        7-1-1-1-1-5 Henry Dean Phillips b. 4 May 1897

        7-1-1-1-1-6 David Crockett Phillips b. 3 January 1903 Kaufman Co. Texas

        7-1-1-1-1-7 Eva Lucille Phillips b. 1 December 1905 Kaufman Co. Texas

        7-1-1-1-1-8 Elizabeth Luella b. 14 October 1908 d. 23 October 1918

7-1-1-1-2 Henry Phillips

7-1-1-1-3 Priscilla Phillips b. 8 May 1866 Ala m. 21 August 1902 Kaufman Texas to Jesse J. Dennis

7-1-1-1-4 Charles Napolean Marshall b. 6 July 1870 Athens Ala. d. 19 Dec. 1966 Dallas TX m. Mary Lavinia Blake 1 January 1905. Terrell, Kaufman County, Texas

    7-1-1-1-4-1 Leonard Stroud Marshall b. 23 October 1905 Kaufman, Texas

    7-1-1-1-4-2 Omera Marshall b. 17 April 1907 Crandall, Kaufman Co. Texas

    7-1-1-1-4-3 Ethel Marshall b. 21 September 1909 Crandall, Texas

    7-1-1-1-4-4 Katie Marshall b. 22 Feb 1911 Crandall, Texas

    7-1-1-1-4-5 Ernest Raley (Billy) Marshall b. 13 February 1913 Crandall, Texas

    7-1-1-1-4-6 Hubert W. Marshall b. 3 October 1914 Crandall, Texas

    7-1-1-1-4-7 Charles James Marshall b. 2 June 1916 Crandall, Texas

    7-1-1-1-4-8 Demetra Marshall b. 16 July 1918 Crandall, Texas

    7-1-1-1-4-9 Mary Sue Marshall b. 19 December 1920 Crandall, Kaufman County, Texas

7-1-1-1-5 William Richard Marshall b. 19 April 1872 Pulaski, Tenn. d. 1932 Garland, TX. m. Elizabeth C. (Tina) Blake 3 October 1897 Forney, Kaufman Co. Texas

7-1-1-1-5-1 Ollie Lee Marshall b. 21 July 1898 Kaufman, Texas m. 7 November 1915 William Edgar Thompson at Crandall, Texas

7-1-1-1-5-2 Willie Myrtle Marshall b. 5 October 1901 Terrell, Kaufman Co. Texas m. 19 March 1927 Vernon H. (Jack) Samuels

7-1-1-1-5-3 Gertrude Eva Marshall b. 5 April 1909 Crandall, Texas m. 20 June 1923 Percy Eugene McCallum d. 31 October 1963 Dallas, Texas

7-1-1-1-5-4 Lonnie Mack Marshall b. 31 March 1906 Crandall, Texas m. 14 August 1932 Kansas City, Missouri to Evelyn Bridges d. 30 April 1967, Sioux City, Iowa

7-1-1-1-5-5 Everette Alfonso Marshall b. 5 April 1909 Crandall, Texas m. 23 December 1933 Annie Laura Corley, Garland, Texas. d. 28 Jan 1948 Garland, Dallas County, Texas

Willie James (Bill) Marshall b. 11 March 1912 Crandall, Kaufman Co. Texas m. 17 August 1947 Sara Beth Axe at Garland, Texas.

Andrew David Marshall b. 23 August 1914 Crandall, Texas m. 11 January 1940 Fredna Pearlene Jackson

7-1-1-1-6 Mary Francis(Mollie) Marshall b. 1874 TN. d. 1 December 1932 Dallas, Texas

7-1-1-1-7 Susan Marshall b. 1876 d. September 1897 Kaufman, Kaufman Co. Texas

7-1-1-2 A girl b. about 1837(Malissa?)

7-1-1-3 W.(William?) Monroe b. ca 1838 m. Louisa Herron

    7-1-1-3-1 son died young

    7-1-1-3-2 - Avellina b. July 21, 1878 in Alabama. married Isaac Hunt.

        7-1-1-3-2-1 Cedric Francis Hunt born Feb. 19, 1896

        7-1-1-3-2-2 (twin) b. feb. 19, 1896 married Lydia Huffman

        7-1-1-3-2-3 Mardell Elizabeth Hunt b. Sept 8, 1898 married John Homer Blackmon.

            7-1-1-3-2-3-1 John Homer Blackmon Jr. b. Aug. 7, 1921 d. June 14, 1964

                7-1-1-3-2-3-1-1 Sharon Ann Blackmon b. Feb. 2, 1946 m. James Van Lutrell

                7-1-1-3-2-3-1-2 John Homer Blackmon III b. Nov. 14, 1947 Dallas, Texas m.

        7-1-1-3-2-4 Thomas Isaac Hunt b. Dec. 26,

1900 m. Glenna Ward d. 1943
    7-1-1-3-2-4-1 Wayne Roy Hunt b. June 8, 1941
7-1-1-3-2-5 Philip Roy Hunt b. Dec. 26, 1900 m. Marie
7-1-1-3-2-6 Vincent Ford Hunt b. May 2, 1902 m. Dorothy Hempy
7-1-1-3-2-7 Joseph Samuel Hunt b. Sept. 30, 1905 m. 1. Nadine Allen 2. Mabelle Thomas
    7-1-1-3-2-7-1 Joseph Samuel Hunt Jr.
    7-1-1-3-2-7-2 Patsy Ruth Hunt
7-1-1-3-2-8 Virgie Marie Hunt b. June 23, 1908 m. Durward P. Elder.
7-1-1-3-3 son died young
7-1-1-4 W.S.(a girl) b. ca. 1841
7-1-1-5 Richard Alexander b. 22 Sept. 1844 d. 27 June 1908 of "Acute Mania" m. 1) Elizabeth Herron, 2) Lucy Ann Howard (Kaufman Co. Records R. A. Phillips to Lucy N. Archer 2 March 1888)

Richard was a member of Co. D. Reese's 12 Alabama Battalion of Cavalry and later a member of Camp Juda P. Benjamin No. 1532 United Confederate Veterans at Kaufman, Texas.

Richard and his brother Monroe operated a photo gallery in Kaufman, Texas. Later he became a painting contractor and did some minor interior decoration. At the time of his death he had a bill-posting agency which his family continued after his death.

    7-1-1-5-1 Minnie Bell Phillips b. 5 July 1871 Morehouse Parish, Louisiana. m. James Calvin Cunningham (born January 25, 1854 Oglethorpe Co. GA.) she died February 22, 1941 Brownwood, Texas.
        7-1-1-5-1-1 Richard Devon Cunningham b. 19 April 1888, Greenville, Texas. d. 29 November, 1955 Little Rock, Arkansas. m. Addie Hoffman, Houston, Texas
    7-1-1-5-1-2 Jesse Leonard Cunningham b. 10 February 1891, Kaufman, Texas d. 28, May 1958 Texas. m. Annie Williams, Dallas, Texas.
        7-1-1-5-1-2-1 Jesse Leonard Cunningham Jr.
        7-1-1-5-1-2-1 J.L. Cunningham III b. 5 October 1943
    7-1-1-5-1-3 Audrey Avelina Cunningham b. 1 November 1893, Terrell, Texas d. December 16, 1895 Terrell, Texas
    7-1-1-5-1-4 Cherrie Isabell Cunningham b. Dec. 16, 1895 Terrell, Texas m. Churchill Lasalle Scott Aug. 6, 1913

Cherrie and Churchill lived for many years in Brownwood, Texas where he operated a barber shop. Cherrie was a fine seamstress, and made the wedding dresses for her granddaughter's weddings.

7-1-1-5-1-1-1 Churchill LaSalle Scott Jr. b. Jan. 29, 1915 Dallas, Texas. d. 12 August 1943 in action over Belgium. m. Mada Sparks. He is buried in Brownwood, Texas.

7-1-1-5-1-1-1-1 Cherry Catherine Scott b. 26 December 1938 San Francisco, California. Married the Reverend James Alvin Jones.

7-1-1-5-1-1-1-1-1 Kerry Nelson Jones b. 12 February 1959, Carthage, Texas.

7-1-1-5-1-1-1-1-2 Rose Kim Jones b. 3 May 1961 Hattiesburg, Mississippi.

7-1-1-5-1-1-1-1-3 Karmen Anita Jones b. 14 July 1962

7-1-1-5-1-1-1-2 April Allene Scott b. 2 August 1941 Barksdale Field, Louisiana. m. Reverend Robert Earl Kelley

7-1-1-5-1-1-1-2-1 Rachel Star Kelley b. 28 February 1964, Chatanooga, Tennessee

7-1-1-5-1-1-1-2-2 Laura Dawn Kelley b. 16 June 1966 Chatanooga, Tennessee

7-1-1-5-1-1-1-3 Sylvia Madill Scott b. 7 February 1943 Brownwood, Texas. m. 31 May 1963 Chatanooga, Tenn. to Dolphus Bradley Price.

7-1-1-5-1-1-1-3-1 Randall Scott Price b. 18 January 1966 Pensacola, Florida

7-1-1-5-1-1-1-3-2 Robert Bradley Price b. 15 June 1967

7-1-1-5-1-1-2 Vernon Mack Scott b. December 21, 1916 Brownwood, Texas. m. Verna Mae Knieff. 28 Dec. 1942 He retired with the rank of Lt. Colonel at Fort Hood, Texas 31 July 1960. He was in the 142 Infantry, 36th Division U.S. Army with twenty seven years of service.

7-1-1-5-1-1-2-1 Vernon Mack Scott Jr. b. 13 September 1943 Brownwood, Texas

7-1-1-5-1-1-2-2 Verna Katherine Scott b. 18 June 1946. m. Thomas E. Burris of Magnolia Mississippi.

7-1-1-5-1-1-2-3 Churchill LaSalle Scott b. 25 July 1950 Churchill, Illinois

7-1-1-5-1-1-2-4 Claudia Lucille Scott b. 30 January 1956 Alexandria Virginia. m. Donald Joseph Kreis 10 Oct. 1977

...1-1-2-4-1 Dena Katherine b. 31 July 1976

... 4-2 Cheryl Lee b. 8 July 1978

... 4-3 Kristopher Alan b. 13 July 1982

... 4-4 Pamela Dawn b. 25 Nov. 1985

... 4-5 James L. Michael b. 27 September 1988

7-1-1-5-1-1-3 Irvin Devon Scott b. Oct. 29, 1918 Mabank, Texas m. 9 June 1942 Brownwood, Texas Johnnie Dell Pike. He retired as a Master Sergeant June 1961 at Tinker Air Force Base in Oklahoma.

7-1-1-5-1-1-3-1 Irvin Devon Scott Jr. b. 23 August, 1943 Brownwood, Texas

7-1-1-5-1-1-3-2 John Frederick Scott b. 24 February 1950

7-1-1-5-1-1-4 James Frederick Scott b. Aug. 8, 1920 Brownwood, Texas d. 8 June 1944 France. He was in the Texas National Guard and was a fighter pilot in World War II. Did not marry.

7-1-1-5-1-5 Frances Carlotta Cunningham

b. January 22, 1899 m. Jott Maxwell August 15, 1916. Dallas, Texas d. 8, October 1955, Houston, Texas.

    7-1-1-5-1-2-1 Jott William Maxwell b. May 5, 1920

    7-1-1-5-1-2-2 Jack Richard Maxwell b. June 4, 1922

7-1-1-5-1-6 Clara Creighton Cunningham b. Oct. 6, 1902 Granville, Texas m. Jack W. Delaney January 1, 1921

    7-1-1-5-1-3-1 Clara Jane Delaney b. Sept 17, 1931 Galveston, Texas m. Robert C. Condon 3 November 1952 Houston, Texas Children

        7-1-1-5-1-3-1-1 Michelle b. 25 February 1954 Houston, Texas

        7-1-1-5-1-3-1-2 Marise Anne b. 12 November 1956 Houston, Texas

    7-1-1-5-1-3-2 Jack William Delaney b. October 4, 1932 Galveston, TX. m. Patsy Carter

        7-1-1-5-1-3-2-1 Christopher Crane Delaney b. 21 December 1956 San Antonio, Texas

        7-1-1-5-1-3-2-2 Susan Anne Delaney b. 13 August 1959 Dallas, Texas

    7-1-1-5-1-3-3 Robert James Delaney b. April 3, 1940 Houston, Texas m. Mary Lou Noble 16 December 1961 Houston, Texas.

        7-1-1-5-1-3-3-1 John Thomas Delaney b. 24 December 1862 Houston, Texas

        7-1-1-5-1-3-3-2 Joseph Patrick Delaney b. 19 April 1964 Houston, Texas.

    7-1-1-5-2 Judge Phillips died young

    7-1-1-5-3 Henry Gaston Phillips b. Feb. 6, 1881 d. May 23, 1957 m. Annie Jeter.

Newspaper clipping (undated 1950)
H.G. Phillips to celebrate Golden Event

Celebrating their golden wedding anniversary with an open house thursday evening will be Mr. and Mrs. H.G. Phillips

An Invitation is extended by the Phillips for their San Angelo friends to call between the hours of 7 and 10 o'clock at the Phillips home 1322 Caddo Street.

March 23, 1900 was the date of the ceremony when Miss Annie Jeter became the bride of Henry G. Phillips. The service was performed at Kemp by the Rev. J.M. Jeter, Baptist Minister and uncle of the bride.

Mrs. Phillips who was born near Wills Point is the daughter of Mr. and Mrs G.A. Jeter. Mrs Jeter makes her home with the Phillips. Mr. Phillips parents were Mr. and Mrs. Richard Phillips of Kaufman County. Mr. Phillips was born in Decatur, Ala.

The Phillips moved to San Angelo in 1907 where Mr. Phillips was engaged in the outdoor advertising business. The couple has five children, George R. of Eagle Pass, Mrs. M.O. Parker of Houston, Louis of Big Spring, Mrs Russell Hendricks of Jennings LA., Mrs Opal Davis and Dr. D.V. Phillips of San Angelo. All children will be present for the thursday celebration.

Grandchildren are Dick Phillips of Cheyenne, Wyoming, Dorothy Phillips a student at Texas Tech; Mrs. Katherine Phillips of Eagle Pass; and John Phillips student at the University of Texas.

Mr. Phillips is now retired and has more time to enjoy his favorite pastimes of golfing, fishing, and dominos. Mrs. Phillips finds housework and flower gardening take up her time.

7-1-1-5-3-1 George Richard Phillips b. March 4, 1901 San Angelo, Texas m. Dorothy Fay

Angelo Posting Service
Ganong & Phillips Proprietors

Bill posting, Tacking and Distributing
Carefully Done
San Angelo, Texas   Aug 25, 1909

Dear Uncle John Dick. Your Papa is soon going to come home I think. how are getting along. We went to the carnival last night and the was a man there that would get under the water and stay and smoke a cigar and drink milk and at last he went under and stayed I think two minutes and a half is what Mama said. What are you doing now times John Dick are you still playing ball. Your Papa is writing to. Am making money now to by distributing and have made about a dollar and a half. How much money have you made on distributing I have got a little feisty pup her name is Penny well as I dont think of much more I'll stop kiss them all for me.
love to all of them
George Phillips. San Angelo
            Texas

George worked as a business manager for many years and after his retirement as a part time buyer for supermarkets.

7-1-1-5-3-1-1 Richard Forrest Phillips b. Nov. 24, 1926 m. Harriet Edith Schmidt. April 25, 1953

7-1-1-5-3-2 Dorothy Ann Phillips b. Dec. 29. 1929 m. E. G. Hill

7-1-1-5-3-3 Kathryn Phillips b. July 20, 1932

7-1-1-5-3-2 Opal A. Phillips b. June 21, 1903

7-1-1-5-3-3 Doyle Vivian (Bill) Phillips b. April 13, 1906 Kaufman Co. Texas d. Feb. 5, 1978.

7-1-1-5-3-2-1 John b. Sept. 1929

7-1-1-5-3-4 Mary Katherine Phillips b. Oct. 10, 1912 d. Dec. 3, 1981

7-1-1-5-3-5 Louis Edwin Phillips b. June 6, 1915 (Twin) d. March 31, 1985.

7-1-1-5-3-6 Louise E. Phillips b. June 6, 1915 (Twin) d. April 6, 1980.

7-1-1-5-4 Susan Allie Phillips b. 1884 Kaufman, Texas d. 1949 Little Rock, Arkansas m. 1. George W. Metcalfe 1901 Greenville, Texas. 2. Henry A. Laughlin 25 April 1920 Dallas, Texas

7-1-1-5-4-1 Richard Chilton Metcalfe b. October 6, 1906 Greenville, Texas m. Jacobina R. Eikren 1942 San Francisco, California.

Richard married Jacobina Eikren from Sweden who was a naturalized American citizen. Richard enlisted in the U.S. Army Air Corps before World War II. He married Bina in 1940 before he was sent on active duty in Europe. He served in Italy and Germany and after the war, Bina and the children moved to Germany to be with him. He retired as a Major in the United States Air Force.

7-1-1-5-4-1-1 Susan Allie Metcalf b. 21 March 1942 Riverside, California. m. John Zeman 1962 Riverside, California.

7-1-1-5-4-1-1-1 Danielle Jean Zeman b. May 8, 1963 Riverside, California.

7-1-1-5-4-1-2 George William Metcalf b. 10 November 1945 San Francisco, California

7-1-1-5-4-1-3 Richard Chilton Metcalf b. 15 December 1947 San Francisco, California

7-1-1-5-4-1-4 Robert Lance Metcalf b. 30 December 1949 San Francisco, California

7-1-1-5-5 Mary Marie Phillips b. m. William Felton Reeves

    7-1-1-5-5-1 Mary Kathryn Reeves b. January 14, 1914 m. 1.) Bennie Rogers and 2.)Lowell V. McAuly

    7-1-1-5-5-2 Martha Nell Reeves b. March 5, 1916 m. George B. Garner

    7-1-1-5-5-3 William Felton Reeves Jr. b. April 18, 1921 San Angelo, Texas

    7-1-1-5-5-4 Elizabeth Ann Reeves b. March 13, 1924 m. Thomas Edward Lakin.

        7-1-1-5-5-4-1 Mary Lynn Lakin b. 12 May 1956(twin). Her brother Thomas E. Jr. died at five days of age.

    7-1-1-5-5-5 Richard Hiram Reeves b. May 14, 1928 m. Virgie _____

        ...5-5-5-1 Robyn Renee Revees b. 18 July 1958 Sioux Falls, South Dak.

7-1-1-5-6 Rupert Hicks Phillips b. 30 July 1894 Kaufman Co. Texas m. Amelia Cooper d. 19 December 1975

    7-1-1-5-6-1 Rupert Hicks Phillips Jr. b. June 14, 1920 Terrell, Texas m. 1. Lela Mae Mosley 24 March 1946. 2.) JoAnn Anderson

Rupert served with the Army after graduation from College and was discharged after the war as a Lieutenant. He worked with the Army Insurance Service for many years, but finally went into his own insurance business. After retirement, he moved to Flagstaff, Arizona and became an Episcopal Deacon and then returned to Texas.

        7-1-1-5-6-1-1 Martha Lucy Phillips b. December 11, 1946 m. Roy Lee Bruner 18 June 1965 Weatherford, Texas

            7-1-1-5-6-1-1-1 Tracey Lynn Bruner b. 13 October 1967 Germany

        7-1-1-5-6-1-2 Lela Ann Phillips b. Oct. 8, 1948 m 22 August 1970 Fort Worth, Texas 1.) Donald Alfred Johnson 2.) George Edward Bryan II 17 June 1977

            7-1-1-5-6-1-2-1 JoAnn Vincent Bryan b. 21 August 1978 San Antonio, Texas

            7-1-1-5-6-1-2-2 Amelia Suzanne Bryan b. 13 April 1982 Stutgart, Germany

            7-1-1-5-6-1-2-3 Margaret Sumner Bryan b. 6 November 1988 Flagstaff, AZ

7-1-1-5-6-1-3 Amelia Marjorie Phillips b. Nov. 18, 1952 Weatherford, Texas

7-1-1-5-6-2 Marjorie Winifred Phillips b. Feb. 27, 1927 m. Horace Lindsay Gunn
- David Cooper Gunn
- John Winston Gunn
- Mark Leslie Gunn

7-1-1-5-7 Charles Alexander Phillips b. 11 January, 1896 Kaufman Co. Texas m. Gladys Ellen Helm

7-1-1-5-7-1 Charles Terry Phillips b. September 11, 1927 d. January 10, 1934 Automobile Accident.

Charles age six was hit by an automobile when returning home from walking a friend to school. He had been a bright happy boy with much promise and was taken suddenly away by this accident. His parents were much grieved by his death.

7-1-1-5-7-2 Barbara Dean Phillips b. September 30, 1929 m. August 30, 1949 Marvin Omer Van Note

7-1-1-5-7-1-1 Carol Deane Van Note b. 12 August 1952 Pasadena, California

7-1-1-5-7-1-2 Stephen Phillips Van Note b. 4 March 1955 Escondida, California.

7-1-1-5-7-1-3 Roger Dale Van Note b. 12 May 1958 Escondida, California

7-1-1-5-7-3 Wallace Stanley Phillips b. July 12, 1932

7-1-1-5-8 Ardis Ellen Phillips b. 31 March 1897 m. Walter L. Knox

7-1-1-5-8-1 Florence Knox b. 3 March 1918 Farris, Oklahoma. m. 1.) Woodrow W. Pooler 2.) James Thomas Morrill

7-1-1-5-8-1-1 Patricia Ann Pooler b. 12 October 1939 m. Don Pendergraft

7-1-1-5-8-1-2 Theresa Jean Pooler b. 30 October 1940 m. Donald Cain

7-1-1-5-8-1-3 Alice Jo Pooler b. 24 January 1942

7-1-1-5-8-2 Mary Alice Knox b. 10 December 1919 McClain Co. Oklahoma. Married Hershall Hawkins 2 June 1939.

They came to California shortly after their marriage and Hershall started his own business called Areo-Fence Service. They built a lovely home near Pomona, California and were active members of the Baptist Church.

7-1-1-5-8-2-1 Gene Hawkins b. 23 September 1940 m. Maija Karpinski

West Covina California.

7-1-1-5-8-2-2 Walter Hawkins b. 1 January 1943 m. Susan Meyer 17 December 1965

7-1-1-5-8-2-3 Sandra Lee Hawkins b. 29 November 1946 m. H. Lee Jensen 3 August 1963

7-1-1-5-8-2-4 Michael Hawkins b. 20 Aug 1952

7-1-1-5-8-3 Ila Joe Knox b. 8 October 1921 Farris, Oklahoma m. Dana A. Clark Lansing, Michigan.

7-1-1-5-8-3-1 Diane Rose Clark b. 1 September 1948 m. Mr. Bender.

7-1-1-5-8-3-2 Dana O. Clark b. 13 July 1949 Lansing Michigan

7-1-1-5-8-3-3 Oren Lee Clark b. 11 September 1953 Lansing Michigan

7-1-1-5-8-3-4 Ellen Dareen Clark b. 9 June 1959 Joliet, Illinois

7-1-1-5-8-3-5 Theresa Dawn Clark b. 4 November 1958 Salina, Kansas.

7-1-1-5-8-4 Walter L. Knox Jr. b. 12 June 1924 Oklahoma. m. Dorothy _____

Walter "Dub" was a construction worker in Southern California while his wife clerked in a drug store.

7-1-1-5-8-4-1 Walter Lee Knox III b. 21 September 1947 Oklahoma City, Oklahoma. m. Kathy Lunsford 28 January 1967 California.

7-1-1-5-8-4-2 Judith Ann Knox b. 8 April 1950 m. B. Felix

7-1-1-5-8-4-3 Martha Rae Knox b. 11 July 1952 Oklahoma City, OK

7-1-1-5-8-4-4 Christine LeEllen Knox b. 9 September 1953 Montebello, California.

7-1-1-5-8-4-5 David Knox b. 1 February 1955 Covina, California.

7-1-1-5-8-4-6 Janice Knox b. 10 August 1956 Covina, California.

7-1-1-5-9 Raymond Ayers Phillips b. Sept. 5, 1899 Kaufman, Texas m. Faith Helen Van Curen 1 February 1944

7-1-1-5-9-1 Raymond Andrew Phillips b. August 24, 1923 Pasadena, California m. Feb. 1, 1944 Loraine Peterson

Andrew served with the armed forces in World War II. After his discharge, he worked with a Chamber of Commerce in Southern California and later was given a responsible position with a large corporation.

In 1969 Andrew underwent surgery for a brain tumor. He seemed to be recovering, but a year later the headache and pressure returned. The tumor turned out to be malignant, and he passed away October 15, 1970.

7-1-1-5-9-1-1 Deborah Ann Phillips b. 31 July 1948 Pasadena, California
7-1-1-5-9-1-2 Jeffrey Andrew Phillips b. 5 April 1954.
7-1-1-5-9-2 Donald Richard Phillips b. May 17, 1925 d. January 23, 1944 Auto Accident

Donald joined the coast guard in California at age 18. While on leave at home, he and his cousin went horseback riding in the Flintridge area. They were picked up by a car of young people which went out of control not far from the stables and Donald was thrown out. He only lived a few hours.

7-1-2 Reuben Frank Phillips b. Oct. 3, 1820 d.ca. 1900 m. 1) Nancy Burtz daughter of Joshua and Susannah() Burtz August 11, 1848 Forsyth Co. GA
m.2) Catherine Galt 20 June 1866

In February 1863 cotton sold in New York for 92 cents a pound, bacon was $1.50 per bushel in Mobile.

Pierce's Memorandum and Account Book - 1876 penciled notes by Reuben Frank Phillips
R.F. Phillips #1878
Catherine Phillips deparid this life on the 26th day of March on Tuesday. Recieved of R. F. Phillips this August 31st A.J. Phillips His Book. The address of Mrs. E. E. Grady Prairie Lea <u>Texas</u>.
1t picing cotton for J. Smith & Co.

Saturday September 26 pict 206	206
Monday September 30th	75
Tuesday October 1st	80
Thursday October 3rd	100
to one half days work	55
Pulling Corn 20 cts	520
to cleaning out well 25.00	
to picing cotton Friday October 4th	73
Saturday octo 5th	69

Monday I recieved of (Eli) Robians 3 bushels of corn this July the 11th 1878. Recieved of MP Robians 4 lbs meat

Hannah Phillips died December 11th 1848
Adam Phillips was born Dec 27th 1762
Eli A. Phillips was born March 11, 1784 the son of Adam and Hannah
James O. Phillips son of Eli Phillips was born April 25th 1810
R. F. Phillips was born October 3d 1820
Sarah P. departed this life July 30th 1855 age 65 wife of E. A. Phillips

Sarah Phillips Consort of E. A. P. her funeral was preached by Joseph Pharr the 17th <u>Oct</u> from Ecclestis ix & 18th verses
Nancy Phillips wife of R. F. Phillips departed this life April 30 1866

    7-1-2-1 Andrew b. ca. 1849 (d. Young)
    7-1-2-2 Alexander Joshua b. ca. 1852

When only 16 years of age he had been working for a man, who died. When the man died, the wife married A.J. for convenience which marriage lasted only a few years. He married again and settled in Chatanooga, Tennessee where he had six or eight children. In the early 1900's, A.J. went to the home of Wesley Pharr Phillips where he died of Tuberculosis about 1903. He gave John Richard Phillips his Railroad watch for taking care of him during his illness.

    7-1-2-3 Wesley Pharr Phillips b. 19 Nov. 1854 Orange, Cherokee Co. GA. d. 17 Nov. 1911 Ballinger, Runnels Co. TX m. Cynthia(Sinthia) Catherine Bradshaw 2 March 1880 near Corinth Mississippi.

Beds might be rope beds attached to the wall. If a straw-filled "tick" were used it was usually made of oat or wheat straw and might start out three feet thick. If a straw stuck through the matress, it stuck the person sleeping in the bed. On cold winter months, people might sleep under eight to ten quilts which during warmer periods were stored in frames near the bed. Babies were rocked in cradles, home made, and rocked by the mother or an older sister to put a crying infant to sleep.

Baths were infrequent, especially since water had to be hauled into the house from the well or a spring and thenheated on the stove or over the fireplace for the bath. This practice ensured that nearly everyone had parasites such as bedbugs or lice at one time or another.

A typical mountain home would have a kitchen with home made table and chairs, a coffee grinder, large wood burning stove or fireplace and a bin for cornmeal and flour. In the nicer homes this might be built in, but often it was part of a dry sink or other kitchen item. Coffee was of the boiled variety which today we would call "cowboy coffee". Near the fireplace there might be a slop bucket for the hogs and chickens into which went dishwater, left over bits of food, and grease from the skillet. In the coldest parts of the winter the washstand would be moved in from the porch and placed in a convenient location. On this stand were often a wash basin, a bucket with clean water with its own dipper, and a bar of homemade soap. Flour or sugar sacks were used for dishtowels, and a colorful oilcloth from the general store was used to cover the table.

A long porch was usually across the back of the house and possibly a well nearby with a waterbucket; a dipper, and tin washpan hung on a nail on the porch. Cedar was preferred for buckets, as it was felt that metal changed the flavor of the water. Nearby there would be an ash hopper for fireplace ashes which were later processed and used with fat to make lye soap.

About 1870, Wesley Pharr Phillips developed Asthma, a condition which bothered him until the time of his death.
An interesting story about Wes Phillips comes from his son John Richard: Once, while at the table, Wes was served potatoes. He didn't like potatoes, so he edged close to the window and when he thought no one was watching he tossed them out the window. His father Reuben F. saw this and made him go out in the yard, pick up his potatoes and eat them dirt and all because food was so scarce for the family that none could be wasted.

Conditions in Cherokee County Georgia were still very rural in nature. The summer term of school began the second week in July and lasted until fodder pulling time in early September, when the boys had to be out of school to begin with the fall crops. The girls wore calico dresses and the boys wore long pants or overalls and checked or striped shirts. Boys all wore straw hats. In the winter they were sewed into union suits which they might wear all winter. Everyone was classed by reading level. Subjects might include spelling, arithmetic, reading, writing, geography, history, and grammar. The children went in classes to the front to recite before the teacher. Smaller students might learn by listening to the older ones recite. It was not uncommon for one teacher to have up to seventy students at one time. If they were not studying or reciting, the children went outside to play. Popular games were town ball a type of chase called fox and hounds, and marbles. The girls plaited blades of grass or played house.

Children of one family would all eat together out of a common lunch pail. Common school food consisted of cornbread, biscuits, boiled roasting ears, ham, or chicken. Salted or pickled fish was common fare. Desserts might include pie, gingerbread, cupcakes, sweet potatoes, or red apples. Poorer children had fat meat and home made bread or biscuits.

At school, friday was set aside for "exercises". Exercises had nothing to do with calisthenics, but were speeches and games to show off what the students had learned. Visitors often came and took part as judges. There was often a spelling bee or an exercise in "polemics" which we now call debate.

Summer school often ended with a grand entertainment during which both students and visitors might recite or say something entertaining. It was now harvest time, and the students might be out until the first frost.

Wesley Pharr Phillips was in school near Corinth Mississippi in 1875. Common school subjects were arithmetic, history, geography, spelling, and rhetoric. It was here that he met Kate Bradshaw, the daughter of Andrew and Catherine (Hefley) Bradshaw. Andrew had died in the Civil War, and Catherine had raised four girls by herself. Indeed, the concept of the "single parent family" which is so common today was equally common after the civil war, since so many fine southern boys died in the war, leaving young wives with children to raise.

In 1879, Wesley Pharr Phillips took a trip to Texas where he worked at Luling Texas and on a dairy farm near Belton, Texas.

Lucius Elmer, son of Wesley and Kate Phillips was born January 18, 1881 at Farmington Community just east of Corinth, Mississippi.

Max Lee Phillips son of Wesley Pharr and Catherine Phillips was born April 15, 1882 at Ellis County, Texas.

In the fall of 1891, Wesley Pharr Phillips taught School at Peede.

On September 23, 1893 Wesley Pharr Phillips was initiated into the Kaufman Lodge of the Masons. On October 13, 1894 he was passed to fellowship.

In 1895, Wesley Phillips was working in Kaufman County at Peede as a carpenter, coffin maker, and blacksmith. On April 6, 1895, Wesley Pharr Phillips was made a master Mason in the Kaufman Lodge, Scurry, Texas.

Wesley Pharr Phillips was appointed Senior Deacon of the Scurry Lodge in 1899.

In 1904, Max Lee Phillips moved to Ballinger, Texas. Wesley Pharr Phillips held the office of treasurer in the Scurry Lodge this year and in 1905 he was Junior Deacon.

Angelo Posting Service
Ganong & Phillips Proprietors

Bill posting, Tacking and Distributing
Carefully Done

San Angelo, Texas　　　　　　　　　　　　　　Aug 25, 1909

Dear Uncle John Dick. Your Papa is soon going to come home I think. how are getting along. We went to the carnival last night and the was a man there that would get under the water and stay and smoke a cigar and drink milk and at last he went under and stayed I think two minutes and a half is what Mama said. What are you doing now times John Dick are you still playing ball. Your Papa is writing to. Am making money now to by distributing and have made about a

dollar and a half. How much money have you made on distributing I have got a little feisty pup her name is Penny well as I dont think of much more I'll stop kiss them all for me.
love to all of them
George Phillips. San Angelo
Texas

Angelo Posting Service
Ganong & Phillips Proprietors

Bill posting, Tacking and Distributing
Carefully Done

San Angelo, Texas   Aug 25, 1909

My dear Sweet Mamma and onliest Babies:-

Your card came this morning. I was glad to hear that you are all well. I was sorry to hear of the suffering of Bros Hodo and Dunn. They had better come to San Angelo. Bro. Hodo was talking of coming before I left home. I feel sure I missed a bad spell by coming over here when I did, for I have suffered considerably as it is. I am getting home sick, but if I had Cricket and the buggy I would be better satisfied, for I would be out pearling most of the time. A nigger found a pearl the other day that he refused $150.00 for and a party of three or four white men has just got back from a fishing trip on the Llano river and brought several pearls with them, the local jeweler says the best one is worth at least $150.00. Yes you may send me those letters. Russells is about Aunt Ad's pension and may require an answer at once. I don't know what Lucy's is about, but I imagine it is about the Simmons land. I have an idea that she wrote and got the agency and some of her customers are jacking her up about the delay in the opening and she wants me to tell her what to tell them.

In regard to my health I will say that it is reasonably good for August health, you know I have had my worst spells in August, or the most of them at least-. I had to get another box of "Tar and Feathers" last night which makes just twenty days for the last box.

We all took in the Danville Carnival last night. It is the same one that was in Ballinger last fall. I saw the big snake Sampson. He surely is a monster. We saw "The Old Plantation". It is hardly decent. We also saw the play wherein the old man and his son-in-law pretend to be Masons. That surely is funny. I would have enjoyed the plays better however, if my hearing had been better. Henry is putting up more bill boards. He ha'n't got room for the work that is coming in. He will have to quit painting if the business bets much better.

Tell grandaddy that I surely miss his jolly old countenance. Tell him we will make up lost time when I come home. Give my

sympathy to Bros Hodo and Dunn. Don't wait so long before you answer. I had begun to think there was something wrong. With carloads of love to everyone of my own precious dears I am still the same old wheezing
                                                                        Daddy

---

The family had paid one hundred dollars down on a three room house in the West End section of Ballinger and lived there for several years. Mary got a job in the county clerk's office because she could write such a nice hand. In 1910, before the census was fully counted there was an order to have Runnels County counted. When it was tabulated it showed that there were enough people for the county and district offices to be divided. Mary ran for the office of district clerk and was the first woman to be elected [in her own right] to public office in Texas.

Oct 19 - 1910
Dear Mamma, Cherokee, and Dickey, It is raining here this morning we are all as well as usual. I have done very well since I have been here. Sunday was my worst day and that day Henry, George, and I went down the river 12 miles. We saw a great many pecans, but didn't gather any.

We all went fishing Saturday and caught 2 very good messes of fish. Monday night we all went to the big show and it was a big one sure enough. There were three rings and some kind of acting going on is all of them at the same time. There were 25 or 30 clowns and they were cutting up all kinds of tricks outside the rings all the time. T. came to see us while he was here. Let me here from U. I am as ever.
                                                                        Dad

Letter from Wesley Pharr Phillips (probably 1911) from San Angelo:

Dear Mama and the children

I got your letter al right was glad to know that you are all well. I am feeling very well this morning. I am not bothered any more with vertigo but I had Asthma pretty badly yesterday morning. I took three doses of Appomorphia and by bedtime last night I had about chased it off. It is real cold here this morning. I am sitting by the fire trying to keep warm [and] am succeeding pretty well. So you are going to move are you? Well I hope it is for the best.

We haven't been down to the river any more. I have not been able to walk even down to the Orient bridge.

With lots of love to each of you [I] am the same old noaccount.
                                Dad

Angelo Posting Service
H. G. Phillips, Proprietor

San Angelo, Texas,

June 31, 1911

My Dear Kate & Eunice:
Your Dear letters came to hand two days ago and I was surely glad to get them. I was getting uneasy. I had begun to think that some of you were sick and so of course I was especially glad to learn that you were O.K.

I have been doing fairly well since I have been over here. I usually go to bed about eleven O'clock and sometimes I have to get up before day. I did this and yesterday morning both tho, I was not very badly smothered.

We went fishing 3 more times last week and once this week. I caught 2 fine Cats both times last week but the last time we went I only caught one perch and a gar. The gar was swimming along near the top of the water. When he came to my cork floating on the water he seemed to smell of it and then took it in his mouth. Just at that instant - I hit him on the bill with my pole, he gave a flounce and wrapped the line around his bill, and there he was with my cork in his mouth and the line you might say, tied around his bill. He couldn't get his mouth open to let the cork out of his mouth and of course couldn't get away. I had him hog-tied and all I did was to throw him out on the bank and kill him. He was over two feet long.

I went down town with Henry yesterday morning intending to write you a letter, but I went off without my "specks", so I had to deny myself that pleasure till today. I hope you wont wait so long next time before you write.

I am glad Elmer has got his shop in operation. I hope he will find an agreeable place to board, where the old man won't be jealous of him. A man is out of luck when another man gets jealous of him.

Tell Dickey I got the medicine he sent all right and many thanks. It is alright but of course I would have preferred it in capsules it would have been so--much more convenient,- especially while camping out on the river.

Tell Mary I am still looking for a letter from her. I will be good when it comes. Did I hear from the Atty General?

I saw a notice in last weeks Kaufman Herald stating that old man Abbott died of cancer of the stomach last tuesday morning a week ago. Harry Gillaspie and Jesse Rupe had come to town that morning for a coffin for his burial.

Minnie Cunningham, the Herald stated had recently been

operated on for appendicitis at Mabank. It did not state how she stood the operation. All right I guess and hope.

The Pros are going to have a big rally here tomorrow. <u>Pine</u> Lester is going to make the main false statements. There never was a greater aggregation of liars than the present Pro organization of this great fair state. I am sorry the state has to endure such a disgrace. With bushels of love for each of you I am just the same
<u>Daddy</u>

Pocket Notebook - Greer and Company Livestock Brokers

My name is W.P. Phillips. I live at Ballinger Texas In case of accident notify my wife at Ballinger or my son M. L. Phillips 628 Delmar St. San Antonio. I am a member of A. F. & A. M. Lodge No. 726 Scurry Texas; also a member of Ballinger Camp W.O. W.

Write to the Woodworth Co. 1161 Broadway New York City for experimental package of Sempine for Asthma. Saw ad in home life for Sept.

Jno. W. Pharr Berclair Tex.

Little Devils Pills. No. @Sig. two to 6 at night Beadine
Dr. M. G. Walker
Pt nf buy G. F. Harvey Saratoga Springs N. Y.

Rx
Phylolaco Decundeng Fl Rxt   3T
Belladona FxRxt   3T
Chronanthos vii   VI
Simple Elixer
Qrs   ZVIII
tm
sig.
one teaspoonful after each meal   Dr. Walker

H. G. Phillips Cr.
1910
Dec. 27 By cash   1.25
1911
Jan   "   "   .05
 "   "   " Spc'l   .60
 "   "   "   .50
 "   "   " Tob   .05
 "   "   " As R   1.00
 "   "   " "   1.00
 "   "   " Tobar   .20

Wesley Pharr Phillips died November 11, 1911 at Ballinger, Texas.

Newspaper clipping:
Death of Prominent Citizen

W.P. Phillips, one of the prominent and highly esteemed citizens of our city died at his home last night at 10 o'clock from a complication of asthma and lagrippe. He was 57 years of age at the time of his death and was a consistent member of the church of christ and died as he had lived in the triumphs of a living faith. He leaves a wife, two daughters and three sons besides other relatives to mourn his early demise. His body was prepared for burial by J.A. Ostertag and remains will await the arrival of relatives until tomorrow afternoon, when Elder M.D. Scroggins will conduct the funeral services after which the masons will take charge of the remains and they will be buried with Masonic honors of which order he was an honored member. The services will begin at the Mater Hotel at 3:30 o'clock sunday afternoon and final services closed by the masons.

7-1-2-3-1 Lucius Elmer Phillips b. 19 Jan. 1881 Mississippi d. 24 May 1947 Laredo, TX m. June 1914 Berta Barbosa

Bible Record: From W.P. and Kate Phillips to Lucius E. Phillips on his 21st birthday Jan. 19, 1902.
Births.
Anna Lee Phillips 7:35 PM
Berta Lee Phillips 8 PM 6-10-1915
L. Elmer Phillips Jr. 9PM mon. 9-11-1916
Katie Belle Phillips 4PM Thurs. 1-17-1918
John Edward Phillips 11:30 AM Mon 8-18-1919
Deaths.
Anna Lee Phillips 1:45 a.m. 3-1-1916
Marriages.
L. Elmer Phillips and Berta T. Barbosa June 24, 1914

Mr. and Mrs William Charles Clober
  announce the marriage of
    their daughter

Berta Teodora Barbosa

  to

Mr. Lucius Elmer Phillips

Wednesday, June twenty fourth.

nineteen hundred and fourteen

  Laredo, Texas

FUNERAL NOTICE

DIED

In Laredo, Texas, Tuesay Evening June 24,
1947 at 6:20 O'clock

Lucius Elmer Phillips Sr.
Age 66 Yrs.

The funeral will occur from the Jackson Chapel,
Friday June 27 at 6 p.m.

Rev. Stanly Haver will preside at Chapel

Funeral Services at the grave will be conducted by the Masonic Lodge
547 A.F. & A. M.

Laredo, Texas, 26 June 1947

———

7-1-2-3-1-1 Anna Lee Phillips b. 10 June 1915 d. 1 March 1916
7-1-2-3-1-2 Bertha Lee Phillips b. 10 June 1915 m. Arthur J. Rossi
    7-1-2-3-1-2-1 Nadine Rose 18 Dec 1946
    7-1-2-3-1-2-2 Arthur Rossi Jr.
        7-1-2-3-1-2-2-1 Ashley Ann Nichole Rossi
7-1-2-3-1-3 Lucius Elmer Phillips Jr. b. 18 August 1916 m. Tommie Fitzpatrick
    7-1-2-3-1-3-1 Lucius Elmer III(Sonny) b. 13 Dec 1947 m. Patty

———

        7-1-2-3-1-3-1-1 Ambry Phillips
        7-1-2-3-1-3-1-2 Bonnie Phillips
    7-1-2-3-1-2-2 Linda Phillips Neecke
        7-1-2-3-1-3-2-1 Angeline Mary Elizabeth Phillips
    7-1-2-3-1-3-3 Wayne Phillips
        7-1-2-3-1-3-3-1 Jordan Phillips
7-1-2-3-1-4 Katie Belle Phillips b. 17 Jan. 1918 m. George W. Shaw
7-1-2-3-1-5 John Edward Phillips b. 18 Aug. 1919 m. June Hazelwood
    7-1-2-3-1-5-1 Karen
7-1-2-3-2 Max Lee Phillips b. 14 Apr. 1882 Terrell Texas d. 12 August 1951 Ballinger, Runnels Co. TX m. Louisa Mussman
    7-1-2-3-2-1 James Donald Phillips b. 18 Jan. 1914 did not marry
    7-1-2-3-2-2 Arthur Blaisdell Phillips b.

19 July 1916 did not marry
7-1-2-3-3 Ethel Belle Phillips b. 19 January 1884 d. 20 Aug. 1884
7-1-2-3-4 Eunice Jane Phillips b. 5 July 1888 d. 18 Nov. 1965 did not marry.
7-1-2-3-5 John Richard Phillips b. 21 Aug. 1891 d. 4 July 1977 m. Ada Maria Hall dau. of John Henry and Lydia Ellen(Thompson) Hall.

John Richard Phillips, son of Wesley and Kate (Bradshaw) Phillips was born August 21, 1891 at Peede, Kaufman County, Texas.

John Phillips: Mary who was two years older than Eunice, started school in the new building that had been built on Mr. Albert Barker's land. The two older boys had been going for several years as had their cousins Stella and Norman Graham. Olin Graham was about the age of Mary and started when she did. Mr. C.D. Long who had been teaching the school since Wes quit was one of the old time school masters. He kept several long hickory switches stashed above the blackboard at the back of the room as a deterrent. He kept a little black notebook on the inside pocket of his coat in which he wrote the names of anyone caught whispering to his neighbor or even getting out of his seat without permission. Any culprit so caught would get what was called a 'black mark' after his name. When he had accumulated four such marks and another was due, it was crossed out with a dozen or more licks with one of the hickory switches over the black-board, after which he could start all over again with what the teacher called a clean slate.

After Mr. Long came a series of teachers: A professor McDougal; Mr. Guthrie; Miss Lillie Steadman; Miss Jennie Simpson; again Mr. Long who taught two more years; then a young man by the name of Mr. Hand who only taught for about three months, got a better job in Dallas and left without telling anyone that he was going to quit. This left the school without a teacher and Mr. McCormick, the head of the School Board persuaded Wes Phillips to again take the job.

The Phillips family had a barn made from oak logs from the back pasture where wood for cooking and heating was gathered. I spent much time in the barn loft day-dreaming about bicycles, guns, new shoes and a warm coat. The family had to go about one hundred yards to a well to get the drinking water.

Every Christmas morning before breakfast the Phillips children started out knocking on doors of all the neighbors yelling "Christmas gift." This was something like the present "Trick or Treat" as every family had something prepared for the occasion. The two days before Christmas were really busy ones for the whole family. Pies, cakes, and custards were always prepared in advance. Hams were baked, chickens and/or ducks were plucked and made ready to be roasted. Sometimes possums, coons, rabbits, squirrels, and other wild animals were prepared and, if the hunters were fortunate, a wild turkey.

Uncle John Phillips owned a coon dog that was full blooded pointer. He could tree squirrels, coons, and possums sooner than the tracking dogs did, and was especially good at night. Uncle John gave the dog to Elmer. When an animal was in a hole in a tree they cut the tree down and held "Bert" while the tree fell. One time they forgot to hold him and he ran under the falling tree and was killed. Everyone cried over the loss.

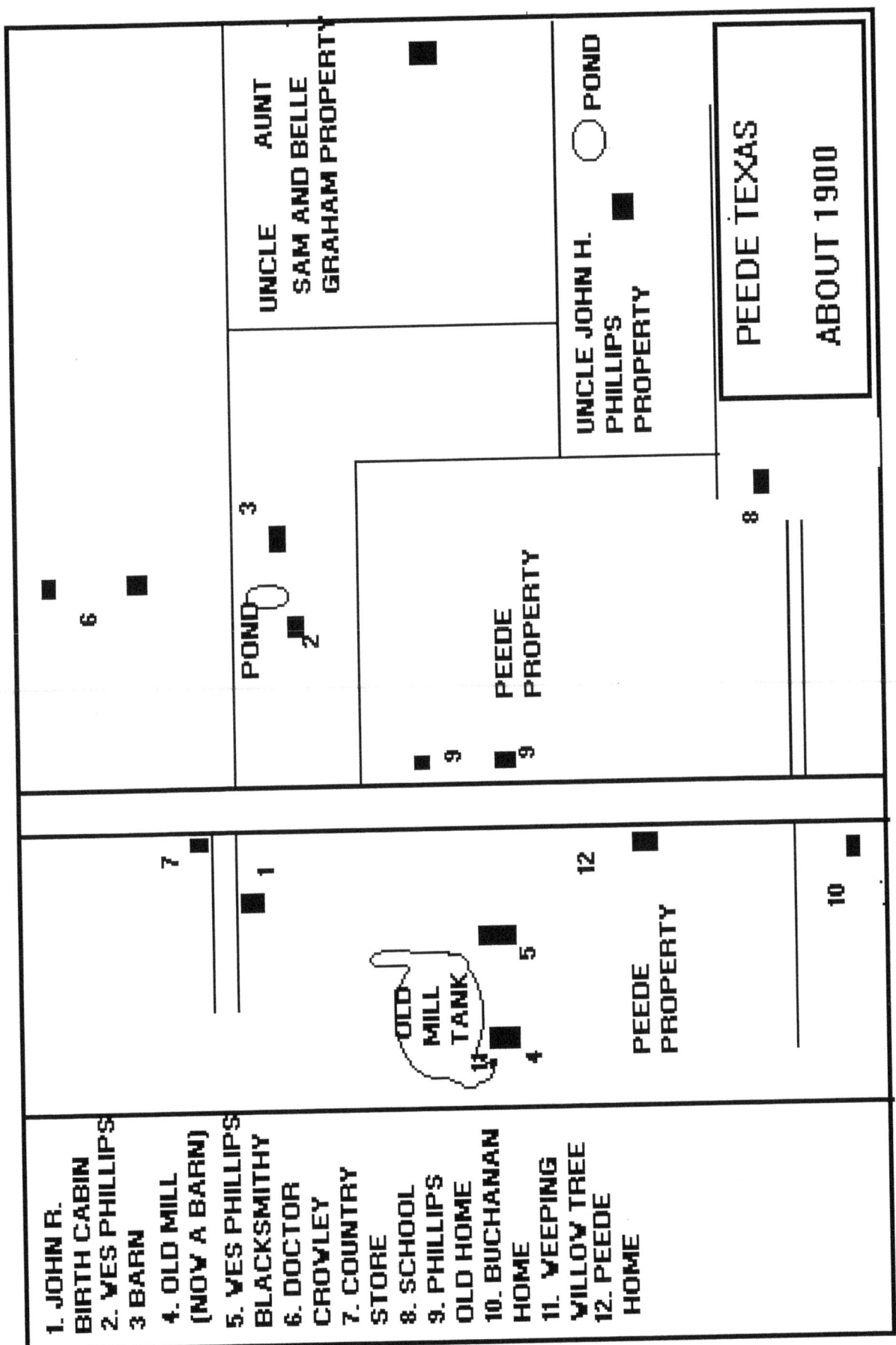

The Fourth of July was never celebrated in the South because the time was considered too close to the hated "carpet bag" days after the Civil War. The kids shot fire crackers and roman candles at Christmas instead of July 4th.

Kaufman County, especially the area around Peede's Mill was at best primitive. No one could go very far in a day unless they went by train and from most places it would take hours to get to a railway station. If you knew when the train was coming through, you allowed time to get there even if you had to start around midnight. King Creek bottom was almost a mile wide and was so muddy during a rainy spell that the farmers had to go to town by horseback or put the rear wheels of the running gear in front which raised the bed out of the mud most of the time. From Peede's Mill if you went to Kaufman you always had to cross King Creek bottom.

There was very little industry in the area at this time. There had been a sawmill at an earlier date but the building had long been abandoned and the machinery moved away. The only machinery left in the area was a cotton gin and a molasses mill. The gin furnished work for a number of men in season and there was always work for the man who kept the gin saws sharp so that the lint could be removed from the seeds. In the fields the cotton pickers used a ten-foot sack which was dragged between the rows until full, then taken to the cotton wagon where sack and cotton were weighed on a scale hooked in the end of the wagon tongue.

Farm wagons were always pulled by two horses or mules. Every animal had his own collar, which if too small pinched, and if too large rubbed blisters which soon became running sores. There were pads which could be used if the collar were too large, but no one would use a collar which was too small. The wagon tongue was about ten feet long and the animals were hitched to the wagon on either side by a single tree. The singletrees were then hooked to a doubletree. If one animal was faster in getting started than the other, one end of the doubletree would swing ahead of the other which would throw both animals off balance. They had to learn to pull together and when they could do this they became valuable workers.

The doubletree was put under the back end of the tongue to raise the front end so that the one who weighed the cotton could suspend the cotton above the ground. When sixteen hundred pounds of cotton had been weighed and emptied into the wagon, the farmer would tramp the cotton down. The wagon had extensions to the sides and ends which permitted it to hold the equivalent weight of unginned cotton. Upon arriving at the cotton gin the wagon was driven under a suction pipe which sucked up the cotton and carried it to the gin saws which stripped the seeds from the fibers. The seeds were dropped into a special bin and the cotton fibers were carried still further aloft and dropped into the compress where it was compressed into a five hundred pound bale ready for the market. The last act

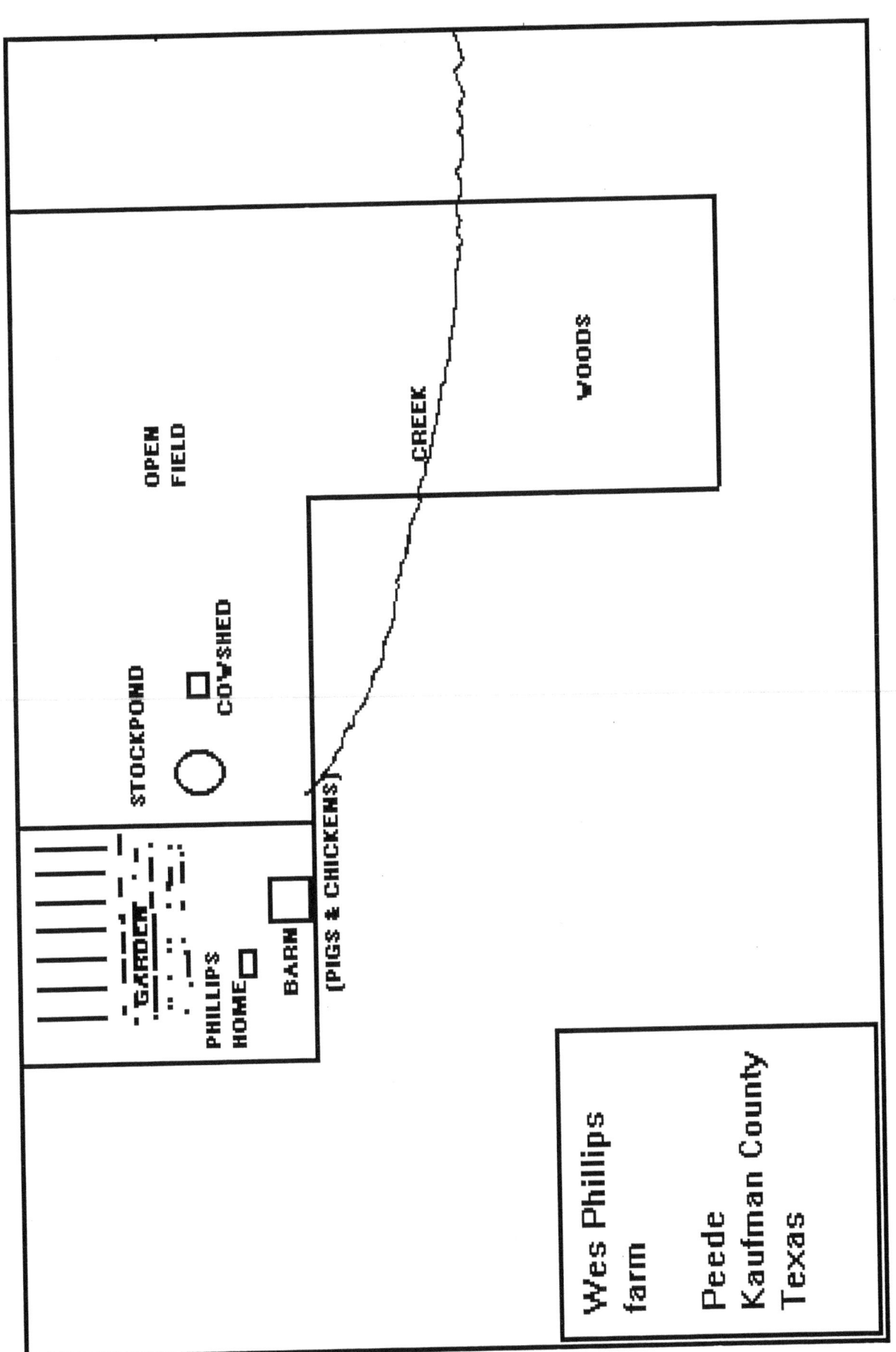

of the compressor was to wrap the bale with jute sacking which was strapped on with metal bands.

The ginner usually got his pay by taking a percentage of the seed. The balance was dropped into the farmers wagon if he wanted it. If he did not want his seed he was paid for it by the ginner.

Molasses was part of the staple diet of the South and in Kaufman County it was a common crop. When the stalks of cane reached maturity and sugar content as well as the seeds were ripe, the field workers stripped the stalks from the leaves and tied them in bundles to be used as fodder for the livestock. When this was done, the seed heads were removed and the canes cut down, loaded into wagons and hauled to the molasses mill. This mill was quite a contraption. Hooked up with two heavy rollers which squeezed the sweet juices from the cane as they were fed through them like an old fashioned clothes wringer, was a long beam to which a mule or horse was hitched. The mule went round and round in a circle which kept the crushing rollers working. The sweet juices were drained off into a large vat under which a wood fire was kept burning. By the time the juice flowed slowly from the end of the long vat, the sugar content gradually became thicker and darker until it reached the con-sistancy of heavy black sorghum which was drained off into containers.

Elmer was quite a character. He got the idea of marking every cat in the neighborhood by clipping a small notch in the ends of both ears. You could hardly find a cat anywhere around Peede's Mill that did not have such marks. Mrs Peede always kept a herd of goats on her place to keep the underbrush eaten off. They were hard to keep in the pasture as the grass was always greener on the other side of the fence. In trying to get through the barbed wire, the goats got their ears hung up on the barbs and most of them had notches in their ears also. Mrs Peede accused Elmer of marking her goats like he did the cats, but Elmer always denied this. Elmer was quite a naturalist also and he knew the names of the plants and animals in East Texas.

Elmer and Lee showed me how to make bird traps using the figure four trigger. I found this very much to my liking and taking the traps down into the woods that grew close to the house I baited them with corn and set them in small clearings. I caught a number of birds including what everyone called Red Birds. I would take them out of the trap, hold them for a while , let them bite down on a twig and turn them loose. The birds would hang in the air for several seconds and then realizing that they were free, fly off. I soon tired of catching birds. I wanted to trap some of the animals which came up from the creek and the forest. I had a small steel trap that had only a short chain, so I got some wire and made a chain about thirty feet long. I did not [at first] know how to bait this trap, but soon learned that if I put the bait on the trigger, the possums pressed down on the trigger with their long sharp noses and could easily wiggle out without much difficulty. I drove down a stick next to the trap and tied the bait on it about six inches from the ground. As soon as breakfast was over the next morning I hurried down to the creek to see if I had caught anything. The trap was gone! I was disappointed, but when I looked up I saw the possum walking around with the trap on his hind leg. What surprised me most was that the animal was a rare black color and made a very valuable pelt.

I found that raccoons would step on the trigger if the bait was placed on it. Corn and peanuts were used as bait and I sometimes caught squirrels with the same set. All winter long I trapped, skinned, and took care of the pelts. I had been corresponding with hide buyers in St. Louis and was agreeably surprised when I got back more than ten dollars for my work and fun in trapping. The black possum pelt brought twice as much as the common gray ones.

In 1904, Max Lee Phillips moved to Ballinger, Texas. Wesley Pharr Phillips held the office of treasurer in the Scurry Lodge this year and in 1905 he was Junior Deacon.

With two strong mules to pull the wagon and horses to pull the two buggies, the family started out on the first of October. The first night they camped at the "cut off" after crossing the Trinity River. This was an old channel of the river before the stream changed its course. Ennis, the county seat of Ellis County was where my mother's mother had died. We visited the graveyard where she was buried and mother came back to the wagon crying. A heavy rain started soon after we left Ennis and continued on into Waxahatchie where a four day stay in a wagon yard was somewhat depressing. We were all elated when the sun came out and the journey recommenced. I saw my first automobile in Cleburn. The crossing of the Brazos River, the largest inland stream in Texas at Granbury was another high point of the trip. In Erath County I saw a quail go into a clump of bushes and told Elmer who was driving the mules. He reached in the wagon back of the seat, grabbed his sixteen gauge shotgun and shot directly into the clump of bushes. There was a flurry of wings as a large covey of quail took to the air. The shot had killed ten and that night the Phillips family dined on quail and corn pone for supper.

The road on which we were travelling ran about six miles north of Brownwood. I said I would eat the first prairie dog Elmer shot, but when one was killed, it smelled so bad that I threw it away without even skinning it. It took a day to drive to Ballinger from Valera.

Ballinger is located thirty six miles east of San Angelo, fifty miles west of Brownwood, fifty miles south of Abilene and a little over one hundred miles north of San Antonio. It is situated on the Colorado River in the center of a rich farming community where

BALLINGER TEXAS ABOUT 1910

RESIDENCES		ELEMENTARY SCHOOL
RESIDENCES		
RESIDENCES / PHILLIPS HOME		HIGH SCHOOL

NORTH TO BALLINGER TRUCKS

P A R K   A V E N U E

FARMERS & MERCHANTS BANK	CITY DRUG STORE	
	1ST NAT. BANK / MY FIRST BUSINESS	
BALLINGER STATE BANK		RESIDENCES

8TH STREET

7TH STREET

H U T C H I N S

| COURT HOUSE SQUARE | | |

6TH STREET

X = DENOTES OTHER PHILLIPS HOMES

cotton, corn, milo maize, kaffir and other crops are raised extensively. In the early days peaches, garden produce -especially tomatoes, onions, beans, cantaloupe, and others were grown as well as especially large watermelons. I saw watermelons weighing over 150 pounds at the county fairs. In 1905 sixty thousand bales of cotton were marketed in Ballinger as it is the trade center for Runnels and adjoining counties.

Morgan Jones built a railroad from Abilene to Ballinger which cut off a large portion of the trade territory. Colonel Stillwell came through west of town and also west of Abilene with the Orient Line which took still more of the vast territory Ballinger was enjoying. To further reduce the trade territory, the Santa Fe Line to circumvent the Abilene Southern being extended to Paint Rock built a spur line from Miles to [Paint Rock]. As it turned out, the railroads which were supposed to help in building the western towns practically killed Ballinger in the early days.

There was only one school building in Ballinger in 1905, but another one was being built. The building was so crowded that there were 72 sixth graders in the one room and this was divided into the low sixth and the high sixth. I was put into the low sixth, but when we went into the new building it was consolidated into one seventh grade.

My father and I used Cricket, the little mare we had bought from Mr. Abbott to work up the first free mail delivery in Runnels County. When the examination came for the mail carrier Dad was sick and couldn't take the exam. The people on the route got up a purse of ten dollars and brought it to him out of sympathy.

I had gone to work at the City Drug Store for Mr. Holman and was determined to become a druggist. I made myself familiar with all the drugs on the shelves. The doctors only used a few drugs in their prescriptions. These had to be mixed and the exact dosage measured and either put in capsules or folded into papers. The powders were folded nicely and after the drugs had been thoroughly mixed, poured out of the mixing bowl onto what was called the pallet where it was formed into a perfect rectangle and measured off into the number of doses prescribed by the doctor. The liquids were put in bottles which I had to keep washed and clean. This was done with small shot. The shot was put in the bottle with a small amount of water, then shaken vigorously for several minutes until the bottle was clean on the inside as well as out and then put on a drying rack.

The main drugs prescribed were castor oil, olive oil, calomel, bicarbonate of soda, milk sugar, carbolic acid, morphine, opium, herbaceous powders, yellow pucoon root, digitalis, ephedrine, and a few others. Aspirin was just coming into use, and few modern drugs had been heard of.

The family had paid one hundred dollars down on a three room house in the West End section of Ballinger and lived there for several years. Mary got a job in the county clerk's office because she could write such a nice hand. In 1910, before the census was fully counted there was an order to have Runnels County counted. When it was tabulated it showed that there were enough people for the county and district offices to be divided. Mary ran for the office of district clerk and was the first woman to be elected [in her own right] to public office in Texas.

I was graduated from Ballinger High School in 1911. The members of my graduating class were Ewing Taylor, Horace and Dallas Hawkins, Elizabeth Alexander, Foy Walker, Kathleen Francis, Kathleen Jones, Idie Voelkel, Bonnie Mae Lawrence, Edith Winkler, Rufus Allen, Selma Lewis, Betty Miller, and Doris Wynn.

Mr. Holman and Mr. Pierce bought out a bakery and put me in charge of it. I delivered bread, cakes, and pies on my bicycle. They soon sold out the bakery, and I bought out the confectionery part of it. The building next door caught fire and the bakery suffered smoke and water damage and had to be closed. I had joined the volunteer fire department and helped fight the blaze. My arms were pretty badly burned and I suffered for several years afterward from smoke and heat inhalation.

John Phillips: About 1912 Emmett Long and I opened up a cafe in Ballinger. It was a hot dry summer and nobody came to town. I saw that I wasn't cut out for that kind of business, so sold my interest in the cafe to Emmett and worked on the farm chopping cotton. In the fall I helped gather the crops including cotton, corn, milo maize, and sweet potatoes.

I was down town one day when Frank Moore hailed me and told me that he had bought out a drug store in Gunter, a small community in Grayson County in Northeast Texas. Since I was a registered pharmacist Frank wanted to know if I would go to Gunter and take charge of the drugstore. He offered me forty dollars a month to go and he would pay my train fare. [When I arrived] I was very disappointed in the layout of the store. Most of the merchandise and drugs were old and out of date. After about three months an old doctor who had his office in the building came down and told me that he had bought the store from Frank Moore for $1000.

I had a chance to go back to Ballinger or go to Wichita Falls which was the liveliest town in North Texas with a population of 12,000 and forty six saloons. When I arrived I had about twenty dollars saved. I got a room in a rooming house and began to look for a job. Every drug store in town was having a hard time keeping their doors open and the druggists salaries at that time were around sixty dollars a month.

I got a job working in a glove factory which was in financial troubles. This job played out in about a month when the factory closed and went out of business. Oil had been discovered near Petrolia and I got a job with the McFall brothers driving a team of horses with a load of pipe for the new field. This job lasted about a month. One day while I was feeding my team at dinner, Clyde Burnett came over and asked me to come to the Cream Bakery and talk to Vic Stamfli the owner. He said that since winter was coming on it would be pretty rough outside and the job in the bakery would be nice and warm. I was hired [the following day] at eight dollars a week as a helper and was given a room upstairs as part of my pay.

The bread was baked in large ovens with shelves in them. These shelves revolved over and over and heating was more economical than in the older ovens. The oven at the Cream Bakery was eight feet square, lined with fire brick and heated by gas. In baking bread I would mix my dough with a small amount of yeast, let it set and when it fell I would put in more flour, water, salt, malt and shortening to make a stiff dough. I let it rise again to double its original size, and punch it down until the air had escaped. I would then let it rise to one third larger than the original size and then put it through the divider. After this it went through the rollers and then was put in pans and placed in a 500 degree oven and baked until golden brown. I did some night baking for several years until a friend who had known me in Ballinger came by and told Mr. Stamfli that I could do him more good in front selling things than in the back baking them. At that time bread sold for a nickel a loaf retail and thirty to the dollar wholesale. Cookies were never more than ten cents per dozen with cakes and pies in like range. The things that we made were the best and remained so until I left the bakery in 1932.

I had been working from sixteen to eighteen hours a day, seven days a week for nearly four years. My boss, Vic Stamfli had quite a bit of influence in Wichita Falls and with the draft board. He kept me from being drafted. I had a friend Bill Lay who looked up draftees and saw that they were sent to camp. One day when Bill was in the shop I called him aside and asked if he could get the draft board to call me up immediately. I was shortly drafted.

On June 23, 1918 after I had placed all my things in my trunk and sent them home to Ballinger, I was sent to Camp Travis in San Antonio and in July on to Waco where I was inducted into the seventh Division, 64th Infantry, K Company. I crossed the Mississippi River at St. Louis. Everywhere people - mostly girls waved their welcome and farewell together. All the boys said they were going back to Decatur Illinois after the war. The part of Missouri we passed was very poor, but in Illinois and Michigan the grain crops were superb.

When the 7th got to New York before going overseas, they were billeted in Camp Merritt on Long Island. Company K. spent a wonderful day at Long Beach where they were fed the most wonderful food they had ever gotten in the army.

Finally we were put in transports and started on our way to Europe. When we had been out three days, a propeller broke on our ship and when we woke up the next morning we were on our way back to New York where we had to stay ten days. One morning when we woke up we found that we had been joined by four submarine chasers. As we had been travelling through sub infested waters the sight of these chasers really brought sighs of relief. They were with the convoy all the way to Brest France. The only way we could get ashore was by lighters as those harbor waters were not deep enough to let the transports dock. When we were sent home after the war, the United States had dredged out the port and installed docking facilities.

After all the troops had been brought ashore we were lined up and marched out of town on an old cobbled road that had been built a thousand years. We were taken to a small field and ordered to stack arms and pitch tents. Every soldier carried one half of a pup tent which could accommodate two persons. The boys unrolled their packs and each took his shelter half and buttoned them together. In a few minutes hundreds of tents were pitched with blankets spread on the ground inside.

After remaining in this camp for four days we were marched to the railroad and loaded on box cars marked in French "forty men or eight horses". The french boxcars were about half the size of their counterpart in America so you can imagine how crowded they were with forty men, their packs, their guns and ammunition and their extra gear. At night the inside of the box car was so dark you could not see your hand before your face and if you had to step outside to relieve yourself, you could not step without stepping on somebody.

After three days and nights, we got off the train and found ourselves within fifty miles of the front trenches. We covered this distance in easy stages of about ten miles a day, camping in the daytime and marching at night. When the march started on the fourth day just after sunset, some of the fellows said it looked like rain as they could see flashes of lightening ahead. I had been doing a lot of thinking and when I had told the boys at the first rest that they were seeing the flashes of the big guns, there was no more talk of rain. The soldiers formed single lines and kept ten yards apart to prevent casualties if they were shelled on the march. The next day, K company came to a little village about ten miles from the front and found the people overjoyed to be freed from the German Army when we moved in.

The troops received some intensive training here for a few days and were being trained to attack in long columns, marching directly into the German Lines. I had been thinking about this method of attack and went to First Sergeant Baker and told him that one bullet striking the head of the column could kill or wound several men. Baker could see the advantage of a staggered attack and no more of that kind of drilling was done by K Company. This idea was evidently carried to the higher command, since I saw no attack made like it had been practiced.

The company went into the front lines after a few days of rest. During this time I was made a member of the intelligence section of the 7th Division and added this to my duties as sniper. Every hundred yards along the Front Line was a P.C. or Post of Command. The Germans watched these P.C.s like hawks. There was a boy named Guffy who came in and sat down on the observer's seat. The observer came back, and when he saw him sitting in his seat, he grabbed Guffy's arm jerked him up and sat down. This slight movement must have been noticed by a German sniper because the observer had just sat down when a bullet hit him right between the eyes.

Company K went "over the top" after being in the trenches for two days. We chased the Germans out of their dugouts and concrete bunkers and held the line until being ordered back to our own lines two days later. One morning about four O'clock, Lieutenant Knobb came down to where the company was stationed and said that the Germans were preparing to attack the 7th Division lines and for everyone to be ready to repel the attack if possible and if overrun to fall back to the secondary trenches and regroup for a counter attack. The trenches were dug in a zigzag line with three soldiers in each sector. While waiting for the Germans to come, I noticed an Italian Soldier in one corner of the zig zag line. He was from southern Italy, and was very dark skinned, but now he was so scared that he was deathly white. For some reason on seeing this boy, it struck me as funny, and I laughed out loud. Immediately, the tension which had gripped us was broken and we were prepared for the enemy to come.

They came in long staggered lines. I crawled up out of the trenches behind a small clump of bushes with two bandoliers of ammunition. Since I had been selected as a sharpshooter, I did not wait for orders, but opened fire. Immediately the whole seventh division opened up and most of the Germans started to fall back, but a few broke through with their bayonets held out at arms length. One German lunged at me but I did as I had been taught and thrust aside his bayonet with my parry. He dropped his gun and raised his arms at the same time yelling "comrad-comrad." I never saw him again.

I had been called to the rolling kitchen which had been moved to the secondary trenches on the morning of November 11th, 1918. As the company could not provide K.P. service because all the men were needed to hold the line, the Mess Sergeant and the cooks had to provide their own, but I was on special service and was told to report to the kitchen. I was going to the Rolling Kitchen with a hind quarter of beef on my back. I met a lieutenant going in the opposite direction who smiled and said. "Have you heard the news." He explained that an armistice had been signed and that the shooting would stop at exactly eleven O'clock.

When I had time to think about what was happening, I became really scared. I had gone through 64 days of "hell on earth" and it was going to end in less than three hours, but the shooting from both sides had grown more intense and would continue to do so up to the deadline. The more I thought about it, the more scared I became. Some officer in command had ordered the 64th to attack even though he knew that the war would be over in a few hours. The Germans were no fools and had placed machine guns in such a position that they had the whole front crisscrossed from every direction . [In the attack] they killed and wounded over 700 men of the 64th when they attacked on the command of a crazy officer. A yellow streak crept slowly up my spine. I got away from the rest of the fellows and sat down on the side of a big tree which would give some protection in case of a direct hit. Pretty soon, wounded and dead were being brought back and by eleven O'clock the litters increased from a trickle to an avalanche. When the firing ceased, I got up and started toward the German line which was less than three hundred yards away. I ran across a man named Boardman and we visited the German lines for about an hour and then went back to our company.
———

(1918)

Dearest Mother and Homefolks
I have been moving some since I last wrote you. France is a large place when you come to move across it especially when part of that distance is covered with full packs on your back weighing in the neighborhood of seventy-five pounds but do you know you seldom hear a murmur from any of the boys for ours is an easy lot compared with what these France people have had to put up with for years.

Just here let me say something about them. They are more like Americans than any other people I have ever known, just like homefolks the kind you are used to seeing every day. And they want to help make the Doughboys stay in France just as [long] as is possible. They will go to almost any inconvenience to themselves to make things comfortable for us.

You want to talk to them so much that you will put in every spare moment in trying to learn their language and it is surprising to see how readily they pick up the American tongue/

France seems to be covered with canals and boats going up and down stream can be seen almost any time and they are almost always loaded down with valuable products of the country. From the way our forces are driving back those detestable Hun-hordes we may be home for Christmas dinner, unless the cold weather puts a stop to our operations, but believe me it is going to become pretty cold before our operations come to a halt for we are prepared for them both with good clothes and with fighting material and food - something the enemy is very short on, so when he is trying to keep warm and free from hunger, we will be fighting and driving him back. You no doubt can tell how things are going by how the papers, and our losses are very light in comparison to the amount and character of the fighting that we have been doing.

Have you heard from my Canadian girl yet? Has Daddy Squires written you yet? I told him to write you occasionally, but he is so old and forgetful that it may have slipped his memory. Do not worry about me for I shall come out alright and we will all be happy once more.

I have been taken out of my company for the time being and put on some special work or preparation for special work and it is not nearly so hard as doing the regular routine and drilling that we did have to do.

If any thing should happen to me, the government will let you know at once so do not be worried about my welfare because you do not hear from me for my letter might get lost coming over.

With love and kisses to all I am as ever.
Your baby boy
John Phillips
Co. K. 64th Inf.   A.E.F. via New York

Letter November 17, 1918

Dearest Mother and Sisters:

I got two letters from you today, the first that I have received for some time. Since I last wrote you there have been some wonderful happenings - was at the front line in three different places - I heard the shrapnel bursting within a few feet of my ears - our platoon was caught in a barrage fire and narrowly escaped being shot to pieces - then the gas came but again all were saved from death by the timely putting on of our gas masks. Our company went over the top with honors and were billed for another drive when the climax arrived - PEACE - not a gun was heard when the eleventh hour of the eleventh day on the eleventh month arrived. Our boys were rather quiet and went about everything they did in a quiet manner but when the time for cease firing came over in the other lines across "Nomans land", such a noise of bugles blowing, hallowing, and singing one never heard before and that night you should have seen the fireworks and bonfires that those boys sent up. Some of our boys went over into their trenches and they were received with open wholehearted handshakes by the boys that a few hours before were considered their most bitter enemies.

I have gone through it all without a scratch and without being sick for one minute and now I like all the rest am anxious to get back home...

John Phillips Co.K 64 Inf Amer. E.F. Via New York

When I returned from the war, things were booming in Wichita Falls. In the summer of 1919 I got a job with the Holiday Creamery at Sixth and Austin streets keeping books for Dan Carithers.

W.A. Squires had been mayor of Henrietta, Texas and had spent most of his years promoting and trying to promote short line Railroads throughout the state. In most cases he could establish a right-of-way, build the road bed, and organize his companies but could never complete the roads to a running reality. Some of these old road beds are still in existence and can be seen running for miles along present day highways. Mr. Squires took a great interest in me and invited me up to his hotel room for a short visit. I was interested in what he told about building railroads as it revived an old desire to be a railroad promoter. As Mr. Carithers did not care, I helped the eighty year old man reorganize the old Oklahoma and Texas Southern just before I left for the war in 1918.

When I returned from Europe, other people had taken over the work that I had started and had left my interests out of the picture. I opened up new contacts that resulted in the organization of four new companies: The Panhandle Short Line; The Colorado, Columbus, and Mexican; The Ardmore, Lubbock, and Vernon Railway, and just before the great depression; the Winnepeg, Kansas, and Gulf which was designed to bisect every transcontinental line in the United States.

In 1920, Congress passed the Transportation Act which was designed to merge all the railroads of the United States into five competing systems. This included all the short lines and feeder lines of the country and would have permitted the newly organized companies to include these short lines in the building of other systems. When I and my companions went to the Interstate Commerce Commission to seek permission to include these short lines in their north and south system, the I.C.C. was enthusiastic and promised to give permission as soon as the request was presented. At all the hearings S. M. Porter and I made such a good showing that the major railroad companies took over and built most of the roads as they visualized.

———

Wichita Falls, Texas,
March 2nd, 1922

Dearest Mother and Homefolks:

It has been snowing and sleeting here for the past week but this morning it was bright and clear but has been very cold all day, however it is thawing out some.

Mr. Lynne sent me a coal bill this month and I see that there is nine dollars and twenty cents more on it than was last month. Don't you think that $15.00 per ton is to much to pay for coal? Wouldn't it be cheaper to buy wood? I think that Mr. Lynne should have some competition to bring the price down to normal

We have a new preacher this week by the name of Smith. He seems to be a good one and everybody likes him. Hope he does some good work here. There is surely a great need of it.

I wrote to Elmer and Berta some time ago but have not heard from them yet. Don't know whether they will write to me or not. Guess they will after so long a time. They sent me the babies pictures Christmas. Elmer sure has some fine looking chaps.

How are Donald and Tiddledee Winks getting along? They never do send me any more word. Guess they have forgotten their Uncle John.

I also wrote to Uncle John some time ago but as yet have not heard from them. I told him about Hoyle borrowing five dollars from me and not paying me back as he had promised. Guess he wants to hear from and get the money before answering.

Give my regards to Lillian when you see her. Hope she is getting along fine with her school.

Love to all

John Richard Phillips
Box 671

Wichita Falls newspapers record some of the events taking place during the late 20s. 1928 seems especially busy, with two tornados occurring on June 27th and an explosion in a fireworks sales area on July first.

Postmark: Oct. 4, 1928 10AM Wichita Falls, Tex.

Dearest Mother:
   I will not be able to send you enough money to pay on the place this month but as I told you in my other letter will pay it off Christmas.
   We had a small rain up here yesterday Oct. 2nd but today is regular summer time again.
   No news at this time..
                         Love to all
                         Dicky

Postmark: June 5, 1929: Return to Cream Bakery
617 Seventh Street   Phone 5029
                        Cream Bakery
                  Milo Connelley, Proprietor
              Fresh Bread, Pies and Cakes Baked Daily
                      Wichita Falls, Texas

Dearest Mother:

    We are mity busy now since the hot weather set in and are somewhat short handed, but I think that I will be able to come home in the next month or in August. Dont know yet just how things are going to turn out.

    We surely have been having some rain up here for the last two or three weeks. It must have rained seven or eight inches in that time.

    I went out to see our big lake up the river several weeks ago. It was the first time I have been out there since it was built. It seems that about all I do is eat, sleep, and work. They have more than 200 miles of canals and laterals. It surely is some lake.

    Please some of you write me once in a while anyway. I know that you have more time for writing than I have.

                                                Love to all
                                                  John

Postmark: July 6, 1931; Return Cream Bakery

Dearest Mother:
    Eunice I wish I was able to send you a real present on your birthday but you know how it is.
    They surely are working me good and plenty this week as I am on the Jury all the week. Besides sitting on the Jury I am working almost my full time down at the store.
    We had some celebration here the 4th but as usual I never got to go anyplace but to work.
    Surely enjoyed your letters. Write me when you have time.
                                                    Love
                                                Johnnie

note: Received with check for $15.00

Undated - mid February 1932

Dearest Mother:

        Sorry that T.D. is sick. Hope he is better now. I also had a small attack of flu but I stopped it right away. When you feel the flu coming on just take a heaping teaspoon of soda - wait two hours and then take another dose then wait two hours more and take a teaspoonful of epsom salts. take it the same was next day but only half as much.

Enjoyed your letters. Please write again when you do not have to entertain so much company.

On sunday the balance that I promised. Hope you can use it.
Love Johnny

[note at bottom] Received Feb. 18, 1932: $5.00

Postmark: Feb. 17, 1932 Wichita Falls, Tex.   Return box 671

Dearest Homefolks:

Got your sweet letters yesterday and surely did enjoy them. Gee but you must be having a good time with so much company all the time. De they ever bring in anything to eat? If they do I kinda believe I'll come home. Things sure are tough up here.

But listen! We just had a dandy rain I [ever saw]. Maybe the drouth is at last broken. Here it is. I managed to borrow a little money the other day and paid off some of the bills I owed but I still owe what I borrowed. If I keep digging and my health keeps up perhaps I will get out of debt some day.

Eunice if I think of it I surely will write Aunt Bell a long letter on her birthday. She surely writes me nice letters Christmas.

Glad to see that Donald is farming even if it is only gold fish and water plants. Say boy you ought to make a gathering of little turtles. They sell as high as fifty cents in the Kress stores and flower stores. If you can gather them in quantities perhaps I can help you dispose of them for ten or twenty cents each. You might write me what you can do.

Tid. how are you and your bicycles? I had to buy me another tire the other day. First one since getting my bike.

Well as it is about closing time will have to sign off at this hour.   Love
                                                                Dicky
P.S. Congratulations Max on turning the half century mark. They say that the first hundred years is the hardest.

Postmark May 9, 1932: Return Cream Bakery.

Dearest Mother,

I want to congratulate you on your 74th birthday. I do not know what I would have done without you all these years. You have been my inspiration.

Seemingly your baby has been negligent of your welfare but because I love you so much, I keep thinking for financial means in order to make you more comfortable in the year that the lord will spare you and the rest of your children.

If, at any time, I should appear to be negligent or fail to do the things that you think I ought to do, just remember that I am still striving and working for you because I love you, My mother.

I am almost broke this week but I hasten to send you sufficient to meet, partially your current needs. Next week and the next I will send you more so do not be discouraged.

The church is having a big meeting here now but I do not get to go any. In fact I work so late at night and all day sunday that I never have time for anything but work. Will write next monday.

                                                            Love
                                                            Dickey

---

Postmark: May 16, 1932. Return Cream Bakery
note on envelope: Received May 18, 1932 with a $3.00 Check

Dearest Mother:

Am sending you $3\underline{\frac{00}{}}$ this week which is all that I have. Will send more next week. It is taking me longer to get on my feet now than before.

Had quite a norther last night and today, monday, is nice and cool. Hope it continues for some time.

Business surely is no good so many of the firms are quitting altogether.

Will write again next monday.

                                          Love
                                            Dicky

[note by Kate Phillips]
Received June 30, 1932 with $3.50 check.

Dearest Mother:

I forgot to write yesterday, so am writing hurriedly tonight. Will write a longer letter next week.

Got a nice letter from Berta today. They are all well and happy.

                                          Love
                                            John

note at top: received with $3.50 July 6, 1932

                    July 4th
Dearest Mother:

Sure is hot here this week but the nights have been cool.

I surely enjoyed yours and Eunices letters. Glad you had such a good time with Aunt Belle and Ophelia. Geraldine must be quite a young lady now.

I have nothing interesting to write about tonight but will try to do better next week.

                              Love,
                                 Johnny

Postmark July 29, 1932: Return Cream Bakery
(written on back of campaign cards for P.A. Martin, Judge)

1
Dearest Mother:

Things are surely getting hot up here in politics but it wont be long now before it will all be over.

We had a dandy rain here yesterday and it was much needed too.

It begins to look

2 more and more like I will be unable to come down this summer. Perhaps I can make it in the early fall.

Mother go ahead and write the insurance I will get it paid some way.

                    Love
                    _John
(note on envelope: Received check of $3.50)

Postmark Aug. 8, 1932: Return Cream Bakery
627 seventh street   Phone 5029
                    Cream Bakery
                 Milo Connelly, Proprietor
            Fresh Bread, Pies and Cakes Baked Daily
                    Wichita Falls, Texas

Dearest Mother:

I am writing this rather hurriedly as I wanted to get it off on tonights train. I have been so busy during the past week that I did not get to write as I had planned but will send you twice the amount in this letter.

We sure do need some rain up here. It has rained all around but not on us.

Since I forgot to write Aunt Belle on the 1st but will try to do so in the next day or two. Maybe it will be a surprise if and when I do write her.

Tell Paul to write to me.
Note: $7.00 check
Love
John

Postmark Aug 19, 1932, Wichita Falls, Tex. Return Box 671

Dearest Mother and Homefolks:

We have been having lots of rain up here the last several days and the weather has cooled down to where the nights are really delightful for sleeping.

Business has been a little better this month. All of us are hoping that the cool weather will bring better business for everybody.

I will send some money on your insurance in a few days.

I did not get to finish your letter last night so will mail it today Friday.
Love
Dicky

Note on back 2.47 light 1.00 water
3,47 from 3,50 remainder 0.03
note on envelope: Received Aug. 22, 1932 with check of $3.50 ct

Postmark: Sept 23, 1932: Wichita Falls, Tex. Return Box 671
note on envelope: Received September 26, 1932 with $3.00 check.

627 seventh street   Phone 5029
Cream Bakery
Milo Connelly, Proprietor
Fresh Bread, Pies and Cakes Baked Daily
Wichita Falls, Texas

Dearest Homefolks,

Wichita Falls is planning to put the big pot in the little'un next Monday, Tuesday and Wednesday. We are having our golden Jubilee. All the old timers will be here with their boots and spurs and cowboy hats. All the women will be dressed as they did 50 years ago in calico dresses, bussels in everything. Every old plow, wagon, and gigg, horses and burros, all the old quilts, spinning wheels, and everything that is ancient, medieval and modern will be represented here during these three days. Yes, and a rodeo with bucking bronks and steers to bring back old memories.

I forgot to mention Mr. Arnett in my other letter ___Abe we call him. If there ever was a freak of nature abe is it. That boy can do anything that he sets his mind to do ____except work for a living he had been going from one end of the country to the other in old rattletrap cars begging and bumming his way __ playing that old accordion wherever they will let him. If he has ever taken a bath nobody around here has ever heard of it. Yes he used to work here with me when old man Stamfli ran the place but not since the last 15 or 16 years. He used to be a fairly decent chap but now he is just a plain bum. If you give him any encouragement he will be there to live with you and will always make that place his headquarters when he is passing through the country. Enough for Abe.

We had a little rain this morning but it has cleared off tonight with a brisk wind from the north. Hope it stays cool, for last week and the first part of this have been hot ones.

Will tell you next week how the jubilee came out.

Love,

Dicky

note: Rec. Sept. 26, 1932 with check for $3.50

Postmark Oct 1, 1932 Wichita Falls. Return Box 671
Letter Missing
Note on envelope Received Oct. 3, 1932 with $3.50

Postmark Oct 6, 1932 Wichita Falls. Return Box 671
Letter Missing
Note on envelope Received Oct. 8, 1932 with $3.50

---

no envelope: note on back sheet Received October 19, 1932

Dearest Mother:

One of my friends is getting a bunch of oil leases down in Kaufman County. He wanted me to go down with him for a couple of days and as it will not cost me anything I think that I will go with him. Maybe my toe will heal better if I can stay off of it for a day or two.

I am looking forward to the trip with the greatest of thrills, wish that he was coming down to ballinger so that I could see you. Will tell you all about it next week.

Love

Dicky

---

no envelope: note on back - Received November 7, 1932

Dear Mother and Eunice:

Was beginning to think that you were angry with me for going down to Kaufman instead of coming to see you. I would not have had any vacation at all but my toe was hurting me so badly that I was going to quit work for a few days anyhow and I found out that two of my friends were going through Gray's Prairie to the Southern Portion of Kaufman County and would be gone 3 days. I asked them to let me go with them and they were just as much pleased to have me as I was to go. They carried me to Mary's getting there just about sundown. They had some little trouble securing some leases which they were planning on so it gave me an extra day of enjoyment.

Ambrose is just the same as always. He married Hulda Wright. She was a widow with one girl at the time they now have two more. Ambrose works all the time but he is the slowest thing you ever saw. His wife says that she never fixes anything to eat until he gets there as she never knows when he is coming.

Old Dick Abbott was pulling off his pants getting ready to go to bed when Lucille, Irene and I got over there on the first night. He just couldn't believe his eyes when they told him who I was.

One of my great regrets of my visit was because I missed seeing Frank Barker and Mary. My toe hurt me and kept me from going several places that I would have gone had it been well. Mary's daughter ... is married and she and her husband are running a store in the corner of what used to be Buchanan's Pasture, just across the road from the new brick schoolhouse.

There has been so many creeks cut out that the land is washing into the creeks and branches and filling them up. The branch that ran through our place is about half as deep as it was when we left and our place is in cultivation clear back to Uncle Sams place altho the trees are still on the branch.

I did not get over to the Clopp place or to Uncle Sams house altho we planned to go to see Mr and Mrs Phelps who live on Uncle Sams place. I thought that perhaps things would look closer together than the used to but they look about the same as they always did.

Miss Mattie Barker is living in Kaufman with Sigmund. Lilly is married and has moved away. I would have liked to have visited them and Mr. Will Jones but we did not have time while in town. I saw Scurry at a distance but did not go there. I think that I could stay a month there and have something to do every minute.

There are sure some large grape vines down the branch behind our place. I slipped off and went down to the old bluffs in Kirby's Pasture. I saw more wild dewberry vines there than I knew existed down there and the prettiest patch of wild black berries that I ever saw.

Well here I am just raving about Kaufman. I dont believe that you are tired of it but I must quit for this time. Will try to think of something else next time.   Love
<u>Dicky</u>

Note: Received Feb. 27, 1933 with check of $3.50

Dearest Mother and Homefolks:

I have been so full of cold lately that I almost forgot to write this week.

Today has been threatening rain but so far only a few drops have fallen.

So Park Avenue is getting paved? Have they opened the Elm Creek Bridge? It ought to be the prettiest street in town now.

I got a musical program from Bertha Lee last week. She must be quite a musician. Is Donald still playing the piano and T.D. and Ralph James still playing their horns?

Wish I could see you all as a I get awfully lonesome.

Will try to do better next week when I feel better.

Love,
Dicky

Postmark March 12, 1933 Return John Phillips Box 671

Dearest Homefolks:

Got your letter several days ago but have been waiting for the bank to open before writing you again but it looks like it might be several days yet before they do open so am sending you 4___ones so that it will be easier for you to handle.

Business is getting so bad that it looks like I will have to leave here one of these days. My cold is about (over) but I have a slight bronchial infection that is gradually leaving.

Hope all of you are well. I guess you still have the large number of kids hanging around.

Will try to write again next week.
Love
Dicky

note on back 9.00
            4.42
   spent   4.58

Dearest Homefolks   3-24-33

Got your letter several days ago but have been so busy that am just now having time to answer.

Hope all of your colds are gone. I am feeling pretty good only when that old flu got into my heart. Perhaps I will be able to throw it off as I grow older.
... The Town is awfully dead now. No one seems to have any business.

Write me when you can find time from your ... company.
Note at bottom: Received March 24, 1933   Love,
                                                     Dicky

John R. Phillips: Twice in the winter, I had attacks of influenza, but I kept up my exercise on my bicycle and by spring had gained my strength back. I had managed to pay off the debts my folks had accumulated in Ballinger including the notes that were held by the bank against the old homestead just before the depression.

The management of the Cream Bakery was in financial trouble and I had to take several cuts in pay in order to keep the doors open. In bed one night I kept thinking how things were going and before I went to sleep I made my resolve.

A man by the name of Henry Gilbert, who had the reputation of being the best gold prospector in the country had been visiting and talking with me about placer gold mining. I did not quit my job immediately, even though my mind was made up. It took me several days to cash in my Government Insurance which I had built up to nearly one thousand dollars; to trade an old army rifle to Pleas Brown for a small trailer; buy a 22 rifle; arrange for Frank Northcut to look after my little house on third street; and numerous other details which anyone had to do when changing from one kind of life to another. I told Mr. Connelly and Mr. Burnett what I had planned on doing and told them that they could give two girls work for what they were paying me, which they did.

Mr. Gilbert had a Model A Ford and I had the trailer. We hitched them together and started out. We went to Ballinger on April 11, 1933 and left on the 13th. I gave my mother all the money I could spare and told her I would send her more as soon as I could. I also told her a fib, that the doctors had told me to go to the mountains to cure my heart ailment - actually they had told me just the opposite. Strangely enough after being in the mountains for less than three months my heart got stronger and soon I was running across the mountains like a mountain goat.

After leaving Ballinger we started for New Mexico by way of El Paso. Between San Angelo and Sierra Blanca we ran into a blizzard in the form of the blackest dust storm either of us had ever seen. We made it into Sierra Blanca about sundown if there had been a sun. It was black as night and the lights from the car could not penetrate the dust over a few yards.

When we got to El Paso the next day, the wind had subsided and the sun was shining. El Paso in 1933 was just a small western town but was beginning to expand. We started up the river to Hot Springs (now Truth of Consequences) where we got a motel room. Since we had all our camping equipment, this was unnecessary. Gilbert insisted on eating in restaurants where thick expensive steaks were his specialty.

We enquired around for someone who had a gold mine for sale. One man took us across the Rio Grande to the other side of the Wild Horse Mountains where we spent an unproductive day looking over a lode lead prospect. Some one told us about the Lings, an old couple who lived in the hills near Gold Dust, New Mexico. Here at the Gold Dust Mining Camp I first saw placer gold being mined. I was completely sold and continued to be sold on placer gold for the rest of my life.

The road to Gold Dust was a plain one having been established by one wagon travelling in the ruts of the wagon which had gone before. Seeing half a dozen tents off to one side of the road, Gilbert asked Mr. Ling who lived there and was told that Mrs Wakeley and her son had traded for gold claims and were holding onto them hoping someone would come along and develop the property. He said that these claims were not considered to be worth much, however we turned in towards the tents as the road to the Ling Property ran right across the Wakeley claim.

We met Mrs. Wakeley and her son and visited with them for about an hour after which we continued over two high ridges to Mr. Ling's diggings. He had dug several holes and had started a well but had not developed any water and not much of a prospect. Using paper bags, we took samples of dirt on both sides of the wash which ran across the property and took them back to Hot Springs where I got my first experience panning for gold in the Rio Grande. With the help of the Wakeley boy we found more and coarser gold than we did on the Ling property.

A LETTER FROM THE GOLDFIELDS about 1934

Dearest Mother and Homefolks:

Am writing you again before getting your letter as I promised that I would send you some money just as soon as I got paid. Will send you some more next week.

Surely has been cold up here. Just as soon as the sun goes down it starts to get cold and it is usually freezing by nine o'clock. The days, however, are wonderfully warm except when the wind blows then it is very disagreeable. We get our cold winds from the west or off the Black Range of Mountains at whose foot our camp is located.

They have moved in some machinery and work is starting in earnest. A big shovel will be in this week sometime. They will really get lots of gold when they get started to operating. Mrs Wakely is still improving but it has been a slow process for her to get her strength back.

Have you had any more rain? We had a few drops of snow a day or two ago but it melted as fast as it fell. I really hope we do not have any snow this winter as I want to work outside all winter if I can. I am getting pretty hard but I hope by spring to be hardened to anything that comes along.

Got a card from Lucille Lowrey the other day. Irene and Virginia and George have all married about two years ago. This only leaves Mary with two children at home - Lucille and Jack. Guess it wont be too long before all of them are gone. It only seems yesterday that George and I played marbles in our backyard but 35 years have gone by since we both started to school. He has been dead nearly thirty years - his brothers and sisters now have grandchildren. Some are old at fifty two and Aggie must be getting close to sixty years of age. None of us are young any more but I am trying my best to remain as young as I can by keeping in good health.

I have not heard from Elmer for over a year. Hope they are getting along O.K. However I guess that he really is better off than any of the rest of us for he is in a climate where he does not have to worry about winter clothes and everything just grows in abundance so they do not have to worry about what they have to eat. Good old Elmer.

Well I have written about everything that I can think about at present. But say do you hear from Aunt Belle, Aunt Callie or Uncle John? I guess that I am completely out of touch with all of them but it is only a few days until Christmas they all come into my mind ____ but they say there is a Santa Claus. May God bless them all and you too.

Write me all the news when you can spare the time for news is scarce out here.

With a world of love to all of you I am the same
                              son, brother, & uncle
                                        Dicky
This is a picture of the cabin where I sleep.

                                   Mother's Birthday 1934
My Darling Mother:

    My one regret today is that I cannot spend it with you and for that matter, all succeeding days would be happier were I only able to see your sweet face and hear your voice as I used in the long ago.

    But, Mother Dear, no matter where I am or whither my life may take me you can always rest assured that I'll be thinking of you and remembering the things you have taught me - honor - truthfulness - honesty - sincerity of life - and the greatest love for you that will never fail.

    Altho we have been separated in the flesh yet we are and shall remain forever as one in love and spirit.

    Your birthdays have been many and it is the prayer of your baby that the lord will spare you for many years to come to be the greatest joy and pleasure that all of your children have possessed _ our mother.

    I can only promise to devote my time to doing things that will make you happy and comfortable. If I succeed - you will succeed. If I fail it will be through no cause of yours and the lord being my helper and with the love which I know you have for me to guide me I will succeed for your sake.

    This is not a long letter but it is written because I love you.

                                        Your baby boy
                                          Johnny
Box 492 Wichita Falls, Texas

note on envelope: This is my birthday letter May 5, 1934

Postmark Sept 15, 1934 Hillsboro, New Mex. Return Box 132 Hillsboro

Dearest Mother and Homefolks:

    Was in town and got your letter so am writing this hurriedly. Everything OK. Hope Max is better by this time.

                                        Love
                                          Dicky
note on envelope: Received ($3.00)

September 18, 1934
Answered Sep 19 1934

[After going from place to place], I was about fed up with prospecting and went with Gilbert's friends the Petersons to California. Big companies came in and took over the Wakeley and Gold Dust property and took out more than six million dollars in gold from the draws and flats.

I came back to Hillsborough alone several months later and after spending the winter with Bill Baines and Slim Brown up in the hills above the town, I figured that the six million dollars recovered had slipped into the valley from the ridges in the Black Range.

When I got to California with the Petersons, I had about fifty dollars. The Petersons had some friends named Wallace who were really wonderful people and like everyone else were hard up for money. I had my sleeping gear with me from New Mexico and got permission to use a vacant room upstairs for two dollars a week. I bought some food for the Wallaces and ate my meals with them for a couple of weeks while I looked for a job. I painted a large sign for a hotel in Wilmington and they gave me a room for a month. Someone mentioned Long Beach, which was down the coast about three miles and I determined to walk the distance to save money. I stopped about halfway to Long Beach in a small Greek restaurant for a cup of coffee and found an add for a shoeshine stand for rent. When I got to Long Beach I rented the shoeshine stand from O.S. Eller who became my lifelong friend. I moved my cot, pad, and blankets inside and opened shop and did a lot of business with the sailors who came by from the ships. Mr. Eller told me that if I kept the place cleaned up I could have the stand and room for nothing.

One day a letter came from Frank Northcutt, telling me that Bert Bean Coffee Company would pay me $100 a month if I would come back to Wichita Falls and take the job of roasting coffee for the firm. A hundred dollar salary was almost a fortune in 1934. I reluctantly accepted the job after talking to my new friends and wrote Bert Bean to send me money for transportation, which they did. I roasted coffee for about six months, and then gave up my job and went back to the gold fields in New Mexico where I stayed several months. I then went back to California and took up where I left off and soon was doing better than ever.

My friend Tom Hart had opened a Booking Business in a small room next to the Pacific Electric Railway Station and asked me to run the business for him at night. [Tom was having financial troubles], and decided to take his whole family to Alaska, and take me with him. Finally, unable to sell the business, he gave it to me on credit, but I soon gave it up.

Post Mark: Long Beach Calif. May 3, 1937. Return Box 1165

A birthday card

Signed: From Your Baby
         Dicky
note inside: Received May 5. 1937
             My 79th Birthday
note on envelope: I was born May 5, 1858
note on bottom of envelope: One of Johnnies friend stoped by to see me his name is Abe. Abe he knew Johnie at Witchita Falls this May 15, 1937

[I had met Ada Hall in Wichita Falls] and in 1937 when she was working on her master's degree at the University of Texas in Austin, we began to correspond. I found that she had not married, so I proposed by mail. We were married December 17, 1937. Ada began to help with the business, but the hotel owners put a liquor store in. Ada and I went to Arizona where we lived in Wickenburg for a time and finally bought a small cafe in Phoenix. We sold the business for a profit of $150 and headed back to Long Beach where Lloyd Larrum offered to rent a space in front of his barber shop. The police soon closed Lloyd down, and he sold out with nothing down, and we successfully operated the place for eight years as a newsstand in front and a barber shop in back.

My sister Mary and I had gone together to buy a nice large house on Park Avenue in Ballinger. Here Eunice and Donald started and ran the floral business which was to support the Ballinger branch of the family for the next 40 years. Without my knowledge, Mary borrowed money on the place in her name and would not pay it back. Mother asked me to do something, so I returned to Ballinger and paid the note off. Mary borrowed money on the house a second time and I paid it off. The third time this happened, I got the house in my name. I went from Long Beach to Ballinger by bus and beat mary in court, and so kept the house for Mother, Eunice, Max and his family.
My mother Kate Bradshaw Phillips died May 5, 1941 and was buried in Ballinger.

On May 3, 1942 our son Wesley was born in Long Beach. We moved to Placerville in Northern California, but did poorly there. We then moved up the mountains toward Lake Tahoe to the little town of Camino, where we lived in a little two room house down the creek. From Camino we moved to Santa Rosa where I worked for Tom Hart on his farm and also worked for J.C. Penny. I spent part of my time here in the pear orchards pruning pear trees.

We moved back to Long Beach where James was born September 14, 1944. We had trouble finding a place to live, but stayed for a while with Mr. and Mrs. Underwood in one room of their house. We finally found a suitable house on Ohio Street which we moved into.

In 1946, I bought a 1932 Studebaker, practiced driving for a few days and then drove back to Wichita Falls. We also drove this car to make a trip to Austin, LaPorte, Colorado, and New Mexico, before it just collapsed in New Mexico and had to be towed back to Wichita Falls.

John Wesley (Wes) Phillips biography: We moved into a small servant's quarters on the back of Aunt Ruth Claypoole's house at 2607 ninth street. We stayed here for a while and then bought an old house and lot on twenty third street from Aunt Velma and Uncle Forrest Jones. Dad tore down the old house and built a new one. During this time we lived in a tent on the back of the lot and used a pit toilet. We sold this house for a profit and then rented a one room building from Mrs. Miller at 1417 sixteenth street. Dad bought a variety store near Reagan Junior High which he ran for about a year until we bought the Griffen House at 1004 fourteenth street.

This was a one bedroom house on the back of a larger lot. It faced 14th Street and had one side near the alley. The one bedroom became James and my room while the former dining room which opened into the living room became our parents room. There was a 12X12 foot kitchen with gas stove and gas refrigerator and a small add-on bathroom probably built after the original construction.

Wichita Falls by this time had a population of around 50,000 and was the independent Oil Capitol of Texas. Shepard Air Force Base also contributed to the economy as did Wichita Falls State Hospital. Midwestern University had around 1800 students enrolled and was a four year school. The business center or "down town" area had around 100 businesses and was booming in the post-war economy of the area. Wichita County had nearly 100,000 population and was a major center of wheat growing and cattle ranching.

Mama had been teaching school as a substitute for a couple of years, and after we moved to fourteenth street, she got a job teaching veterans who reported to our house for school. In 1949, she moved this operation to a basement room at Austin school where I was in second grade. In 1950, she got a job with the Wichita Falls Public Schools, teaching Downs Syndrome children, and in 1952 she became a regular teacher at Barwise Elementary School.

Late in August, James and I always went with Mama to buy our school supplies.

The most important item was clothing, and for this we stopped at Penny's. We walked to the back of the store where we descended the steps to the basement. This was the children's section of the store with shirts, pants, socks, suits, and underclothes. The smell was fabulous! Everything smelled new and fresh, but the best smelling of all were the blue jeans. We got two or three pair of these apiece and picked out three shirts apiece; socks, belts, and later on when it got colder we purchased coats, warm caps, and gloves.

From there we went upstairs to the shoe department where the attendant measured and fitted us for shoes. The new shoes smelled good too and in the shoe department there was an interesting gadget known as a drinking fountain. When we pushed the lever, the water would arch out and splash back into the bowl and here it seemed to taste better than anywhere else.

Penny's was the main stop down town, but we had to have paper, pencils, crayons, rulers, erasers, and such. Dad always took us over to the corner drugstore to purchase these.

By the first day of school we were decked out in our best clothes as were the other students and all the smells made the first day really a marvelous experience.

After I had finished third grade, and James had finished at Mrs. Gregory's first grade across fifteenth street from Austin School, we took a trip out west gold mining.

The night before Arthur had driven up from Ballinger with his car a 1946 Chevy. James, Dad, and I helped load the car. First we put the dry washer in along with the large metal washing pans more commonly referred to as gold pans. We also loaded buckets, bags, cots, blankets, and all the other paraphernalia we would need to camp out.

We left the house about 6AM and drove all day. We spent the first night in Hot Springs New Mexico and arrived mid morning on the second day at Gold Dust New Mexico. Here we rented a house for the night. Gold Dust was a ghost town, and most of the houses were unoccupied. There were two rooms with two steel cots, one table and two rooms full of junk.

That night I slept on the cot with my father and James slept with Arthur. James got in bed early and went to sleep but Arthur went for a walk first. When Arthur got back he sat down on one end of the cot. James was asleep on the other end. Arthur weighed 250 pounds and James weighed 60 pounds. As soon as Arthur sat down, James end of the bed flew up and James sailed through the air and landed on the floor. Both were unhurt and James didn't even know what had happened.

At 4 AM the next morning, just before sunrise, we got up and decided to go to Hillsboro five miles away on a dirt road for breakfast. Arthur was looking everywhere for his keys so we could get into the car, which he had presumably locked to keep the ghosts out. He finally found them - locked in the car. When we finally got them out, it was time to go for breakfast.

My father had recently finished off the attic, with a board floor and had put in a steep staircase to allow us access. James, Wendell, Ronnie, and I now adopted this as a sort of clubhouse, and often spent hours there, especially in the winter time, since the temperature in summer was over 130 degrees. We also began storing things here, and soon had quite a number of things there. Some of the things my parents had stored in the shed in the backyard now went here as well.

My mother had long ago joined Floral Heights Methodist Church, but my father had been Church of Christ, and for a while they attended separate churches, but soon my father saw that this would not work out, so he also began attending the Methodist church. At first we took the bus or a taxi, since it was about two miles from our house to Floral Heights. My mother taught the B.O.P. class, and my father joined the Mens Bible Class where he sometimes played the organ for the songs if the regular organist was not available. They got him a shape note song book, since he knew only this system, and he could play from it.

Dad was forced to retire in 1956 when he reached the age of 65. Actually he was in good health, but no one would hire him at this age. To keep busy he worked in the yard and went on occasional gold mining trips to New Mexico or Northern California. He read almost every day, and soon started to write poems and short stories which he sometimes sent off to publishers to see of they would buy them.

About October 15, 1969

Dear Wesley and Roberta:

I guess that Mama has told you how thrilled we were that you called us the other night. Please do it again any time the urge hits you. Next time have the call reversed so we can share in the cost of the fun.

The leaves are just about gone from the Paradise trees and are turning yellow on the pecan and other trees on our street. I took the bull by the horns and picked up the leaves as the fell (almost) and am standing around with my rake and shovel in my hands waiting for the others to start falling. I put the others in Gertrude;s cistern and the rains have packed them down so that I may have room to put the rest of the leaves in the same place.

We got several messes of beans on the last planting which we did around the cherry tree, which died, but I guess that will be all for this season. The tomatoes put on really good but I was afraid that the freeze would come before they got ripe so gave them to the Normans across the alley. This was the second crop. The first one turned out real well as we got about 150 large ripe ones from it but as tomatos stayt green until frost I just left them to see what they would do this fall. Now I know.

The enclosed family tree covers almost in detail, the complete history of the Phillips- Graham- Heffly- Hudspeth lines. Anyone wanting more details can do their own research from there or write me just what they need and I will be able to supply it.

I know that you fellows are in your glory there in the Everglades. I have just finished reading about the old conquestodores and one of them was of particular intrest Cabeza de Vaca as we ran across one of his descendent our in San Antonio, New Mexico on our recent trip out there.

He, as well as his father, grandfather and generations beforehim were born there on the Rio Grande since before the discovery of America in 1492. I have a story completed that explains everything but am not trying to sell it at the present until I sleep over it for several weeks and maybe able to thrash out any bugs that I might have put in in my haste to get it written.

Mama has really found her grandfather Hall and along with his father and she is delighted as this gives her almost all the things she has been looking for for the last thirty or more years.

More later.   Love   Dad

Dear Wesley and Roberta:

I am so proud of both of you that I have burst off all my buttons and my head has swelled to abnormal size.

Since Wesley has now become elegible for the gormete club it will take a lot of worry off the minds of both of you.

While Mama was gone I got my meal ready, put it on my plate and not only started soaking the pots and pans but I also put a small amount of detergent in each so that it would clean easier.

As soon as I got through eating immediately the dishes and pots and pans were cleaned and put away and guess what I did after that--- I took a nap and I knew that I would not have a lot of dirty dishes to contend with when I woke up.

I guess Eleanor has gone back to Arizona by now. Wish all of us could go out there and stay period. I love the mountains so much that I tell Mama that when I get too old to be useful to her to take me out to theedge of the desert, take off my bridle (clothes) and turn me loose so that I can go out to the mountains where there are plenty of holes and gullies to jump in and die.

James wanted us to look up a car for him when he gets home. I found just the car he asked for only it is two years older than the year he suggested. It is a Dodge sedan, white wall tires, automatic transmission, power brake, power steering, which fits his description of the kind of car that he wants. It also has air conditioning and only 32,000 miles. It is a '65.

Summer is beginning to bear down on us as the degrees have been hovering around the century mark now almost since Mama left to come to Florida.

Mr. Flake still has his paper route and plans to keep it aslong as he is able to handle it successfully.

Wesley you have heard me speak of Sammy Hunt who lived with for a number of years in Ballinger. After he went back to Dallas he became a restaurant cook and finally got a chefs job in Houston. Several months ago, while working at night, two negros came in the back door of the kitchen, robbed him of his wallet and then shot him directly in the face with a shot gun at close range. It blew away most of his face and throat including his voice box. Fortunately his eyes and hearing were not damaged. Cherry Scott, another cousin in Brownwood, wrote us about it and asked me to write to Sammy and cheer him up as best I could and this I did. He answered right back and asked me to write again soon. He said that the doctor is going to try to restore his voice box and build back his face from flesh and skin from his hip. If his voice box is restored it will be the first successful operation of its kind. If

I can get the information that I need and want I will write this up and try to get the Reader's Digest to publish it. If they buy it I will send most if not all the money to Sammy to assist him and his family as he rehabilitates. Hope I can write a successful story.

Take care of yourselves and let us know every few days how Wesley is progressing. We think and hope that now most of your troubles will be over. He willnot mind it so much even though he does have to stay on the desk five days a week. He at least will have two days off each week to do the things he likes to do and you will be able to do them together and be happy doing them.

Please write or call (at our expense) any time.

      Love   Dad

June 29th, 1970

Dear Wesley and Roberta:

Thanks for your nice letters of a day or two ago and we know how glad you were to get home after almost a month away from it. We know how glad we have always been upon seeing the old home after a long trip somewhere in the U.S.

The apricots began to get ripe on the first of June and the birds and squirrels also began eating them so I had to stand out there with rocks inmy hand to ward them off. Within ten days I had them all gathered, cooked and put in the deep freeze. Wish there was some way we could send you frozen fruit but perhaps we can keep some of them until you come again.

The ancestral books came and they are very interesting but so far we have been unable to hook up Adam with their Phillipses.

There is a chart in the book which shows the beginnings of the Phillips name and how it has evolved. It is quite interesting and we know you will enjoy it also especially has the exploits of David Phillips during the Civil War been interesting to me as it brings back some of my own times in W.W. One.

I seem to have a hard time getting back on my memoirs but I will one of these days and you know me when I start something I like to see it through as soon as possible.

So far we have had very little rain. It has come down in bucketfulls all around us but the people of this city just seem tohave done something to anger the gods as we have been in a hole as far as rain is concerned.

John Rader had an awful time trying to bring his girl back

from McAllen. He had to drive almost day and night for five days and after getting the girls things all packed her mother raised such a hullaballew that they had to post pone the wedding until August and he came back without her. I sometimes wonder why God made women like they are but after all they are part of the human race. Claud, Irma, John, Betty and Linda left immediately after John got back and Mama has had a letter from Irma so we know they reached home safely although they must have driven almost all night.

I do not know whether Mama has written you about John Stanfill, Stella Graham's husband. He was 93 and his mind was wandering and he kept trying to wander with it. Sometimes he would go off and someone would find him eight or ten miles from home and they would have to go after him. The last time this happened they did not find him for a week and of course he was dead when they did and he was about twenty miles from home. He had gone off by the side of the highway and lay down to rest and it seems whenever woke up.

Please forgive me for not writing more often but these days are so long and hot that it is almost impossible for me to get started and when I do I just keep on whether I have anything to say or not and this is one of those times.

We will send you your book in a few days and hope you will enjoy it like Mama and I have.

I have written a long letter to the author and together we may be able to work out something tangible on Adam's father and Grandfather. I have it figured pretty well but it is not authentic and does not really prove anything. Perhaps when he gets my letter it may clear up some things for him. We hope so anyway.

Take good care of yourselves and write us some more of your wonderful letters.

                         Love to both of you.

                             Dad

7-3-71

Dear Wesley and Roberta:

Well, it rained. Yesterday brought us over and inch and today the weatherman has promised us some more of the same. We are all hoping which is about all that any of us can do.

I have prepared another chapter of Johnny's memoirs which is herewith enclosed. Hope you like it. We sent you your ancestor book several days ago. Did you get it along with several chapters of Johnny's life. I guess that you forgot to mention them or they may have been slow in arriving.

Mama and I are taking long walks - I say long walks with reservations - they are around eight blocks in length especially while the weather has been so hot. Over 100 for a whole month and most of the time above 104.

We got a nice letter from James Friday. He really is happy with his work and, as we knew, is doing wonderfully well with it.

Mama and I have three things, especially, to look forward to every day - the postman; the paper; and our walks. If we can keep up this interest until our grandbaby arrives when we can add another interest to our lives, we will try to struggle along even without gold prospecting.

Our neighbor Mr. Jones, went down to the bank and got each of us a rain guage. So far neither of us can figure out where to put it so it will not be obliterated by houses and trees and things. Perhaps today we may be able to put it up for the next rain that comes.

The squirrels are getting so numerous that we may have to eliminate some of them as they are now trying to get in all the houses including ours but so far I have kept them scared away from us.

We also have a redheaded woodpecker that comes every day and lights on the electric light pole at the corner of the yard next to the old mesquite. When the pole was put up they had put a hole about an inch wide through the top of it. The bird lights first on top then comes down on the side and pokes his bill into the hole then he sidles around to the other side and does the same to the same hole on the pole. He never seems to get anything out of the hole but may be looking for spiders which would be about all that he could find anyway. He also has a mate which comes with him now and then.

I know how much you are enjoying your swimming. Wish that I could be with you but since my legs have a tendency to cramp I guess my swimming days are over but I could swim better and dive longer than most boys in my younger days. Believe it or not I could stay under the water for a minute and a half and used to be able to dive across the Colorado River, reach up and pat the bank while still under water then turn round and dive back to the opposite side. Hope you think I am not bragging but I am.

Take good care of yourselves and write us more of those wonderful letters.

                Love   Dad

7-24-71

(undated - summer 1971)

Dear Wesley and Roberta:

We enjoyed your letter (and) talking to you very much. As the hot weather is getting a little better I have finished up the fourth chapter of the story.

I amy also be several weeks getting out the fifth chapter but will do just as soon as I can.

We got a letter today from Ed and Eleanor. They seem to be having a ball buildingon to the house and Ed even allowed your mother to nail on part of the roof.

They may come to see us after meeting you up north. We hope so.

Ethel Rinefield has taken the Jones family (Our minister, his wife, two sons and the wife of the minister that died about two years ago to Europe where I hope they have a wonderful time and am sure that they will.

We had a good rain last Friday and hope for more in the near future as we surely do need it.

I have finished out at Aunt Ruth's place with the exception of trimming those large trees on the west side of the house which have nearly been killed by mistletoe. If I can cut them back I may be able to save them for the shade that she and mama want on the west.

I have been all morning and part of the afternoon copying the fourth chapter and am pretty tired so will not write or cannot write a very interesting letter at this setting but will try to do better next time.

Both of you sound as if you are enjoying life to the fullest. Keep it up. It will mean a longer life and a happier life for both of you.

                                    Love

                                    Dad.

Dear Wesley and Roberta:

First I want to thank you for the nice letters plus the candy and cookies which also came today. It is hard to keep Mama out of them even if she is trying to keep her weight down. By the way she is down to a hundred twenty pounds today the astronauts lift off from the moon.

We got to see it all. It was much smoother than it was when it was simulated on the last moon walk.

I have all those logs sawed up over on those lots the other side of the Norman lot. There is still lots to do over there but I have heaps of time to do it in. It is looking 200% better now and should look like decent folks live near when I finish.

Mama is going to the library to look up something for Clovis as she thinks the people who had all those books out on Latin America have brought any or all of them back.

I am sending you my "gold" chapter. Hope you like it. If you will clip each chapter together as I send them to you when I get down to the last chapter I will number each one so that they will come in sequence.

Some of the old boys who had been in the hospital from my sunday school class were back sunday and are doing real well it seems.

Mama insists on ironing out the wrinkles in my suit every sunday morning. I am not sure when she does it because she is proud of me or ashamed to be seen out with me full of wrinkles.

Bozo the little Jones dog almost scratched out of his pen this morning but the old lady found it before he did and threatened to give him a licking. He knew what she said as he curled over on his back and whined like all get out. He is one smart pooch.

I have just about ran out of anything to write about but the gold story should keep you reading a little while longer.

    More later.   Love   Dad.

Dear Wesley and Roberta:

I wrote you a long letter last week that had some vital information about becoming an octogenarian but last evening I was outside counting the birds when it occurred to me that I ought to send you some supplemental stories of Johnny's life that might be of interest to you and future generations.

After I had finished I find there are eight pages of them and I hope they will be to your liking.

You fellows now have most of my history and sometimes I just cannot believe it myself so help me I at least think it is true.

Of course you just cannot set down in eight pages the complete history, the joys, the sorrows, the hardships and the happiness of a life of eighty years.

The old TV went out last night and it is now in the shop waiting to be analyzed. If it is too much we will not have it fixed and Mama wants a smaller machine anyway and I guess that that is what will happen eventually.

I started this paper in wrong and now it will not come out straight but will at least have all the words on it.

Roberta you remember the bugs I told you about. I think you were right as they are thicker around those China trees and are of the description of the ones you described.

I guess Ed and Eleanor are home before this. I have not written them now since they have been away but will do so in a few days.

I will try to run my memory back over the years and see if I can find something else for you to put with this supplement and when I do I'll write it down and expand on it like these enclosed.

We are calling James tonight to see if he is coming home on Labor day. It kinda keeps us up in the hill not knowing whether to expect him or not.

Write us another of your wonderful letters. We lap them up just like they were candy.

         Love Dad

9-1-71

Dear Wesley and Roberta:

You will note in this package and in previous ones that I have included most all the things you have asked for except Elmer and the cat's ears; giving the boys cabbage and hot cakes on the front line in France and other incidents in the trenches.

We have had four inches of rain in the last three days and it is still threatening. There surely is a big difference in rain water and this hydrant water. Since the rain everything has greened up to such an extent that most of the yellow is gone and it reminds you more of spring than summer in its last throes of burning everything up.

If you can think of anything that I used to tell you just ask me about it and I will respond. You now have my life, that is the better part of it, down in writing and I made some drastic actions this past week as I told Raby Hampton that I wanted to buy the cheapest coffin and burial that he had and he said that the cheapest one was $650 which was the price I paid for Eunices burial and coffin and pink robe. She looked so nice that I want the same for me. I also told him that instead of a lot of flowers on top that all I wanted was a United States flag. I also told Glendall Jones, our pastor at the Church, that I wanted to have him preach my funeral. He said he would only asked me to postpone the action for about twenty years as he is pretty busy at the present.

I have already selected the songs that I want sung so there will not be much to do except for the family to mourn if they are so inclined. You already know that we have our lot in Crestview.

As you also know I am not going to die until I have to so do not think anything about my getting everything ready as I think that that is the only thing for anyone who loves his family to do before a tragedy occurs.

Mama and I had a very nice three day visit over in Oklahoma last week and even left there in the rain. Minnie had the nicest tomatoes that I have eaten in years and years. They were big Beefsteak ones and red all through. Hope you will enjoy this last report as this may be the last one for several weeks or until I get the urge again.

        Love Dad

8-16-71

Dear Wesley and Roberta:

I guess by now you have those memoirs sent you last week. I have written out a few more which completely covers all the things you suggested and these are included with this letter.

We did not know what you wanted for your birthday but Mama and I are sending a small token of our love which she thinks will cheer you up while waiting for the baby to put in his appearance.

It is raining here pretty hard at the present time but we are expecting much more when the new cold front gets in this afternoon as that is what is predicted.

We are having baked potatoes, pork T-bones and apricot jello for dinner. Wish that you both were here to enjoy them with us.

Mama and I started to town and old man Jones came out and warned us that it would rain before we could get there and it did. Mama had to buy a parasol that she has been wanting a long time to keep her hair from getting wet on the way home. Dad already has one that he bought with S&H Green Stamps but as he did not have it with him his hair got wet but dried off soon after getting back home.

I will make a complete story for you on gardening and fruit growing just as soon as I can get around to it. It will cover just about everything that you will need to know to get a good garden and fruit. Peaches are the hardest to grow in this part of the country but can be made to bear prolifically with a small effort.

I guess that I had better leave something for Mama to write. Will try to do better next time.

                Happy birthday Roberta!

                                      Love, Dad

9-22-71

Dear Wesley and Roberta:

This is just a short letter to supplement the letter that I mailed you yesterday.

As I promised you will find out why I am able to grow fruits, vegetables and flowers that do so well.

Of course with the limited space Mama and I have here in Wichita Falls to grow much of anything is the reason that we have gone mostly to fruit. I made a big mistake by not using the soil testing kit on our apple and peach trees but I did so on the apricot and you know how it turned out.

By using the garden encyclopedia I would have been able to keep our peach trees from dying--also the apple tree that is almost half dead and would have been had not the rains come when they did.

Those packets of seed that you gave me came up and flourished 50% as only the Zinnias and Marigolds did so. As I am completely out of soil testing chemicals I really did not know what the other two needed so they did not even come up. The zinnias and marigolds are blooming their heads off at the present time and so are our roses.

You remember that beautiful pink rose down in front of old man Kidds store on Lamar. Nell Thompson, Ada's cousin from Enid Oklahoma gave me some hints on putting out rose cuttings and I got several from the Kidd rose and I believe they are all going to live. I hope so as Mama wants them to do so Very much.

It has been raining now for four days. Not heavy but a drizzle that has added up to over three inches. This is the kind of rain that all the farmers and ranchers have been praying for for several years. Of course it has come too late to do this years crops any good but will put a wonderful soaking that will be good for winter grains, mostly wheat.

When I think of other things to write about I will do so.

9-24-71   Love   Dad

Dear Wesley and Roberta:

We got your letter this morning and enjoyed it very much. You write such interesting letters that they always give us a lift when they come.

The pictures enclosed are duplicates of some of those you asked us to have made. Hope you like them. The rest we will save until you come to see us or we come to see you before having them reproduced.

The two pictures of my mama and her sister Belle will give you some idea of the change in dress from the early 1860s to the present. In the colored picture they are both still old fashioned and always wore their dresses down to where their ankles could not show.

The one of Ada, Velma and Henry when they were children also gives you an idea of what children wore some fifty odd years ago. We are very proud of the way they came out in the reproduction.

Of course the four sisters are very modern in their picture taken together and are they all beauties. Its the best picture they have ever had taken together as they are so happy by being together.

The picture of the Phillips family is really great. It was taken out to one side of our little farm down in Kaufman County in front of a forest of trees on Old Doc Crowley's place. Note especially the collar on your dad's shirt. That was typical of the times around 1900. My shoes were worn out and I had a hole in my stocking is the reason for the hat being in front of me. It and the grass covered up the hole.

The pictures of Wesley's grand parents are good reproductions. The Thompsons were a great clan and you can be proud of such stalwart forebears.

Pat Runge is in town and will be until after next sunday. Mama and I are going to visit with her this afternoon at four thirty out at Aunt Ruth's.

Bob Gant is out of the hospital and has put in two whole days work on his job. He really has had a hard go of it. Hope he snaps out now especially on his and his families standpoint.

As I want to get this in the mail will stop.

        Love   Dad.   10-14-71

Dear Wesley and Roberta:

If we could be certain of a "hole" in the weather when it comes time for the baby I would be tempted to drive through as we can pick a route around the big cities and the roads are good all the way. Wish that the little fellow could have been born on August 21st as we have air conditioning in the car and would not have been bothered by the summer weather. For some reason babies are unable to pick their time to make their appearance and I guess that that is for the best as everyone would have wanted to be born on my birthday--- or am I bragging?

Mama is going to write and may be able to get her letter in this one. She will tell you about James calling to tell us about his trip out to Pasadena, Calif. He had to fly on account of the weather as it was snowing cats and dogs when it was time for him to go.

Hope you will like my Christmas story which I was able to condense into three pages numbered 91,92,and 93. I numbered them myself so as to keep the record straight.

We are having a slow drizzle this morning but the weatherman says it will clear off during the day but as the moon is now going into conjunction with the sun and evening star I think the chances of a downpour of either rain or snow for the next week or ten days are good.

I am still enjoying the bird book and the binoculars and will continue to do so as long as I can get outside to watch the birds and other things that mother nature has to present.

I have been nominated to become an officer in the church which some would consider quite an honor but at my age I think they should choose younger men for the job. The first meeting of the board will be this coming wednesday and the next week will be Methodist Men so my activities are planned for me for this week and next.

The car seems to have a smile on its windshield this morning as it stands out there under its new carport which I completed and painted white last week. It really is attractive even if I did build it myself with help from no one. I find a drawing here on the table that I made before starting to build. I am enclosing it so that you can see what it looks like. It is covered with clear plastic strips that are twelve feet long. They enhance the looks and value of the carport. Hope you like the story.

Love   Dad.

Dear Wesley, Roberta, and Theresa:

In my eighty years being a Texas I have never seen such beautiful weather like we have been having for the last three weeks, or, for that matter, the last three months.

The old Mesquite is already out which is at least two weeks before it has ever come out before. The apricot tree has fruit that is as big as those glass marbles you boys saved up and up for years.

Two nights ago we had almost a half inch of rain which was the first we have had this year-- even drier than last year and last was the driest we had known since the year one. But even that half inch has given a new lease on life to everything that is supposed to green up this time of the year. Of course I have been giving them some help with the hose and water from the hydrant, but that is nothing compared to rain from the skies.

Mama teaches sunday school tomorrow and of course we will be there with bells on and with all of them ringing. She enjoys teaching and I am glad for her to teach as it gives me time for meditation while she is preparing her lesson.

Mrs. Brown is getting to be a regular gad-about as this month she has made almost a weeks visit up in Oklahoma also about as long in Abilene. She thought she was going to dance with Lawrence Welk in Oklahoma but found that it would cost ten dollars just to get in to hear him let alone dance.

Aunt Ruth is planning on moving by the middle of June. She and Mama do not think that I can sell the place but to show them that I can I have advertised in the weekly papers at Henrietta, Iowa Park, and Burkburnett and am enclosing a copy of the ad with this paper. We may have to take a loss on that property but not counting the taxes, the insurance and other things that we have spent the twelve years she has been there we have received back a little over $5000.00 in rents. She has been a good renter and has taken care of the place just as if it were her own. We will not lose even if we have to sell for less than we paid for it and she has been happy there.

When you come for your visit in June you will see how well I am. In fact I am sure that I will be here for many years. I had my doubts for a while but am doing so well under the doctor's and Mama's care and am really enjoying being coddled for a change. At that time also the apricots will be ripe for all of us to enjoy.

Jay tore off the porch from his house last weekend and is over there now figuring out what to do to fix up the place so that he can rent it. I guess Mama has told you that they bought a high priced place up on Rivercrest and have bought a riding mower to mow the large front and back yards. He is over there this afternoon working and I will go around and give him my moral support even though Mama and the doctor have turned thumbs down on my doing anything to help. I tried to get Jay to let me fix up the place just after they moved out but he did not me to do so which relieved me of my worries.

Mama and I have not been going to church at night since the doctor slowed down and has restricted my driving until next monday and as Mama had been doing all the driving and as I do not want her to drive at night-- we just stay home and look at the T.V. or in my case play solitaire on the kitchen table.

My chimney swifts have not returned yet but if the weather continues like we think it will they should be here this afternoon or tomorrow. They are pretty prompt every year and this year should be no exception.

We have a $120.00 insurance bill on the new car which came in this week but as it is not really due until after the middle of April we will not have to pay it until then and our bank account can remains intact.

Theresa should be saying a few words by June and we can have more fun with her then than we could now by either my flying down there for a very short visit or Roberta flying up here for a longer one. We may try to take her away from you when you get here so you had better put your brand on her just in case.

When I start to write to you I never know when to stop so I guess I'd better.
March 25, 1972   Love   Dad

Dear Wes and Roberta:

One thing we missed telling you is that Donald says that he is going to start his social security in another 15 months when he is 62. He can still work almost what the Wares need him at the florist shop. He did mention that they could move to Graham, Mineral Wells or some other place then if they wanted to. I doubt they will for Arthur is pretty well situated there at Hico Nursing Home. He knows the nurses and most of the people living there. He is well liked. Donald probably could get to work part time at just about any place he moved to, but he has a wonderful friendship with the Ware family that bought him out. That might not be true of any other place he moved to after retirement.

Do you remember that when we went to see them at this last place they have that there were no flowers there? Now there are flowers around the front of the house, flowers on the porch, and the back yard has flowers and fish pond like he had at the 7 acre tract and at the florist shop location. Besides the fish tanks at that window between hall and kitchen and at the kitchen window, he has what I think is a couple of slender, side by side tanks that are just about filling the wall over in the corner where his dinette table is.

Letha is one of the thousands of women who became concerned about breast cancer after Mrs. Ford's trouble. She found a lump and has had surgery. It was benign so she was one of the lucky ones. Her son Randy is in college and is taking biology. This semester he seems to have the course on water and water life like the one you took, Wes.

The way Johnny is developing and learning it may be that in a few months he will be able to understand and do it when you tell him "Say 'More please'" when his plate is empty. That will make it easier on all of you, and he can still get as much food as he really needs.

I finally looked up my father's obituary. It said he was born in Racine, Wisconsin when I have verified that he was born in or rather near Friendship, Wisconsin. That is the place(Racine) where I need next to look for the Lester Brown family in 1907. Ruth and Velma both remember that he talked about that and thought he was born there. I must ask Irma what she remembers hearing him say about Racine, Wisconsin.

Roy's ear is a lot better and Velma is also doing well. Roy will probably have the prostate operation before long. They think it is just enlargement and they think it has no malignancy there. Velma is thinking seriously of having her crippled foot operated on. They can remove damaged joints (from arthritis) now and install plastic joints. After that she could wear shoes that would be suitable for wearing to church. She may have fingers done too, for then she could manage better the things she needs to do.

Bobby Jones son Bobby Junior is in his last year in high school. He is in Germany with Henny. Henny and family will be coming back to the U.S. in March, but Bobby will stay with his German Grandmother and finish out the other couple of months to get his work finished with his class.

Tina, Bobby's daughter, is with him. She is bright enough that she has taken extra work so that she will be graduating from high school this next june, too. She is quite serious with the boy friend, but I hope and so does Velma, that she will not get married next summer. These young marriages have not worked out at all well.

Wes, Maybe those nearing retirement will soon be taking advantage of it and will make way for some naturalists to move on up faster. We will hope so. Besides they will eventually get that budget finished and in action. I saw in the paper the other day that they had needed to bring pressure to bear on some in the military service to get them to retire. It may also be true in the Park

Service.

Yesterday I went to Dillards (Fedway) to take in their removal sale. They will re-open at Sikes Senter Oct. 30. I got a set of sheets for the single bed, and some everyday shoes.

Roberta would really enjoy browsing that shoe counter. The one where I found mine was the $3 counter. I expect the shoes had been $6 or $7 originally. Penny's is doing the same thing getting ready to move, so I'll go there this afternoon. Yesterday I got the stationary to give Hazel for Christmas. This afternoon I'll dome past Woolworth's and get one of those photo albums for Irma's Christmas Present. She liked so well the one you gave her that she wanted to fix one like it for her other child to have later on. I'm going to get Ruth a bubble rain umbrella and some small thing to go with it. Linda wants a book that will help her learn to do needlepoint. James wants a book too. I may get him Coronado's Children by Dobie. It is one that came out about a generation ago, but I doubt if there's anything better. To my surprise James said he would like a book about Coronado!

It will not take your package as long to go and I wanted to wait a little before putting something back for you. If you should get moved by Christmas, I have in mind small shells for Wesley. I haven't decided what to send Roberta. I have been trying to find some payons. They are made like crayons but you dip them in water and paint with them. I thought it might provide an interesting experience for Roberta. They introduced them to us at an art teachers meeting once (3rd grade art), but I have not seen them since. Maybe they did not go over and they were discontinued. Maybe I'll think of something else that might be better.

Maybe next time I'll have a letter from James and Linda to send on.

Did you get a day off for Columbus Day? If so, what did you do with it? Here's hoping all of you are well and will stay that way.

Now that we have been to see both Irma and Velma, we probably will stay right here for quite a long time. Velma and Roy think of going to Irma's next spring. Maybe they will let us go with them. They have a big old bus about 20 or 23 feet long that can sleep four, so Dad could take his nap while riding. They might even go on to New Mexico. Roy was in the Civilian Conservation Corps in the middle '30s and would like to go back over there and see what the territory looks like now. It is not too far from Hillsboro, so it just might be Dad would do it.

Larry and Family are still at Ft. Campbell Kentucky, but will soon go back to Germany.

Now! I have some potatoes and some meatloaf in the oven, so that will be the basis for an easy noon day meal. We already have jello and pudding ready.

I'm thinking that next week Dillards(Fedway) will be having an <u>Everything Goes Sale</u>. Of course, on some things they will not mind as much moving them. Things that will go in the gift shop will soon be in demand, and might cost merchants more than what those things cost. Maybe Penny's sale will be somewhat that way too. They haven't had as many sales, nor as big ads about them. I really should try to decide on some other Christmas gifts. I generally get Dad's about last, for he is so hard to please, if I do not he will talk me out of it.

It is good to hear the children's voices in the background while talking to you. Even when Johnny yelled so loud it told us that he is beginning to be decided in his likes and dislikes. They sound like two very bright children.

I'm glad the art teacher is there and will soon be checking with you. Really I know art about like a third or fourth grade child is instructed. "Make just a few big things. Make the skyline uneven/not a straight line. Repeat your colors. Make trees look as if they grew out of the ground. Let them extend up against the sky, too."

We tried to show them just a bit about perspective, too. Roads, paths, streams grow smaller, but never do the lines meet. We had some mechanical proportions to help them with getting fair proportions on people. If you do otherwise legs and arms are too short.

If we do not call you this Monday evening, you will know its because we are waiting for an important report after seeing the doctor. I think we'll have it all by Monday evening. Will write you early next week.   Love
                                      Mama

Wes Phillips: My father was not doing so well any more. I took off on June 16, 1976 and took Theresa with me and we went to visit him in the Hospital in Wichita Falls. They removed a large hernia in his bowels, but the cancer seemed to be catching up with him.

On November 25 we took another trip to Wichita Falls. Dad was not well, and though he still got around well, he had recently had several accidents and seemed somewhat confused when he went out.

On December 29th we went to Wichita Falls again. We found him weak, but in pretty good shape for 85 years old.

On February first, we drove to Lubbock, visited the Sorleys and continued on the second to Wichita Falls. We found Dad weak, depressed, and with some pain in his back, but otherwise alright. We returned home on the fourth.

On February 11th Mama called and said that Dad had fallen and broken his arm. He had gone to mail a letter, and forgotten his cane, slipped in front of the Kemp Library and broken his arm.

Dad went into the Nursing home after his hospital stay. Mama spent much of her time there visiting and caring for him.

On April 2, 1977 we left for Wichita Falls. We found Dad to be bedfast for the most part, and unable to get out of bed without help. He could only take liquids and had to be fed these. Aunt Irma, Uncle Claude, and Ross Campbell arrived in the evening. We helped all we could with Dad and cleaned out the sheds on the back of the small lot.

On April 16th we made another trip to Wichita Falls. Dad's arm had not healed properly, and he was in Lane's nursing home.

My mother called on April 25th to tell us that Dad was failing even more, and now had kidney failure to add to his other problems.

On May 21, Mama called to tell us that Arthur Phillips had died in Hico. I called Larry, took the day off, and drove to Wichita Falls. We picked Mama up and drove on to Hico the following day. We ate at the Wares and returned to Wichita Falls. Dad was some better while we were there.

We returned to Wichita Falls on June 29th on news from Mama that Dad was not expected to live very much longer and wanted to see the children before he died. Aunt Ruth Claypool is in the same nursing home where Dad is. Pat Runge, Aunt Ruth's daughter came in from Wyoming while we were there. We returned home July first.

Dad died on July 4, 1977. We drove back to Wichita Falls. We picked James and family up at the Airport at 10PM. On July 5th Aunt Velma and Uncle Roy came up for the Funeral. They stayed with Bob and Jeanne Gant. The funeral was July 6th. The next couple of days James and I helped Mama clean up the attic and other areas of the house.

7-1-2-3-5-1 John Wesley Phillips b. 3 May 1942 Long Beach, California m. Roberta Ellen Safarik dau. of Edgar Robert and Mildred Eleanor (McJunkin) Safarik 6 Apr 1968 Wickenburg Arizona

John Welsey Phillips Autobiography

PRE-THOUGHTS

How can I express a life of more than fifty years? How can you sum up the songs you have sung, the dances you have attended, the interminable hours in class and the free hours out doors? How can you express your thoughts so as to make them exciting for others? How about the changes of season - the long summer nights, the cold blustery days as Pooh says? How do you sum up a flower or a butterfly?

How much of my parents lives should I include? Surely they are part of mine. How about Children or grand-children? Surely the hours spent changing baby's diaper; the happy times of feeding your infant; the times swinging her or being swung. Surely these are parts of my life. How about my spouse? Her life has been mine for these many years. She is part of my life history. The special trips with my son; the special relationship I have with my daughter and with her husband. Friends, both childhood and adult - these are my life!

How have I changed the earth? Pogo says, "We have met the enemy - and he is us" Surely, though I have loved nature and the out of doors, I have also loved the good life provided by my country and by my style of living. I live in a consumer driven economy. We are using up the earth at a rapid rate. My grandchildren will never experience the things I have known first hand.

I have lived throughout my life in search of truth. I **MUST** know about the world. I long to know about every plant and animal, every rock and fossil. I want to know about the past - In the beginning - how was it? Not just on earth, but in the universe. The universe is so large and I am so small. Though I might make a difference on earth - how can I make a difference in the universe?

INTRODUCTION

I have lived in a truly miraculous age. Jet Planes, rocket ships to the moon, computers, CD players, space exploration both by telescope and through rockets have expanded our horizons to infinity. We have explored the solar system through remote sensing. Television brings the universe into our living room.

I live in a free country where I am free to worship as I choose. Yet the country I live in has a larger proportion of its population in prison than any other country in the world. I am told that there are more people in prison in Texas than in Europe.

We are also a country of consumers. I as well as my fellow americans are using up our resources at an ever-increasing rate. Our forests, our petroleum reserves, our land, our water, our air is all degraded from what it was 500 years ago when the Native Americans had this country.

Yet, I live a life of luxury on a moderate income. I have an automobile, a house, and a computer of my own. I have cable television and a VCR with which to bring the world into my home.

I am content with my life, though worried about the future for my descendants. What will life be like in 40, 80, or 120 years? Will it be better, or worse? What will the world be like in 500 or 1000 years? Someone has to ask these questions and give answers for the future of this nation and for the world.

The following is a glimpse of my life over the past 50 years. The changes observed are tremendous! Will I live to see the third millennia? I will only be 58 years old. My parents both lived past 85 years. I have a good chance to see it all, and yet, much of my life I have been sick - rheumatic fever, asthma, ulcers, arthritis, gall bladder surgery, spinal surgery have all taken a toll on my body. My health remains good, but my future may not be secure past the year 2000. We shall see. Here is my story.

I was born on Sunday, May 3, 1942 at Community Hospital in Long Beach, California. I was born at 6PM which my mother told me was "just in time for supper."

Long Beach at that time had a population of 165,000. It lay on the coast opposite Catalina Island in Los Angeles Harbor and was the home port of the Pacific Fleet. The major industries at the time were Oil which was best represented by signal hill whose back looked like a porcupine with all the oil derricks; auto factories, and Sea Food Canneries.

At the time of my birth, the United States was at war and I was issued a Ration Book for commodities. My parents operated a newsstand and barber shop just above "The Pike" amusement park where the sailors would visit during their trips to Home Port.

I remember one sailor in particular. He was John Edward Phillips, son of my father's brother Elmer. John had his Home Port at Long Beach and paid us several visits when I was young. He seemed so big and handsome to me that I called him "Big John" to distinguish him from my father who was John Richard and myself John Wesley. It was always an exciting time when he visited because he was something special. He wore a dark blue uniform with a white hat and I was told he was a sailor. I was very young and didn't know exactly what that meant, but I was sure that he must be the most important man in the world.

Another visitor was my cousin Arthur Phillips, the son of my father's other brother Max. If John was big, Arthur was HUGE. He stood five feet ten inches tall and weighed over 250 pounds. Arthur's job was unknown to me at the time, but I understand he worked in a munitions plant in Washington State.

Arthur was important in later years, after my parents moved back to Wichita Falls. He would drive to Wichita Falls and spend the night. The following morning we would all pile into his 46 chevy coupe and he would drive us to Ballinger to see Uncle Max, Aunt Louise, and Donald.

When we got to Wichita Falls, we moved into a small servant's quarters on the back of Aunt Ruth Claypool's house at 2607 ninth street. We stayed here for a while and then bought an old house and lot on twenty third street from Aunt Velma and Uncle Forrest Jones. Dad tore down the old house and built a new one. During this time we lived in a tent on the back of the lot and used a pit toilet. We sold this house for a profit and then rented a one room building from Mrs. Miller at 1417 sixteenth street. Dad bought a variety store near Reagan Junior High which he ran for about a year until we bought the Griffen House at 1004 fourteenth street.

This was a one bedroom house on the back of a larger lot. It faced 14th Street and had one side near the alley. The one bedroom became James and my room while the former dining room which opened into the living room became our parents room. There was a 12X12 foot kitchen with gas stove and gas refrigerator and a small add-on bathroom probably built after the original construction.

Wichita Falls by this time had a population of around 50,000 and was the independent Oil Capitol of Texas. Shepard Air Force Base also contributed to the economy as did Wichita Falls State Hospital. Midwestern University had around 1800 students enrolled and was a four year school. The business center or "down town" area had around 100 businesses and was booming in the post-war economy of the area. Wichita County had nearly 100,000 population and was a major center of wheat growing and cattle ranching.

Mama had been teaching school as a substitute for a couple of years, and after we moved to fourteenth street, she got a job teaching veterans who reported to our house for school. In 1949, she moved this operation to a basement room at Austin school where I was in second grade. In 1950, she got a job with the Wichita Falls Public Schools, teaching Downs Syndrome children, and in 1952 she became a regular teacher at Barwise Elementary School.

Dad got a job with Crestview Memorial Park selling cemetery lots. He bought a racing bicycle with narrow tires, something unusual at that time, though so very common today, and rode that out to the cemetery and around town selling door to door. We had no car.

When I was five years old, Mama took us to Floral Heights Methodist Church where James and I entered Sunday School. During church, we would stay in the church nursery. I remember very little about this time, though I know that the regular attendance over the years gave me a love of bible study which I have kept until the present. I don't remember ever believing that all the stories in the bible were more than stories, however. My mother often read stories to us at home, and these seemed similar to those.

Late in August, James and I always went with Mama to buy our school supplies. The most important item was clothing, and for this we stopped at Penny's. We walked to the back of the store where we descended the steps to the basement. This was the children's section of the store with shirts, pants, socks, suits, and underclothes. The smell was fabulous! Everything smelled new and fresh, but the best smelling of all were the blue jeans. We got two or three pair of these apiece and picked out three shirts apiece; socks, belts, and later on when it got colder we purchased coats, warm caps, and gloves.

From there we went upstairs to the shoe department where the attendant measured and fitted us for shoes. The new shoes smelled good too and in the shoe department there was an interesting gadget known as a drinking fountain. When we pushed the lever, the water would arch out and splash back into the bowl and here it seemed to taste better than anywhere else.

Penny's was the main stop down town, but we had to have paper, pencils, crayons, rulers, erasers, and such. Dad always took us over to the corner drugstore to purchase these.

By the first day of school we were decked out in our best clothes as were the other students and all the smells made the first day really a marvelous experience.

My love of nature and nature study began before I reached first grade. By the time I was in second grade, my parents had provided me with the golden guides for insects and birds. I began an insect collection and soon learned common names for several species. My father was always pointing out birds to me, and I learned birds at an early age as well. My best experiences were, however, with insects.

After I had finished third grade, and James had finished at Mrs. Gregory's first grade across fifteenth street from Austin School, we took a trip out west gold mining.

The night before Arthur had driven up from Ballinger with his car a 1946 Chevy. James, Dad, and I helped load the car. First we put the dry washer in along with the large metal washing pans more commonly referred to as gold pans. We also loaded buckets, bags, cots, blankets, and all the other paraphernalia we would need to camp out.

We left the house about 6AM and drove all day. We spent the first night in Hot Springs New Mexico and arrived mid morning on the second day at Gold Dust New Mexico. Here we rented a house for the night. Gold Dust was a ghost town, and most of the houses were unoccupied. There were two rooms with two steel cots, one table and two rooms full of junk.

That night I slept on the cot with my father and James slept with Arthur. James got in bed early and went to sleep but Arthur went for a walk first. When Arthur got back he sat down on one end of the cot. James was asleep on the other end. Arthur weighed 250 pounds and James weighed 60 pounds. As soon as Arthur sat down, James end of the bed flew up and James sailed through the air and landed on the floor. Both were unhurt and James didn't even know what had happened.

At 4 AM the next morning, just before sunrise, we got up and decided to go to Hillsboro five miles away on a dirt road for breakfast. Arthur was looking everywhere for his keys so we could get into the car, which he had presumably locked to keep the ghosts out. He finally found them - locked in the car. When we finally got them out, it was time to go for breakfast.

When I was in second grade, I developed what was called "Wry neck". In third grade, this became a dislocated neck, with the muscles pulling my neck completely out of joint. I was admitted to the hospital and my neck was placed in a stretcher which straightened it back out. At about the same time I developed Rheumatic Fever. Since Wendell Willis had already had this disease, my mother recognized it, and took me to the doctor. I was ordered home and to bed for strict bed rest for about six weeks. I was on sulfa drugs for several years after this, and had regular blood tests to determine if the disease had returned.

My father had recently finished off the attic, with a board floor and had put in a steep staircase to allow us access. James, Wendell, Ronnie, and I now adopted this as a sort of clubhouse, and often spent hours there, especially in the winter time, since the temperature in summer was over 130 degrees. We also began storing things here, and soon had quite a number of things there. Some of the things my parents had stored in the shed in the backyard now went here also.

After third grade, I had been sick, and I went to spent the summer on the farm of my mother's sister Irma Campbell.

"The Campbell Farm"

I woke up and looked around. The room I was in had two large beds in it. My bed was the one on the right. On towards the front of the room was a large chimney which came from the fireplace downstairs. The walls slanted in above my head and there was a window over each bed.

The first thing I did on waking up was to stand up on my bed and look out the window. I could see the seldom used front gate, the road, the woods, a large field, and the small rustic wooden bridge across Turkey Creek. It was a beautiful day without a cloud in the sky.

I immediately jumped down from the bed and ran across the room where I jumped up on the other bed and peered out of its cupula window. Here, the back gate, which everyone used, led into an open yard. On one side of the yard was a large sprawling dobé building, which due to lack of maintenance looked even older that it really was. Just across the lane from this large building sat a small one made of logs, which I knew was the granary. The lane passed between the two buildings to the outdoor "two holer", which was the first place I visited after I dressed.

The air outside was cool and crisp as it always was in the mornings, even though it was the middle of August. After visiting the outhouse, I took a look in the pigpen where the pigs greeted me uncommitedly since I never fed them. I then wandered back past the outhouse to the chicken house and yard. I gathered the eggs and then went back to the house. Aunt Irma and Uncle Claude were up now, and Aunt Irma was making a fire in the wood stove for breakfast.

"Good Morning," she said cheerily, "Have you been up long?" "Not long," I replied.

I liked Aunt Irma. She was almost always happy and she always took time out of her chores to play with me. Sometimes it would be cards or checkers and sometimes we would go outside and I would be tarzan and live in a tree house and she would be Alley Oop and live in a cave (actually the cellar of the old adobe house).

We had pancakes for breakfast and then walked the quarter of a mile to the barn to milk the cows. I got to milk once in a while, but mostly I just watched. Aunt Irma would start at one end with Snow White an old and very gentle cow while Uncle Claude would begin at the other end with Betty, an old roan cow who was too mean to be trusted since she was prone to kicking over the bucket and maybe the milker too if she had a chance. I sat there for a while, on my own one legged stool, but I soon grew restless and walked outside. On one side of the barn was a barnyard with its large pile of what Uncle Claude called manure. I had seen the cows make it, so I knew what it _really_ was. On the other side of the barn was a large straw stack and a small haystack. The straw was thrown into the barn and the hay was thrown in to the cows, but I wasn't really sure which was which. Aunt Irma and Uncle Claude came out, each carrying two buckets of milk. "Would you like to carry one?" Aunt Irma asked.

I accepted gladly, but in a few feet I was beginning to regret that I had been so generous. 'These are heavy," I remarked, straining under the load. I sat the bucket down and changed hands. We walked farther and I changed hands again. "Want me to carry it now?" Aunt Irma asked. "No," I replied "I can manage." I had gone this far now and I wasn't about to give up.

We finally got back to the new cellar next to the house, and carried the pails down to Uncle Claude who was operating the separator. "Would you like to turn the crank." he asked.

"Sure." I quickly agreed.

"Not too fast now." he instructed "Just slow and even."

I watched fascinated as the milk came out of one spout and the cream came out of another. After we finished the separation, we poured the cream in one large milk can, and the milk in another. We also separated the foam from the milk simply by pouring the milk out from under while holding the foam in.

By the time we had finished this operation and taken the separator in to be washed, it was time to go to the fields to pitch hay. During the previous two weeks, we had first cut the hay with a horse drawn mowing machine, and then raked it with a ten-foot wide rake.

Jim Wilburn, our next door neighbor who lived just a mile or so away, had just arrived with two large plow horses pulling his hay wagon. He unhitched the horses and we put them to raising the haystack pole, which had a basket like fork to life the hay from the wagon to the stack. It took some work, but we finally got the pole up.

We all gathered up our pitchforks and put them on one of the hay wagons and rode the wagons to the hayfield. There were seven of us in all including two Wilburns, Uncle Claude, myself, and three Trojillos.

When we got out to the field, we divided into two groups,

one man on the wagon and the rest on the ground. The driver would drive among the small stacks and the people on the ground would pitch the hay up to him. When we got a wagon load, we went back to the barn, and the stackpole quickly emptied the wagon.

At noon, we knocked off for lunch; and what a lunch! Aunt Irma was a good cook and she fixed Chicken, Mashed Potatoes, Green Beans, Brown Beans, Beets (Which I didn't care for), and gravy. For dessert there was a choice of apple pie and chocolate cake. We ate like starved beasts.

I was too small at ten years old to be of much help to the workers in the hayfield, so I declined to go back in the afternoon and instead went up into the hills. I slid out under the large wooden gate and ambled up the road past the barn on the right and the field and horse corral on the left. The road turned opposite the horse corral, but I slipped through the barb wire gate leading to the pasture and followed this road instead.

The road crossed Dry Creek where it split; one fork leading to the Trojillos and the other to the Campbell Pasture. Just past the fork, there were the beehives. There were about 25 in all and I always kept well away from them and got past them as quickly as possible. I sure did enjoy the honey though.

Shortly, the country became quite hilly, and the road went up a steep incline. When I reached the top, the difference was astounding! Down close to turkey creek there were willows, cottonwoods, elms, chokecherries, and oaks. Up here there were mostly pines; both piñon and the long needled ponderosa. In places they gave way to sagebrush and short grasses and at times to open meadows where the cattle grazed. This was the pasture and it was large enough for a boy to get lost in for an entire afternoon.

I wasn't interested in finding the cattle today as I had come "up on the mountain" to be alone. I headed right to my favorite spot - an oddly shaped rock called the armchair, and looked out over the wooded valley in front of me. I could see the trees stretching away in the distance and hear their branches singing in the wind.

I didn't sleep, but I did dream; daydreams as any little boy might have while in such a majestic setting, but I was young, and couldn't sit still for very long. I reluctantly left and retraced my steps down the mountain. On the way down, I collected some pretty rocks (mostly white quartz) which I could use for building stone forts when I got back. I saw where a porcupine had eaten the bark all around a Ponderosa Pine and a magpie swore at me for interrupting his meal.

By the time I reached the bottom, the sky had clouded and a few drops of rain were falling. I hurried back to the house, but by the time I reached it, the sky was clearing, so I went down to the creek.

I took off my shoes and waded down into the water. It was icy cold coming from the melting snow up on "Old Baldy", but once used to it, it wasn't so bad. A water strider glided across the still water near the bridge and I grabbed for it. It was too fast and got away, but I caught the next one and examined it closely before letting it go.

I went up on the road and crossed the bridge. Down on the other side there was a large sand pile, which afforded me hours of fun. Here I took the many small twigs from under the willow trees and formed them into opposing armies which fought back and forth in pitched battle until the one I favored won a decisive victory. I was just about to leave when a large black 'pinch beetle' caught my eye lumbering across the sand. I caught it and played with it until I finally heard Aunt Irma calling me to supper.

After supper, we sat around and read by the light of a kerosene lamp . I was a little behind in school, so Aunt Irma helped me with my spelling until bedtime. Finally, tired and happy, I ventured back up the stairs to bed to dream sweet dreams until the following day when I knew there would be new adventures awaiting me. Aunt Irma would often read to me from books we had checked out from the Walsenburg library.

My mother had long ago joined Floral Heights Methodist Church, but my father had been Church of Christ, and for a while they attended separate churches, but soon my father saw that this would not work out, so he also began attending the Methodist church. At first we took the bus or a taxi, since it was about two miles from our house to Floral Heights. My mother taught the B.O.P. class, and my father joined the Mens Bible Class where he sometimes played the organ for the songs if the regular organist was not available. They got him a shape note song book, since he knew only this system, and he could play from it.

I was not a good student, and my recent illnesses had not

improved my grades. My writing suffered from what today would be called Dysgraphia - No matter how hard I tried, it just wouldn't come right. I continued printing through third grade, but changed to cursive in fourth.

In fifth grade, we began the system of changing classes every period. It was a simplified system of what we would have to do in Junior High School, but all on one floor. My Social Studies Teacher was Mr. Hampton, for Mathematics I had Miss Tipps, for Reading Miss Claypool, for English Mrs Robinson, for Music Miss Fern Fowler, and Mrs Marvel for Art. For a while I took Violin lessons, but it proved too complicated, so I dropped these.

We had recess morning and afternoon, during which time we usually played baseball or football. I was not a good athlete and was often the last chosen for a team.

I excelled in English, Reading, and Social Studies, and my knowledge of these continued to grow, but my writing held me back. I continued to be interested in plants and animals, especially insects and soon knew common names for many local species.

During these years, I formed a lasting friendship with Wendell Willis and Ronnie Sanders, whose parents were about the same generation as James and mine. The four of us were inseparable, and hiked or played together much of the time. This friendship lasted until James and Ronnie graduated from High School when James went off to Texas Tech in Lubbock and Ronnie joined the army.

Dad was forced to retire in 1956 when he reached the age of 65. Actually he was in good health, but no one would hire him at this age. To keep busy he worked in the yard and went on occasional gold mining trips to New Mexico or Northern California. He read almost every day, and soon started to write poems and short stories which he sometimes sent off to publishers to see of they would buy them.

I went to Jr. High School in the fall of 1956 at Reagan Jr. High, just a block north of Austin School where I had attended Elementary School. In 1958 I went on to Wichita Falls Senior High School. I was not a scholar, and still spent much of my time in nature study activities which interfered with my schooling. Mathematics were perhaps the hardest for me, as I just couldn't concentrate enough to become interested.

Christmas was a special time. For us, it really began with the Saturday after Thanksgiving, when the Christmas

Shops down town in Wichita Falls opened up and the toys went on sale. James, Ronnie Sanders, and I all piled into Wendell Willis' green 1956 Chevy and drove down town where we parked about a block from Fedway, which was a large department store. We usually walked the eight blocks down town, but since it was windy, we short circuited the normal activities and rode.

We went across the large Fedway parking lot, already packed with Christmas shoppers and entered the south door, made our way to the escalator, which at that time was the only escalator in town, and quite a novelty.

The toy shop was upstairs, and though we were all in High School, we were still more interested in toys than in girls. It was early, so we were "just lookin'" as we told the clerk. James and I had been given twenty dollars each, which in 1959 was still enough to buy quite a few presents. The prices at Fedway were however a little beyond our modest means, so we soon left and walked a block down the street to Noble Hardware or "Noble - Little" as Dad would say, recalling the name from thirty years previously.

The upstairs toy store was perhaps our favorite store. At Christmas shopping time, it was loaded with toys of all varieties, and the prices were better. It was here that we purchased new cars for our electric train which we ran jointly and it was also here that we bought many of the board games such as Monopoly and Clue which we played relentlessly during the year. There was an entire table with pull-string musical instruments, and another with toy forts made of logs or more modern looking forts with contemporary soldiers in military gear.

Just down the street was Lovelace Book Store where we shopped regularly. I bought my mother another volume in the "Interpreters Bible" which she used in her Sunday School Class at church. In the 1930s, she had joined the B.O.P. class, then the Buds of Promise, but now she said it was the "Blossoms of Prudence", and she was the teacher, with the ladies in their late 40s and early 50s.

We had each set a maximum price which we could spend on each other of $1.00, and this we usually spent at the "five and ten cent stores" - Kresses, Woolworth, or McRorys, where we could buy a deck of cards, toy soldiers, or sundries.

On the way back to the car, we stopped at Skaggs Drug Store across from Noble Hardware. We usually picked out our "gifts" for ourselves and then let someone else "buy" them for us, though sometimes it was a surprise. Skaggs was another favorite store. Before Thanksgiving the basement toy store opened up, and we all could really find interesting things here. This ritual continued many nights, and on the weekends until Christmas time.

I entered High School in the fall of 1957. I had developed Asthma in Junior High, and it continued to plague me in High School. My neck was still stiff from the Rheumatic Fever and I was shorter than my class mates.

High School began for me in the tenth grade, since Junior High went through the ninth. American History and Civics were required as was Three more years of English. I took Plane Geometry and Algebra as mathematics courses. Science was Biology and Chemistry. Surprisingly the only course I failed was Biology, the subject I was so interested in. I also had a year of Art which I also nearly failed. I wish now that I had taken foreign language in High School. The school had an excellent language department, and I later really learned to love language studies. I had a course in salesmanship, and one in business.

I enrolled for three years of R.O.T.C. or military training to count for physical education which I had grown tired of in Junior high.

In my junior year in high school, I joined the Biology Club, and my senior year I was elected Vice President. We made annual field trips to the Wichita Mountains and Platt National park in Oklahoma. We would travel by car to the various areas and would take along a picnic lunch. Here I learned how to key out trees with a booklet on the forest trees of Oklahoma. By my second trip, I knew quite a good number of trees.

Things have changed since I was young. For one thing, there was segregation. The black people literally lived "across the tracks" in the section of town known to the whites as "Niggertown". The streets were unpaved for the most part, small lots with no lawn with a small house usually in disrepair. There were two sets of schools, with the whites going to Wichita Falls Senior High, while the blacks went to Booker T. Washington High School on the other side of town. I was unaware of the system, and was disappointed when a child to find that the water in the "Colored" drinking fountain wasn't anything special, just water.

The automobile was different too. First the cars had

"fast backs" with a sloped trunk, but later they grew fins and became longer. When I was small, many people still travelled on the train, but as I grew up, more and more people bought cars, and the trains disappeared. My father bought his first car when he was in California, but didn't have another until I was about 14 years old when he bought a 1948 Plymouth. There were no interstate highways and few divided highways. Most were narrow two lane roads and dirt roads or gravel roads were not uncommon. The speed limit was 60 in Texas and at night 55. Later it was increased to 70 and night 65. The Oil Crunch of the 70s put a halt to that, with the 55 mile speed limit.

Clothes were different too. Boys in school wore blue jeans while girls wore dresses of skirts and blouses. Girls never wore pants in school. Boys wore their hair short and girls wore their hair long.

Frozen foods were not common. All food was fresh or canned. There was a butcher counter at Wagonner's Grocery, two blocks from our house. Kenneth was the butcher, and he would cut it like you wanted it. Milk and soda pop were in returnable bottles and aluminum cans were unheard of.

No one had television until the mid 50s. There were no microwave ovens, home computers, slow cookers, or video cassettes. Tape recorders were reel to reel. Fluorescent lights were found only in businesses.

Trash was collected in dump trucks. The men came down the alley and it took two men to pick up the 50 gallon oil drums we used for trash.

When I visited my Aunt Irma and Uncle Claude in Colorado, it was like stepping back in time to the turn of the century. They did have a 1930 Chevy pickup truck, but there was no electricity, no radio, and no running water. We kept the milk in the cellar by the house.

My father was somewhat of an amateur geologist, and we picked up rock specimens in the dirt roads around Wichita Falls which he identified for us. Most of them were what he called "Silicon" which I later learned was Silicon Dioxide or Quartzite, a sandstone which had been cooked through heat and pressure to form a resistant rock. In the mid 1950s, James and I made a trip with Dad out to California to do some placer gold mining with shovels and a rocker system. On the way we stopped at the Petrified Forest and the Grand Canyon and I picked up a set of mineral specimens pasted on a card. I sorted these in the back seat as we drove and began to learn my minerals this way. Later when I was a senior in High School, Wendell took me to the Rock and Mineral Club show where I purchased individual specimens pasted to separate cards and learned more about the various kinds.

A Visit to Hico

My father had gotten up at 4 o'clock and fixed breakfast. My mother had followed him and was also working in the kitchen packing a meal to take along.

At 5, Dad came into my room and "woke me up" - actually I had been awake for 10 or 15 minutes already and was perfectly ready to get up. While I was dressing, Dad called James and coaxed him out of bed too. We ate breakfast and then packed the car. We carried suitcases, pillows, boxes of food, blankets, and a variety of "extras" which we were sure we would need. I took along several books on nature study just in case something unusual turned up.

At 6 o'clock we left the house, and in about 15 minutes we were on the open road. The sun had not yet risen, but it was already light and we could see faint tinges of pink on the clouds. This deepened into a golden glow and in a few more minutes "Mr. Sun" appeared in all his glory.

The country around Wichita Falls was rolling prairie, now mostly covered by mesquite trees and thorn brush. In another hour we had entered a forest of scrub oak near Mineral Wells. On south, we saw Juniper bushes growing among the oaks. Shortly after 7:30 we entered the fertile Brazos River Valley with its beautiful green fields and pastures.

Around Morgan Mill, there were quite a lot of Beef Cows in the pasture and as we approached Hico, sheep farms were in evidence.

We got to Hico about 9:30 and turned by the Conoco station to go to the Phillips home. We passed the stadium and turned on North Mesquite Street. At the end of the street on the right was the familiar white house with the rock foundation which we knew so well.

Arthur was sitting out in the back yard and as we drove in, he got up and hollered into the house, "Uncle John's here."

Aunt Louise and Donald came out and after a full round of hugging and kissing we all went in and sat down in their spacious living room.

James and I couldn't stay seated very long, so we left the older folks to visit and went into the yard in back. The first place we visited was the florist shop. Since this had changed only a little since the last time, we went on through to the large green house in back.

"Hey, look at those cactus." I said pointing to nearly half a shelf full of various prickly plants. We browsed on through the green house which had everything from exotic plants planted in apple cider jars to tomatoes growing in pots. We left by the back door on the path which ran by the garden.

Before we got to the bird pens and chicken yard, I saw the cage about four feet square behind the greenhouse.

"Let's see if they have any squirrels now." I suggested.

"There he is," I said. Sure enough there was a large fox squirrel sitting up on his hind legs and nibbling a tidbit. When he saw us, he immediately had to show off, so he jumped onto his "merry go round" and ran around and around in it without going anywhere.

We watched him for a few minutes, and then went on to an even larger cage about ten feet long and six feet high. By peering through the wire, we could see about 100 parakeets flying around or sitting on perches in various parts of the cage. We next went to a large gate and stepped through in to the chicken yard. Here we were met by an outstanding variety of chickens all of which declared in loud and emphatic voices that they hadn't been fed in weeks or perhaps months, even though there was feed still scattered on the ground from the morning's feeding.

We passed on through this melee and went on to a series of cages around the edge of the enclosure. In each cage, there was a different kind of bird -- Chinese Pheasants, Golden Pheasants, Ring Necked Pheasants, Muscovy Ducks, Turkeys, and several others which seemed exotic to us.

As we returned to the house, we met Arthur, who asked if we wanted to go with him to the Post Office.

We all climbed into the 1953 Chrysler Station Wagon and drove on down the street. We turned at the corner and went down the hill and across several more streets to "Downtown". We went into the Post Office and picked up the mail and then drove another block to the store where we got some groceries. By the time we got back, it was time for dinner.

And what a dinner! Two pheasants, two chickens, a duck, and part of a turkey, ham, and roast beef. For vegetables there were string beans, potatoes, brown beans, carrots, cabbage, and cole slaw. There were two kind of gravies and for drinks we had coffee, iced tea, and milk. Dessert consisted of ice cream, with our choice of apple pie, fruit cake, chocolate cake, angel food cake, or lemon meringue pie. James ate the most, finishing off an entire pheasant, a chicken, and about half of the other meats available and sampling all the desserts and having three helpings of ice cream.

After dinner, the "men folks" sat out in the yard and talked while Mama and Aunt Louise did the dishes. This was the old fashioned method of air conditioning. The trees surrounding the house, and especially the back yard protected both the house and the loungers from the heat of the day. There was always a cool breeze, and even if the temperature was near 100 degrees, it felt cool in the shade. Quite a few people came by both to buy flowers and to visit with the folks. I took my collecting bottle and walked around the yard and garden catching insects for my collection.

In the afternoon, James and I went with Arthur to Dublin to deliver flowers for a funeral. The rocks were all white and Arthur said they were limy. I later learned that they were of Cretaceous Limestone and had fossils in them.

When we returned, we had a scrumptious dinner and then sat around and talked until bedtime.

The next morning I was awakened by the chiming of the Grandmother Clock on the floor at the head of the couch where Donald and I had slept. Now since a "grandmother clock" is in itself an unusual object, it may take some explaining. This clock was a floor clock, but smaller than the grandfather clock, and was only about five and a half feet tall. It had the base with the swinging pendulem, and a face with a picture of a man in 18th century costume with a thin mustache. It was right at the head of the couch where Donald and I slept, and struck during the night. I was a light sleeper, but the sound of the clock lulled me to sleep.

Dad was already out in the yard somewhere, but no one else was awake. I slipped quietly out of bed and dressed without waking Donald. Arthur and James, in the other couch were dead to the world and heavy sleepers, so there was no fear of waking them. While I was in the bathroom, I heard some movements in the house, so I hurried up and slipped out as it was a popular place early in the morning.

I was only out for about ten minutes, but when I returned, everyone was up except James and Arthur. I went with Donald to feed the birds while breakfast was cooking. After getting all the birds fed and cared for we returned to the house. We all sat down to eat except James and Arthur who were still asleep. When we had almost finished breakfast, James and Arthur finally arrived, but neither wanted breakfast. They both slurped down the coffee however.

After breakfast, James went with Arthur to get the mail while I went with Donald to see about a parakeet cage out towards Dufaw.

We returned, rested, talked, and had lunch about 1 o' clock. Dad decided we had to leave. We all tried to talk him into staying a while longer, but once his mind was made up, it was hard to change, so about 1:30 we left and arrived home at 5 PM. The phone was ringing. It was Aunt Ruth wanting to know how the trip had been, How was it? It was great!

In the early 1960s, Dad began his first bout with cancer, a fight he kept up for many years. I began college at Midwestern University in Wichita Falls in the fall of 1960 with a major in Biology and a minor in Geology. My biology professors were Dr. Art Beyer in Botany and Dr. Walter W. Dalquist in Zoology. My Geology professors were Dr. J.L. Watkins in Paleontology and Mineralogy and Loren Wicks in Geography and Geomorphology.

Halloween was always an exciting time at our house. When we got too old to go trick or treating, we went into decorating the house in a big way. I found an old chicken fence thrown away about a block from our house and drug it home. It was just about long enough to go across the corner of our yard along the old fence in front with enough left over to turn the corner and cover part of the yard. We cut up old boxes and made a series of tombstones across the east part of the yard, and had an old file cabinet on its side as a "coffin" lying near the steps. Ronnie was stationed in the attic with a black cat made out of cardboard on a string which he would pull across the steps as a person turned into the yard, and a bat on a string which was supposed to swing down and hit the people in the face when they got on the top step, though this never seemed to work right. Wendell was hiding behind the old Mesquite tree by the street and as the victim approached, he crept up behind him and tapped him gently on the shoulder, just as I sat up in the "coffin". James was in the house to give out the treats to anyone who could make it through our maze. It made quite a show.

May 5, 6, 7, 1961 was the Midwestern University Field trip to the Arbukle Mountains and the Criner Hills in Oklahoma. The Texas Society of Geology Clubs attended. We left Wichita Falls on the afternoon of the 5th. Johnny Graham, Glenn Collier, and I rode on the Geology Society Bus. We spent the night in a motel in Ardmore, Oklahoma. At 8Am the following morning We assembled at the intersection of U.S. Highway 77 and 12th street in Ardmore, Oklahoma opposite the English Village Motel.

Our first stop was an outcrop of the Caney Shale, Sycamore Limestone, and Woodford Formations of Mississippian and Devonian ages. The Lions Club had marked the highway very well with signs which showed the outcrops and marked which were important. The Arbuckle Mountains is one of the most important Paleozoic outcrops in the country, since it covers many formations which are now laid on their sides and easy to explore. We stopped also at outcrops of Devonian and Silurian Systems, Ordovician system, and finally around noon at the Cambrian System. We were not exactly on schedule, so we varied our lunch stop. This turned out to be a mistake, since the ranch foreman found us eating at a spot not designated and forbade us to ever come back on the ranch.

After lunch, we continued to Turner Falls and walked up the creek to the falls. We returned to our cars and went to another Ordovician outcrop near the highway where there were Graptolite fossils. The end of the trip for the first day was the McLish formation which was a white loosely cemented glass-quality sandstone.

On May 7 we met at the intersection of US highway 77 and 70. We went first to the Overbrook Anticline which represents a nearly complete section of Pennsylvanian age sediments. Next was the Vanoss Conglomerate, then the Paluxy formation and finally the Brock Anticline where we saw the Criner Fault. Our lunch stop for the day was the Woodford Quarry where we saw the Sycamore Limestone. We then returned to the bus and back to Ardmore.

We had been having radiator trouble on the Geology Club Bus, so we had to stop every little while to fill the radiator but we finally got back to Wichita Falls.

Beginning in the 1950s we made several trips to the seashore at La Porte to visit my mother's sister Velma and her husband Forrest Jones and to Galveston Island to sight see. I began collecting seashells during this time, and when in high school we had a speaker on seashells, I also began buying shells for my collection. I bought several books on the subject and begin to identify the species which I had collected. Lovelace Bookstore set up a seashell and rock shop in the rear, and in a few years, Mr. Lovelace moved out near the armory and set up a rock shop.

A Visit to the Farm

Mama and her sister Velma had been writing back and forth for more than a month, planning for the trip, and now it was the morning to leave.

We awoke early, packed the car and left the old house on 14th street. We travelled due east across the mesquite covered Permian hills and soon entered a belt of scrub oak growing on younger rocks of Cretaceous age.

Finally we turned north and went through Denison, the birthplace of President Eisenhower. We could see the old house from the road, but we never stopped for a closer look.

Finally after many small towns and villages, we came to the crossroads store of Darwin, Oklahoma. Here we turned back west along a dirt road for about a mile until Uncle Roy's house came in sight around a bend in the road.

The house was small and unpainted and the furnishings were simple but it was one of my favorite places. Aunt Ruth had come with us, so while Mama and Aunt Ruth visited with Aunt Velma, James and I went out to explore the farm. We didn't have much time before lunch, so we just took a hurried look at the buildings and the animals. There were pigs, and a goat which Uncle Roy had bought since our last visit and several new fences were proudly built to keep them in.

Dad came out to fetch us for lunch so we interrupted our explorations for a simple but filling meal. After lunch, Aunt Ruth wanted to go for a hike so James, Dad, and I went with her while Aunt Velma and Mama finished the dishes.

We walked through the cow corral, past the barn, and on across the pasture to the stock tank Uncle Roy had had built by the Department of Agriculture. We knew from previous visits that the stock tank contained catfish and turtles so we passed on by it and out into the meadow.

Aunt Ruth was praising the outside air, and the walk, and the fields, and the flowers, and anything else that came up so we boys said very little. I kept my eyes out for plants and animals and Dad and James just kept their eyes open and looked at what Aunt Ruth was pointing out at the moment.

After crossing the meadow, we came to a woods with a pretty little stream meandering through it. The moss here was thick on the sides of the big trees and it was quite cool all around.

We rested here for several minutes, studying the stream, the moss, and the accumulated artifacts such as tobacco tins which lined the creek. We left this lovely area with reluctance and headed over a marshy area to a cornfield.

The road ran along next to the field so we crawled through the barb wire fence and the blackberry bushes and emerged scratched but still in one piece, on the road. A short walk of about half a mile brought us back to the house where we relaxed for the afternoon.

I swatted wasps and flies for a while, but as the insects thinned out, the sport became more difficult so I tired of it and went back outside. James, Dad, and Uncle Roy were sitting on the porch watching a gopher digging in the yard so I joined them. After about 15 minutes this too became tiresome so James and I hiked off down the road.

"What's this?" James asked. Pointing to a large green ball. "That's an Oak apple gall," I informed him. "Its where an insect laid an egg."

There had been quite a bit of rain and we could hear the tree frogs and the cricket frogs singing in the bushes. It was sunny today and the birds were competing with the frogs in nature's chorus.

I was collecting all kinds of rocks from the road bed and James wondered what they were.

"This one is ferrugineous Sandstone and this is a limonite chert pebble conglomerate..."

"Wait a minute!" James broke in "Say it in english!"

"Oh, sorry," I said "Both of them contain Iron. Limonite and hematite are Iron oxides which turn the rocks yellow or red. Chert is a form of quartz common in lots of sediments - it's kinda like flint."

"OK," James replied "Go ahead."

"A ferruginous sandstone, then is a sandstone with limonite or hematite in it and a chert pebble conglomerate is a lot of chert pebbles stuck together with some kind of cement - in this case limonite."

These were the most common kinds of rock present, so James had no trouble with most of them after that. We walked about two miles down the road and then turned back. By the time we returned it was suppertime.

After supper we sat around, read magazines and talked until after dark. James and I slept on the couch, Aunt Ruth on the porch, and Mama and Dad in the spare room.

The next morning dawned bright and clear. I was up early, walking along the road, collecting insects, fungus, plants, and rocks. I returned after about 30 minutes to find everyone up and about.

We had eggs for breakfast and afterwards, James, Dad, and I walked across the road and climbed the barbed wire fence into the neighbor's pasture and woodlot. No one was ever there so we had it all to ourselves.

We walked through the high grass for about 3/4 of a mile and then came out in a small woodlot. There were several large boulders in among the trees and in turning them over we found two very small rat snakes. One got away, but I kept the other and took it home with me the next day.

Dad spotted a large shelf fungus over eight inches across high up in a large post oak. It was too high for anyone to reach, so I got a long stick and knocked it down. It was really a beauty! I turned it in with my fungus collection when I took Mycology in 1963, and so lost it.

After lunch, Uncle Roy took James and I with him to pick up a cow he had bought the week before. We rode over in the cab of the truck. We all went out to the pasture and drove the calf up to the loading ramp. With everybody pushing and shoving, we finally got the calf into the truck and tied down so it wouldn't hurt itself. We got back, unloaded the calf, and began packing for the trip back to Wichita Falls the following day.

My sophomore year in college, I took Plant Propagation and my Junior year Plant Taxonomy. For these courses I had to learn my trees on a higher level than I learned during high school. In my senior year of college, I took a special problem with Clarence Shay to make a book on the trees of Wichita Falls. We photographed each species and I made up a key to identify them through leaf and stem characters. The year after my college graduation I took another special problem in which I identified beetles and grasshoppers to species level.

I had spent a year in Graduate School at Texas Tech in Lubbock, and now my first Job was with the National Park Service as Park Naturalist. We had a short seasonal training program, and I went to work talking to the visitors, working at an information-sales desk, and walking on the trails contacting park visitors.

Petrified Forest is located in the high desert country of North Eastern Arizona, not far from the New Mexico line. Typical plant life is rubber rabbit brush and broom snakeweed, low plants. Some juniper is present, and along the water courses some cottonwood. Wildlife consists of rabbits and coyotes with such birds as the horned lark and the golden eagle.

The main attractions are the Petrified Forest with its colorful petrified logs, and the Painted Desert with its red, blue, gray, and yellow soils, also with petrified wood.

My boss was Larry Henderson and I roomed in a small trailer house with Jim Ballard, the other interpretive seasonal that summer. I spent much of my off time studying the flora and fauna of the area, and made a small insect collection. Jim and I went into Holbrook Arizona some evenings to eat in the Chinese Restaurant. For two single guys, this town was a disappointment, as there were no girls our ages.

During the time after working at Petrified Forest, I was diagnosed with an ulcer. I had been having pain in my back for a number of years, perhaps since 1956, but had never associated it with my digestive tract. I had a lower GI series at the hospital and they confirmed the doctor's suspicians. I was placed on medication including antacid tablets to relieve the symptoms and a diet to cut out foods which might cause problems.

Eunice Jane Phillips died November 18, 1965 in Abeline, Texas. She had started the florist business, but her health had been poor, so Donald took over the business and ran it for over 50 years both in Ballinger and later in Hico. The funeral was in Ballinger, and Dad, Mama, and I attended from Wichita Falls. Katy Bell came up from Laredo, but didn't arrive until after the services.

In December 1965, I went to work at Organ Pipe Cactus National Monument at Ajo Arizona. This area was a desert paradise. The day I arrived in December it had been 82 degrees, and continued mild most of the winter. I gave guided walks and evening programs, and sold postcards, books, and slides to the park visitors. My boss was Vic Jackson and the other seasonal was Bill Hoy.

The main attraction was the Sonoran Desert Flora and Fauna with Saguaro, Organ Pipe Cactus, Palo Verde and Ironwood trees plus the mesquite so familiar in Texas. Wildflowers became a passion of mine here, and I learned nearly all the species in the two years I worked there. Birdlife was abundant, and I learned such exotic birds as the Phainopepla and the curved billed thrasher and noted the more common Cactus Wren and mockingbirds also. The Harris Hawk was a common species here.

My second year, my boss was Dick Cunningham. He was an ornithologist of the first rate, and taught me some more about birds. On several occasions when he couldn't make his bird walk, I stood in for him.

I had not kept company with girls during most of my high school and college years, and during my time at Organ Pipe Cactus National Monument, there was only one person of my age who came through as a tourist. Roberta Safarik came with her parents Ed and Eleanor Safarik to camp at Organ Pipe. Like myself, Roberta had not had a lot of contact with the opposite sex, but we made friends while I worked there, and began corresponding after she left.

In May 1966, I went to work at Big Bend National Park in Texas. My boss was Bruce McHenry. I came in a few days early, so I explored the area and made a trip with Bruce and his family into Alpine, Texas. Dr. Jon Barlow of the Royal Ontario Museum in Ontario Canada was in and Dick Fisher an ornithologist, so we did some bird watching.

I became interested in the flora of the area. When Frank Judd and Alan Sartain came in, we worked up a natural history of the Giant Dagger Yucca area on the Eastern Edge of the park. Frank was a mammalogist and Alan a herpetologist, so with my knowledge of birds and plants, it proved to be a good workup.

On June 7th my parents and brother came in from Wichita

Falls. My father at nearly 75 years of age easily made the climb up the hill for the Basin Nature Walk.

During my stay there Harry Gregory and Dr. Roger Conant both herpetologists were in the park collecting. I learned a great deal about reptiles and amphibians from them and from Allan Sartain.

In July, we got word that Bruce McHenry was going to be transferred and Roland Wauer was going to be the new chief naturalist for Big Bend. When he arrived, he soon changed the schedule, but failed to notify everyone of the changes, so the schedule was mixed up for a while.

In mid July, Gene Phillips a seasonal Ranger from Alabama and I checked on some Mexican wax factories just across the river in Mexico. There were five men cooking wax plants(Hectia scariosa) in a large caldron and using the dried weed for fuel. This weed eventually ended up as wax for cars in the United States after being smuggled across the border.

My main jobs here were working on the information desk, giving evening programs, and giving nature walks. The material I learned helped considerably with my talks in the evening and my walks. One of my talks was a history of the Big Bend area which was titled "Rio Bravo".

My parents visited again in August. We celebrated my fathers 75 birthday while he was there. On September 2 I took a special trip to the top of the Chisos Mountains, about a five mile walk. I collected numerous mushrooms, dried them and identified them for the collection.

I left Big Bend National Park on September 25, 1966. I visited Langtry, saw the Judge Roy Bean Museum and spent the night at Del Rio with Uncle Roy and Aunt Velma. I took Aunt Velma on to Copperas Cove where her daughter in law lived. I went on into Hico, visited with Arthur and Donald Phillips and arrived in Wichita Falls at 6PM.

On October 26, 1966 I took off for a trip to the Everglades. I went to the Big Thicket and then on into Mississippi. My car broke down at Bay St. Louis Mississippi on the Gulf of Mexico. I had the car towed to Gulfport Mississippi, but it wasn't fixed until November 4th. I spent the last of my vacation money to get it fixed, so returned to Wichita Falls. My vacation wasn't entirely ruined on this trip in spite of the circumstances. I had my bird book and the weather was nice so I walked around town watching birds and then walked on the beach picking up shells. The plant life was a jungle like second growth forest and I knew many of the plants.

Beginning on December 3, 1966, I travelled to Organ Pipe Cactus National Monument. I stayed with Bill Hoy until my quonset was ready to live in. On December 7 I moved into the Quonset. The Safariks had a trailer in Wickenburg, so on the 12th I drove to Wickenburg and visited Roberta and her parents.

December 21 was the Christmas Bird Count. I was assigned Alamo Canyon, a beautiful desert canyon. The 27th was the second day of the count, and I went with Jimmy and Sandy Taylor in the residence area and the Senita Basin.

On January 12, Roberta and her parents brought their travel trailer down to the park. We visited off and on for several days and took the driving trails into the desert. On January 22, 1967 I visited Fred and Jan Carter in Phoenix. On the 23rd I drove into Wickenburg and we went out to see the Safarik's new house.

I worked out a Plant Checklist for Organ Pipe Cactus, worked on the desk, gave walks and talks as usual. I had an offer from the Army for a full time job and another from the National Park Service which I accepted. I left Organ Pipe Cactus National Monument on March 3, 1967 and drove to Wickenburg. The following day I reported to the Grand Canyon Training Center. I visited Larry Henderson in the evening. Classes began on March 6th, 1967.

We studied and played hard. I learned the common plants and birds of the Grand Canyon and renewed my acquaintance with the Geology of the area. The Grand Canyon is perhaps the best place in the country to study the Geology of the earlier rocks up to Permian Age. Some of the oldest rocks exposed anywhere on the earth are found in the depths of the canyon and a nearly complete sequence of paleozoic sediments is found here.

I gave several talks. On the 24th we took a test over what we had learned. I drove to Prescott in the evening. I drove on to Wickenburg the following morning and visited the Safariks for a couple of days.

Back at the training center I gave talks on Appomattox Courthouse and Glacier National Park. We had classes on first Aid, obstetrics, dark room techniques, archeology, and other subjects.

On April first 1967 we left for a field trip to Lake Mead National Recreation Area. On the second we went on to

Zion National Park and on the third to Pipe Springs National Monument. Back at the training academy we worked on accessioning of museum objects, and had training on Building Fire Control. I was assigned fire inspection of the Training Center and gave a conducted walk on the park Insect Collection. On April 9th John Ray, Trevor Arthur and I went to Navajo National Monument and walked down to Betatikin Ruin. We had classes also on Law Enforcement and accident investigation. We went into a long session on Park Planning using a model of an imaginary park to base our studies on. We also had a presentation several days long by the FBI and fired on the pistol range.

On May 3rd, 1967 My 25th birthday, I was assigned to Colonial National Historical Park as an Intake Park. I went the following day off to Wickenburg. Roberta was upset about my being transferred so far away, but she said she would visit me there.

We worked a week with the park staff, studied rapelling and search and rescue. On the 20th I put five new tires on my car. I hiked down into the Canyon for the first time since I had arrived on the 22nd. Graduation exercises were May 26th and after graduation I drove to Quemado New Mexico for the night. I drove into Lubbock on the 27th and stayed with Gene and Imogene Sorley, and the following day on home to Wichita Falls. I made arrangements to have my things shipped to Yorktown Virginia. June first I visited Russell Cave in Northern Alabama and spent the night in Tennessee. The second I was in North Carolina and on the Third I spent the night in Virginia. I arrived at Jamestown Entrance Station early Sunday Morning June 4th. My new boss, Virgil Leimer was on his way to church and had stopped at the entrance station, so I met him first thing.

I was oriented to the park over the next few days, and met many park staff people. I also began patrols which soon became routine. My job here consisted of road patrol of both the Colonial Parkway and both Jamestown Island and the Yorktown Battlefield. There had been a drowning in the James River on June 17, so I spent some time walking the shoreline looking for bodies. On the 19th The Safariks came for a visit and stayed until the 25th. I soon learned all the plants.

The York and James Rivers are branches of Chesapeake Bay, and are tidal rivers or estuaries where the tides go several miles up the river at high tide and then are flushed with fresh water during low tides.

The fauna and flora here was the best developed of any where I had been in the National Parks. Oaks, elms, hickories, walnuts, tulip trees, virginia pine, beech, dogwood, spicebush, broomsedge, asters, horsetail weed, pigweed, red maple, southern red oak, chestnut oak, green brier, poison ivy, willow oak, bayberry, red bay, and red cedar were common here.

Possum, red fox, gray fox, box turtles, white tailed deer, striped skunk, cottontail rabbit, white footed mice, raccoon, gray squirrel, moles, porcupine, mink, and muskrat were all common.

Bald eagle, great blue heron, wild turkey, osprey, field sparrow, grasshopper sparrow, meadowlark, cardinal, mockingbird, catbird, blackbirds, crows, wood thrush, salamanders, garter snakes, great horned owl, pine warbler, red-eyed vireo, red-tailed hawk, and ovenbird were to be found here.

I also became interested in the long and varied history represented by Jamestown and Yorktown, and read as much as I could on those areas. Colonial Williamsburg was a fabulous area which showed all of the good things about colonial life and none of the hardship, and I spent much time there.

On July 3, My parents and brother James came in from Wichita Falls. I took them all around to Yorktown, Jamestown, and Williamsburg as I had the Safariks. They left the 9th. On the 11th I visited Jamestown Festival Park. It is a reconstruction of the original fort at Jamestown and except for too many talking boxes is a good interpretive medium.

My ulcer flared up several times this year. There would be indigestion, followed by gas and swelling of the stomach which caused pain in my back. I had several kinds of medicine for it, but probably the most effective was simple antacid.

On September 25, I went with Roger Giddings to Greenspring Plantation, the former home of Governor Berkeley, who was governor of Virginia is the mid 1600s, and on September 29th I went to Norfolk, bought tickets at the airport to fly to Wichita Falls. The fare was $175 round trip. I visited the botanical gardens while in Norfolk.

On October 5th and 6th I made a trip to Shenandoah National Park. I visited Bruce, Martha, Keith, Brucie, and Dolly McHenry. We picked Bruce up at Harpers Ferry.

On the 7th Bruce and his family took me into Luray where I saw Luray Caverns and the Car and Carriage Museum.

On October 14, Linda Stanton and Kathy Kirby, two new historians came in. They were slightly younger than myself, and we soon became good friends. October 19 was Yorktown day, and I helped with traffic control and logistics. Fall color was very good in November, and in December there were a number of parties.

On December 19, I flew from Norfolk to Washington D.C., from there to Dallas where I met James. We flew on into Wichita Falls where Ronnie Sanders and our parents were waiting for us. On Christmas day, we all drove the 142 miles to Hico where we had our annual Christmas visit with the Hico Phillipses. I flew back to Virginia on the 31st.

In February and March of 1968, I was included in Intake Training, which consisted of cross-training with all the various divisions. I was busy reading a number of classics in the evening.

Roberta Safarik and I had been corresponding since 1966 and in the course of events we had become engaged by mail, so to speak. I spent much of the time during this period making up lists of people for wedding invitations and planning for a trip to Wickenburg. On April 1st I flew to Baltimore and on to Chicago and from there to Phoenix where the Safariks and Fred Carter picked me up.

We worked the next few days in final plans for our wedding which was at the Wickenburg Presbyterian Church, where we were married April 6, 1968. We flew back to Virginia and set up housekeeping in the Moorehouse Kitchen. I had kept it pretty austere, but Roberta wanted some comforts such as a bed, so we soon bought one. I had not had a Television, so we bought a TV also.

News clipping undated: **PHILLIPS - SAFARIK**

The wedding of Roberta Safarik, daughter of Mr & Mrs Edgar R. Safarik of Wickenburg to J. Wesley Phillips of Yorktown, Va., took place April 6 at 7 p.m. in the First Presbyterian Church. Rev. W. Howard Blazer performed the double-ring ceremony. The father of the bride gave her away. Paula Jean Safarik of Brea, Calif., was the bride's attendant. James R. Phillips, brother of the groom, was best man. Fred Carter of Wichita Falls, Tex., and Robert Safarik of Brea, Calif., were ushers.

The bride wore a white gown of peau de sole, a fine lustrous silk material with grain texture. It was made in simple a-line style, ankle length. With it she wore a shoulder - length veil of silk illusion, and carried a colonial bouquet of white carnations.

The church was decorated with baskets of gladioli, carnations and 7-stick candelabras. A reception in the church parlor followed the ceremony.

The young couple will make their home in Yorktown, Va. The groom is park naturalist at the Colonial National Historical Park in Williamsburg, Virginia.

Out of town guests were Mr & Mrs John R. Phillips, Wichita Falls, Tex., parents of the groom, Mrs Lily Brown, Sherry & Sarah Rasbury, and James Middleton, Phoenix; Mr & Mrs Larry Henderson, Grand Canyon; Mrs Margaret Miller and Mrs Eloise Sullivan, Compton, Calif.; Mrs Otto Safarik, Palm Springs, Calif.; Mrs Robert Safarik, Brea, Calif; Mr and Mrs John Schmidt, Burbank, Calif.; Mr & Mrs Hub Dutton, Corona Del Mar, Calif.; & Mr and Mrs Frank Reed, Scottsdale, Arizona.

I had to show Roberta all the sights, so we took frequent trips around the Yorktown tour road and to Jamestown Island or along the Colonial Parkway, or to Colonial Williamsburg. It was a fabulous time, as we were both interested in nature study, Roberta in animals and myself in plants. Roberta was well versed in art, so she would sketch plants and insects for me as we went.

On April 21, 1969 Roberta's parents came for a visit. We made a trip to Washington D.C. with them, saw Jack Safarik, Roberta's brother, and visited many of the museums and other places around including Mount Vernon. We visited the Lederers, Nancy Safarik's parents and drove back to Colonial on the 28th. On the 29th we turned around and went to the Blue Ridge Parkway where I had a school on Environmental Education. We returned to Colonial on my birthday May 3rd. We stopped at Appomattox and Petersburg on the way back.

On July 22, Virgil Leimer left for Whiskeytown. He was replaced by Gunnar Guardipee as district Ranger for the Yorktown District.

Gunnar Guardipee came in the second week in August, and on the twelfth I gave him the grand tour. Roberta and I had taken up square dancing, and we went dancing about once a week.

I hung up the phone and sat back in the chair in the district ranger's office. I had finally received the call I had been waiting for all my life. I had been offered a naturalist job at Everglades National Park. It was a goal I had long been working toward, and now finally I was to have my chance.

For the past two and one half years, I had been a park ranger - law enforcement - at Colonial National Historic Park at Yorktown, Virginia. It had been a bitter-sweet experience. At 5 feet four and 110 pounds I was not built for hard and heavy law enforcement. Fortunately, there was little in the way of lawlessness as yet on the Virginia Peninsula, and much of my job had been such mundane tasks as reading traffic counters, putting up battlefield flags, and opening gates to tour roads at both Jamestown and Yorktown. The closest I got to real law enforcement was running radar on the Colonial Parkway and stopping speeders.

I had some very understanding supervisors at this time however, who gave me some responsibilities which better fit my qualifications. I got to do some work on wildlife management and I worked on preparing an environmental study area at Ringfield plantation site. Perhaps the most interesting part of my job was the work I did after hours on Jamestown Island. I had early-on began to learn the flora and fauna of the area, and soon I knew the vegetation better than anyone else on the staff. At some time in the distant past, there had been a deer exclosure put on Jamestown Island, to find out what the vegetation would be like if the deer couldn't get into a fenced off section. I began by sampling both inside this plot and inside the plot, and worked around the island, finding out about the vegetation in bits and pieces.

The wildlife was fabulous! I saw more deer on the Yorktown tour road than I have ever seen together in one place anywhere else I have worked. Raccoons, opossums, skunks, little dark swamp rabbits, turtles, snakes, lizards, frogs, and especially birds were seemingly everywhere. I had watched a mink chasing tree frogs on the tour road at Jamestown Island once.

But, now - now I was going to a place where the natural history was incredible! My wife Roberta and I had long wanted to move to a natural area where I would have full use of all the things I had learned in school. I had told Pat Miller that I would have to talk to my wife, but that there was very little doubt that I would accept the position. I called Roberta up, and she was delighted with the prospects, so I called Everglades back and accepted the job.

It took a few weeks to gather up our things and get the move scheduled, but by Roberta's birthday on October 1, 1969, we were just about packed and ready to go. We spent the night of October 2nd in Charleston South Carolina and called Paul Gordon. I had worked with Paul at Colonial, and he was a good friend.

We took the coastal Highway, Highway 1 most of the way down and arrived at the entrance to Everglades National Park on the afternoon of October 4. I was never so shocked as when I drove past the entrance sign and realized that the area which we had driven over between Homestead and the park was the remnants of a magnificent pinelands of 100 years before. At the entrance sign, the pines stretched away into the park, in sharp contrast to the flat farmland and grassland we had just driven over. It took little time to realize that the adjacent lands had been butchered by the hand of modern man and that the land within the park was much more pristine than anything I had driven over south of Homestead.

My introduction to the Pinelands of South Florida, then was sudden. Two other habitats were soon added - the Everglades and the Hardwood Hammock. I spent the months of October and November getting oriented to the park. We visited Flamingo, Everglades City, and all the trails along the main park road. In December, the real tourist season began. I was assigned to go to Flamingo at times to give nature walks on the Christian Point Trail, or along the edge of Florida Bay.

I was assigned to the Royal Palm Area of the park. The Anhinga Trail took off from the Royal Palm Visitor Center and led across the Everglades to Taylor Slough. At times the wildlife here was ubiquitous. The Anhinga also known as Water Turkey and Snake Bird was a regular visitor here and nested along the boardwalk close enough that the nests could be easily viewed by a casual visitor.
The flora was really exotic here. The Royal Palm Area had a boardwalk out over the marsh itself, but the Gumbo Limbo Trail ran through a subtropical jungle or Hammock area with the Gumbo Limbo or Naked Indian Tree, wild coffee shrubs, palms, ferns, live oaks, orchids, wild pineapples, and many other exotics. On the boardwalk, the primary attraction was the alligators, plus such birds as the Anhinga and various herons and egrets.

The Alligator was, however, the star of the show. Just to see a twelve foot reptile weighing over 1000 pounds at a distance was a treat, but here, a huge 'gator called

"Big George" was sprawled right under the public's eye. I was told by the experienced guides that the way to estimate the size of an alligator was to estimate the length between the end of his nose and his eyes in inches and then change inches to feet. So, if it was 11 inches from the tip of George's nose to his eyes, he was eleven feet long.

The truth of the matter is that George was a bum. He made his living from tourists who threw crackers and other tidbits his way, and didn't have to fish for a living as conscientiously as before. I was soon leading the night prowl around the Anhinga trail, and here I had the chance to see a real alligator in action! This lithe creature was only about five feet long, but he was swimming after fish for all he was worth. It was a dance in the water, with the gator coming out ahead. I marvelled at the sinuous curves he could place in his body and the graceful way he darted after the fish. No, Big George was not a real alligator.

Great Blue Herons stood in the shallows waiting for that fish to get in just the right position to spear, while coots dove into the depths after water weed or other plant life. One day I saw a large Florida Bass about two feet long which appeared to be proud of herself. She had just killed a water snake about four feet long and was parading up and down by the boardwalk as if she was showing off her prize.

This was a great introduction to the Everglades and its wildlife, but equally fascinating to me was the Gumbo Limbo Trail which took off from the Royal Palm Visitor Center as well. It plunged right from the well-mowed yard into deep, densely canopied, tropical hardwood forest. It was named for the "Naked Indian Tree" or Gumbo Limbo. This common tree looked as if it had been sunburned, with its thin, red, peeling bark standing out against a green underbark. The Gumbo Limbo Trail dove straight into a hardwood hammock, known as Royal Palm Hammock. This hammock, one of the largest in the park had been the backbone of the Royal Palm State Park, set aside by the Ladies Garden Clubs of Florida. This in turn had become Everglades National Park in 1947.

I was placed incharge of two visitor centers - one at Park Headquarters, and the other the Royal Palm Visitor Center. The V.C. at headquarters was a major sales outlet, with perhaps 50 titles for sale. There was a slide program here which often went haywire, and soon I was the major fix-it man for this operation. I supervised Ruth and Sam Mendlen and Maude Harriott as tour guides and information receptionists at the visitor centers. They were well experienced interpreters and could give excellent programs.

The Royal Palm area soon became my favorite spot, especially the Gumbo Limbo Trail area. I learned all the exotic plants and discovered all the trails used when the area was a state park. The Anhinga Trail with the alligators and wildlife was also exciting. At times I was detailed to Flamingo where I gave the Christian Point walk through a swampy area out to a spot called "Snake Bight", which was a cove off of Florida Bay. Once or twice I gave the bayshore walk along the bay and Cape Sable. Mary Jane Inman who I had known at Grand Canyon was the area interpreter here.

October 10, 1969 - I worked Royal Palm with Maude Harriott. Opened the building at 8:00. Took the Anhinga Trail and saw Yellowthroat and my first Black Crowned Night Herons. Observed Limpkins along the road near the marsh. I went on Maude's tours. She went all the way around the boardwalk and pointed out a great number of plants and birds.

October 24, 1969 - I got up at 6 o'clock and left at 8 for Everglades City and the Gulf Coast. It was raining when I left and continued till I got there. I went with Bill Truesdale in his car. First we went to Chockoluskee Island where we saw Yellow Elder, Croton, Cabbage Palm, Short Leaf Fig, and several others. We visited the Post Office and trading post established in 1910 by E. M. Smallwood. It had survived several hurricanes with no damage. Many antiques were inside and it still had an early 20th century flavor. I ate the lunch Roberta fixed at Bill's house and met his wife and two girls. After Lunch we got in the boat and went out to Sandfly Island where Bill's Environmental Study Area is located. His trail is about one mile long and starts at the boat dock. New plants were numerous including Guava, Tamarind, Bag Pod, Gumbo Limbo, Jamaica Dogwood, Catclaw, Cat's Paw, Spiny Acacia, Cassia, Red Mangrove, Black Mangrove, Buttonwood, Snowberry Vine, Prickly Pear, Dildoe, Lycium, Pigeon Plum, Coco Plum, Verbena, Lantana, Baccharis, Corkscrew Air Plant, Cardinal Air Pine, Spanish Moss, Wild Grape, Sisal Agave, American Agave, Century Plant, Golden Polypody, Marlberry, Possum Grape (<u>Cissus sicyoides</u>), Nicker Bean, Spider Lily, Stopper, <u>Foresteria</u>, Live Leaf (<u>Kalanchoe</u> sp.), Poor -man's Patches.

We got up and drove to the Pinelands Trail. The water in the potholes is slowly drying up. This is Fantastic country! The ground is covered with gaping potholes, some of which are ten feet across. The deeper ones have water weed, arrowhead, and fish in them, while others have diving beetles and whirlagig beetles.

We got up at 7:00 and left for Flamingo. We ate a picnic lunch under the Coconut Palms along the bayshore and fed the gulls. We saw terns, two kinds of gulls, yellowlegs, peeps, skimmers, pelicans, and cormorants from our picnic area as well as some cute "chicks". We then went over to the visitor center where we looked at the eagle's nest and then went on the bayshore walk with Dan Scurlock. On the walk we saw turtle grass, hermit crabs, lined bubble shells, stone crabs, fiddler crabs, red, black, white, and button mangroves, cabbage, thatch, coconut, and Wright's palms; sea grape, sea oxeye, and a variety of other plants. Under rocks along the shore we found amphipods and small snails and shells.

On the way back, we stopped at Mrazecks Pond where we saw roseate spoonbills, white ibis, great white herons, american egrets, great blue herons, a little blue heron, and cormorants. I picked flowers near nine-mile Pond - blue eyed grass, wild morning glory, white topped sedge.

We had real naturalists at the parks in those days. Both Mary Jane Inman from Flamingo and Bill Truesdale from Everglades City were naturalists of the first order, and could name every bird and plant and tell stories about them.

November 30, 1969 - Roberta and I went to Royal Palm this morning and walked out the Old Ingram Highway until it became so overgrown that we could go no farther. On the way we picked a sour orange. On the way back we freed a large dragonfly from a spider web and Roberta sketched plants including a fern which I didn't know.

December 5, 1969 - Mary Jane Inman and I went out on the Christian Point Trail first. We waded across the ditch and then started through the brush. The trail was well defined until we came out into an open field. Here it disappeared completly. Mary Jane stopped and looked around and then decided which way it should go and struck out in that direction. We came to a large christmasberry shrub where she told me that the plant marked the site of an old charcoal processing plant. The dead trees in the field had been used to make charcoal between 1880 and 1900.

We went on across the field and into another woods. Here the trail still didn't appear but Mary Jane pushed on, gaily marking plants as we went. In a few minutes we came out into another field.

"Isn't this the same field we were in before?", I asked her, since it seemed to me we had gone in a semicircle.

"No, we've been following the sun all the way, haven't we?" Mary Jane stated confidently. "See, here's one of the orange markers from last year!"

Sure enough, there was a marker and just a little ways further on there was another.

"Well, you've got me lost" I confessed " Do you have a map or something that you could show me.

"Sure," she stated " Everybody gets lost on this trail."

She produced a map and pointed out the trail and the old road it would join up with and finally Christian Point. Then just for emphasis she said. "We should be able to see the standpipe and the radio tower ahead of us."

We looked carefully out across the open field we had just entered but all we saw was a lot of dead trees lying around in the field just like the first field we had come to. We walked a little further and I looked behind us. "There's the standpipe." I said.

We had gone through the woods in a semicircle and come out in the same field that we had started in, but just by chance we had come out on the actual trail.

"Well I guess it's true that you go in circles when you're lost." Mary Jane said.

On May 3rd, my 28th birthday, we left Everglades for a vacation trip to Wichita Falls. We travelled by bus day and night until we reached Wichita Falls 11 O'clock on May 5th. We drove to Hico, and then after several days took the bus to Beatrice Nebraska where Roberta's Uncle Eddie Brier picked us up and took us to DeWitt. We visited with Aunt Irene and Uncle Eddie and also with Aunt Viola and Uncle Glen Sire. We went out to the old Zwonecek Mill and visited John and Faye Zwonecek, and Aunt Clara Jewell. We also went to Wilber and visited Aunt Mae Zwonecek and Tina Chabb her sister. They took us to the Czec Museum and the library. On the way back, we stopped at the Arch in St. Louis. It was pretty new then, and we rode in the elevator to the top where we could see the vista all around. We stopped and visited Al Garcia in Jacksonville, Florida. We returned to

Everglades on May 23, 1970.

I had been having trouble with my ulcer since 1966 and at a training course at Harper's Ferry West Virginia in April I had developed a severe pain with it. Roberta talked me into going into the doctor who referred me to a surgeon Dr. Tully who operated on me in June 1970, correcting my ulcer problem, or at least the worst symptoms of my problem. The operation also uncovered the fact that I had gall bladder problems, so that was also removed. After the operation I was laid up for about six weeks under doctor's orders, though I felt pretty good most of the time.

Roberta had been on birth control pills since we had been married, but early in 1971 we decided to start a family. Early in March Roberta went off the pill, and in about two weeks the doctor said she was pregnant. The due date was early in December, but the days drug on and then weeks, but finally on December 27, 1971 Theresa Ann Phillips was born. She was named for Theresa Lianzi, a good friend of Roberta's. Theresa was born in the Hospital in Homestead, which was about ten miles from our Pine Island Residential Area in Everglades National Park.

Much of our life now became centered in the baby. Roberta especially felt the pressure of the extra work, but there was extra joy also. Theresa proved to be a very beautiful and easy going child and was frequently happy and singing in her crib in the morning. My brother James Richard Phillips married Linda Kaye Porter on September 30, 1972 at Ogden, Utah.

July 15, 1972. (Roberta) - Today Wes & I "waded out in the swamp" toward Royal Palm. For the 1st time in approx. 2 yrs. I spotted a little blue heron beside the bridge, which is now _really_ overflowing. There has been lots of rain in the 'glades since we've arrived back from Texas. In fact, while going out hunting for insects, fish, etc, we all got caught in the rain _including_ little Theresa! She didn't seem to mind it, tho, and Wes _liked_ it!

August 27, 1972. I went out to look for millipedes today and found three _Mastigoproctus giganteus_ (Giant Whiptail Scorpions) and one _Schizomus floridanus_ (White Whiptail Scorpion).

On October 30, 1972 I attended a course on Urban Problems in Park Management in Washington D.C. Before returning home I went to the National Archives and obtained the Revolutionary War record of Adam Phillips.

On November 18 James and Linda came in for a visit. We had just been informed that we would be moving to Everglades City, so we all went over and looked at the house. It was a huge place, up on stilts to keep it out of the high tides if a hurricane struck. Roberta flew to Phoenix on the 21st to visit her parents. I finished packing everything and moved to Everglades City on December 4th.

At Everglades City I had two seasonal naturalists, an information receptionist, and two welcome center hostesses to supervise. I was also supposed to help Sammy Hamilton with his boat tours in any way I could.

The Everglades City or Gulf Coast district of Everglades National Park was one of the most interesting areas I have worked in. When I arrived, no previous naturalist had really come to grips with the fabulous story of the mangrove zone of the park, but I went to work, detailing the growth of the mangroves, the fish which fed on the shed leaves, the birds which fed on the fish, and the story of the shell mounds scattered around the area. Another aspect of the area was the sinking coastline which produced mangrove peat. The sinking also produced the Ten Thousand Islands, which were constantly reworked by the tides.

December 14, 1972. Bill Murray and his wife, Leah Bowen and Frank Buono went with me to Corkscrew Swamp today. We left the office around 8:30 and arrived at Corkscrew about 9:30. We talked to Jerry Cutlip and then took the mile and a half nature trail. I had my camera along and got pictures of squirrels, birds, and gators as well as other animals & plants. It is a very beautiful area.

December 15, 1972. Went on the maintenance men's boat today. We went out Sandfly Pass to Rabbit Key, Turtle Key, Rat Terd Key, Mormon Key, Duck Rock and Pavilion Key. We stopped at Lostman's River Station then went up the Turner River through Onion Key Bay to Onion Key, Camp Lonesome, and finally back through the Inland Waterway to Alligator Creek. Just as we got out of Alligator Creek and were heading out in the middle of the channel, the steering cable broke and we plowed into the mangroves. John Russell was injured slightly but it didn't appear serious. John Galvin undid the steering system and steered it by hand until we got back.

Saturday December 17 was Sammy Hamilton's party at the Rod and Gun Club. I attended and ate a lot. It was a great party. During the night the newer part of the Rod and Gun club caught fire and was destroyed. It was believed to be an electrical fault.

I now started a history study of the Everglades region and Everglades City/Chokoluskee area in particular. This lasted much of the time I was at the West Coast District, and included a genealogical study of the local residents.

Roberta and Theresa arrived back at the Miami International Airport at 8:48 PM on December 19th. By December 25th the Boat tours were booming. Sammy liked the naturalists to go along on the tour, so Frank Buono, Bill Murray, or myself went on many tours and often talked and gave information to the visitors. I became involved with the Everglades Area Chamber of Commerce and attended some of their meetings, and joined the Everglades Lions Club.

Because of my interest in ancestors, Roberta began painting portraits of our ancestors. I wrote frequently to the National Archives, State Archives all across the country, and every relative I could get my hands on. Doug Bowen, The District Ranger and I formed a friendship and things went along smoothly.

In September, 1972 Roberta became pregnant again and on June 13, 1973 John Edgar Phillips was born. He was born with a full head of black hair, and a jaundice condition called bilirubin which they cured by placing him under a blue light. He was named for his grandfathers John Richard Phillips and Edgar Robert Safarik. My folks came in on June 8th and were there for the birth.

June 29, 1973. I read "Environments of Coal Formation" which deals with the mangrove zone of the park. This volume just about completes my knowledge of how the mangrove zone formed, how it operates and how it will disappear. It is a fabulous environment, and perhaps one of the most productive in the park. The story is one of mangroves living in a rising sea. As the sea rises, the mangroves encroach on the fresh water swamp and the Everglades. The outer edge of the mangrove zone is dissected to form islands by the tidal currents.

July 10, 1973. This morning while I was going to work, Stanley Brown from Chokaloskee Island stopped me and told me he had just seen a manatee going up Halfway Creek. I told Doug and he took me out in the boat. The manatee was going up the Paradise Bay Canal, sculling gently with the tide. It was on its side, and apparently nursing the calf that was with it. It was afraid of the boat propeller & dove whenever we started the engine. It was about 12 feet long and the calf was around 5 feet. The calf only came up for air once while we were watching them.

On September 2, 1973 we left for Wichita Falls and all points east. We arrived at Rogers Arkansas on September 5th, where we visited with Otto and Louise Safarik, Roberta's aunt and uncle, and Bob Safarik and his wife Margaret. Bob and Margaret's children, Monica and Carl were also there.

We drove on to Wichita falls on the 7th and visited with my parents. The Safariks from Wickenburg came too. We visited Hico on the 27th. Aunt Velma and Uncle Roy Ogletree came in also on the Third of October. We left Wichita Falls on October 6th and were home on the 10th.

On October 15, I started a series of classes on Supervision and Group Performance in Miami. During part of this time I lived in the Bunkhouse at Pine Island and then two nights at the Tamiami Ranger Station.

Chuck Millikan was my seasonal this winter. It must have been quite a contrast with him six foot three inches tall against my five feet four. Roberta was sick during much of this winter, partly run down from having two babies, and partly recuperating from a virus caught the previous fall.

Roberta continued with her art work, and sold a painting of Nancy Brown, the daughter of Roxie Brown who ran the Everglades Welcome Station. By this time we had our walls decorated with pictures she had painted of various family members all the way back to Adam Phillips. I continued family history research, and our interests reinforced each other. The children were growing like weeds and getting into everything, so it was a busy time.

Bruce McHenry transferred out this year, and was replaced with Pat Crosland. We were ready for a move ourselves, and had applied to numerous parks, but none of them panned out, in spite of the fact that so many seemed like sure things.

November 14, 1974. (Roberta) Last Monday we went for a canoe outing -- the first time in ages! We paddled almost all the way around Everglades City. I saw a horseshoe crab _alive_ for the first time -- also a manatee, a few great blue herons, white ibises, several yellow-crowned night herons. We were stiff & sore from our outing the next day. We'll just have to do this more often, as I'll admit, I was impressed by the ride with seeing Everglades City from the water. It is truly a typical fishing village and to really enjoy it you have to see it from the water.

Ed Safarik died January sixth 1975. He was 75 years old, and had suffered from tuberculosis and emphysema. He had a heart attack while being treated for his lungs in the Wickenburg Hospital. Early in 1975 Dad had some problems with his heart. It slowed down to 25 beats per minute. He had to have a pacemaker installed to regulate the beats.

James and Linda were living in Germany, but we corresponded regularly. We had found a royal line of ancestry, and we were both interested in finding all its ins and outs.

Johnny proved to be quite a handful. He was intelligent, but since his speaking ability was not yet developed, he couldn't communicate, and would scream or beat his head on the floor to make a point. We were recovering somewhat from our chronic flu-like symptoms, and all were feeling pretty well. With the death of her father, Roberta began to have some trouble with mental illness, a problem which persisted for about ten years.

In March and April 1975 I worked on a community genealogy for the Everglades City/Chokoloskee Island area. I also joined the Sons of the American Revolution on the Adam Phillips line and became a member of the Collier County Historical Commission.

On April 26, we left Everglades bound for Wichita Falls. We visited Andersonville Prison and the archives in Atlanta. We toured the battlefield at Kennesaw Mountain and visited several cemeteries. We arrived in Wichita Falls on May 1. Roberta's mother came in. Both she and Dad were feeling well. Dad was especially anxious to show everyone his new pacemaker.

On May 12, we visited Hico. Arthur had been pretty sick, and been in the hospital, but was home for the day. Dad was not feeling well, and had to lie in the back of the station wagon most of the way. Dad and Donald gave me many of my Grandfather Wesley Pharr Phillips carpenter tools.

On October 6, 1975 I received a phone call from Lake Meredith Recreation Area in Fritch Texas offering me the position of Interpretive Specialist for Lake Meredith and Administrative Assistant for Alibates National Monument. We were thrilled, as this was just the area we had been hoping for.

We left Everglades on October 30, 1975. On November first we visited Judge Samuel P. Burtz, a distant cousin who lived in Canton, Georgia. He took us around and showed us the sights in the hills around Canton and we spent some time in the Cherokee County Court House searching for Phillips and Burtz records.

We arrived in Wichita Falls on November 4th and left 8AM on the 7th for Fritch where we arrived in the early afternoon. I called Johnny Graham and visited with him some in the evening.

We immediately got us an efficiency apartment at the motel and began to house hunt. We had never bought a house before, so we were inexperienced, but we found a nice one, reasonably priced at $15,000 near the Park Headquarters in Fritch. The address 412 Nara Visa was to be our residence for many years.

The first week I was at my new job I was given the grand tour by my new supervisor Larry Nielson and assigned to write up a folder for use in metropolitan areas. Ed Day was my only employee. His job was as tour guide for Alibates Flint Quarries National Monument.

The Texas Panhandle is an area with deeply entrenched river valleys in a sea of grass. Rainfall is scant. Winds are often severe, and winter temperatures often hover near the zero mark.

The Canadian River forms the major river system in this region with the North Canadian and its tributary Beaver Creek to the north and the South Canadian in the central Texas Panhandle. The Canadian River Breaks, where the land is broken by erosion, is the area of abundant wildlife, and the area where many Indian groups often camped or lived. Permian Redbeds form the general substrate, though the hills are capped by a Permian gray limestone called the Alibates Dolomite within which is the Alibates Flint so useful to the peoples of the past. The Ogallala formation common on higher ground away from the river is absent in most areas along the river, though gravel remnants provided hammerstones for working the flint.

Grasses typical of our region include blue grama, side oats grama, hairy grama, buffalo grass, sand dropseed, sand bluestem, little bluestem, and along the valleys switchgrass, indiangrass, and reeds. Trees typical of this area include mesquite, cottonwood, hackberry, soapberry, one seed juniper, and a variety of willows. On the hillsides typical shrubs include aromatic sumac, sand sagebrush, gray sagebrush, yucca, catclaw mimosa, and feathertop dalea, while in the stream bottoms plums, chokecherries, grapes, currents, and cattail predominate.

Mammal life typical of the area include mule deer, white tail deer, bison, pronghorn, coyote, wolf, black bear, mountain lion, bobcat, skunks, badgers, porcupines, beavers, jackrabbits, cottontails, and a variety of small rodents. Birds include turkey, prairie chicken, bobwhite, scaled quail, eagle, osprey, red tailed hawk, great blue heron, and a variety of smaller birds. Reptiles of importance include the western diamondback rattlesnake, prairie rattlesnake, bullsnake, coachwhip snake, snapping turtle, softshell turtle, and box turtle. Fishes include blue catfish, flathead catfish, bass, and sunfish.

Eleanor Safarik came for a visit on December 10 and on December 11 we moved into our new house. Eleanor stayed through the 22nd and on Christmas morning we drove to Wichita Falls to celebrate Christmas. We returned to Fritch on the 28th.

James and Linda had their first child on December 30th, 1975. Cynthia Heidi was born in Tucson Arizona. She was named for my grandmother Cynthia Catherine Bradshaw and for Linda's Grandmother Heidi Heikola.

On December 31 we took a trip to Ordway Colorado to Visit my mother's sister Irma Campbell, her husband Claude, and her daughter and family Lula May and Francis Rader. While we were there, Aunt Irma gave us several things which had belonged to her parents. It was 17 degrees there and spitting snow, though there was no accumulation. Billy and Jewell Rader came in and we had a good visit with them also. We returned on January 3rd, 1976.

On February 12 we took the eagles for the new museum with us and left for Albuquerque where we left them at New Mexico Taxidermy. We continued on to Arizona, arriving there on the 13th. Theresa was especially interested in the new baby, but Johnny was still pretty willful and threw a fit. We continued on to Wickenburg where we arrived on the 17th. Eleanor gave us some pictures and some of Ed's things. We returned home on the 21st of February.

On April 4, we went to Wichita Falls. James and his family were there, and we had a group picture made of the entire family. Roberta and I celebrated our tenth wedding anniversary in Wichita Falls.

I found my Bradshaw ancestors this month. Andrew Bradshaw was the son of Samuel and Dorcas (Prigmore) Bradshaw of Tennessee, and grandson of John and Nancy Ann (Clendenin) Bradshaw. The Bradshaws, Clendenins, and Hustons are from Pennsylvania. They came to North Carolina before the Revolution and moved to Tennessee before 1800.

On April 10, we took our Czec materials to Mrs. Joe Spinhirne of Vega Texas for translation.

On April 23rd we got a dog which we named Clio. She looked like a husky, but on a smaller scale. We had her until she was quite old.

My father was not doing so well any more. I took off on June 16 and took Theresa with me and we went to visit him in the Hospital in Wichita Falls. They removed a large hernia in his bowels, but the cancer seemed to be catching up with him. I returned home June 18.

We opened the Lake Meredith Aquatic and Wildlife Museum this month. It had three large aquariums and LaNelle Poling's dioramas, and other exhibits.

On July 4, the 200th anniversary of the United States, we had a big party and fireworks at Sanford Yake. Eleanor arrived early enough to help celebrate with us. She went with us on the ninth when we all returned to Wichita Falls. Dad was up, and fixed hot cakes for us all on the tenth.

Beginning on the 21st of July I spent every wednesday at the Boy Scout camp near Mobeetie, Texas. My job was to give various merit badges to the boys, mostly to do with nature study.

On September 10 we made another trip to Wichita Falls. Aunt Ruth had told us that she had made arrangements to have Roberta's paintings exhibited at the Memorial Auditorium, but when we arrived, there was no such arrangement. This was the first sign we had that Aunt Ruth was beginning to suffer from Alzheimer's disease.

On the 18th we arrived in Wilber, Nebraska where we visited with Bertha McJunkin, John Zwonecek, Clara Jewell and other relatives and found the graves of many of Roberta's ancestors. At the library in Wilber we found printed biographies of many of Roberta's ancestors. At a restaurant, Theresa lost her first baby tooth while eating a piece of lettuce. We had a new room added where our garage had been, and when we returned from DeWitt, we put wallpaper on one wall.

On October 9, 1976 we were in Borger, and somehow Johnny became separated from us. He walked about two blocks down the street and ended up in a beauty parlor where they called the police. We had to pick him up at the police station. He was never afraid during the entire time, though Roberta was terrified.

On October 27th James and Linda came in for a short visit on their way to Wichita Falls. They had recently joined the Mormon Church and were all fired up for us to join as well. Since my boss Larry Nielson was a Mormon, the idea did have some appeal, but we attended the Mormon Church, and found some of their doctrine hard to swallow. We took the entire course of study, but it only strengthened us in our attendance at the Fritch Methodist Church. I feel as if the Mormon Church has in some ways improved on typical Christianity, but like some other churches it is too much a leap of faith for me to make.

On November 25 we took another trip to Wichita Falls. Dad was not well, and though he still got around well, he had recently had several accidents and seemed somewhat confused when he went out. We returned to Fritch on the 28th. In early December, I finished A Short History of the Phillips Family, Descendants of Adam Phillips. I got it to the printers December 9th. We got it back on the 16th and mailed out copies all across the country.

On February first, we drove to Lubbock, visited the Sorleys and continued on the second to Wichita Falls. We found Dad weak, depressed, and with some pain in his back, but otherwise alright. We returned home on the fourth. On February 11th Mama called and said that Dad had fallen and broken his arm. He had gone to mail a letter, and forgotten his cane, slipped in front of the Kemp Library and broken his arm. Dad went into the Nursing home after his hospital stay. Mama spent much of her time there visiting and caring for him.

In March, 1977 I attended training in Lawton Oklahoma, Albuquerque, and the Grand Canyon. On the trip to Grand Canyon, I had a layover in Phoenix and got to visit with Eleanor.

On April 2, 1977 we left for Wichita Falls. We found Dad to be bedfast for the most part, and unable to get out of bed without help. He could only take liquids and had to be fed these. Aunt Irma, Uncle Claude, and Ross Campbell arrived in the evening. We helped all we could with Dad and cleaned out the sheds on the back of the small lot.

On April 16th we made another trip to Wichita Falls. Dad's arm had not healed properly, and he was in Lane's nursing home. We visited Clovis, Garland, and Susan Russell. My mother called on April 25th to tell us that Dad was failing even more, and now had kidney failure to add to his other problems.

On May 21, Mama called to tell us that Arthur Phillips had died in Hico. I called Larry, took the day off, and drove to Wichita Falls. We picked Mama up and drove on to Hico the following day. We ate at the Wares and returned to Wichita Falls. Dad was some better while we were there. We returned to Wichita Falls on June 29th on news from Mama that Dad was not expected to live very much longer and wanted to see the children before he died. Aunt Ruth Claypool was in the same nursing home where Dad was. Pat Runge, Aunt Ruth's daughter came in from Wyoming while we were there.

Dad died on July 4, 1977. We picked James and family up at the Airport at 10PM. On July 5th Aunt Velma and Uncle Roy came up for the Funeral. They stayed with Bob and Jeanne Gant. The funeral was July 6th. The next couple of days James and I helped Mama clean up the attic and other areas of the house.

On July 12, James called with information on Adam's father from Corinne Philips of Jacksonville, Florida. Adam Philips was the son of Reuben Phillips who died in Oglethorpe County Georgia. With this new Information, I began more intense genealogy researches.

On August 13, 1977 Roberta and I moved into our new bedroom, giving Johnny our old room. On August 30th Theresa started school at Fritch Elementary School.
In September Eleanor arrived from Wickenburg. She brought her new pickup camper, and took Roberta and Theresa camping with her. She left on the 22nd, and Mama arrived the same day from Wichita Falls. She remained until the 25th. From Fritch she went on to Oklahoma, Nebraska, Colorado, Arizona, and visited three spots in Texas, all to visit relatives.

Aunt Ruth Claypool had been failing for some time, and now moved into the Clampitt Retirement club in the old Marchman Hotel in Wichita Falls. Mama moved in with her, and they shared a double room, though Mama maintained her own home on 14th street also. By mid October, it was becoming obvious to everyone that Aunt Ruth had Alzheimer's Disease. On October 22 we made another trip to Wichita Falls, the first since my father died. We found all doing nicely, except that Aunt Ruth was failing mentally.

On October 31st I left for training in Albuquerque, New Mexico. We were trained in Library Operations. Roberta had been taking macrame training beginning in mid October, and continued through Mid November.

Johnny was now into a dinosaur stage in which he learned the names of many dinosaurs, and something of earth history. On November 17th I was elected president of the Hutchinson County Genealogical Society.

We left Fritch November 23rd for Thanksgiving at Wichita Falls. Eloise Benson, Mama's best friend came over and ate with us on Thanksgiving the 24th. Aunt Ruth was badly confused when we visited her at Wood's Nursing Home. Eleanor was married in Early December to Huber Foster.

On December 14th Ed Day, Larry Nielson and I began excavating a slab-lined cyst above McBride Canyon. It was of Panhandle Aspect age, or about 500 to 1000 years old.

On December 23rd we drove to Wichita Falls to spend Christmas with Mama. We visited Aunt Ruth in the nursing home and found her unable to carry on a good conversation with us. Mama's friend Eloise Benson will enter the Nursing home after Christmas. Early in January, 1978 we were all sick with colds or flu. Johnny was especially bad with a temperature of 104 degrees.

On January 29th I sent my book "Phillips Family Papers" to Frank Rademacher for publication, first in his Phillips newsletter and then as a separate booklet.

On February third, our pastor at the Fritch United Methodist Church, Brother Vernon Willard died. He was 65 years old. He had been especially good to our children, taking them to the dairy queen for treats and visiting with them.

On February 18th we went to the Library in Amarillo. Johnny somehow wandered out and we had to pick him up at the Amarillo Police station, the way we had to do previously when he was lost in Borger.

On April 2, I flew out of Amarillo to Phoenix and on to Tucson where James and Linda met me at the plane. They were in a natural childbirth class and I went with them to that. They took me to my motel room on the 3rd after spending the night at their house. From the fourth through the seventh I attended the Southwestern Interpreters conference. While at this conference, I had a portrait painted of Roberta by an artist in the hotel.

James called me at the Marriott and told me that Nathaniel Joshua Phillips son of James and Linda Phillips was born April 7, 1978 in Tucson, Arizona. He was named for Joshua Burtz and Nathaniel Temple, two of his ancestors. On April 8th we picked Mama up. On the 9th James took me to the airport and by 2:05 I was home.

June 7, 1978 Eleanor and Huber Foster, the newlyweds, came for a visit. We all liked Huber as he was easy going and knowledgeable. They stayed for a few days and we had a good visit. On the 16th we took a trip to Wichita Falls, Fort Worth where we visited the zoo, and the Botanical Gardens, Kaufman and Gray's Prairie and found someone who could show us where Peede was. We returned to Wichita Falls on the 24th. During this time, the daily temperatures were over 100 degrees everyday. On the 25th it was 110! Temperatures at night dropped to around 90. We returned to Fritch on the 28th. Aunt Ruth was better this time as was Eloise who had a new home.

I had been secretary of the Lions club this year, and I relinquished my materials to John Houston on July 8th. That evening Mama, Aunt Velma, and Uncle Roy came in for a visit on their way back from Aunt Irma's in Ordway, Colorado. Mama brought back many items which belonged to her parents which Aunt Irma had.

We received a phone call from James on August 21st stating that in December he and Linda and family were transferring to Hill Air Force Base in Utah. They were excited about the move. When we called Tucson on September 2nd, James said that the transfer would be in October and that they were to Enter On Duty October 8th. Mama called on the 28th and told us that James and Linda had bought a five bedroom house in Utah.

On September fifth Ed, Paula, and I started school at West Texas State University, auditing a course on Southwestern Archeology. Roberta began an art class at Frank Phillips college. She was working on a study of Bigfoot in her spare time. On October 14th Roberta displayed 14 paintings at Frank Phillips College.

Ed Day started a class on the Archeology of the Texas Panhandle at Frank Phillips College in Borger on November 2nd. It met once a week. Roberta continued her art classes.

Mama moved out of the house at 1004 14th and into an apartment in the building where Aunt Ruth used to have an apartment. It was close to the store and within easy walking distance of the church. We made a trip to visit Mama in her new apartment beginning November 22nd. We helped move some things over to the apartment from the house. On the 23rd, Thanksgiving, we picked Eloise up at her house and brought her to the apartment for the noon meal. The house on fourteenth street was rented out, and Mama was in the process of selling it to the Times and Record News. We had lived in this small one bedroom house since April of 1948. We returned to Fritch on the 26th.

Early in December the Park Staff was informed that Bill Dyer was transferring (being transferred would be more precise). He went to Santa Fe. We got in his place John Higgins from Chickasaw Recreation Area in Oklahoma. Ed, Paula and I continued our classes at West Texas State University. Ed gave his last class on the Archeology of the Texas Panhandle on December 14th.

On December 22nd, we left Fritch, headed for Wickenburg. We spent the night in Gallup, New Mexico. We visited Petrified Forest on the 23rd and headed south to Phoenix. There had recently been flooding, and the roadway was partly washed away near Phoenix, but we arrived in Wickenburg at 4PM. They have a nice new trailer house in a scenic location just off the highway. We opened presents December 25th. James, Linda, and Mama called us from Utah while we were there. We celebrated Theresa's birthday on the 26th. She was seven years old.
We left Wickenburg on Theresa's birthday the 27th and drove to Tucson where we visited the Arizona Sonora Desert Museum. On the way across New Mexico and Texas, we stopped at Guadelupe Mountains National Park and Carlsbad Caverns National Park. We got home at 6:30 on December 29th.

John Higgins came in the last of January. He had been a real take charge individual at one time, but had recently had heart trouble and was not so perky, though still knowledgeable. Theresa was now in the girl scouts, and in February, Roberta took her around to sell girl scout cookies. On February 23rd we went to Wichita Falls. We visited with everybody on the 24th and returned on the 25th. Aunt Ruth was better when she was with other people and away from the nursing home. On the 27th there was a multiple drowning with four victims. These drownings occur at most lakes, and are usually caused by too much alcohol. This was no exception. Not only was alcohol involved, but many other judgement errors were committed resulting in the deaths of two men and two women.

In March 1979, Meeks Etchison and Beverly Schmidt came in to look for sites to excavate with the YCC students. We selected the South Ridge Site near the Ranger Station area.

On April 11th, 1979 a huge tornado struck Southwestern Wichita Falls, destroying many homes. It just missed the nursing home where Aunt Ruth was, but tore Clovis and Garland's house up pretty bad. None of our relatives were hurt.

Theresa and Johnny came down with Scarlatina during April and missed some school, but were not uncomfortable with the rash.

Mama went in late may to help Aunt Velma who had been sick, but ended up in the hospital herself in Rockdale, Texas suffering from her hiatal hernia. Aunt Velma had a perforated ulcer. I called James and found that Linda's mother had just had open heart surgery.

I continued with my job, working with scout groups, school groups, clubs, regular tours of Alibates Flint Quarries, nature walks, off site programs, and day to day paperwork. We began our regular season on Memorial Day as usual and continued tours on a regular basis until Labor Day. After Labor Day tours were by reservation only.

July fourth we had another fireworks demonstration at the lake which was very well attended. On July 12 we left for Wichita Falls. Jeanne Gant was very sick. She had been a smoker and it had damaged her heart. She tried to quit, but this caused severe edema which was also life threatening. 1980 was a bad year for our family. Bob Gant and Garland Russell both passed away. Roberta began treatments for Mental Illness which helped her considerably. Aunt Velma and Uncle Roy moved to Wichita Falls, but Aunt Velma had terminal cancer and soon was involved with chemotherapy which made her violently ill. Aunt Ruth continued to decline and was soon bedfast. In spite of all the bad news, there was joy also. Adam David Phillips son of James and Linda Phillips was born April 5, 1980 in Sunset, Utah.

Meeks Etchieson was employed by the Bureau of Reclamation in Amarillo and helped us with a number of archeology projects this year, the major one being the mapping of the Alibates Ruin. In October 1980, I began teaching the sunday school class at church. The first series I taught was "Archeology and the Bible".

1980 and 1981 were years in which I surveyed a number of the archeological sites around Lake Meredith. Ed and I visited over 150 sites during this time. On May 18, 1981 We began a shoreline survey of Lake Meredith. Ed Day, Meeks Etchieson, Mary Barger, and I were on the survey team. This was a walking survey in which we searched for any remnants of previous occupations around the shoreline of the lake, and was impaacted by shoreline erosion. My main job was to identify the fauna and flora of the area. This survey lasted about a week, but a large publication resulted from the work which proved valuable in increasing knowledge of the area.

Johnny began piano lessons, and progressed quickly. His teacher was frustrated since Johnny had both the ability to read the music and the ability to play it by ear. He progressed quickly, but his dyslexia kept him from doing as well as otherwise might be expected. His teacher was Mrs. Billie Simmons. I continued teaching Sunday School in 1982 and 1983, teaching sessions on the History of Christianity, the History of Methodism, and Evolution and Creation.

Aunt Ruth Claypool died on April 5, 1984. We went to the funeral in Wichita Falls. Others attending the funeral were Dale Russell, Clovis Russell, Henry and Hazel Hall, Lynn and Bob Mohrs, Ralph and Jeanne Claypool, Allan Gant, David and Anna Gant, Elisha and Jenifer Mohrs, Amber Gant, and Pat and John Runge. Uncle Roy Ogletree helped us move Aunt Ruth's recliner into Mama's apartment. We stayed until April 8th, celebrating a somewhat subdued anniversary.

On Easter Sunday, April 22, 1984 Johnny joined the Fritch Methodist church. I was now the Lay Leader for the church. Our Lady pastor Kimberly (Kim) Poole had appointed me to this position. Beginning in April I taught a session in sunday school on comparative religions. When our next Preacher Brother Bob Brown was on vacation, I preached the sermon from Isaiah 66:6 " The voice of the Lord"

Theresa now went into the rabbit business in a big way. She had a rabbit which we named Jumping Jehosephat (Jumpy for short). He was a LARGE California Rabbit and extremely tame. The children at church enjoyed him during the easter egg hunt. At this time, she had a lop rabbit with floppy ears and several others. In May 1984 Theresa's friend Kathy Jones gave her a kitten. It was

Black and White and we named it Boots. Our dog Clio was now getting older. She was still friendly, but not quite as active. We had a cat Spunky also, so we had quite a menagerie.

On July 5 we made a trip to Wichita Falls. During our stay we heard Art Linkletter speak at the First Baptist Church about his daughter's death from drug overdose. We returned home on July 12, leaving Johnny at his grandmothers. When I was back, I worked on getting Dad's autobiography ready for photocopying. We returned to Wichita Falls on August 14th to pick Johnny up. I had been working on the history of the Wichita Indians and Wichita Falls, and continued at the Wichita Falls Libraries. We returned home on the 19th. Mama came with us. On the 20th we called James. Adam's broken collarbone was better. Mama continued on to Ordway to visit Aunt Irma.

On September 2nd, we went to the Tri-state Fair in Amarillo. Theresa got another lop rabbit. This was the year that Theresa became interested in BOYS. I continued teaching Sunday School, giving a session on the twelve apostles.

On September 10, 1984 I left for Albuquerque. I attended a class on Museum cataloging. In the evenings I went to the Albuquerque Genealogy library and studied Family History. I returned home on September 14th, James 40th birthday. On September 24th, Brother Bob Brown and I made five copies of Dad's Autobiography on the Church Xerox machine.

We went to Wichita Falls on October 12th. On the 13th, we packed all Mama's things at the apartment. Uncle Roy Ogletree came over and helped us pack and we finally got everything in by 4PM. Johnny and I were in the U-haul, while Mama and Theresa rode with Roberta in the Pontiac. The U-haul truck broke down in Clarendon and Roberta didn't notice I was missing. Johnny and I spent the night in a motel. A mechanic came in the following day and got us back on the road. We took Mama's refrigerator off the truck, and then on the 15th, we continued on to Ordway. I got her unloaded at Aunt Irma's house and then took the bus back from Rocky Ford. The snow slowed us down on the way home, and I didn't arrive home until 9PM October 17th.

For Thanksgiving we went to Ordway, where we met James and Family. We had a good visit both with James and family as well as Aunt Irma, Uncle Claude, Lula May, Francis, Ross, Pat, and a number of Lula May's children and grandchildren. While we were there, the water which has selenium in it caused Johnny and I to become sick. We returned November 25th. The water at Ordway made me sick, and during December I continued sick off and on for a number of days.

I continued teaching Sunday School, with a series of lessons on Old Testament characters.

January 1985 was colder than usual, and on the 31st school had to be closed. It was back in session on February first, though the temperatures that morning were 2 degrees below zero. On the 6th we got in Chris Lintz Doctoral Dissertation on <u>Architecture and Community Variability within the Panhandle Aspect Phase of the Texas Panhandle.</u> On February 20, 1985 I found Andrew Bradshaw in Marshall County Mississippi on the 1850 census. This was the tying up note to prove Andrew Bradshaw's ancestry.

On March 2, 1985 We made a trip to Ordway. Uncle Henry was supposed to come in on March 7th, but he never showed up. We later found that they had started, but that he was beginning to suffer from Alzheimer's Disease, and couldn't find the way. We returned home on March 8th. Johnny took a spell at this time of riding long trips on his bicycle. Some of these trips were up to 15 miles in length. I began working on some columns for the newspaper this month, but they were not continued for very long.

March 31 was Palm Sunday. Theresa gave the opening and Johnny was a singer in the program. We all came down with the stomach flu in early April. On towards the end of the month, Roberta painted the ceiling in the living room. In May, I began a sunday school lesson series on The Prophets.

On June 29th we began our vacation. We camped the first night near Ruidosa New Mexico, and the second night in Tucson. We arrived in Wickenburg on July first at 10:30AM. I checked on the Bradshaw Mountains in the Wickenburg Library and found that they had some information, but not as much as I had, so I agreed to send them more information. It got up to 115 degrees in the daytime. We left on July 3rd and ate in Flagstaff. After we left Flagstaff, we began to have car trouble, and not realizing it was vapor lock, we had the engine worked on which only made it worse. We spent the night in the Forest Service camp just outside Grand Canyon National Park. We had our car worked on two more times, before finally getting to Ordway on July 6th, where we remained visiting everyone until the 15th.

On September 11th, 1985 our cat Spunky was run over on the highway near the Park Headquarters. I saw her as I was going out on tour, and called Roberta to pick her up and bury her. When Roberta picked her up, she meowed, so Roberta took her to the Vet, where he fixed her up. She later had a litter of kittens.

I taught a session on Methodist beliefs in Sunday School.

In 1986 we moved Mama to Fritch, where she got an apartment near the Dairy Queen. We had gotten a VCR and the VCR rental was in the same complex, so we often rented videos while we visited Mama. There was a swiming pool, and the kids loved to swim, so they frequented the apartments just for that reason. It was a good time. We could visit anytime we wanted and were often there five or six times a week.

In June 1987 I went to Lake Fryer and took part in the Courson Archeological Project and the Texas Archeological Society Field School. I was in the lab identifying what was brought in from the dig. In August James came down from Utah, we loaded Mama into another U Haul, and took her back home with him.

In October Midge Savage and I gave the first-ever Dinosaur Days program at the Fritch Museum. We got posters, specimens from West Texas State University, dinosaur quilts, dinosaur models, dinosaur calendars, and other appropriate displays, and wrote a letter to the schools, The schools turned out in large numbers and I talked daily tuesday through friday for the entire month of October.

On October 10th (Saturday) we had our Take Pride in America Lakeshore cleanup. I was the principle organizer of this event. Hundreds of boy and girl scouts, campfire girls and boys, and other organizations turned out and we picked up tons of trash.

I continued teaching Sunday School, with a lesson on Philemon. On October 29th we ran the vegetational transects on the north side of the lake at Plum Creek, Devil's Canyon and Big Canyon. On Halloween, Theresa went off to Wichita Falls to compete in a band competition. We had the house all decorated and had several trick or treaters come by.

Johnny had gotten a computer and video games and during this time he was constantly playing with these. he went into River Road School in Amarillo to try out for the Tri-state band and made first chair tuba.

On November 26th, 1987 (Thanksgiving) we drove to Norman Oklahoma where Jack, Sharon, Eleanor, and Huber were then living. They fixed turkey, baked potatoes, sweet potatoes, waldorf salad, mixed vegetables, dressing, gravy, and had wine and pepsi. For dessert there was pistachio pudding and pumpkin pie. On the 27th Huber took us out to eat at Picadilly cafeteria and in the evening to Longneckers for hamburgers. We looked at Jack's slides in the evening.

We returned home on the 28th and on the 29th I gave the sermon on King David. Mama was at James in Utah, but she was not feeling very well. She was nearly bedfast, and had to be waited on much of the time. She was also having trouble with her eyes and had implanted contacts. Theresa was now into boys in a big way. Her boyfriend was Red Rogers from Borger. In the evenings she would often talk for hours on the phone, laughing, talking, giggling, and having fun. I was really into Texas and New Mexico history at this time, and was reading everything I could find and taking notes on everything. In the middle of December we had a nice snow. Eleanor had given us a Video Player (VCR) and we often bought movies to watch on cold and snowy days. On December 16th it dropped to five below zero. We had to let our pipes run to keep them from freezing.

On December 17th I was called out to take some people to Vernon. We had a hunter out, who had failed to return, and we had called in dog handlers to track him, but they had had no luck, so Chuck Clark of the maintenance division and I drove them on the ice slick roads the 200 miles to Vernon. They finally found the body on the Kritser ranch, perhaps a twenty mile walk from where he started.

We had a big christmas dinner on December 24th. Theresa's friend Monica McIntosh came over and we fixed turkey, dressing, mashed potatoes, zucchini squash, cooked cabbage, and cooked onions. Johnny fixed a lemon souffle for dessert. We opened our presents after supper. We woke up Christmas morning to a White Christmas, the first we had for several years.

On December 29th I took some of my artifacts and heirlooms up to the museum for display. We filled about five of the seven cases, and Wilda Page filled the other two with some of her things. Johnny was becoming interested in family history and could recite his ancestors back for four or five generations.

On January 5th, 1988 we took Theresa and Johnny out of school and took them into Borger where we got their Social Security cards. The new requirements for Income Tax required that they have them. On January 8th, Midge Savage and I worked up a postcard display for the museum, using all the old postcards from the old trunks.

Midge and I began to work up displays for our Rare and Endangered Species program in March. We visited the Big Texan Steakhouse and Bob Lee promised us some specimens. The Big Texan is a large restaurant on Interstate Highway 40 East of Amarillo, and for floor displays, they had stuffed mammals. On January 23rd 1988, we drove into Amarillo Civic Center where Johnny played his tuba in the All Region Band Concert. Johnny had a solo part and did very well. Theresa had broken up with Red Rogers and Haley Mayberry was her boyfriend.

February turned off cold again, with temperatures down near zero again. We talked to James on the phone and found that he was moving to Marquette Michigan. Mama was unsure whether to move with him or to come back to Texas. We borrowed $650 from Buster Hodges at the bank and bought Theresa a car; an old Suberu.

The church youth sold pizza and on the 22nd, Johnny sold 64 by himself as a project to raise money for a sunday school class trip. February 27th we set up our Rare and Endangered Species Program at the Museum. A Mr. Dixon of Borger loaned us some large cages and over 100 rare birds. We had displays, animal mounts, skins, posters, pictures, and all kinds of exciting things on display.

In March, the classes poured into the museum and I was busy nearly every day giving programs and answering questions. I talked to over 3000 people during the month. On March 17th, the roads were Icy and the wind was blowing, but we left for Norman. It cleared up nicely after we reached Oklahoma. We stayed until the 20th and then returned home. Roberta had been having trouble with high blood pressure, and was taking medicine for it. We had a large tree planting on the 29th at Plum Creek in which we set out 250 saplings.

Early in April, we had a wet slushy snow which melted nearly as fast as it fell. On the second, Theresa met a new boy, Jeff Younger. On the 6th Roberta and I celebrated our 20th wedding anniversary. On the 10th I was honored with a plaque naming me as <u>Museum Supporter of the Year</u> for the Lake Meredith Aquatic and Wildlife

Museum. On April 11th James and Mama came in from Utah, and on the 12th we moved Mama into the University Park Nursing Center, near Clovis Russell's home. This was a moderately nice facility with friendly staff, situated on a slow side street with pretty lawns all around and nice trees. She was in pretty good shape, but just felt as if she was too big a burden for James and family. Clovis said we were welcome to visit and stay at her place any time. On April 27th, Theresa and Jamie Collette were out practicing driving in Theresa's Subaru and while trying to adjust their seat belts, they struck a parked car, demolishing Theresa's car. Nobody was hurt.

In May Theresa got together a flower project for school. She ended up with over 60 identified specimens, a new record for Fritch High School biology classes. May 7th was Take Pride in America, and once again we had a big turn out and lots of trash picked up. On May 9th we hired Donna Otto to work up our Museum Collections. To work with her we hired Kathy Balser and Steve Schumate. Theresa got her driver's license on May 13. On May 17 Ed Day, Keith Taylor and I went to Capulin Mountain to help them with their Seasonal Training Program. The same day, Johnny was proclaimed outstanding band member of the Fritch High School Band.

May was a busy time for school groups and off site programs too, with tours, off sites, and a visit to Palo Duro Canyon. On the 20th we made a trip to Wichita Falls to visit Mama. Mama was much improved and getting about nicely.

In June we continued our cataloging project, and by the 11th we had cataloged over 40,000 artifacts. Theresa and I went to Lake Fryer and worked on the archeology dig there. Theresa worked on Courson D. under Joan Few and I worked on Courson B under Meeks Etchieson and Jim Couzzouart. This was a Plains Village Ruin, perhaps somewhat earlier than ours at the National Monument, and dated perhaps from 1000 AD to 1450 AD. The houses weren't as well built, but the artifacts were similar.

We found out on the 24th that my cousin Pat Runge had terminal cancer. She lived in Wyoming and was only 57 years old. She died in just a few days.

The summer season was well under way by this time. Keith Taylor was our Alibates Seasonal and being from Houston he was not familiar with wildlife. There was a large Rattlesnake which enjoyed coiling up on the trail and after a couple of encounters, Keith killed it, which is a no-no in a National Monument.

On August 1, 1988 Johnny and I went on a trip. We visited Camargo, Oklahoma where Mama lived when young, and on to Wichita Falls where we had a brief visit with Mama. We spent the night in Arlington and visited with my Cousin Marjorie Phillips Gunn. I visited the Fort Worth Genealogy Library on the third and on the fourth I drove to Kaufman County and did some research there. On the fifth I visited the Dallas Library. During this time, Johnny was seeing the sights at Six Flags and taking in the Wet and Wild Water Park. We spent the night in Stephenville, and I drove down to see Donald. He was doing pretty well, still working for the Florist who had bought out the Wares. On the sixth we returned to Fritch, stopping for another short visit with Mama on the way.

During this summer I made a survey of the vegetation around perhaps 75 gas wells. The wells in question were on Lake Meredith property, but had recently changed hands, so they were required to make a "Plan of Operations" which included an Environmental Survey. I had Kathy Balser type up my list of edible and useful plants onto the computer, and then worked on revising it. Steve Schumate indexed it for me. Donna Otto and I visited Panhandle Plains Historical Museum on the 25th and surveyed all our artifacts in storage there.

In Mid August, James and family moved to Marquette, Michigan.

On September 16th, we went to Wichita Falls for a visit. We arrived at about 2:15 and Mama told us that Clovis wanted us over for supper. We took Mama over about 5:30 and had a good meal. We returned her to the nursing home at 8:15. We spent the night at Clovis House and had breakfast and lunch there before going home the following day.

On September 21st, Midge Savage and I went to the Geology Department at West Texas State University where we picked up some display materials for our Dinosaur Days program in October.

Theresa was now seeing Jeff Younger on a more steady basis since she and Haley Mayberry had had a fight and broken up.

On September 29th we sent in our catalog cards for our collection. We had cataloged over 100,000 artifacts.
In October we had our Dinosaur Days program at the Museum. It was a huge success with lots of classes in to learn about dinosaurs. It was also a busy month at

Alibates Flint Quarries, and Ed and I had lots of tours there as well as the museum programs. On October 31st I left for Albuquerque where I attended the regional interpreters conference.

On November 12th I began putting my notes in the computer on the Indian and Spanish History of the Texas Panhandle, and On the 24th we left for Norman for Thanksgiving. Johnny and I slept at Jacks while Roberta and Theresa stayed with the Fosters.

On December 3, 1988 we learned that Linda had a nervous breakdown and had returned to Utah with the kids. James would have to stay in Michigan until his year was up and then return. This had happened in the middle of November, and we hadn't known it before. Linda stayed with her sister in Utah.

Theresa continued seeing Jeff on a regular basis. He came over once or twice a week, usually on Friday evening. They would go out to a show and a meal and then return. If Jeff wasn't there, Theresa was always "bored" and if he arrived later than she thought proper, she was mad.

For Christmas, Johnny had received the game "Dungeons and Dragons" and now he insisted we play it often. It turned out to be quite educational, and increased his vocabulary considerably.

On January 23rd, I had a Physical Examination by Dr. Muthalli at the Texas Tech Clinic in Amarillo. I had a blood workup which showed my Cholesterol level was 286. He suggested I go easy on red meat and dairy products.

On February 4, 1989 Johnny's band took first division which gave them the privilege of going on to Austin to compete in state tryouts.

I had been working for some time on the park insect collection, and now I had reports back from Texas A&M on identification. I began to compile a list of insects. Richard Howard of Amarillo College now began to help me with the identification and did some excellent work, both on identification and labeling.

On February 17, 1989 My Uncle Henry Hall died in Goliad Texas. He was 78 years old. He had been failing gradually, and finally passed away. Theresa was doing a cartoon for the Fritch Newspaper called "Edgar Eagle" which featured an Eagle (Fritch H.S. mascot) and other characters including Freedom the dove which had hatched during our Rare and Endangered Species program in March.

The Rare and Endangered Species Program began again in March with much the same success as before. In mid march we had linoleum installed in our kitchen to replace the worn out carpet. It really brightened up the room!

On March 18th we visited Wichita Falls. We spent the night in Trade Winds Motel and returned on the 19th. On the 23rd we called James who told us that he had sold his house and would move into an apartment in May. Roberta had begun painting Civil War Soldiers for people across the country, and sent off two paintings near the end of march. I was busy at work with the upcoming Lakeshore Cleanup and Archeological Awareness Week.

Jeff Younger was by this time a regular guest at our house, often spending the night, so he and Theresa could see more of each other. He had to work during the week and often put in 20 or more hours of overtime at his job, so they had little time together during the week, though he often came by mid week if he didn't have to work overtime. On April 8th I went to the Scout Skills show with Midge Savage. We had reptiles, amphibians, and animal skins which fascinated the scouts. On the 15th we planted 187 trees at McBride Canyon with the help of 55 scouts both boy scouts and cubs. I took 42 of them on an Alibates Tour afterwards. Our lakeshore cleanup was progressing nicely. By this time I had assigned all the areas, placed the troops, and gotten lists out to the participants. Alicia Reban, from Texas Lakeshore Cleanups had worked out all the prizes, food, and entertainment. April 22nd was the big day. We had about 800 boys and girls out and really cleaned things up. This was followed by our annual "Trash Bash" which was food, prizes, and entertainment.

May was a busy month in 1989. Many school groups showed up, some of them with over 100 students. Ed and I divided them up into groups of up to 80 apiece and took them into the flint quarries. May 6th was the Junior-Senior Prom. Jeff took Theresa and Jamie Collette and Monica McIntosh went with them. There was a banquet at the Borger Country Club, followed by the dance at Fritch Middle School. It was an all night affair with a breakfast at the middle school the following morning. Theresa and Jeff came home and said they would go to Sunday School and church with us, but went to sleep. We got them up in time to go to the 11:00 service where Johnny sang the solo.

We were busy with tours, off site programs, and museum

groups the entire month. The students and the teachers are all tired by this time of the classroom, so they schedule either field trips or classroom visits, so Ed, Midge, and I were kept busy the entire month. Midge and I worked on a nature study program at the museum for June which would include reptiles, amphibians, fish, birds, and mammals.

On May 23, 1989 Eleanor, Huber, Jack, and Sharon came in from Norman. It was a short visit. Jack and Sharon camped at the lake.

Our summer season started as usual on Memorial Day. Our seasonal this year was Betty May from Stinnett. She was the Biology Teacher at the Stinnett High School. On the 31st we had Ed Benz and the Adobe Walls Indian Dancers in for a special Chamber of Commerce program to promote Alibates Flint Quarries.

On June first, Johnny left for Band Competition in Austin. He returned Sunday Evening at 6PM. On June 6th we had Charlie Williams from the Lake Meredith Marina in at the Museum to talk to the kids about fish and fishing. On June 8th I drove to Dalhart and gave nature walks at Rita Blanca Lake to the cub scout day camp. On the 9th I visited Camp M.K. Brown and Old Mobeetie. I gave a flint chipping demonstration to the scouts and made a plant list for Mobeetie. In the evening I gave a program at the Soil Conservation Service banquet at the museum in Fritch. On June 13th I gave the Reptiles and Amphibians program at the Fritch Museum. We had numerous snakes, lizards, frogs, salamanders, water dogs, toads, turtles, and other creepy crawlers for the kids to see and touch. On the 14th we had the visually handicapped children in for the same program. On the 20th it was birds and on the 27th it was mammals, each program being more heavily attended than the previous. During this month, we also had the Charles Harper Travel Display at the museum, and many were in to see this as well.

On July 3rd I traveled to Palo Duro Canyon where I gave a nature study program to 140 people in conjunction with the Panhandle Plains Historical Museum. On July 8th we had Senator Sarpaulius in for an Alibates Tour. This was another Chamber of Commerce extravaganza with the Adobe Walls Indian Dancers.

Roberta and I were now walking regularly over to the high school track, exercising and then returning. I would bathe and get ready for work, and then lead tours or give programs. We still had quite a menagerie with cats, a dog, ducks, and chickens. I spent much of my spare time reading and writing.

Beginning August 8th, 1989 Theresa, Johnny, and I took a trip to Rocky Mountain National Park. We also visited Garden of the Gods and Cave of the Winds at Colorado Springs and stopped off for a short visit with Aunt Irma Campbell at Ordway. We returned home on the 12th. We bought Theresa a new car, a 1981 Pontiac. It was a really beautiful car, but because of its love of fuel we nicknamed it "Greedy Gut".

August 19th was Howdy Neighbor Day at the Fritch City Park. Midge, William Savage, and I sat with the snakes and other displays. The kids came by the hundreds to handle the snakes and see the touch and feel box. The following day was Charge Conference at the Fritch United Methodist Church. We found we had 48,000 of the needed $50,000 to begin our building expansion program. On the 24th Midge and I set up a Back to School display at the museum.

We were watching numerous movies on our VCR, and Jeff was over regularly. Roberta was painting and I was reading and writing, an well as collecting insects to send off for identification. James had returned to Utah in August, and they found a home in Layton, Utah. It was a happy time for all.

Midge and I were preparing for Dinosaur Days again, looking for materials and writing off for films, posters, and display materials. We had a new Park Superintendent. Pat McCrary had been in the Regional office in Santa Fe, but transferred here when John Higgins announced his retirement.

On September 16, we left for Wichita Falls. We stayed at Clovis house, but took most of our meals out. Mama was doing fine. We celebrated her 84th birthday on the 17th. On the 18th we returned to Fritch.

On the 28th we finished the Dinosaur Days display thanks to Duane Gall who loaned us his tropical plants. We also had a 18 foot long "dinosaur" in the form of the Stinnett dragon for the Halloween parade and fun house.

October was as usual a busy month. School groups were in nearly every day, and we also had off site programs and Alibates Tours. On the 8th, James came by for a short visit on the way to Wichita Falls. We found out that Aunt Irma was suffering from cancer and on the 12th she died.

On October 27th we had the Texas Archeology Society meeting at the Park Inn in Amarillo. I attended and listened to as many of the talks as I could. We also met with representatives of the Texas Historical Commission who were not happy with the way the National Park Service was handling its cultural resources. On the 29th the same individuals came out to the lake and we visited several sites around the area.

On November 11th I went to Canyon and gave Flint Chipping demonstrations for "Indian Days" at the Panhandle Plains Historical Museum. Theresa and Jeff painted the house, and had done the North, East, and West sides by this time. I spent some time typing up some letters Dad had written between 1922 and 1938.

We were in a period of extreme fire danger, and on the 14th we received extra fire fighters and fire trucks from New Mexico to help in "pre-suppression" of fires around the area. I was spending much of my time off at the Amarillo College Library searching for life history information on insects of our area. I also read in some of the classics.

On November 23rd, we went to Norman for Thanksgiving. Theresa and I slept at Jacks and Johnny and Roberta at Eleanors. On the 24th Jeff and Larry came in and we had pizza at Eleanor's apartment. We returned home on the 25th. Theresa won second place for her art work at the state level competition.

On January 7th we made a trip to Wichita Falls. Mama was doing well. We saw Janna and family and spent the night at Clovis house. We heard the president of the nursing home talk in the evening of the 8th. We spent the following night at Clovis also, and returned home on the 9th.

On January 29, 1990 I made a trip to Lubbock where I left some of my insects for identification and checked more information for common names and life history data.

On the 20th of February there was a good snow, which continued for some time. Janet Ferguson the new museum director and I began plans for the rare and endangered species program. I took a course at Frank Phillips College this winter on the American Sign Language for the deaf.

On March 12, 1990 Theresa voted for the first time in an election, and as a democrat, voting on the Democratic ticket. March 14th was the graduation banquet for the sign language class and Roberta and I attended. On the 16th I worked up my application for the position at Chickasaw Recreation Area. March 17th was the Boy Scout Camporee at Plum Creek. I arrived in the area at 7:30 to find that the scoutmaster had fallen and been rushed to the hospital the night before. I had all the people lined up and we went ahead with our Nature Merit Badge program.

On April 8th Theresa and Jeff visited with Eddie Marcum about their wedding plans. The date was set for August 4th, the anniversary of her Grandma Fosters wedding to Ed Safarik. On the 10th Theresa and I voted democratic. We had a call from Jack on the 24th stating that Huber had died quietly in his sleep. He was 87 years old. I spent the rest of the month working on the museum inventory. April 28th was the annual lakeshore cleanup. I ate breakfast at Mullinaw Canyon the next morning with Johnny Graham and his scouts.

May was busier than usual if that is possible. We had over 850 kids through the flint quarries plus numerous other tours and groups. On May 24th Jeff was laid off at Celanese. The subcontractor he was working for let all but five of his 185 people go, and Jeff was among them. On May 31, Theresa graduated from High School. We all attended the ceremony.

On June 3rd Johnny went to Austin for Band Competition. June fifth it was 108 degrees. Tours were underway. We had Betty May back as a seasonal and during the summer we had two volunteers who helped us. Patsy Sims and Jonathan Pierce. On the 18th Mama fell and broke her hip. James flew in from Utah to be with her and on the 22nd I drove down. I stayed the first night with Uncle Roy Ogletree and then when James left I spent the nights of the 23rd and 24th at Clovis house. By the time I left, Mama was up and walking with the help of a walker. We took her back to the nursing home. I left the morning of the 25th. There was a fire raging out of control on the north side of the river in Plum Creek and Big Canyon, so I spent the next few days with little sleep.

Huber had left us some money, so we spent much of July replacing carpet, fixing our carport, and buying things for the wedding. It had been a hot dry summer, but finally on July 20th it rained nearly three inches in Fritch and one or two inches in other areas.

Theresa and Jeff got their marriage license on the 20th also. On July 29th there was a wedding shower for Theresa at the church. The wedding went nicely, and

Theresa and Jeff spent their honeymoon in Amarillo. They went to a play, went horseback riding, dined out, and relaxed. Eleanor came for the wedding. They had a two bedroom house in Skellytown where Jeff had already set up housekeeping. Jack Safarik drank all the wine.

On September 15th we went to Wichita Falls to celebrate Mama's birthday. Johnny stayed home, but Jeff came along. We all shared a motel room. We returned home on the 16th. I had been having trouble with numbness in my right hand and arm, and during the last part of September I went through a number of tests including a Magnetic Resonance Imager which showed me to have Stenosis of the spine. James called on the 28th and said that Clovis could no longer take care of Mama.

We celebrated Roberta's Birthday on October first, and on the second, I entered High Plains Baptist Hospital in Amarillo for SPINAL SURGERY. The surgery went well except that I had a reaction to sublimaze which caused me to stop breathing temporarily. I went home on the 4th. It took me about six weeks of recuperation before the doctor and the National Park Service would allow me to return to work. On October 6th, Johnny won a trophy for his acting. I was allowed to return to work on November 13th.

There was some confusion as to whether Mama was to stay in Wichita Falls or move elsewhere. Clovis just couldn't handle the extra burdens so was unsure if she wanted to take care of Mama or not. On November 22nd we all made our annual trip to Norman for Thanksgiving. We returned on November 4th, with a side trip to Wichita Falls and a quick visit with Mama. On the 28th we learned that the decision had been made and we would have to move Mama to the nursing home in Borger.

On December 8th, Jeff and Theresa took their car and I took my car and we went to Wichita Falls, picked Mama up and brought her to Fritch. On the 10th we got her into the nursing home and in to see Dr. Steve Elston in Borger. We worked to get all of her checks coming into her new account at the Fritch State Bank.

The new Nursing Center was somewhat older than the one in Wichita Falls, but similar in many ways. It did lack the nice lawn around the facility, but had a well kept lawn with trees in front. We soon began learning some of the other residents. My friend Bee Holmes was also a resident there.

Our life now was actually pleasant. We could visit

Theresa and Jeff in Skellytown, and stop by to see Mama either on the way there or on the way back. We brought Mama back to our house for Christmas and had quite a party.

On the 28th, Eleanor, Jack, and Sharon came in for a visit. We learned the same day that my cousin Donald Phillips had died of complications from pneumonia. The weather was awful, and we couldn't get to the funeral, but we called Matt Ware and found that he had a nice funeral and that Matt was taking care of all the estate for us. Eleanor visited Mama at the Nursing home and said she would like to move in some time in the spring.

On January 11, 1991 we took Theresa to Frank Phillips College in Borger where she enrolled as an art major. She took two art classes, zoology, orientation, and aerobics.

Theresa went two years to Frank Phillips College and has gone on to West Texas State University to complete her degree.

In the winter of 1991, Johnny decided to join the army. The reason for this was the chance for $25,000 for college and the chance to specilize in electronics.

CERTIFICATE OF MERIT
*John Edgar Phillips

is awarded this certificate in recognition of
Honorable Mention All State

Presented at *Evening of One Act Plays*

This 19th Day of May 1989

Lydia Fowlkes

CERTIFICATE OF ACHIEVEMENT

SUPERSTAR

THIS AWARD OF DISTINCTION IS PRESENTED

To _John Edgar Phillips_

For Superior Achievement & Excellence of

Performance in *TOM JONES* and *ROOMERS*

This 14 day of May 1992

Signed _Lydia Fowlkes_

I had been given the job of Environmental Protection Specialist which is concerned with keeping the area around Oil and Gas wells clean and looking good. I have been to training in environmental compliance, spill prevention and cleanup, and use of a Geographical Information System computer.

Johnny went into the Army on September 8, 1992. He is a communications specialist. His basic training began September 8th at Fort Jackson Near Charleston, South Carolina and has continued up to the present.

[sept 26, 1992]

Dear Mom & Dad,

    I finally have enough time to tell you about what all is going on. The entire platoon is lined up to wash their clothes in 1 of 2 working washers. Perhaps I can briefly sum up what all is going on and what will hopefully happen in the near future. I spent the first four days after I left in the reception battalion going through processings, attending briefings and learning the army way. Then I was shipped three days early to basic training and I am here today.

    I met my three drill sergeants the first day. They are Drill Sergeant Stephenson, Drill Sergeant Harris, and Drill Sergeant Logan.

Drill Sergeant Harris is the most relaxed of the three. His philosophy is that if you yell all the time, the privates won't be concerned when the drill sergeants mean it. The reason he joined the army is because the judge gave him a choice: go to the army or go to jail.

Drill Sergeant Stephenson is the head drill sergeant. He was involved with the war in the gulf . He helped several Iraqis meet Allah. Drill Sergeant Stephenson is anything but even tempered. He isn't happy unless he's screaming at the top of his lungs while one of the privates is "beating his face" which means beating your face until you can do it no more. He reminds me of Dad when Dad loses his temper. The main difference is that he loses his temper about ten times a day. He is hispanic, but he sometimes talks with a Black dialect.

Drill Sergeant Logan is a Black Female. Yes, a woman. And because she is, she always tries to prove how she is tougher than any of the rest of us. When we're around her were getting smoked about half the time. (Getting smoked means doing exercises until we achieve muscle failure.) Of all drill sergeants, she is my least favorite. I want you to write me as often as you can. Get Theresa and Jeff to write me too, because Drill Sergeant Logan makes us do pushups if we don't get any mail. This is her first job as a drill sergeant, so she has something to prove.

The first day of basic training was quite challenging. We had to assemble our LCE's. An LCE looks like a very heavy duty belt with suspenders that go over your shoulders. Upon assembly I discovered that I was missing a First Aid Kit, so I informed drill sergeant Harris, and he got me another first aid kit with nothing in it. Then I asked him, "Put it on now sir?"

And he responded,
"Yea, after you beat your face. Figure out why later."

So I got down in the front leaning rest position and started doing pushups. After about 20 pushups, the drill sergeant spoke, "Get up private," He said?"

I thought he was punishing me for losing my first aid kit "Yes sir," I replied.

"I guess not. Get back into the front leaning reps!"

As I was beating my face, the drill sergeant gave the platoon a lecture over how to address a non-commissioned officer. Never call them "Sir"! If he is a drill sergeant, call him "Drill Sergeant"

Well, Its about time for my wash to be ready, so I'll have to sum up the rest of the week. Despite a few blisters, I'm in good health, I'm learning new things, i'm getting in shape, I'm getting organized. I <u>passed</u> my

P.T. test on the second try. I did 37 push ups, 66 situps, and ran 2 miles in 16:42. We are starting basic rifle marksmanship this week. I know I can handle it! And I can Hang!

    Mom was right. I am homesick. I miss my family, my home, and my former life style, but I'm all grown up now, and all in all, I'm having fun.
    Sincerely

<u>Private</u> John Edgar

RSVP
RSVP!
RSVP

3 oct 92

Dear Mom and Dad,

Today was to be an easy fun day. We were gong to go on a "fun run" and have the rest of the day for R&R, but we blew it as well as our fun weekend we had planned. While half of our platoon was on post detail, a scrimmage broke out between Private Robinson and Private Scholte. The other private tried to stope the fight, but no one told the Drill Sargent which at that time was Drill Sargent Stephenson. Because no one told him, he took away all our privileges, including getting our hair cuts in a longer style, our television privileges, our going to the PX without a Drill Sargent, and most importantly, our phone privileges. <u>I will not be able to call you until we get our privileges back</u>.

The time I'm using to write you this letter is time that I'm on "CQ" which stands for Charge of Quarters.

My shift is between 0200 and 0400. That means that I have to wake up at 0145, get ready, and walk down to the CQ desk to relieve the last shift. When my shift is over and my relief comes, then I get to go back to the barracks at 0400 and sleep the rest of the night. (Wake up is 0430!)

So far the highlights of my shift have been the drill sargent walking in to make sure that I and my partner, Private Quinones, were in line, and a phone call by some Commissioned Officer who asked for the time.

Before, I mentioned the PX. If you don't know what that is, it's like the army general store. It's where we go to get odds & ends like soap, shoe polish, envelopes, extra pt uniforms, etc. We go there about once a week. During this phase of training, we were supposed to be able to go to the PX on our own, but this incident put a stop to all that.

If you have any problems with those traveler's cheques, please write & tell.

Sorry I couldn't call.

When you send me a letter, try to include any events in the news. Remember, I'm isolated from the world as it is, but I'm still curious.

Love
Private Phillips

On October 2, Roberta got a birthday present of a puppy. It was a Lhaso Apso which is a long haired small breed.

---

21 Jun 93

Dear Mom and Dad,

I have received numerous letters from you, but haven't answered any of them; sorry about that. I'll try to write a little more often.

Don't worry about me going to Bosnia right away, but I may possibly be headed to Somalia. Someone from my platoon has already gone there.

Unless something goes wrong, I will be P.F.C. by the time you receive this letter. I was eligible to get it with 9 months in service, but the paperwork didn't go thru, so I'm still a PV2, but that's alright, I can deal with it.

I finally broke down and bought a TV, and a very good one at that. It's a Goldstar 24 inch remote control TV with a VCR built into the bottom of it. Here in Europe, It is sold for $450, but I bought it for $245 second hand. AFN or the Armed Forces Network is the only channel I get on it that I can understand. All the other channels are in German! The reception is better than cable.

Oh yeah! I passed another P.T. test, and with flying colors;
    I did 65 set ups   and
       70 push ups,   and
      ran the mile in 14:07.

I also qualified on the M 16 rifle again, shooting 34 out of 40, and I got a new badge for that, I'm not a marksman any more, I'm a Sharpshooter, so I'm doing alright.

Well, That's about all the news.

Love,
John E. Phillips

Oct 2, 1992

Dear Johnny,

Well, it is Friday evening. I have been home long enough to have eaten supper (vegetable dip) and to have watched the news.

Theresa has gone to Amarillo to get Mom a dog for her birthday - which was yesterday. She seems to be lost. It is now 7:40 and she hasn't shown up. We had cake and ice cream at Grandma Foster's yesterday. I got Mom some towels, sheets, and two new pillow cases. She also got a hooded sweatshirt and a long-sleeved pullover shirt. Theresa <u>and</u> Jeff are on a diet, so they couldn't eat any cake and ice cream. Mom helped herself pretty heavily though, and we all had a good time.

Sergeant is the preferred spelling for Sargent, in spite of the fact that you see it spelled the other way in the comics. The sergeants probably can't spell, so you won't have to do any push ups for the mistake.

Theresa and Jeff say they have written, and I wrote yesterday, so you should get several letters about the same time. I am thinking of sending your address to our cousins in North Carolina, so they could write sometimes too.

We have stayed pretty much on our diets, though Mom has bought some margarine - I guess she just can't live without it. Mom has been practicing with the bench press and has upped the weight so she is moving up to be a professional weight lifter. (She lifts 30 lbs now.)

I am scheduled to preach at church the last Sunday of the month, and then I have made them take me off all the lists of church workers while I make up my mind about going back to church.

Today I went around the lake early and across the Kritser ranch down into Big Canyon. It has been dry here since you left, and the roads had just been graded, so they were a foot deep in dust at spots. I wasn't sure I could get out, since the egress was a steep road up a rocky hill which had recently been graded, and I did slip and slide around a bit, but I came through it O.K.

In spite of the lack of rain, Big Canyon was beautiful. The big rains earlier this year have made it green and it just refuses to brownup. After frost it will cure out, and then -- **WATCH OUT!** We may have a really bad fire season.

Well, it is 8 o'clock and Theresa isn't back yet. Jeff is getting worried and wants to leave Skellytown and look along the road to see if she has had car trouble, but I suspect she just had so much to do that it is taking longer than she figured.

Mom is getting somewhat worried too, but she has Herbert out and is playing with him. We have the cats locked in your room waiting for the dog, so everything is in suspense. Pum-bum Pum bum Pum-bum Pum bum Pum bum bum bum bum bum bum bum.

We got the bad news in our staff meeting today. The Park Service budget has been cut again. This is the third year in a row that we have had this happen, but only the first time that Lake Meredith has been affected. It will probably mean that we can't fill one of our vacant positions for a while.

They have given me a new Dodge Ram pickup which is really nice. It gets good milage and is nice and clean. It only has 4000 miles on it. They have promised me a new 4-wheel drive next spring.

Well, Theresa finally called about 8:45. She said she didn't have a watch and the time caught up with her. She got Mom a purebreed - an afghan hound - no a laso apso or some such breed. She was so late getting home that they didn't bring it over tonight, but will bring it tomorrow morning. I go to Men's breakfast at the church at 8, but I expect they won't be over until after 10.

I will close and see if Mom wants to add some. Perhaps we can wait to mail it until Theresa and Jeff get here.

Love,

Dad

Dear Johnny,   Oct 7, 1992

We got another letter from you today, plus one from the base commander saying that **IF** you make it through basic, you will graduate November 11. That is only about 4 weeks. I have used up a lot of leave this year and may not be able to come for this one. We are sure proud of the way you are doing. Keep up the good work.

We also got your money. I hope you have devised a direct deposit from your paycheck to your mutual fund. That would really make it easier. Mom put it all in the savings account. Coincidently we got your previous statement. You had 156.73 balance before the deposit. This plus the $530 makes your total $686.73

You asked about the news. Most of the news is about the political races, especially the presidential race. Clinton is still **WAY** ahead. It is something like 53% to

38% to 7% ±. There are going to be three presidential debates and one vice presidential debate. Perot has been invited to the first, but there is speculation that with such a small following he will be dropped from later tussles.

He isn't entirely out of it, though. He has bought TV time and will give 30 minute segments on everything. In other news there are tornados, plane crashes, murders, and all the regular havoc which always dominates our violent country.

I don't know anything about sports, except that there is going to be a world series again this year. I don't know who the teams are.
Theresa and Jeff were still on their diet the last I heard. Theresa hardly eating, and Jeff taking it hard.

The new dog is very small and pretty quiet. The first day it barked at Pericles and Big P. let him have it. The dog has been quiet around cats ever since, though he feels that if he could just get to Herbert he could dominate him.

I am indexing the latest variation on my Phillips Family Chronicles. It is 268 pages and the index will probably be 32 pages making a 300 page document not including appendices and bibliography.

Jeff and I trimmed up the cherry tree and the rose bushes and Jeff hauled off the limbs in the pickup. They filled the back of the pickup completly.

Grandma Foster cried when she read your letter - the part about you being homesick and missing your family. She thought it was the best letter she ever read.

I will close and let Mom add some.
Love,

In November 1992, Johnny moved to Fort Gordon in Georgia for A.I.T. (Advanced Individual Training). Mama was recertified to stay in the nursing home.

The first week in December we set up my new computer at work, and loaded several programs on it to allow smooth operation. The new computer is especially powerful and will draw maps using the information in various geographical systems such as soils, geology, flora, fauna, oil and gas, archeological sites and others.

Johnny got to come home for Christmas this year, so it was a special time for all of us. We had a big Christmas and on Theresa's birthday Jack and Sharon were here from Norman to help us celebrate it.

My mother had been gradually failing for many years, and now at 87, she developed several related problems which ended up with Congestive Heart Failure on January 24, 1993. She lingered on for a week in the hospital in Pampa, but passed away January 30, 1993.

Newspaper clipping Wichita Falls Times Record News dated February 2, 1993:

Ada Maria Phillips

Ada Maria Phillips, 87, died Saturday in Pampa, Texas. Services will be at 3 p.m. Wednesday at Floral Heights United Methodist Church with the Rev. Paul Goodrich, pastor, and the Rev. Merwin Turner, associate pastor, officiating. Burial will be in Crestview Memorial Park under the direction of Hampton-Vaughn Funeral Home.

Mrs. Phillips was born Sept. 17, 1905 in what is now Dewey County, Oklahoma. She was a member of the Daughters of the American Revolution and the Texas Retired Teachers Association. She was a resident of Borger, Texas for the past two years and was a former longtime resident of Wichita Falls. She received her Bachelor's of arts degree and Master's of arts degree from the University of Texas. She taught in Miami, Texas and Wichita Falls for about 25 years. Her husband John Richard Phillips died in 1977. She was a homemaker and a member of Floral Heights United Methodist Church.

Survivors include two sons, John Wesley of Fritch, Texas, and James Richard of Salt Lake City, and five grandchildren.

Johnny flew in from Georgia, and James drove out from Utah, and we buried her next to my father at Crestview Memorial Park in Wichita Falls.

In a few months, Eleanor, Roberta's mother who had been suffering from Parkinson's disease became so bad that she asked to be placed in the nursing home. She was miserable at first, but after about three months she began to become reconciled to her condition, and although she didn't enjoy the nursing home, she at least tolerated it. She continued to improve, and made some friends.

In April 1993 we learned that Theresa was pregnant, and on December 23, 1993 our first grandchild Ashley Dawn Younger was born. Jeff was there all the way!

       7-1-2-3-5-1-1 Theresa Ann b. 27 Dec. 1971 Homestead Fl. m. 4 Aug. 1990 Jeffrey Lowell Younger Fritch, Hutchinson Co. TX
         Ashley Dawn Younger b. 23 Dec. 1993
       7-1-2-3-5-1-2 John Edgar Phillips b. 13 June 1973 Naples FL

7-1-2-3-5-2 James Richard Phillips b. 14 Sept. 1944 Long Beach, California m. Linda Kaye Porter of Ogden Utah.

       7-1-2-3-5-2-1 Cynthia Heidi Phillips b. 30 Dec. 1975 Tuscon AZ
       7-1-2-3-5-2-2 Nathaniel Joshua Phillips b. 7 Apr, 1978 Tucson, AZ
       7-1-2-3-5-2-3 Adam David Phillips b. 5 April 1980 Sunset, Utah

7-1-2-4 George Phillips b. about 1857

7-1-2-5 Jane Callie Brilla Phillips b. about 1859 m. James Madison McKee 28 November 1878

Orwood, Miss 11/8/1903

Mr A. J. P.
Peede, Tex
Dear old Bud

Will answer your letter with the girls too Cant write Much

Monday Morn Nov. 9th He is able to be up thro morn He may have a high fever this eve, but hope not Dr. has given him another through of Medicine

Well, Yes me are doing very well amd me will still make another hole more cotton than me thought Me would got 10 cents last Fri, have sold 8 willhave 3 more(.) gathered 245 bush. of good corn sold it all to one man at 50 cnts, but you see me have boys in Tex. and that makes Tex. a whole lot better. but me have me toleave here of course me hate to to leave her here but she knew me intended easing into fall(.) She said she had rather stay with Felix and of course she has that right(.) I dont never expect to try to get them to go they can use their own pleasure about it. And we think where so many million people live some are rich and some millionairs. Me think me can make some kind of a living.

Well I must go to the office mill close. Love to all as ever
Your devoted Sis
J. C. McKee

7-1-2-5-1 Walter Dean McKee b. October 13, 1879 d. July 22, 1956 m. Florence Spears

Walter and his friend Edward Beck were the first of the McKee family to come to Texas about 1900. They both went to work for Norman Phillips on the farm. A year later, his brother Will came from Mississippi. He too worked on the farm. A year later the rest of the family came to Kaufman County, Texas with the exception of the eldest daughter Lela, who had married and would not leave Mississippi.

7-1-2-5-1-1 Bennie b. 5 November 1904 Cottonwood, Texas
7-1-2-5-1-2 Clifton b. 26 August 1906 Gastonia, Texas
7-1-2-5-1-3 Ralph S. McKee b.

30 July 1908 Palmer, Texas
7-1-2-5-1-4 James U. McKee b. 7 February 1911. Forney, Texas d. 1964
7-1-2-5-1-5 Lottie McKee b. 19 February 1913 Palmer, Texas
7-1-2-5-1-6 Otis McKee b. 4 March 1914 Scurry, Texas
7-1-2-5-1-7 Winifred McKee b. 9 January 1918 Cushing, Texas
7-1-2-5-1-8 Walter McKee Jr. b. 27 August 1920 Bardwell, Texas
7-1-2-5-1-9 George McKee b. 21 December Cottonwood, Texas
7-1-2-5-1-10 Ola McKee b. 27 September 1925 Cottonwood, Texas
7-1-2-5-1-11 Lola McKee b. 27 September 1925
7-1-2-5-1-12 Billy W. McKee b. 12 July 1928 Cottonwood, TExas
7-1-2-5-2 William Harvey McKee b. May 18, 1881 d. Sept 10, 1958 m. Commentine E. Perkins 28 May 1905
    7-1-2-5-2-1 Ruby Estelle McKee b. 21 July 1906 Cushing, Texas did not marry.
    7-1-2-5-2-2 William Felton McKee b. 14 April 1908 m. 16 November 1935 Maurine Smith
        7-1-2-5-2-2-1 Jerry Wayne McKee
    7-1-2-5-2-3 Arthur Benton McKee
    7-1-2-5-2-4 Clovis McKee
    7-1-2-5-2-5 David Paul McKee - b. 31 October 1913 Prairieville, Texas m. 26 May 1940 Dorothy Kay
        7-1-2-5-2-5-1 David Paul McKee Jr.
    7-1-2-5-2-6 Annie Belle McKee b. 17 June 1915 Kaufman, Texas m. 24 December 1936 Carl White
        7-1-2-5-2-6-1 Micky Ann White m. Tom Lear. Children Ted Norman, David Wayne, Christopher Kyle, Mary Lois
    7-1-2-5-2-7 Louise Inez McKee b. 28 July 1917 d. 1 December 1938
    7-1-2-5-2-8 Earl Webster McKee

b. 20 September 1919 m. Mary Lee Hamm; children: Linda Marie, Debra Sue, Jean Lee

7-1-2-5-2-9 Jay Durward McKee b. 9 April 1923 Kaufman, Texas

7-1-2-5-3 Lela Mae McKee b. August 11, 1885 Georgia d. May 31, 1964 Panola County, Mississippi m. Felix L. Mills 11 January 1903

    7-1-2-5-3-1 Annis Quebelle Mills b. 15 December 1903 m. Burnie Tidwell

        7-1-2-5-3-1-1 Doris Kelley Tidwell b. 12 November 1926

        7-1-2-5-3-1-2 Charles Tidwell b. 5 November 1928

7-1-2-5-3-2 Elmer Leslie Mills b. 25 November 1904 m. Thelma Doris Nelson

        7-1-2-5-3-2-1 Betty Jo Mills b. 5 January 1929 m. Donald Wilson. Children: Ricky, Larry, Randy, Jimmie, Michael

        7-1-2-5-3-2-2 Reba Jay Mills b. 23 June 1931 m. Leon McMinn. Children: Leticia, Ronald, Stephen, Phyllis, Denese, Cynthia

        7-1-2-5-3-2-3 Patsy Nell b. 14 December 1938 m. Billy Carisont

        7-1-2-5-3-2-4 Leslie Wayne b. 31 December 1940 m. Nancy Griffin. Children: Leslie Scott, Allen Wayne.

7-1-2-5-3-3 Ethel Ross Mills b. 7 February 1907 Mississippi m. 1.) Coleman Cooper 2.) Herman Dugard

        7-1-2-5-3-3-1 Horace Coleman Cooper b. 12 February 1926 m. 1947 Clara Scalon

            7-1-2-5-3-3-1-1 Linda Cornelius Cooper b. 2 October 1948

            7-1-2-5-3-3-1-2

Michael Anthony Cooper b. 15 November 1948

7-1-2-5-3-3-1-3 Stephen Philip Cooper b. 12 November 1952

Horace Coleman Cooper married 2.) Ruthann Small 14 September 1963

7-1-2-5-3-3-1-4 David Clayton Cooper b. 9 June 1964

7-1-2-5-3-3-1-5 Donald Coleman Cooper b. 2 September 1966

7-1-2-5-3-3-1-6 Dana Christina Cooper b. 28 June 1968

7-1-2-5-3-4 Vivian Clyde Mills b. 20 January 1909 m. Thomas Houston Locke

7-1-2-5-3-4-1 Barbara Jean Locke b. 3 July 1936 m. Billy Glenn Haupt.

7-1-2-5-3-4-1-1 Billie Carol Haupt b. 5 November 1957

7-1-2-5-3-4-1-2 Michael Glenn Haupt b. 26 September 1965

7-1-2-5-3-5 Francis McKee Mills b. 4 August 1911 m. Milton David Childs

7-1-2-5-3-5-1 Martha Jo Childs b. 4 December 1935 m. Kelley Eugene Hutchins

7-1-2-5-3-5-1-1 Kathy Merle Hutchins b. 2 April 1957

7-1-2-5-3-5-1-2 Lisa Hutchins b. 12 January 1961

7-1-2-5-3-6 Noel Douglas Mills b. 22 December 1913 m. Mary Elizabeth Fisher.

7-1-2-5-3-6-1 Douglas Eugene b. 6 April 1937 m. Ophelia Anthony.

7-1-2-5-3-6-1-1 Jeffrey Owen Mills

b. 9 August 1961

7-1-2-5-3-6-1-2 Debra Lynn Mills b. 12 November 1964

7-1-2-5-3-6-2 James Drew Mills b. 9 December 1939 m. Martha Dodson

7-1-2-5-3-6-2-1 James Ronald Mills b. 3 July 1964

7-1-2-5-3-6-2-2 Michael Douglas Mills b. 12 January 1967

7-1-2-5-3-6-3 Gloria Sue Mills b. 10 August 1945 m. Calvin Johnson

7-1-2-5-3-6-3-1 Greta Carol Johnson b. 10 April 1963

7-1-2-5-3-6-3-2 Gregory Scott Johnson b. 31 August 1964

7-1-2-5-3-6-4 Samuel Ray Mills b. 18 October 1948

7-1-2-5-3-6-5 Donald Wayne Mills b. 7 February 1955

7-1-2-5-3-7 Felix Webster Mills b. 18 September 1916 m. Ruth Helms

7-1-2-5-3-7-1 Marilyn Linda Mills b. 23 January 1946

7-1-2-5-3-7-2 David Webster Mills b. 17 August 1948

7-1-2-5-3-7-3 William Terrel Mills b. 16 August 1950

7-1-2-5-3-7-4 John Michael Mills b. 22 February 1954

7-1-2-5-3-8 Heron Don Mills b. 18 June 1920. m. Ann Loyd Williamson

7-1-2-5-3-8-1 Ann LaRue Mills b. 25 June 1943 m. Lewis Patrick Haynes jr.

7-1-2-5-3-8-1-1 Tracy Renee Haynes

b. 3 September 1963

7-1-2-5-3-8-1-2 Lewis Patrick Haynes III b. 3 August 1967

7-1-2-5-3-8-2 Peggy Louise Mills b. 18 August 1952

7-1-2-5-3-9 Marion Swan Mills b. 28 June 1920 m. 2 September 1939 to James Drew Carr

7-1-2-5-3-9-1 Yvonne Carr b. 19 September 1942 m. Don Edward Hunt 21 January 1964

7-1-2-5-3-9-2 James Larry Carr b. 11 June 1947

7-1-2-5-3-9-3 Phillip Allen Carr b. 11 September 1960.

7-1-2-5-3-10 Callie Mae Mills b. 29 October 1926 m. Jesse Glen Weeks

7-1-2-5-3-10-1 Barry Len Weeks b. 30 June 1955

7-1-2-5-3-10-2 Timothy Weeks b. 2 April 1959

7-1-2-5-4 Hershall Edward McKee b. September 19, 1888 Panola County, Mississippi d. October 8, 1928 Kaufman Co. Texas

7-1-2-5-4-1 Roland J. McKee d. 1961

7-1-2-5-4-2 James L. McKee

7-1-2-5-4-3 Robert Leon McKee d. 1923

7-1-2-5-4-4 Lloyd N. McKee

7-1-2-5-5 Reatha Alma McKee b. June 13, 1891 d, October 23, 1952 m. Connie D. Wiser

7-1-2-5-5-1 Avis Brilla Wiser b. 27 December 1909. m. 29 April 1926 Sam Smith

7-1-2-5-5-1-1 Billie Ruth Smith b. 26 October 1928

7-1-2-5-5-1-2 James C. Smith b. 9 September 1930

7-1-2-5-5-1-3 Avis Pauline Smith b. 21 June 1933

7-1-2-5-5-1-4 Coleman D. Smith b. 29 August 1939

7-1-2-5-5-1-5 Sammie Sue

Smith b. 19 May 1943

7-1-2-5-5-1-6 Linda Joyce Smith b. 3 August 1947

7-1-2-5-5-2 Nolan Douglas Wiser b. 4 March 1912 m. Francis McKee

7-1-2-5-5-2-1 John Wiser b. 2 July 1935

7-1-2-5-5-2-2 Charles D. Wiser b. 10 September 1939

7-1-2-5-5-3 Velma Scottie Wiser b. 26 October 1914 d. December 1916

7-1-2-5-5-4 Forrest Young Wiser b. 2 January 1917 d. 27 January 1968

7-1-2-5-5-5 Connie McKee Wiser b. 3 September 1920

7-1-2-5-6 Minnie Boyd McKee b. September 18, 1893 m. Albert Cheek

7-1-2-5-6-1 Noel Douglas Cheek b. 15 July 1911 d. 28 June 1966

7-1-2-5-6-2 Elbert J. Cheek b. 19 August 1915 d. 28 January 1966

7-1-2-5-6-3 A.C. Cheek b. 2 August 1917 d. 22 October 1918

7-1-2-5-6-4 Barney James Cheek b. 28 August 1919

7-1-2-5-7 Barney Eugene McKee b. October 23, 1896 m. Mollie LeeAnn Long

7-1-2-5-7-1 Hassel Eugene McKee b. 4 March 1918

7-1-2-5-7-2 Mural Dean McKee 13 March 1919

7-1-2-5-7-3 Eugenia LaVern McKee b. 29 June 1921

7-1-2-5-7-4 Silas Franklin McKee b. 3 February 1923

7-1-2-5-7-5 Harold Ray McKee b. 22 December 1925

7-1-2-5-7-6 Jewell Owen McKee b. 18 May 1930

7-1-2-5-7-7 Betty Ruth McKee b. 14 April 1934

7-1-2-6 Franklin Phillips b. about 1863 m. Ollie McKee

7-1-2-6-1 May Phillips m. Sanford Lawson

7-1-2-6-2 Bonnie Phillips m. Johnie

McGowan
- 7-1-2-6-3 Eli Philips
- 7-1-2-6-4 Lester Phillips
- 7-1-2-6-5 Marie Phillips

7-1-2-7 John Henry Phillips b. 1866 m. Juliette Johnson 14 August 1905 Kaufman Co. Texas
- 7-1-2-7-1 Byron Phillips b. 1898
- 7-1-2-7-2 Hoyle Phillips
- 7-1-2-7-3 Parks Pharr Phillips b. 13 March 1901
- 7-1-2-7-4 Maurice Sheppard Phillips
- 7-1-2-7-5 (daughter)

7-1-2-8 Theodosia Phillips b. about 1867
7-1-2-10 Sarah C. Phillips b. about 1870
7-1-2-9 Eli E. Phillips b. 5 February 1872 d. January 9, 1945

7-1-3 Christenberry Phillips b. November 21, 1821 m. 1) Caroline Honea 2) Emily Waddil

Declaration for the Increase of an Invalid Pension

State of __Georgia__, County of __Cherokee__, ss:

On this 17' day of February, A. D. one thousand eight hundred and seventy __two__ personally appeared before me __W.R. D. Moss Ordinary and Judge of probate__ the same being a court of record within the county and state aforesaid, __Christenby Phillips__ aged __48__ years, a resident of _____, county of __Cherokee__, State of __Georgia__, who being duly sworn according to law, declares that he is a pensioner of the United States, duly enrolled at the __Washington City__ Pension Agency at the rate of __Four__ dollars per month, by reason of disability incurred in the __Military__ Service of the United States while __a private in Capt. Birds Company & Regt Georgia Vols__

That his physical condition is such that he believes himself entitled to receive an increased pension, and that he herewith returns his present pension certificate.

He further declares that he is disabled n the following manner, to wit: __That he is totally disabled from doing manual labor to earn his living; that he has no profession by which to do so & that he is dependant on charity to a great extent. He can do but little work of any kind.__

that he appoints __B. D. Hyam__ his true and lawful attorney, to prosecute his claim; That his residence is no._____. in _____ street, of _____ county of __Cherokee__, and State of __Georgia__; and his post office address is __Canton, Georgia__

Christenberry Phillips

Certificate
of
PERIODIOCAL EXAMINATION BY CITIZEN SURGEONS

State of Georgia, County of Chattooga, ss:

The subscribers, practising physicians or surgeons in the town of Summerville do hereby certify that we have carefully examined Christenberry Phillips, who states that he is to be paid an invalid pension at the agency in New Orleans, in the State of Louisiana Age, 56; height 5feet 5 inches; weight 112; pulse 90 respiration, 25, He is suffering from Chronic Diarrhoea, contracted in the service of the United States in the War with Mexico, which has resulted in indigestion, hemeroids, and Spinal Weakness. He is left with...Two Dollars per month paid by the Government dependant on an almost helpless and needy family. He is very frail and emaciated.
and that his present disability for obtaining subsistence by manual labor is Total
Dated at Summerville } R. Y. Rudicil
28th day of September 1877} G.A.R. Tucker

MEXICAN WAR PENSION
act of January 29, A.D. 1887

Declaration of Survivor for Pension

State of Georgia
County of Floyd

On this 25th day of March, A.D. onethousand eight hundred and eighty-seven personally appeared before me, A. E. Ross Clerk of Superior Court, Christenberry Phillips, a resident in the county of Chatooga, in the State of Georgia, who being first duly sworn according to the law, deposes and says:

I am the identical Crisenbury Phillips, who served under the name of C. Phillips as a private in the company commanded by Daniel H. Byrd, in the 1st regiment of Georgia Infantry, commanded by Col. Henry R. Jackson, in the war with Mexico; that I enlisted at Canton GA., on or about the 5th day of June A.D. 1846, for the term of 12 months, and was honorably discharged at New Orleans La., on the - day of May A. D. 1847.

That being duly enlisted as aforesaid, I actually served sixty days with the army or Navy of the United States inMexico, or on the coast or frontier thereof, or en Route thereto, in the war with that Nation, which service was as follows: Landing at Brazos Island & Marching up the Rio Grande to Monteray & thence to Tampico & Vera Cruz.

That I am 65 years of age, having been born at Habersham Co. Ga. on the 27th day of November 1821.

That I am disabled by reason of Chronic Diarrhea, which said disability was not incurred while in anymanner voluntarily engaged in aiding or abetting the laterebellion against the authority of the United States; but that said disability was incurredat Brazos Island on or about the - day of July A. D. 1846 in manner as follows; Severe Diarrhoea.

That being actually enlisted as aforesaid - I was actually engaged in battle with the enemy in the war withMexico, to wit: in the battle of Siege of Vera Cruz on the 22nd day of March, 1847.

       7-1-4 Matilda b. ca. 1822 m. James Pendry
       7-1-5 Martha b. ca. 1829 did not marry
       7-1-6 through 7-1-12 three more girls and four more boys names may have included Alexander, Hiram C. and Martin.
       7-1-13 Ira Lorenzo Dow Phillips b. ca. 1856
       7-1-14 Susanna b. ca. 1857
       7-1-15 Cicero b. ca. 1859
   7-2 Elizabeth March 27, 1791 d. 15 March 1874 m Henry Wells 21 Feb. 1814. He d. 6 Feb 1873
       7-2-1 Lucretia b. 15 Dec. 1814
       7-2-2 Hannah b. 15 Dec. 1814 m. Robertson Hicks(Nathan Robertson Hipps)
          7-2-2-? Lawrence b. 1850
          7-2-2-? Anna b. 1853
       7-2-3 Mary Ann b. 23 April 1817 d. 28 Nov. 1902 m. Eli Kennerly Hutsel

On July 24, 1852 Eli K. Hutsell died of Tuberculosis. He is buried at Sulphur Springs, Buncombe County North Carolina. He was born December 3, 1815 in Wythe County Virginia. When only twelve years old he joined the Methodist church and at the age of 18 was a licensed exhorter. On October 22, 1837 he was ordained deacon by Bishop Thomas A. Morris at Lafayette, Georgia.

On April 15, 1840 Eli K. Hutsell was married to Mary Ann Wells daughter of Henry and Elizabeth(Philips) Wells.

The Reverend Hutsell put religion first, and the order of temperance second. A most remarkable sermon was preached by him at Walker's schoolhouse near LaFollette, Tennessee in June of 1842. At that time he was a preacher in charge of Tazewell circuit, and preaching with him was Dr. Jackson Buckley a local preacher and medical doctor of Fincastle Tennessee. Only twelve persons besides the preachers were present, and only one of these was a professing christian. Reverend Hutsell noted a young lady who had been present at another service, and thinking that she might profess christianity, he called for mourners, when to his surprise all eleven unconverted persons came forward for prayers. The services continued for some time, and three of the penitents were converted that night. During the next six days hundreds of people flocked in to hear the preaching, and many of them became soldiers for the Lord. By the time the meeting closed, people were coming in for miles around to profess christianity. A few weeks later, a second meeting was held, and as many who were present knelt in the schoolhouse and were baptized by sprinkling, and then a large procession went down to Big Creek, where they were baptized both by pouring and by immersion.

He continued to preach for a few years, but his health began to fail and in 1845 he was placed on the list of worn out preachers. He is buried at Sulphur Springs, Buncombe County, North Carolina.

Eli K. Hutsell

Eli K. Hutsell died July 24, 1852. He was a good preacher, magnetic and fascinating. He travelled only a few years, and was placed on the superannuated list on account of feeble health from pulmonary disease. While in the active work he was unusually successful in winning souls to Christ. He preached occasionally while a superannuate, and always with acceptability. He enjoyed the blessing of perfect love. His wife was Mary Ann Wells who was born on Turkey Creek, Buncombe Co. N.C., April 13, 1818; and died at the home of her son-in-law, Mr. Silas Sharp, near La Follette, Tenn. November 29, 1902. Her vigorous intellect was an inheritance from the Philips stock, her mother being an aunt of the Reverend Sewell Philips. At the death of her husband she was thrown upon her own resources; but with an excellent English education and a happy talent for governing and imparting instruction, she made a good living at school teaching, and reared an excellent family. She gave to the Church one of our most gifted travelling preachers, The Reverend R. A. Hutsell, now (1909) a member of the conference.

Eli K. Hutsell spent his last years in Buncombe County, N.C. as a farmer and part of the time as a merchant. When he was dying he asked a friend if he thought he was dying and on receiving an affirmative answer he said: "If this is death, thank God for death!" Dr. Samuel Patton preached a memorial sermon of Brother Hutsell at the Conference of 1852. It was a written sermon, and the preacher scarcely lifted his eyes from the manuscript; but such was the affection of the preachers for the deceased and such was the spiritual power that accompanied the reading that when a lively song was sung after the sermon there was a delightful pentecost. There was a general weeping and rejoicing throughout the congregation.

In the October session of the Buncombe County Court for 1852, A.J. Plemmons brought the last will and testament of Eli K. Hutsell into the court. His wife Mary Ann and Samuel B. Gudger were appointed executrix and executor.

On Friday morning, April 13, 1855 Mrs Mary Ann Hutsell was appointed guardian of Julia E., Robert A., and Mary Ann Hutsell orphans of her husband Eli K. Hutsell.

Buncombe County Court Records April session 1861: Susan Huggins is bound out to Mrs Mary A. Hutsell until age 18 now being 11 to learn to read and write, Geography, Grammer, History, and Housekeeping.

Mary Ann Hutsell died at the home of her son-in-law Silas Sharp near La Follette, Tennessee on November 29, 1902. She was born in Buncombe County North Carolina on April 13, 1818. She was a woman of bright intellect and strong character. After the death of her sainted husband she found herself with a number of children to support, and very little means. She had quite a good english education for her day and turned it to account in school teaching. She was popular and successful, and thus enabled to do much good while she was supporting herself and her children.

She professed faith in Christ in her thirteenth year and joined the Methodist Church. Her religious life was not only orderly and consistent, but zealous and useful. She was a constant and extensive reader. While she kept up well with the general literature of her time, she delighted in reading the standard religious books of her church and was a regular and careful bible reader. She thus became an intelligent and mature christian, with strong faith and bright hope of eternal life. Her reverence for the memory of her husband, which she held and nurtured to the last, was beautiful indeed.

She spent the last several years of her life in the home

of her daughter, Mrs. Silas Sharp, where everything that the tenderest affection could suggest was provided for her comfort. When age and infirmity would no longer permit her to go abroad, she spent her time in reading and instructing her grandchildren in letters and religion.

She is the mother of Reverend Robert A. Hutsell, of the Holston Conference, who has inherited the gifts and graces of both his father and mother in an eminent degree. Such a life could but have a good ending. As she stood on the banks of the Jordan and looked over into the beautiful land of promise, she said in the confidence of the faith which she had so carefully kept and cultivated, "I am almost home."

Buncombe County Court Records April session 1861: Susan Huggins is bound out to Mrs Mary A. Hutsell until age 18 now being 11 to learn to read and write, Geography, Grammer, History, and Housekeeping.

> 7-2-3-? Robert A. Hutsell b. 16 Dec 1847 Asheville NC d. 7 Sept 1913 Fountain City Tenn m. Lucile Seabolt 1878

Robert A. Hutsell died September 7, 1913 at his home in Fountain City Tennessee after an illness of several weeks. He was born December 16, 1847 at Asheville, North Carolina and was the son of the Reverend Eli K. Hutsell, who was one of the most successful revivalists in the history of the Holston Conference. His mother was Mary Ann Wells, a woman ... of vigorous intellect and unusual force of character. At the tender age of ten he was converted and joined the Methodist Church. He was married in 1878 to Miss Lucile Seabolt. To them were born four children: Robert K. who lives at Fountain City and who is one of the most successful sunday school superintendents in this conference; Harry who is a travelling preacher of promise and ability; Mrs. J.L. Bragg of Chatanooga, and Miss Pearl Hutsell.

The subject of this sketch joined the Holston Conference in 1872 and served among others, the following charges: Dandridge, Decatur, Sweetwater, Spring City, Jasper, King Memorial, Mary Street, La Follette, Welch, Wise, and Straw Plains. In 1889 on account of continued ill health, he located, and for thirteen years he engaged in the practice of medicine at La Follette, Tennessee, but during this time he preached with remarkable regularity. Partially regaining his health, he returned to the pastorate in 1897. As preacher and pastor he served each charge with conspicuous fidelity and success. He never sought preferment but went cheerfully to whatever field he was assigned.

        7-2-3-?-1 Robert K. Hutsell
        7-2-3-?-2 Henry(Harry) Hutsell
        7-2-3-?-3 _____ m. J.L. Bragg
        7-2-3-?-4 Pearl
    7-2-3-?? _____m. Silas Sharp
7-2-4 Maria Elizabeth b. 4 May 1819 d. 5 May 1908 m.1) Bevil McEntire 2) William Clontz

7-2-5 Francis Marion b. 5 June 1821 m. Elizabeth Miller 29 Nov. 1845 Buncombe Co. NC d. 27 June 1915 she d. 21 May 1908 Madison Co. NC

"WHAT GOD HATH JOINED TOGETHER LET NOT MAN PUT ASSUNDER"

This Certifies
THAT THE RITE OF
Holy Matrimony
WAS CELEBRATED BETWEEN

F. M. Wells of Buncombe County
and Elizabeth Miller of the same county
on the 29 November 1843 at the brides house
by John Brown Esq 1843

Witness: Cathrn Church

Births

(all in same hand and similar ink)
W. H. Wells was born March 13, 1845
A.D? Wells August 23 1846
E.K. Wells Sept the 6 1848
G. F. Wells March the 5 1850
M.J. Wells Feb the 23 1852
J.P. Wells April the 27 1854
Harriet E. Wells March th 27 1856
Joseph R. Wells March the 1 1860
Hiram J. Wells Feb the 3 1858
Robert H. Wells April the 11 1862
Bessie A. Wells January the 4 1865
Laura A Wells Sept 21. 1867
Carrie S. Wells Sept 5 1870

(in a different hand)
Selma S. Wells June 26, 1885
Daughter of G.F. Wells & Nannie Clark - Wells

Marriages

W.H. Wells to M.J. Smith December the 26, 1877
H. F. Wells to Anne Robin Sept the 25 1867
M. F. Wells to John Cheakley January th 21, 1881
John P. Wells to Janie Stoner September the 1 day 1887
Hiram J. Wells to Anas R. Wise Oct 26 day 1887
R. H. Wells to Florence Haworth April 23, 1895
G. F. Wells to E.L. Blair March 17, 1891
Laura Wells to David H. Gardiner Novemb 4 day 1891
Bessie P. Wells to J. C. Logan Jan 19, 1893
John P. Wells to Adda Mathus Jan 1 day 1894
Carrie Wells to J.L. Larue Febr 17, 1896

Deaths

Elisha K. Wells June the 21, 1855
Hariet J. Wells June the 23, 1858
Elizabeth Wells My GMother May 21st 1908

Francis Marion Wells June 29th 1915

G.F. Wells dide Jan 12 -- 1920

Henry S. Wells Feb 6 day 1873
My Father

Elizabeth Wells died March 15, 1879
My Mother

M.A. Hutsell died November 25, 1902

Francis Marion Wells and Elizabeth Miller. By Virginia Skinner Wainwright 1989.

It was the year 1821 and James Monroe from the state of Virginia was president of the United States. In Buncombe County, North Carolina, Francis Marion Wells was born 15 June 1821 to Henry S. Wells and Elizabeth Phillips. His brothers and sisters were Lucretia, Hannah (they were twins), Mary Ann, Maria Elizabeth, Tilithia Cami, Hirom, John Haney, Decater, and Ruphus.

Francis fell in love with a young lady, Elizabeth Miller. The wedding bells rang for Francis and Elizabeth and they were united in Holy Matrimony 29 November 1845. Elizabeth was born 12 December 1826 to Henry Miller (Revolutionary War Patriot and Soldier) and Mary Glance. Elizabeth's brother and sisters were: Anch, Katie, and Hannah.

Great indeed must have been the pride and satisfaction of Francis and Elizabeth of their family. They often reflected on the great blessings and love that God had poured out upon them. Their children were: Henry, Andrew, Decater, George Franklin, Mary, John Phillips, Jefferson, Robert, Bessie, Laura Alice, and Carrie Shields.

Elizabeth was a wonderful mother, grandmother, and homemaker. In the summer she was busy preparing fruits and vegetables for the winter. She enjoyed drying apples and beans, making apple butter, apple jelly, churning butter, growing herbs and the berry patch. Elizabeth took pride in weaving, knitting socks, sewing, and reading her bible.

Francis, although an unassuming man of quiet disposition, had many friends who admired his upright standards of living and his fine character. He was a staunch Methodist and very active in church work. He loved his church, his family, farmland, and farm life. He was a well known citizen and landowner of Madison County. He and Elizabeth were members of Antioch Methodist Church, Rt. 2, Hot Springs, North Carolina.

It was the year 1861 and the nation was going to war. The Civil War disrupted families and lives with far reaching implications. The Wells family was no different from any other Southern family. They knew the pain of war and the loss of a son. General Sherman began his invasion of Georgia in the spring of 1864 and captured Atlanta by 1 September, 1864. It was during the battle of Atlanta that Henry Wells lost his life.

The Wells family lived in the area of Paint Rock, Madison County, North Carolina. Paint rock is part of the Appalachian Mountains, which geologists say are very old mountains. Some declare that they are the oldest in the world. They are inspiring, uplifting, challenging, and seem to beckon to higher things. Summer and early fall the mountains are enhanced by the beauty of rhododendrons, mountain laurels, fireweed, and many other wild flowers.

Paint Rock is beside the French Broad River, part in Tennessee and part in North Carolina. The cliff is nearly 110 feet high and has been characterized for centuries by colorful figures and formations on the rock, which resemble paintings, presumably Indian paintings. It is Hot Springs, North Carolina's next door neighbor. The two places are separated by five and one half miles of French Broad River. When Hot Springs was the

Gatlinburg of the South, around the turn of the century, Paint Rock was down the road, down the railroad, or just down the river. There is a sign located on U. S. 25 - 70 at Hot Springs at the south end of the bridge that spans the French Broad River "Paint Rock - Early landmark. Site of blockhouse to protect settlers from Indians, 1793. Figures on rock resemble paintings. It is 5 1/2 miles Northwest."

The settlement of Paint Rock used to be a bee hive of activity. It had stores, churches, schools, railroad yards, a huge lumber operation and a post office. Farmers, traders, and merchants were as familiar with Paint Rock as they were with their own homes. Countless herds of cattle, goats, geese, turkeys, and other livestock have been driven up and down the river by the painted rock. If the travelers were caught away from home by darkness, Francis Wells' was a stopping place for them. He never refused. In return they would share part of their goods with him.

The flood of 1916 put an end to all the activity around Paint Rock. Everything that wasn't tied that came under the tide went downstream. The lumber operation never reopened after the flood.

Francis, a most conscientious father and indulgent grandfather, after long years of generosity, sharing his services, his talents, his warm kindly spirit, and his earthly possessions, passed away 27 June, 1915, and was buried in Antioch Cemetery beside his beloved wife who went to be with the Lord on 21 May 1909.

It is my pleasure to share with you some of the events in my Great Grandparents life as it was told to me by my mother Selma Wells Skinner who is 104 years old. She has been a mountain top experience for her children and we are deeply grateful.

Francis Marion Wells died June 27, 1915 in Madison County, N.C. He was the son of Henry and Elizabeth (Phillips) Wells and was born June 15, 1821 in Buncombe County, N.C. He married on November 29, 1845 to Elizabeth Miller daughter of William and Mary (Glance) Miller. Their children were Andrew D. 1846 who married Rachel A. Robison; Henry who served in the Confederate Army; George Franklin born 5 March 1850; Mary born 24 February 1852 who married John Chockley; John P. born 1854; Jefferson born 1858; Robert born 1862; Bessie born 1865 who married the Reverend James Logan; Laura Alice born 1867 who married David H. Gardiner; and Carrie born 1870 who married Joseph LaRue.

7-2-5-1 W. Henry Wells b. 13 March 1845 m. 26 Dec 1877 to M. J. Smith

7-2-5-2 Andrew Decatur Wells b. 22 Aug. 1846 d. 1 Nov. 1911 Madison Co. NC m. Rachel Ann Robison

7-2-5-3 Elisha Kennerly Wells b. 6 Sept. 1848 d. 21 June 1855

7-2-5-4 George Franklin Wells b. 5 Mar. 1850 Buncombe Co. NC m. 1.) 19 March 1884 to Nannie Click 2.) 17 March 1891 Emma L. Blazer d. 12 January 1930 Madison Co. NC

    7-2-5-4-1 Selma S. Wells b. 26 June 1885 m. E.G. Skinner 2 Dec 1915

        7-2-5-4-1-1 Guy Skinner

        7-2-5-4-1-2 Virginia Skinner

7-2-5-5 Mary J. Wells b. 23 Feb. 1852 Madison Co. NC d. m 1) 21 January 1883 John Chockley 2) Samuel Best 3) Wilson Green

    7-2-5-5-1 Walter Chockley

    7-2-5-5-2 Eugenia Chockley

    7-2-5-5-3 Stella Chockley

    7-2-5-5-4 Bessie Chockley

7-2-5-6 John Phillips Wells b. 27 April 1854 Madison Co. NC 29 May 1935 Madison Co. NC m. 1.) 1 Sept 1887 to Janie Stoner 2.) 1 January 1894 Ada Mathus

7-2-5-7 Hariet E. Wells b. 27 March 1856 d. 23 June 1858

7-2-5-8 Hiram Jefferson Wells b. 3 Feb 1858 Madison Co. NC m. 26 October 1887 to Annie R. Wise d. Washington DC

    7-2-5-8-1 Raymond

7-2-5-9 Joseph R. Wells 1 March 1860 d. 15 June 1862

7-2-5-10 Robert H. Wells b. 11 April 1862 Madison Co. NC m. 23 april 1895 to Florence Haworth d. Clearwater Florida

7-2-5-11 Bessie Wells b. ca. 1865 Madison Co. NC d. Bristol Tennessee. m. 19 July 1893 Rev. James C. Logan

7-2-5-12 Laura Alice Wells b. 21 Sept 1867 Madison Co. NC d. 1965 Buncombe Co. NC m. 4 November 1891 David Harris Gardner.

Newspaper Clipping (undated) Mrs Laura Wells Gardner, 98, of Asheville died Saturday in an Asheville nursing home after a long illness. She was a native of Madison County and had come to Asheville in 1950 to make her home with a son Charles M. Gardner of 15 Conestee Pl. She was a granddaughter of Henry Miller, Revolutionary War

Patriot and soldier, and was the last living member of Antioch Methodist Church near Hot Springs. Known affectionately as Aunt Laura, she was quoted on her 90th birthday in 1957 and commenting: "I don't feel like running any footraces, but I take care of myself, my room and the flowers." She was a daughter of the late Francis Marion and Elizabeth Miller Wells. Surviving in addition to son are two daughters, Mrs. Ruth Johnson and Miss Mary Gardner of Asheville; three other sons, Hugh of Asheville, Hiram of Hot Springs and John L. Gardner of Mountain Home, Tenn.; eight grandchildren and 15 great-grandchildren. Services will be held at 3pm Monday in the chapel of Morris-Hendon Funeral Home. The Rev. Lee Barnett will officiate and burial will be in Lewis Memorial Park. Pall-bearers will be Walter Chockley, Harold Bowling, Joe and Eugene Lanning, James David Gardner and William Marshall Gardner. The family will receive friends from 3 to 5 p.m. Sunday at the funeral home.

    7-2-5-12-1 Leslie Gardner
    7-2-5-12-2 Frank Gardner
    7-2-5-12-3 Wells Gardner
    7-2-5-12-4 Hugh Gardner
    7-2-5-12-5 Charles Gardner
    7-2-5-12-6 Hiram Gardner
    7-2-5-12-7 Maurice Gardner
    7-2-5-12-8 Ruth Gardner m. Hugh Johnson
    7-2-5-12-9 Mary Gardner
  7-2-5-13 Carrie Wells b. 5 Sept 1870 Madison Co. NC d. Knoxville Tennessee. m. Joseph Lafayette Larue
    7=2-5-13-1 Ruth Dexter Larue m. Thomas Charles Tedder
      7-2-5-13-1-1 Charles Richard Tedder(d.y.)
      7-2-5-13-1-2 Robert Wells Larue Tedder m. Edith Smith
        7-2-5-13-1-2-1 Ruth
      7-2-5-13-1-3 Kenneth Allen (Joe) Tedder m. Elizabeth Nickle
        7-2-5-13-1-3-1 Claudia Tedder
        7-2-5-13-1-3-2 Jodie Tedder
      7-2-5-13-1-4 Frederick Wells Tedder
      7-2-5-13-1-5 Ruth Ellen Tedder m. Bill Crowther
    7-2-5-13-2 Ruby Larue m. Claude Rutherford

7-2-5-13-2-1 Claudia Elizabeth Larue
7-2-5-13-3 Mary Larue
7-2-5-13-4 Paul Larue
7-2-6 Tilitha Cami m. Jack Plemmons
7-2-7 Hiram Phillip b. 1823 m. Susan Pence
7-2-8 John Vaney m. 1) ___McDonald 2)___West
7-2-9 Decater
7-2-10 Ruphus

7-3 Elisha b. ca. 1793 d. April 29, 1891 m. 1. Clarissa Evans, 2. Nancy Hall.

Reverend Reuben: I purchased a farm from my brother in law Joseph W. Pharr lying near my brother Elisha in Haywood County. He had a distillery and was to pay several hundred gallons of whiskey that winter and could not give possession that year unless I would take the corn and distillery off his hands. I consented to do so and about the first of September I moved to my farm and commenced operating and preparing to make the whiskey. My brother lived within half a mile and he assisted me some and at it I went. Day and night I attended to that Devil's Tea Pot; made the whiskey, paid the debt, sold the distillery, and got out of the whole arrangement.

In 1824, Elisha Phillips moved onto a farm which had been bought by Reuben Philips. They formed a partnership by which Reuben would make money teaching and Elisha would farm.

Reverend Reuben (1825) My brother (Elisha) proposed to take the new place.

Hannah daughter of Elisha and Clarissa Phillips was born in 1826.

To give an idea of some of the conditions in Haywood County N.C. I quote from a court record of October 1827: The commisioners who were appointed by court to allot to Rachel Brown, the widow of Ezekiel Brown dec'd depose thus - A list of the articles of crop, stock, & provisions alloted to the said Rachel as follows (to wit) Choice of three cows with or without calves, 1050 weight of pork the quantity supposed now killed. Three small hogs on foot not exceeding fifty weight each gross, one hundred bushels of corn, six bushels of wheat, one of barley, three bushels of salt including the salt made use of on her pork already killed, thirty weight of sugar and fifteen weight of coffee or in lieu of the sugar and coffee to be optional with the widow. Half the hemp, the whole of the flax, five pounds of wool if that quantity on hand, thirty weight of cotton including what is now on hand and if any difficulty the balance in cash at the rate of six pounds to the dollar, and ten dollars worth of leather and five dollarsfor making the leather into shoes and binding thread. half a pound of pepper, some quantity of alspice and some quantity of ginger and the whole of the corn shucks on hand, three gallons of vinegar if that much on hand, all the cabbage of this fresh or pickled, with all her other pickles, what candles are now on hand and a part of a small cake of tallow not made up.

Elisha Phillips served on the Jury in Haywood County in April 1829 to lay out a road from William Scotts on Beaverdam Creek to the top of Sandymush Mountain.

Elisha Phillips served in Haywood County North Carolina on a road jury in December 1829.

In the July 1830 session of the Haywood County Court Elisha Phillips was appointed election judge for the August Elections. On August 20, Sewell Phillips son of Elisha and Clarissa was born.

On October 29, 1833 Benjamin Robertson(Robeson) of Habersham County Georgia was married to Alissa Phillips daughter of Elisha and Clarissa Phillips of Haywood County, NC at the home of the Reverend Reuben Philips.

Mary Ann daughter of Elisha and Clarissa Phillips married James Washington Alexander on July 30th, 1835.

On the April session of Court for 1836 Elisha Phillips was ordered to serve on the superior court jury for the next session. Bynum son of Elisha and Clarissa Phillips was born May 16th.

Lucinda daughter of Elisha and Clarissa Phillips was married September 15, 1836 in Habersham County Georgia to Andrew Robinson(Robeson).

Elisha Phillips was appointed Election Judge for Haywood County, NC in the April 1837 session of court for the upcoming elections.

Irenia daughter of Elisha and Clarissa Phillips married Andrew J. Fain October 9, 1843.

Hannah daughter of Elisha and Clarissa Phillips married Archibald Russell on December 10, 1844.

On December 29, 1845 Adam Philips sold 65 acres on Whitson Creek to Elisha Philips.

In the March session of the Haywood County Court 1850 Elisha Phillips paid a fifty dollar bond to bind Ellen Amanda Clark to himself, she being the daughter of J.R. and Elizabeth Clark.

Althea Phillips daughter of Elisha and Clarissa Phillips was married to William Alexander on September 21, 1851.

In the March session of the Haywood County Court for 1856 Elisha Phillips asked to be relieved of his obligation for Ellen Clark and the bond was rescinded.

In the June session of Haywood County Court for 1858 Elisha Philips was excused from Jury duty, and never again appeared on the jury roll. At age 65 jurors were no longer required to serve due to age.

Will of Elisha Phillips Haywood County, North Carolina

I Elisha Phillips of the County of Haywood State of North Carolina being in common health, and of sound mind and body do make this my last will and testament.

First
I direct that when I die my body be decently buried that my just debts be paid and the remainder of my property be divided as follows, I direct that all my property both real and personal be cared for according to the law of the state.

Third
That my three living sons to whit - Christenberry, Sewell, Bynum be given four hundred and fifty dollars each the amount that had been paid to each be deducted from each ones share.

Fourth
I direct that the lawful heirs of my deceased son have four hundred and fifty dollars, and my money previously paid be deducted.

Fifth
I direct that my daughters, nine of them vis - Aliff, Lucinda, Mary Ann, Irene, Elizabeth, Hannah, Althea, Catherine, and Emily each have sixty five dollars and the amnount paid to either of them be deducted from this.

Sixth
I direct that my daughter Laura have all the remaining both real and personal, I direct that my executors take it in hand and use it for her support to the best advantage.

Seventh
I do hereby make my close friends Francis B. Evans and A.J. Murry my executors to carry out my Will.

In Witness hereby I set my Hand and Seal
January 12, 1864
Book 3 Page w63   Elisha Phillips

Reverend Reuben to son Elisha, July 1882: My youngest sister Catherine Bell now lives in the house that you were born in. She is in her 80th year and my brother Elisha for whom you were named lives in the same place he first settled 68 years ago. He is nearly three years older than myself. His post office is Pigeon River in Haywood County.

Bynum Philips, Haywood County N.C. Dec. 20, 1882: My father [Elisha Phillips] is yet alive and able to walk around at times [very pert] living at the old homestead. Also Aunt Salley Hall living with him [both] old and feeble. Aunt Harriet Rinehart is yet alive. [I] read your card to her; she sends her best respects. Aunt [Mahala] Shook is yet alive [but] E. Hall, John Hall, [and] Henry Johnson [are] all dead. George Hall [is] alive; William Sohart, (&) David Shaad (are) dead.

In 1882 Elisha Phillips of Haywood County wrote his brother Reuben in Alabama stating that his health was poor and he had lost his sight in one eye and nearly lost it in the other. Reuben was still at Hanover, Coosa County.

Elisha Philips; Pigeon River, N.C. Aug. 27, 1883;

Dear brother Rubin, This is in answer to a letter which I received last Saturday the 25th of August. I was glad to hear from you once more.

I am getting weak and feeble. I have very sick spells at times, at other times, I am able to walk about. I am at times almost blind in one of my eyes. My wife is not very stout, though she takes as much care of me as if I was a baby. My mother in law Sally Hall is yet alive though very old and feeble. She is living with us. We are all old and nearing eternity, and by the grace of God, we hope to meet in that temple not made with hands, eternal in the heavens.

I have one child living with me, my youngest child named Laura, an Idiot Girl. She is now about forty [years old]. I have six children dead and nine living. I have three boys living. Two of them are preachers. Harriet Rhinehart and Mahala Shook are both alive.

Rev. Reuben to gr. son Shelton March 10, 1885: My brother Elisha Philips has lived on the same place since 1815 and his first wife gave birth to 15 children and died and went to Jesus I have no doubt. Three of their sons are good industrious Methodist preachers, two of them itinerants in the Holston and North Carolina conferences, one with them at home. My brother is now in his 92nd year. I never knew my brother to go in debt in his married life nor go anybodies security!! His oldest daughter Aliff married Benjamin Robeson of Habersham County Georgia in my house is now a good citizen near Jonah Mountain Nachoocha Valley in Habersham County. Her sister Anna came to visit her awhile and was also married to his brother Andrew Robison [who] has been a noble itinerant preacher for years. [He] went to the Tennessee conference and I learned died a few months since and gone shouting to Jesus!!

Florence Alabama Times - 30 May 1891. Phillips, Uncle Elisha, died in Western North Carolina on Wednesday at the advanced age of 107 years. (note - born in 1792 or early in 1793) [died May 29, 1891]

      7-3-1 Mary Ann m. James Washington Alexander July 30, 1835
      7-3-2 Christenberry b. ca 1823 m. Elizabeth Patton Oct. 3, 1843 (dau of James Patton)

Christenberry was active in the court records of Haywood County N.C. as witnessed by the following:

June term 1848 - The court proceeded to appoint judges and Justices of the Peace to hold the next august election for governor and members to both branches of the legislature & also shff. The following are names of persons appointed: ...

Beaverdam - Green Moore and William M. Robinson   Gov.
        Elisha Philips and P.A. Penland   Sent.
        H.P. Haynes and J.M. Cabe   Cong.
        C.B. Philips and Jesse Smathers   Shff.

Ordered by the court that William P. Roberson be overseer of the public road from the forks near Christenberry Phillips up Beaverdam to the top of the mountain at the Buncombe line.

December court 1848 - A deed from Elisha Philips to Christenberry Philips dated the 25th day of June 1847 was proven in open court by the oath of A. M. Russell, the only subscribing witness thereto and ordered to be registered.

A deed of conveyance from Wm Clark and John Hall executors of the last will and testament of George Hall dec'd to Arch M. Russell dated the 11th day of December 1848 was proven in open court by C. B. Philips one of the subscribing witnesses thereto and ordered to be registered.

March session 1849 - Ordered that C.B. Phillips be overseer of the state road from the forks of Pigeon River to ... Bailey Mingus.

December court 1849 - A deed of conveyance from Elisha Philips to C. B. Philip for 121 acres of land dated the 25th day of September 1849 was acknowledged in open court and ordered to be registered.

Wednesday morning 23rd June 1852 Court met according to adjournment and proceeded to draw a jury for sept term of the Supr. court as follows:(42 names in all)
7. Elisha Philips
15. C. B. Philips
19. A. M. Russell

June session 1854 - Jury sworn included 7. C. B. Philips. C. B. Philips also drawn as a juror for the September term and appointed election judge in the "Sherriff's" race.

Jury list December 1854 included C. B. Philips as did lists for 1855 and 1856 and again in 1856, Christenberry served as election judge this time in the senate race. Both he and his father Elisha were drawn to serve on the Superior Court jury in 1856.

March session 1857, C.B. Philips was a security for Sarah P. Moore who was guardian to the minor heirs of James Moore deceased.

In June 1857 he was judge for the constable race, and at the same session asked to be released from his bond for Sarah Moore. He was on the Jury list for December 1857.

In the June session 1858, C. B. Phillips was selected to be on the Grand Jury and in December on the Jury again.

In the September session 1859 a list of the "waits and measures" of Haywood County was returned by the standard keeper. - 1 half bushel; 1 Galon Measure; 1/2 Galon Measure;1 Quart; 1 Pint; 1/2 Pint; 1 Yardstick and Box; 7 Weight; 1 Brand - N. Carolina

In the June session 1861 C.B. Phillips was drawn for the Grand Jury.

In the September Session 1861 The execution of a deed from C. B. Phillips to Elisha Phillips was duly proven and ordered to be registered.

December 1861, C.B. Phillips was appointed patrol for Beaverdam district of Haywood County.

A list of Jurors to serve in the October Session of court included C. B. Phillips in May 1863, and again in the August session 1865 he was selected for the October court asa was his brother B. R. Philips (Bynum)

April Session 1868
Lavisey Robinson)
Expartee) Petition for Years Provision

On motion of L.C. Hollifield a Justice of the Peace and A. J. Murry, Joseph Christopher, and C. B. Phillips Freeholders are appointed commissioners to view the estate of her late husband dcd and to allot and set apart to his widow Lavisy Robinson now so much of the crop stock and provisions belonging thereto as may be adequate to the support of herself andfamily for one year and if there shall not be sufficient on hand to afford such an allowance then to access the deficiency in money. Said commisioners are to report to the next session of this court.

7-3-3 Hannah b. ca. 1826 m. Archibald Russell Archibald Russell died in Haywood County North Carolina. He was a soldier of the Confederacy and after the war a successful farmer in the Pigeon Valley. He married Hannah Phillips, daughter of Elisha and Clarissa (Evans) Phillips.

Their son, Joseph Hascue Russell was born in 1848. He was educated in the common schools. At the age of fourteen he ran away from home and enlisted in the twenty fifth North Carolina Regiment, Company C, Ransom's Brigade, Longstreets Corps. He served three years in the war.

After the war, Hascue Russell entered the Louisville Medical College at Louisville, Kentucky, and graduated in the class of 1876. He was a practicing physician in the town of Canton for twenty eight years in both general practice and surgery. He was a democrat and a Mason. He died in 1904.

Dr. Russell married Tina Smathers of Canton and they reared the following children: Dora who married J.O. Kinsland, a teacher and farmer; Daisy who died at the age of 25; Jesse Milton, a physician of Canton; Grover C., a deputy sheriff of Canton; Arch G., Chief of Police of Canton; Fred, a clerk in the Wachovia Bank and Trust Co. of Asheville, who was first sergeant in the 115th machine gun battalion and served in France during the World War; Bertha, wife of Samuel Moses, a contractor of Washington D.C.; Joseph Faine, Tax Collector of Canton; Annie, wife of Ralph Bass of Canton; and Emily who lives in

Asheville.
        7-3-4 Irenia m. Andrew J. Fain Oct. 9, 1843
        7-3-5 Alief(Alissa or Airliss) b.about 1818 m. Benjamin Robeson(Robertson) Oct. 29, 1833.
On October 29, 1833 Benjamin Robertson(Robeson) of Habersham County Georgia was married to Alissa Phillips daughter of Elisha and Clarissa Phillips of Haywood County, NC at the home of the Reverend Reuben Philips.
           7-3-5-1 A.E. b. about 1835 (boy)
           7-3-5-2 S.S. b. about 1838 (girl)
           7-3-5-3 V.L. b. about 1840 (boy)
           7-3-5-4 W.J.B. n. about 1847
        7-3-6 Sewell b. Aug. 20, 1830 m. Ada Gillespie

THE METHODIST EPISCOPAL CHURCH SOUTH ET.AL VERSUS ATHENS FEMALE COLLEGE ET. AL. July 2, 1866... On March 1, 1858 the Tennessee Legislature incorporated in Athens, Tennessee a school for young ladies called the Athens Female College. The M. E. Church South and its agents apparently took over this institution from the Independent Order of Odd Fellows by purchase, and added to the acreage so as to increase it to twelve or fourteen acres plus the original improvements. When the Reverend Erastus Rowley took over the administration of this building in 1858, the school was already in debt. Because of the Civil War, Rowley became unable to make the payments, and asked the court to allow him to sell the property to pay the debts. In the mean time, he had begun school in the building, renting it to a teacher who lived on the premises and had his home nearby. The M.E. Church asked that it be given time to make the payment, and <u>Reverend Sewell Phillips</u> was appointed by the Holston Conference as an agent to raise the money to acquire the school.

August 30, 1875 to Elisha from Rev. Reuben: You have a cousin who now ranks among the talented of the Holston Conference. Sewell Philips. His address is Eagle Furnace, Roane County, Tennessee. You may wish to open a correspondence. He weighs 300 pounds and is wealthy.

The Reverend Sewell Philips died at his home in Roane County, Tennessee on February 27th, 1896. He was born August 20, 1830 in Haywood County, North Carolina, the son of Elisha and Clarissa(Evans) Phillips. From his youth he was taught the scriptures by his parents who were plain old-fashioned Methodists. In his early youth he was converted to God, and became a power for good in the community where he was raised. He was licensed to preach on July 12, 1851 by the Reverend William Hicks, Presiding elder of the Asheville District, and was admitted on trial in the Holston Conference. In 1853 he was ordained deacon by Bishop Robert Paine at Wytheville, Virginia, and in 1855 ordained Elder by Bishop Paine at Jonesboro, Tennessee.

On August 1, 1856 Sewell married Ada A. Gillespie, daughter of R.A. and Hannah Gillespie. This couple had the following children: Ema, Robert, John, Edward, Catherine, William, and Mary A. These were all born in Roane County, Tennessee.

Sewell inherited a large estate from his wife's father, and though he came from a frugal home, his great intellect allowed him to manage the large interests involved with his wife's farm. He developed a good business sense and made handsome profits on the farm. From this money sprang the beautiful church at Asbury Campground.

Sewell Phillips was a powerful preacher, and except for his involvement with the farm, would have probably become one of the greatest in Methodism. He preached in churches all across Roane County and beyond, and no small country church or backcountry schoolhouse was too shabby for him to enter and preach the gospel. He was much in demand, and often a small country congregation heard a sermon from his lips which would have delighted a large metropolitan congregation.

Though a man of God, he struggled with Satan, and his farming business often caused him to appear irritable and harsh. On his deathbed however he wished to make peace with all mankind, which caused an awful struggle to erupt within his being. Finally through the grace of God, he found the power to forgive all who had sinned against him in the secular world.

On his dying bed he told his friends gathered around him that he had been resentful of the physical suffering, but now he saw the way clear and his soul was in an ecstacy of joy. His Voice grew faint and [as he died] he whispered a mighty "Hallelujah".

> 7-3-6-1 Ida b. ca 1858 m. Rudder Hood
> 7-3-6-2 Ema D. Phillips b. 1860 m. ____ Long
> 7-3-6-3 Robert N. Phillips b. 1862 m. Helen R. Johnson
> 7-3-6-4 John M. Phillips b. 1864
> 7-3-6-5 Edward B. Phillips b. 1867 m. Vida Collins
> 7-3-6-6 Catherine M.(Bird) Phillips b. 1869 m. Euclid Waterhouse

7-3-6-7 William Eugene Phillips b. 1872
7-3-6-8 Mary Anne Phillips b. 1875 m. Charles Montgomery
7-3-7 Catherine
7-3-8 Bynum b. May 16, 1836 m. Elizabeth Herren Oct. 1, 1838 d, May 15, 1906

Bynum Philips died May 15, 1906. He was the son of Elisha and Clarissa(Evans) Philips of Haywood County, North Carolina and was born May 16, 1836. He remained in Haywood County all his life as a farmer and a stationed preacher on the Methodist Church.

7-3-8-1 Emily C. b. March 17, 1859 m. George Renno. d. June 24, 1898
7-3-8-2 Ada L. b. July 16, 1861 d. Oct. 15, 1885
7-3-8-3 Philetus Benson b. May 8, 1863
7-3-8-3-1 Edith Evelyn Phillips b. 1 Oct 1896 Canton, NC. m. December 1917 to Robert Russell
7-3-8-3-1-1 Robert Phillips Russell d. in World War II
7-3-8-3-1-2 Billy Martin Russell d.y.
7-3-8-3-1-3 Betty Lee Russell b. 5 January 1921 m. Louis Charles Hurd (b. 17 Nov. 1918)

Betty Lee Hurd took her B.S. Degree in Music at the University of North Carolina at Greensboro and her M.M. in Music at the University of Michigan. Louis Hurd also received his M.M. in Education at the University of Michigan. Upon retirement, they returned to the old Farm where Elisha Phillips had built his house about 1814, where they reside at present (1994)

7-3-8-3-1-3-1 Leslie Jean Hurd b. 16 December 1948 m. 1984 Terry Roberts.

Leslie took her Bachelor's degree in Psychology at the University of Connecticut.

Charles Andrew Roberts b. 5 July 1985
James Michael Roberts b. 9 Jan. 1987
7-3-8-3-1-3-2 Phillip Charles Hurd b. 10 May 1952 m. Beverly Betz 1981

Phillip Charles Hurd toook his Master's degree in Hospital Administration at Duke and is the Director of Finance and statistical analysis Medical Service Plan Johns Hopkins.

Nathaniel Hurd b. 9 Oct. 1982

Caitlin Elisabeth Hurd b. 25 December 1984

7-3-8-3-1-3-3 Gary Russell Hurd b. 15 Sept. 1955 m. Jane Watson 1983

Gary Russell Hurd took his degrees in Landscape Architecture and Accounting at Colorado State University and Western Carolina University. He is the Director of Finance at the United Church of Christ Retirement Center.

7-3-8-3-1-4 James Frank Russell died in WWII

7-3-8-3-1-5 Evelyn Jean Russell b. 18 December 1927 m. Mack Neel Adams 28 Dec. 1950

Evelyn took her degree in Social Work at the University of N.C. at Greensboro.

7-3-8-3-1-5-1 Bobby Neel Adams b. 9 July 1953

7-3-8-3-1-5-2 Thomas Turner Adams b. 17 August 1954

7-3-8-3-1-5-3 Kent Russell Adams b. 13 July 1956 m. Linda Larson 1989

7-3-8-3-2 Tymah Phillips b. 1898 m. Narvel Crawford

7-3-8-3-2-1 Narvel James Crawford b. November 1929 N.C. State Representative

7-3-8-4 Evva Leona b. July 15, 1867

7-3-8-5 Mary Ann b. Jan 1, 1865 d. Jan. 1, 1866

7-3-8-6 Tinna E. b. Oct. 17, 1869 m. J. R. Moffitt d. July 17, 1898

7-3-9 Lucinda b. about 1820 married Andrew Robeson September 15, 1836 Habersham Co. GA.

Lucinda daughter of Elisha and Clarissa Phillips was married September 15, 1836 in Habersham County Georgia to Andrew Robinson(Robeson).

7-3-9-1 C.E. b. about 1838 (boy)
7-3-9-2 R.K. b. about 1843 (boy)
7-3-9-3 C.P. b. about 1845 (boy)
7-3-9-4 J.R. b. about 1847 (boy)
7-3-9-5 J.W. Robeson b. about 1849
7-3-9-6 Jackson Robeson b. about

1840(living with Elisha Dion in 1850 census; probably bound out.)
7-3-10 Allie m. Duncan Herren
7-3-11 Althea m. William Alexander Sept 12, 1851
7-3-12 James
7-3-13 Emily
7-3-14 Elizabeth
7-3-15 Laura did not marry

7-4 Reuben b. Dec. 4, 1795 d. 12 Feb. 1887 m. 1) Elizabeth King October 20, 1820 2) Caroline(Owen) Sadler Dec. 7, 1847

Biography of Reuben Philips

At the request of some of my children, I write in short synopsis of the most particular events of my life. I was born in Mecklenburg County, North Carolina in A. D. 1795 on the 4th day of December, twelve miles S.E. of Charlotte on Crooked Creek. My grandmother on my father's side was a Welsh Lady. My Grandfather on my mother's side was an Englishman, and a clergyman of the Baptist Church. My father and mother were both members of the Methodist Church, but my mother always retained strong preferences in favor of baptism by immersion.

My father settled in the bounds of a Presbyterian Congregation and being inconvenient to the knowledge of his own church he became a subscriber in the support of Mr. Barr the Presbyterian Minister and communed with his congregation, he and mother, and received pastoral visits and had his children regularly catechized by Mr. Barr.

When I was four years old, my father taught a small neighborhood school and when the weather was pleasant he took me with him. On seeing the other children learning, I became anxious to try. My father made me letters on paper and pasted them to a paddle and I soon learned them all... I now think in one day! He then gave me a Dikes Spelling Book and I was allowed to say a row in the short words as often as I could learn them. I would say some forty or fifty lessons per day and by going to school a few days I was enabled to learn at home, so I soon could read in the testament and shorter catechism which was required of us all that could read at all. The first verses I ever memorized was in Dikes Universal Spelling Book as follows:
> "A town besieged they held consultation which was the best method of fortification. A grave skillful mason gave in his opinion, that nothing but stone would save his dominion. A Carpenter said, that was very well spoke, but better by far to defend it with Oak. A currier wiser than both these together said, try what you please, there is nothing like leather."

I was at this time about four years of age and loved my book very much. I soon memorized the shorter catechism and was examined by Mr. Barr, and received encomiums for so early learning to read. I can truly say as did the Apostle to Timothy that from a child I knew the scriptures.

My father was poor and could not board me out to school and there being no English school within reach I was not permitted to go to school any more while we lived in that country. There was a German school not far off and on being with the Dutch boys I learned to spell and read easy books in that language, and also read a little in the Dutch Testament. All that I can now remember of religious exercises was that my father kept up family worship and took us to church on Sabbath. We had a pew in the Presbyterian Church where Father and Mother and all the children sat during divine service. We were kept under close and ridged discipline at church and during the Sabbath. I also remember when I was baptized. A Methodist Minister called at my fathers by the name of Gazaway. He was an old itinerant minister whose circuit came within some twelve miles of my fathers. Hearing my father was a Methodist, he called on him to learn his situation as to his soul. While there he baptized all my father's children that had not been baptized. Though I was only in my fifth year I remember after baptism that he laid his hand on our heads and talked about us. As he laid his hand on my head, I had strange feelings something like tremors. As my mother was greatly affected during the exercises, I felt my heart ache, but do not recollect that I felt any guilt for sin as I was unconscious of any law except parental prohibition and injunction.

In my sixth year I remember feeling the first alarm from any danger. While at play with my little brother and sister, near where my father was at work with some flax a huge rattlesnake crept into our midst and my sister younger than myself was playing with it as it was at full length. There appeared no disposition on its part to harm us. As she put her hand near its tail it drew itself up into a coil and began to rattle. My father then suddenly told us to run, being greatly frightened and then cut off its head with a hoe. When he explained to us the great danger we were in and our merciful preservation I then trembled with <u>fear</u>.

In the year 1803 my father moved to the mountains and settled in the western part of Buncombe County and lived one year in the neighborhood of Turkey Creek and as he rented land we had a hard year. In the fall of 1803 he purchased a piece of land unimproved on the beaverdams of Hominy Creek and we moved to it on the 10th of March 1804.

There being but few inhabitants we had no church, no school, and no Sabbath except at my fathers. He still kept up religious exercises in his family and was able to govern his family on the Sabbath. Gradually the older children formed association with the youth in the county and, there being no church, all began to retrograde in morals.

In the year 1806, Daniel Asbury came to my fathers as a Missionary and I remember how thankful he and mother were to see one more minister of the gospel. He being Presiding Elder of the district adjoining that county had a tour to see whether a circuit could be formed. At the request of my father he left an appointment for the preacher that was to be sent. Accordingly, a Brother Jesse Richardson came and preached at my father's house and formed a society which prospered greatly. My father became Class Leader and if I remember correctly Brother Samuel Mills succeeded Brother Richardson and as he was a great revivalist many were added to the church and my mother became greatly stirred up in religion. She had a regular hour for secret prayer and kept her testament all the time where she went morning and evening for prayer and meditation. She often came home shouting from her place of secret prayer which was a large hollow chestnut tree where she resorted every day. On one occasion she took me with her and told me she wished me to assist her in putting some bushes around the tree to make it more secret and to turn off the evening sun.

While we were there she said to me that I might recollect when she was dead that she had a place where she regularly prayed in secret. Before she left, she took me into the tree and prayed for me and talked with me about my soul. Here I felt the first impressions to save my soul and the first moving of the spirit. I was truly concerned and did make solemn promises to seek religion. I had not as yet learned the ways of sin, but I was thrown into bad company and saw and heard wicked boys talk of things that I am sorry until now that I ever heard. I was not wickedly disposed but in changing nights with other boys I thought that what was told me was true. I therefore lost confidence in almost everybody on finding myself so badly deceived in some that were making great pretension to religion. I became disgusted with the usages of the church, especially classmeeting because so many had gone back to wickedness that had been so religious in classmeeting. I should have become an infidel even at so early a period but for the regular religious life of my mother and her prayers for me. I went to church and delighted very much to hear good preaching but my impressions about my soul became weaker and I became more careless.

It was my regular business to attend to the stock and bring them from the mountains [where they wandered many miles]. I found it necessary to carry my gun to protect me from the vermin that I might be exposed to. There were bears, panthers, wolves, and catamounts in abundance. Being fearless, I often camped out at night alone, and in those solitary regions I thought a great deal on religious matters. One of the leading members of the society had become a subject of many censures and was called a notorious hypocrite, altho he made unusual pretensions and was prompt to duty, it was said that if he was not a hypocrite there was none. I watched him faithfully to be convinced of his sincerity. He also followed the mountains in search of game. On one occasion I had wandered so far as to find it necessary to camp out and being some eight or ten miles from where any person lived, I rested badly that night. The wolves were howling in different directions.

In the morning I left camp and crossed a large mountain quite early and when going down on a headwater of Mills River I heard a human voice at some distance in the cove below. I thought at times it was a sound of distress. I drew nigher until I could hear the words of prayer and praise. I ventured quite up and found my old friend walking without his hat with his face turned up towards heaven. He would clap his hands and shout and walk to and from and then he would sit down and be quiet for a short time and then burst into loud hallelujahs. I stood and looked on for a long time, knowing that he was unconscious of any person being within ten miles of him. All my infidel temptations left me and I fully gave into the truth of religion and that he was one who possessed it. I at length approached him which at first surprised him. On being informed how I came there he was so happy as to shout aloud. I in my heart felt that I wanted such religion as he had and set a determined resolution to seek for it. This was in the fall of the year 1808. I was remarkably small for my age being not quite 13 years old. I knew but little, only to hunt for stock and kill game which I was fortunate in doing.

My father and mother at length became alarmed for the welfare of their children, there being no school to which they could send their children so my father sold out his farm and purchased a situation some 20 miles east near Asheville. In the fall of 1809 he moved the family leaving me to winter the stock. During that winter a school was opened by a good teacher, so I went to school two months and studied arithmetic and worked through the rule of three [today called proportion]. I made fine improvements in writing and as I was alone most of the time I had a fine chance at night. The school terminated. I was very sorry. It cost my father nothing as I worked for my teacher in the days and fed the stock at night. In April my father came and took his stock all home.

On the way home an application was made to my father to let me teach in a small neighborhood. My father consented on the condition that three of the principal people be trustees and guard my interests. On the first monday in May 1810 I commenced my first school on the Swannani River. Jeremiah West, Francis Sluder, and Cornelius Sale were my trustees. I weighed precisely sixty pounds. I had 22 scholars - a mixed school. I mustered the boys every day according to Duanes Military Tactics. At the end of three months our examination was largely attended and general satisfaction expressed by all involved. A new school was made up for more scholars than I ought to have had. That school was made for twelve months and I taught for fifty cents per month, two thirds in trade. I closed that years school at Christmas in the year 1812. I then spent the winter at my fathers and assisted him in making some improvements on his plantation and in removing some buildings.

I also assisted in making a crop the next summer which was the year 1813. In the month of January 1814 I left home to go to school and commence at the single rule of three and in seventeen days I went through the square and cube root. I arranged to pay my teacher $10 to teach me the art of mapping and surveying with plane table and compass and went thirty days in all and then broke up. I could not help showing my disappointment but having learned to survey, my teacher took me to my own house and in two days I learned the use of the quadrant and how to find the latitude, so I paid him for everything.

I returned home and some two weeks after that I came back to see him and we took a tour into the mountains to gather Fir Oil from the native fir tree called Balsam. We went up the east fork of Pigeon River passing Mount Pisgah which was an exceedingly high peak so high so as to be seen all over the surrounding country to the distance of thirty miles. This mountain lay in a Southwesterly direction from Asheville and we circled it, leaving it on the east and Northeast of us. We next ascended the Shining Mountain which lay in a south direction from Mount Pisgah. We made our camp near The Star which was an uncommonly large rock as white as snow and crystallized as clear as transparent flint. It could be seen at a distance of 15 or 20 miles like a star of great magnitude!

We returned home, rested on the Sabbath and parted, never to meet again. His name was W.G. Berry and he very soon moved to Indiana.

I then returned home to my fathers near Asheville and commenced school on the 14th day of July 1814 some 18 miles from home in the neighborhood of Newfound Creek on the west side of French Broad River. I taught one session of six months and closed up at Christmas. At this examination we had a treat given by the principal employers, and my school was full to overflowing. [There were] some 40 scholars and on that day there were a great number of persons in attendance. There was sweetened brandy and cakes and pies in abundance. Some of my small students became intoxicated. From this time I resolved to never allow any spirits at an examination over which I had any control.

On the first monday in January (1815) I commenced again at [the French Broad River] for twelve long months! I had to teach a night school for persons who wished to study arithmetic three nights in the week until 10 o'clock. In order to keep up the copybooks and copies on paper I went nearly every morning at four o' clock, made fires, warmed up the house and set copies in readings for all the day. A cold breakfast was sometimes sent to me by some of the scholars and if not I done without until dinner. This was a charming school.

I was envied by a Mr. Silas Green who was a school teacher. He tried to break up my school, asI was so young and a poor scholar. My friends stood by me to a man and when we wrote against each other, the judges gave it in my favor. He became so enraged that he left the country.

During this 18 months I boarded among the employers, going where I choose and as often as I chose. The people were mostly Baptist of the old school, now called Hard Shell Baptist. Their pastor was an old man by the name of Thomas Snelson; very ignorant and bigoted. I attended his ministry once a month on both days of their meetings. In this church I heard the old pastor preach a sermon on the text <u>Nine and Twenty Knives</u> that were used in Solomons Temple. Altho I had been somewhat concerned about my soul I must confesshis sermon on that subject was not profitable to me, but rather amusing and disgusting.

In the fall of the year, the old pastor sold off and moved to Missouri. I do not remember that any person was baptised that year. The church elected another pastor by the name of Moses Freeman who preached the doctrine of <u>Particular Election and Reprobation</u> and the churchmembers with whom I boarded were mostly of that belief and from hearng the doctrine preached so much and the people vindicating the doctrine, I became wretched in my feelings and disgusted at the whole gospel system

During the fall, Lorenzo Dow preached in the country and left a tract called his <u>chain</u> which was a complete answer to all the system of calvinism. I read one of them over and over, and being so well pleased with his doctrine I betook myself to composing pieces. At length I wrote a poem on the subject of Calvinism which in part has recently been published by the Elyton Times. This I read to some of the prominent members of the church and they ceased to annoy me any more.

At the close of this term an application was made for me to teach in an adjoining neighborhood near old Thomas Forrester's. In January 1815(1816?) I commenced teaching for twelve long months (with) some thirty grown scholars. I had some fifty regular scholars. I was exceedingly busy and but for teaching a night school, I could not have managed at all. I remained all night at the school and very often caught up the writing on copybooks that were behind.

In the spring of that year the wife of Alexander Starrett died. I attended the burial and my heart was unusually affected on seeing one of her daughters (a twin) whose name was Ruth jump into the grave when her mother was let down. The little girl lay on the coffin and could not be prevailed on to get out until she was taken by force and carried away until her mother was buried. The father married again within two or three months and the children were all scattered, but I took the twins into school and the oldest single daughter and on my own expense gave them as much as I could well teach; Ruth and Polly in particular.

I spent the most of my Saturdays at Esquire James Gudgers, writing in the Register's office, recording deeds for which he gave me one dollar per day.

That year I purchased a farm from William Eaton in Haywood County on the head of Homney creek. I let my brother <u>Elisha</u> live on it as he had just married and had no farm, we united our interest as one; he farmed while I taught school and our interest was as one until the year I married and he still lives on the place and raised some seventeen children.

In the year of 1816 I took a school in Haywood County. I taught in a Baptist Church called Locust Old Fields. The Reverend Humphrey Posey was the pastor and I enjoyed myself remarkably under his ministry. He was a Missionary Baptist and preached free Salvation for all. He was a great revivalist and many were added to the church that year.

I taught one year at Locust Old Fields and then took a school for six months on the beaver dams of Hominy Creek near my brothers. The neighborhood was so dissipated that I taught in that place only six months commencing a few days before christmas. For the first time I was barred out at christmas and it proved a serious matter. My employers collected and demanded the house and those within refused to give it up. The parties were armed and ready to engage in a general Rain Countre. I at length went to the place; dismissed all and returned home unmolested; so the trouble ceased.

During the winter we engaged a Mr. Moses White to teach a music school in the school house. I was a scholar. He taught six or seven days and gave it up, so I only got to know the rules and a few tunes in the different parts. I was truly sorry as I had a good voice to sing and a talent to learn.

In the fall of that year I commenced a school on Sandymush Creek in the west part of Buncombe County near Colonel James Lowrey. The neighborhood was composed of about forty families and no church but the Methodist and an excellent community. I enjoyed myself very well and being anxious to learn music I applied to the same Mr. White to come over and teach for us. He accordingly sent articles and the school was made up. He employed me to make the manuscript books. The school commenced. He attended and taught two days and at the close of the second day he informed us that he could not teach any more so the school was done. The young people had a meeting and resolved that I should take his place and that they would sustain me. I concluded to try, so I commenced in good earnest, only knowing four or five tunes in the parts. [I] appointed the next saturday for the first day. I soon memorized the rules and practiced some more tunes on saturday. The first saturday in October 1816 I commenced my first music school. I taught on saturdays only and sang on Sabbath gratuitous.

The young people that were the scholars at Newfound 10

miles east of my school hearing that I had commenced teaching music and was succeeding very well came over by numbers and applied to me to give them a school. I agreed to do so and I alternated one saturday and Sabbath at each place. My reading school continued the following season which embraced the year 1817. I still kept my music schools and got old Brother Nathan Harrison to preach on the Sabbath at both schools.

My good success was published all over the county and a petition was sent from Locust Old Fields where I had before taught school for me to teach a reading school and a singing school for them. I was violently opposed by the community of Sandymush but by getting me to promise to return to them they gave up, so I opened a school at Locust Old Fields on the first monday of January 1818 and a music school also for saturdays and sundays gratuitously. Old father Shook came to hear us sing and was so delighted that he proposed his house [five miles west] for me to sing in. Old Father Shook had a fine house and in the third story he had a room 40 feet square well finished for preaching for the Methodist. I made a large school at that place some fifty scholars and had the assistance of my old friend Humphrey Posey who was an experienced music teacher. This school drew together a vast concourse of young people from both schools.

I felt this year the great necessity of religion and did seek for it, but being opposed to the doctrine of the Calvinist and the Altar Exercises of the Methodist, I was unable to obtain religion.

Towards the end of the summer my friend Posey and Parson Byers requested that we should call all the Sandymush and Newfound music scholars for a three day singing - two at Father Shooks and on sunday at Waynesville five miles further west. We had over 120 singers; the greatest singing ever witnessed in that county. On sunday we went in procession to the muster field where a stand was erected for preaching. The hymn was sung that effects my heart. I was so overcome as to be scarcely able to stand on my feet. The hymn was commenced "Oh tell me no more of this worlds vain store etc."

Just as prayer was closed a runner was sent to tell us that Mrs Welch who had been sick was dying. This produced some confusion for a few minutes until the doctor and the relatives got away. There remained a congregation like a Campmeeting and we had a most extraordinary good sermon from the text in the psalms "He sitteth between the cherubims, let the earth be moved."

This day humbled my soul and I was truly anxious to obtain religion. I wept and sobbed under preaching and felt some tokens of joy, but would not excuse that faith which brings salvation. This ended up our schools for the music line but I carried on my reading school until Christmas and then returned to Sandymush for the purpose of opening a school according to promise.

In 1818 I took a singing school in the north end of Buncombe County after the schools at old Father Shooks was done. This school in Buncombe was the hardest task I ever undertook to perform as it was fifty miles from Locust Old Fields where I taught my reading school. In performing the duties of this school, I left my Reading School at 3 o'clock on thursday evening and rode 25 miles that night and rose next morning at 4 o'clock and rode 25 miles by 10 o'clock and sung until 3 o'clock Saturday and on Monday morning. They paid me well for all my trouble as I had 60 scholars and prompt pay.

On the first monday in January 1819 I commenced teaching. I had a splendid school as I only engaged for nine months intending to travel in the fall. During this school, Elizabeth King attended as a scholar. She was 26 or 27 years old I thought she would suit me for a wife. Her widowed mother lived in the state of Virginia. She had one brother in the neighborhood who had a family, but she made her home at Robert Bell's Esquire. After she quit school I contemplated the matter prayerfully and as I seldom ever kept female company privately I determined to propose to her my hand and heart. I sought an opportunity and without much ceremony told her my determination. In a few weeks I called and she gave me her hand and we solemnly covenanted to be true to each other though I was to travel first. No mortal was to know of our engagement but ourselves.

During the year 1819 a public controversy took place between Humphrey Posey and Allen Turner the travelling Methodist preacher on the subject of Wesley's Testament. Posey said the scriptures were altered and for the worse; turner asserted to the contrary. Dr. Coffin of Green County, Tennessee and Francis H. Porter of Asheville, Buncombe County were referred to on the subject of translation; they being Presbyterian Ministers and linguists it was thought proper to refer the matter to them. Both decided in favor of the translation of Wesley's Testament as being a better translation than our present version. It was soon ascertained that Daniel Witt and Thomas Wear the book agents of the Methodist Episcopal Church had taken the translation out of Wesley's notes and bound them into a testament and sent them out as

Methodist books, without the knowledge of the book committee of the General Conference. This matter made a great stir among the Baptist and created much hard feelings between the two denominations. At length the best informed Baptists became reconciled with the translation except where it related to baptism by immersion. The preposition from the water in our saviours baptism was never reconciled. The copy used in debate is now in the library of Thomas W. Sadler Esquire being retained by myself until Elisha Philips was licensed to preach when I gave it to him. He sold it with other books to T. W. Sadler Esquire. I felt greatly grieved that a difficulty should take place with my old particular friend and the people among whom I was teaching, and it was carried on in my school house. The Reverend Posey preached from second Timothy 3rd. 16th "All scripture is given by inspiration of God". The Reverend Turner preached from a passage in Job "I will also show mine opinion". The day was taken up in this controversy. The Sabbath following the Reverend Joseph Byers (Now of this county) and Stephen White answered all the controversies at the house of Mr. Mason a citizen of the same neighborhood, so the fire went out among the common people and much excitement ensued and no real good that I could ever see. And I must confess it was calculated to harden my then tender feelings about my soul. Altho I had determined to seek religion that year, these circumstances did me no good in obtaining that good blessing.

After I finished my schools and made some collections I purchased a splendid horse and began to prepare to travel. [Thomas Siler, a young man who lived about six miles away agreed to go with Reuben]. We travelled only two days, being in the first part of October and my horse took the sore tongue. We lodged at Jacob Calers on Jonathans Creek; he was an old friend of mine, and had been sent to school to me at Newfound my second school, so I had to stop until my horse could travel. My companion went on to Macon County where he had brothers living; it was still Indian lands. He waited there some ten days until I caught up with him. We rested one day and then on October 15 we started on our journey. We soon got into the Indian settlement but had good luck and struck Alabama at Wills Creek and from there to Jones Valley. We came to Village Creek four miles Northwest of where Elyton now is. Siler was anxious to teach school somewhere, and the people finding out that I was a teacher solicited me to take a school. I went with [Thomas Siler] to Tuscaloosa. It was a town mostly built of clapboards. We went to McCowans Bluff where he made up a school.

I returned to Village Creek and drew up articles and Jonathan and David Prude rode with me to make a school at Frog Level ... The people set to work; built a schoolhouse and I commenced first monday in December, 1819, with only seven scholars the first day [as I] had Parson Owens influence against me. My school so increased that on monday morning of the second month there were 40 scholars and Old Parson Owen came over and put under my care his little son William. This was the first monday in January 1820. I boarded among the scholars and taught a night school three nights in the week and was kindly treated by all the people.

Biography of David Gardiner Phillips (probably unrelated)
Then there were no electric, gas, or even lamp lights. We had tallow, sometimes molded, candles, but more often simple "dips". Our main dependence for light at night was a pine knot blaze. Our three months winter schools of that day, the only schools we had, would have put Goldsmith to the blush.

We made no cotton in those days, but we made plenty of everything [we needed] and lived comfortably. We had no money, and no opportunities except those of laboring country boys. I had never seen a buggy, a railroad, a pistol, or a playing card.

At night by pine knot fires I had made myself a fair english scholar. With my mother's assistance I had mastered Dilworth's Speller, Pike's Arithmetic, Woodbridges Geography, Kirkham's Grammar, Obey's Philosophy and had become a good scribe.

I had been partially seeking religion for several years but was unsuccessful up to that time. I invited Parson Lockhart of the Cumberland Presbyterian Church to preach every round in my school house and Matthew D. Thomason and a Mr. Rennoc Circuit Preachers of the Methodist Church also preached every two weeks. Soon after the circuit commenced, M. D. Thomason had a fight and left the work. Ebenezer Hearn came on the circuit or Mission. I was pleased with his company. He advised me how to seek religion and I made it a rule to remain every evening that I could until sundown and wright for the school and invariably attended to secret prayer before I left. I became very anxious on the subject of religion and visited old brother Miles the class leader. He was an experimental christian; this was what I desired as I was well versed in the theory of religion.

I also formed an acquaintance with Parson Hosea Holcombe a minister of the Baptist Church and formed a music school in one of his churches, called Ruhama some six or seven miles up the valley. But I could not profit much by his conversation as he invariably lugged in the doctrine of baptism by immersion and as I had been baptized and felt satisfied on that subject, it became rather irksome than otherwise to me to talk on that subject. And in the meantime some things were reported among which was that he would take spirits too freely at times for a minister of the gospel. I received but little spiritual information from him altho we were very friendly socially speaking. At length I opened my true condition to old Sister Prude who was an acquaintance of my parents and who was a good christian. I kept my washing at her house and also had my horse kept on her farm. I found her a practical christian and a constant bible reader. My heart was affected when I prayed, often I went to church and read the scriptures and on the 14th of February 1820 about sundown while I was engaged in secret prayer in my school house, I verily thought I saw a storm of wrath coming down upon me. I felt as though I was lost forever! But I prayed fervently and cast myself wholly on the mercy of God and looked with an eye of faith to the atonement. I felt that God was reconciled with me for what Christ had done for me. I felt an inward peace and the gathering storm turned to a sweet calm. My heart melted down into tenderness and thankfulness. I fully believed my sins were forgiven and I claimed the mercy of Christ as mine. I could not leave the place for a time; I sat calmly down and wept tears of joy I did truly wonder why I had been so unbelieving. I had felt for years in prison that God intended me to work in his vineyard somewhere. I there promised to take up the cross and try to do all that I felt enjoined on me to perform, whether it pleased the world or not. I went down to Colonel John Browns who lived but a few hundred yards, to spend the night. He was from home. His wife was a good christian woman of the Baptist Church and very diffident on all subjects but that of religion. She would talk freely on that subject. I told her what I had just experienced. She wept and laughed and talked and thanked the Lord, so I went to rest that night for the first time in my remembrance free from guilt and fear.

The next Saturday I had singing and on Sunday we all met for singing and no minister present. My old friend Miles was not in attendance that Sabbath who always prayed when I called on him and I felt it impressed on me to close the exercise with prayer, and I proposed to take a vote whether we would invariably open and close our singing with prayer, and begin that evening, and when put to a vote it was unanimously adopted. I accordingly made an attempt for the first time in my life publicly. I told them of the great change that I had experienced and it had a similar attempt on them. There being a great many in attendance, the word went out every where around the neighborhood and from that time forward when I visited religious families, they asked me to hold family worship. I did so, but it proved the greatest cross I had ever experienced as I was not gifted in prayer; in fact I could scarcely pray at all, but being determined not to yield to temptation, I continued to try. Sometimes I felt happy in the attempt; at other times I felt miserable, but having a music school in Cahaby Valley and in a pious neighborhood, I received great assistance. A young gentleman by the name of Joseph K. Sparks who had taught music some came into school and on seeing my plans, and hearing me lecture made himself known to me as a christian. We talked much on the subject and as neither had joined any church we showed no sectarian feelings, but became like Jonathan and David, in love.

At the close of one session he proposed a partnership in teaching one more session and it was soon made up. We taught together and loved God and one another as christians. I still kept up prayer and moral lecturing, and in this way satisfied my feelings as to public exercises. My music school went on alternately and having a great many grown scholars in my reading school I proposed to them to spend every other day with them in singing at recess, and it was adopted in the room of common play. So I made little manuscript books for the whole school and we had the best music that had ever been had in the valley. Old Parson Owen came in to hear us at noontime and was so well pleased to see and hear the infant voices mingling with the larger that he seldom failed to be there on the days when we sung. This excited others and we often had room for as many as would come, and we invariably stopped at the minute, and all but the school left, though sometimes very reluctant. We had a pleasant school, no difficulty whatever, but the Devil was uneasy and at length did us harm. Elyton as is now, was then called Frog Level -- nothing but a pair of race paths and some of the citizens made a horse race and the sum was some thousand dollars and a great excitement prevailed. The time came, and I prevented the young men and boys from going to the race. They were angry but obeyed my law, and when the race was run, one of the horses flew the track and threw the rider leaving him lifeless for a long time. The other ran through and claimed the money. The parties and their friends engaged in a riot and many fought, some with weapons, some with knives, and so great evil resulted to the assembly. When my young men learned how things turned out, they returned to me and expressed great thankfulness to me for having kept them away as it was their relatives that were in the fight. This circumstance gave me many friends among the religious and parents.

I closed my reading school last day of July, but my singings were not out by something over a month. It was proposed that I would teach one month and let all sing that would and end all my schools at once as I was going to return to North Carolina. That month [on the seventh of September] I had over 50 scholars in attendance [and] I closed. Old Parson Owen preached a sermon and I left for Cahawly Valley the same day.

When I closed up my last school in Alabama, many wept at our parting. On closing up in Cahawly Valley I met with the Reverend Francis K. Porter, a Presbyterian Minister. He was going to North Carolina and we gladly accompanied each other as he lived as a neighbor to my parents. We set off on Monday September 11 and soon got among the Indians. He preached at Lassleys to a congregation of Indians. This was the first Indian congregation I had ever seen. He next preached at Major Ridges a native Indian. There we read several letters from John Ridge and John Ross who were then in Cornwall College in Connecticut. These were interesting letters to me. We then turned up the Oustanella River to Charles Nixes. He was a religious Indian. I heard him read and explain the bible and to my mind made it plain that the Cherokee Indians were descendants of the Jews, from the custom of sacrifices of the first fruits of all they raised from the earth and from the manner of burying the dead.

From thence we went to Spring Place, an old missionary station. Old father Gambold was the minister and teacher and his lady. They were Moravians and they received us cordially. We spent the Sabbath at that place and I heard the preaching to the Indian school and heard them read in their own tongue. I felt like I wanted to stay among them, but we went from thence to Talena, a missionary station by the Presbyterian; Thomas Butrell was the missionary. Here we found John Arch, a native Indian who had been converted and professed to be called to the ministry. We took him along with to North Carolina and he was of great use as a linecaster being acquainted with both languages. We all went together to the Valley Towns Missionary Station. Humphrey Posey was the minister and teacher. We remained only two days and then struck for home and found all well.

I called on Miss Elizabeth King and found her rather impatient as I had been gone so long and still had to go some two hundred miles below to pay some money, but at the time when I would have singing in the neighborhood we would consummate our intended union. That sabbath after singing I rode a few rods with Elizabeth and told her that I would go on by where she lived and ride with a brother that was going home and return at sundown and we would be married before supper. The gentleman and lady (the Bells) with whom she lived were still ignorant of the whole matter, but when I arrived I found it necessary to give him notice as we intended him to celebrate the rites, as Justice of the Peace. I asked him to take the book of discipline and select the place and I informed his wife, and the company and we went upstairs and she accompanied me down to the hall where we were married (October 20, 1820). The news spread that night all over the neighborhood.

Next Morning we started to the State of Virginia to see her mother from whom she had been separated for seven years. On the day we reached her residence my wife appeared all day to be in a melancholy frame of mind as she said it was strange to think she was so near her mother. It was an interesting sight to me to see them meet. Her mother did not know her, but on being informed that it was her daughter she was quite overcome, but on recovering from the excitement we engaged ourselves very well for a few days, but as the time of parting drew near our pleasure was very much mingled with pain, as my wife's mother was old and no reasonable expectation that they would ever see each other any more.

I contemplated to move to Alabama. On Thursday morning on the first day of November we started back to Buncombe County, North Carolina. On our return we were induced to move to my fathers on Swannani River and I had a room inmy fathers house and we boarded ourselves.

On the first monday in January 1821 I commenced a reading school at Alexanders, four miles from home, and also carried on a music school on saturdays.

Reuben Philips taught school at Alexander's again this year and began building a house on his father's land. Schools at this time often had no floor but the earth. In the center burned a fire under a cat and mud chimney supported by four posts placed about six feet apart and about three feet above the floor. Around this in a hollow square were backless benches (half logs). If there was a window, a split log was placed under it for a writing desk. There was a shortage of paper, but what writing that was done was with goose quill pens and homemade ink made from pokeberry leaves, oak galls, iron rust, and inner bark. Later the school would have a puncheon floor and a fireplace at the end of the room. Spelling was often the main object of the lessons. Advanced students read in the New Testament.

Reverend Reuben. In the Month of September on the 9th day we were blessed with the birth of our first child, a daughter. We called her name Clarinda, and as we had not as yet joined any church, I felt it my duty to dedicate our babe to god in the ordinance of baptism. I accordingly went as soon as my wife was able to a small church east up the Bull Mountain and gave myself and child to the Methodist Episcopal Church and my heart to God. Brother Malcolm McPherson was our circuit preacher and his first year as a christian and a minister. He was exceedingly uncultivated and ignorant, so much so that many societies in the circuit rejected him and would not go to church, but I thought him a good man so I gave him my hand in church and my house as a resting place. He made great improvements and became a powerful man under God. [He] was Presiding Elder for many years, wore himself out and died happy and to Heaven.

On the 27th of September I commenced to build myself a [good] house on my father's land and conditionally purchased 100 acres from him and here I built a good house.

When I finished my school at Alexander's the people were so well pleased that a proposition was made for me to take the English school at Asheville in the Academy. I felt inadequate to the task and dreaded it as no man could govern the aristocracy of the place, so I took a winter school on Sandymush, 20 miles from home. I had a very good school, but many boys had grown so large as to trouble me greatly. There were 27 distilleries in the neighborhood and the boys had taken to drink and were so hard to manage that I had to resort to measures of punishment so disagreeable to my self that I returned home in the spring. I succeeded so well in conquering the boys at Sandymush that my old friends at Alexanders sent me an article filled with subscribers and instead of making a crop myself, I hired a young man to work my crop and I went to teaching at Alexanders again. I engaged only for nine months.

I engaged in a music school at the Academy [in Asheville] during the summer and also at Big Ivey some 20 miles north of where I lived. This employed my Saturdays and Sabbaths. I managed the young people of town so well that the parents of the youth determined to have me try one session in the english department. Mr. Porter was still teaching in the Academy; had only ten or twelve scholars and discouraged me so much I felt it hazardous to undertake. He was anxious to have me connected in the same house with him and cordially gave up one of the rooms, he occupying the other. On the first monday in January 1823 I opened a school in the Academy. It was an excellent brick house well furnished for school and also for church services... There were in attendance 30 scholars the first day and very soon the school increased to 45 and some of the summer session I had fifty scholars. I had to go four miles to school, but I was punctual, and gave my whole attention to it.

I had gone the fall before to East Tennessee and brought my Mother-in-law to live with us. She was old and had been a widow 23 years and my wife being her youngest daughter, she gladly made my house her home, as she had not kept house for many years. This circumstance was attended with a great blessing to her and ourselves. She was devoutly religious and read much, and my wife and her enjoyed life to equal any I have before or since known. I being away so much in the day time they were company for each other. I also kept a man hired to make my crop. On the 8th of March, my first son came. We called his name Elisha after my brother next older than myself, with whom I had a partnership for many years, but dissolved it at my marriage. Inasmuch as my mother-in-law lived with us, I lost no time from school. Also my ownb mother lived within 300 yards of us and my father spent a great deal of his spare hours with my wife. They were all religious and Methodist of the old stock and great biblereaders; many bible conversations had they.

I had never had the measles and they were in school. I took them about the 25th of March and not thinking what was the matter, I went to school and during the day they came to the surface. I was advised to go home by my friend Mr. Porter. I started home very sick. Unfortunately for me I was overtaken by an alarming storm of rain, hail, and wind. I got very wet and cold and the measles disappeared from the surface and I verily thought I should die that night. Every effort was made to drive them out, but all in vain. When all gave me up, old man William Gudger came to see me and brought a bottle of peach brandy. He proposed to give me of it assuring me that it had been instrumental in saving his life a short time before under similar circumstances. I commenced using it with great reluctance as I was a <u>sworn</u> enemy to the use of ardent spirits. I continued to drink freely of it during the night; still it had no inebriating effects on me and by sunrise next morning the eruption came to the surface partially...I felt so much relieved as to astonish all my friends, and Elisha King my brother in law in particular.

In 1823, Reuben continued teaching at the Academy in Asheville. He was given a house on the grounds.

Reverend Reuben: In the latter part of the summer of that year, Mr Porter closed up his classes, but having never studied English Grammar, I was greatly at a loss to manage those more advanced, but as those who had been studying grammar had passed over Orthography in a superficial way, I found it important to instruct them in that department which I found myself very capable of doing, to the entire satisfaction of my patrons. I was quite successful in my reading school and also in my singing schools. I finished the term Christmas week and commenced another session on Monday after New Years day.

The winter of 1823 / 1824 was cold and disagreeable.

Reverend Reuben: A few days after the school commenced one of my scholars,[the daughter of Brannon Patton] took sick and died. Mr Porter was now moved away [so] there was no minister at the burying. Her grandfather, Colonel James Smith, asked me to sing and pray and, if I would, make some remarks on the subject. I did so and in addressing the children there was much excitement and her grandfather was seen to shed tears freely which he had scarcely done on any occasion. I had felt for some time a powerful impression to exercise in public and this case aroused in me new convictions and as it was my first attempt I was encouraged to believe that God intended me to labor in his vineyard somewhere. As others thought so, likewise I continued to pray in public at my schools and in my family and elsewhere when called on.

It so happened that in a few months old Colonel Smith died also and among his requests to his family and friends he requested that I should perform the religious services at his grave. This was a trying time as he was a wealthy man and his relatives of the first class of the rich in that country, and he also requested to be buried with honors of war being an old Revolutionary officer. This circumstance drew together an unusually large assembly among whom there were several ministers. I tried to evade the service, but could not as it was his particular request. His children insisted in my making the attempt. I must confess that the drum and fife and solemn procession did sink my feelings very much, but before the firing of platoons commenced we were all marched around the grave in military order and I was called on to hold forth. I accordingly opened my mouth and truly God filled it with suitable words. I now suppose that I never up to this time have made a more successful effort.

I had not yet been licensed to speak in public and after all was over a brother reminded me that I was breaking the rules of the discipline. This mortified me very much, as I could not think of asking liberty to exhort for I felt no impressions to exhort, but I did to preach and I saw no chance for me to do that. So I lay still, satisfying my conscience by admonishing the youth committed to my care. I however named the matter to our preacher and he told me to go ahead when called on. I son had to perform on occasions of death for the burying ground was near my house and almost invariably I was called on to perform the burial service.

I at length found my school to be burthamsome in my house and I purchased a farm from my brother in law Joseph W. Pharr lying near my brother Elisha in Haywood County. He had a distillery and was to pay several hundred gallons of whiskey that winter and could not give possession that year unless I would take the corn and distillery off his hands. I consented to do so and about the first of September I moved to my farm and commenced operating and preparing to make the whiskey. My brother lived within half a mile and he assisted me some and at it I went. Day and night I attended to that Devil's Tea Pot; made the whiskey, paid the debt, sold the distillery, and got out of the whole arrangement.

In 1824, Elisha Phillips moved onto a farm which had been bought by Reuben Philips. They formed a partnership by which Reuben would make money teaching and Elisha would farm. The school building Reuben was teaching in caught fire and burned to the ground, and he had to teach the scholars in his own house on the grounds.

Brother David Cummings was sent as our preacher that year from the Holston Conference and he travelled the French Broad Circuit. He soon found I was on background and learning all around his circuit the feelings of the people with me he used great efforts to get me out from the encumbrance. At length he brought me several singing schools already made up round his circuit. I was persuaded by my wife and brother to go to teaching music again. I hired a man to make my crop and I turned out to teaching. I took one at Hominy Creek, one at Mills River, one at Davidsons River, one weeks work every day singing. I took a school also at Newfound, one at Rims Creek, one at Big Ivey. This was another weeks work. I sing at all these schools one in two weeks alternately. All these schools were in Buncombe County.

On the third day of January, 1825, my wife had her third child born. We called his name Ewell Petty for one of our circuit preachers. He was a remarkably cross child and so troubled his mother that she was well nigh giving over any further business but to attend to him. Her nights were nearly sleepless, and I being gone so much, she was left with a great task, but she had her mother to help. Ruth Starrett was still with us and Jane Clark was a hireling and with us to gain her health, so my wife had company overflowing, so to speak.

Brother David B. Cummings was our circuit preacher and travelled pretty much the same route [as that] of my schools. Learning that I was very useful among the youth where ever I went in every way, he in my absence asked the society to grant me license to exhort. Accordingly on the 11th of August 1825 my license were recorded on the church book of the circuit steward and he handed them to me and told me to go on doing good and let the church feel my influence.

I could not pick any conscientious scruples about being called to work in the church in some was, but thought if I could do anything it would be to preach as I was inclined to systemize, and to order. On his next round, Brother Cummings asked the society where I lived to recommend me to the district conference to be held in East Tennessee where I might be examined and licensed if worthy of the calling.

They readily granted me a recommendation and I wound up all my schools and in company with Brother Cummings, Brother Jacob Weaver, Brother McMahon, and Brother Andrew Pickens started to the district conference to be held at Clear Creek, Green County, East Tennessee. There were a great many ministers in attendance and there were 14 candidates in the class that I was examined in, and we all passed readily except those who had slaves. There was hard debating and rough sailing before they could be licensed at all. On hearing the arguments for and against the subject of slavery, I became disgusted and moved to withdraw my application. As I had no slaves and there was no objection tome, I was persuaded to hold on. My Brethren Weaver and McMahon both had slaves and were the subject of debate. We had with us an old travelling preacher Brother Andrew Pickens, who was a member of the General Conference when the rule on slavery was adopted, so he at length settled the matter much to my notion and we were all licensed and left the meeting with good feelings.

On my way home, I called at old Brother Forsters on

Turkey Creek and attended church on Sabbath and found Brother Andrew Hamil and old Presiding Elder of the South Carolina Conference who was resting to regain his health. At the close of service he appointed a meeting at old Father Silas at candle light and, said he, "Brother Philips will preach."

This was like a clap of thunder to me, having no arrangements made to preach, but not being disposed to back out, I made a choice of the Psalm " The Lord hath established his throne in the heavens and his kingdom ruleth over all." I of course made a poor sermon as the subject did not suit my congregation and but little good was done on my part, but old Brother Hastus Harrison followed with an excellent exhortation and we closed with a good meeting. I have never tried to preach from that text since.

I arrived at home and found my brother (Eli A.) anxious to look for a better country. He persuaded me to accompany him to the new part of Georgia. We set out and travelled as far as the Nachoocha Valley on the Chatahoochi River in Habersham County. Here we found a man by the name of Samuel Farris who informed us that he owned a quarter of a section of land on the head of Soquee some twelve miles back that would suit our notions being in the mountains and fine range, but we could not see it as the next day was Sabbath and we wanted to return. He proposed to go with us on the next day and if we liked it we could remain until Monday. He gave us the price and payments on Saturday evening and we started back Next morning he came and we road over the land; it being all in the woods except an Indian Hut and patch. We were much pleased with the land and the price. How to do it was the tug. There were several men along and all wicked but myself. All intended that we should draw the writing there on Sunday as it was, rather than ride 12 miles back, but I remonstrated and would return. So we went back to his house and remained until morning. I was cursed by some of the company for a Damned Methodist. This I bore. However, General Wafford applauded me for my constance. My own brother insisted to have it arranged on the land, but I arose at daybreak on Monday morning and before the family was up I had the bond and notes drawn and we all assigned them by sunrise and we returned home.

I mentioned this circumstance to show how important it is to do right, for when I moved to the place and set out an appointment to preach, Samuel Farris was with his family to hear me, and was a constant hearer and when I raised a society at Claytonsville in Rabun County where he then lived having moved from Nauchoochy, I had the pleasure of joining into the church his wife. He then told me that if I had consented to draw and sign the papers for the land that he never would have had any confidence in me as a Christian and also that the course I pursued gave him confidence so he required no security for his money not fearing that he would not get his money. His wife became a bright and constant Christian and raised a religious family. All of this as she said was from the firm stand I took on the side of God and Religion. She has since died a happy Christian and gained her reward in Heaven. Amen & Amen.

After our land trade we returned home and intended to move but times were hard and we could not sell our lands. My brother (Elisha) proposed to take the new place. I turned out to make the money by teaching. I went back to my old neighborhood on Sandymush and took a winter school, but found the young people grown up under the influence of whiskey so that I could scarcely govern them at all. In the spring I turned out to music school again. I taught nine schools that summer mostly in Buncombe County: one at Mills River; one on Davidsons River, One at Glouster, high up on the French Broad River near the Blue Ridge.

There I became acquainted with a fashionable and interesting family by the name of Pageton, all wicked, but polite and wealthy for that country. I was solicited to visit the family and as I preached every other day at the close of singing, the gentleman got to hear me at singing. I told him I would like to preach at his neighbors and his family when I visited him. He was pleased to have it so.

On my next round I went to his house four miles up the river. The evening was very inclement and when the hour for preaching came on, no person came out. I proposed to him to call his servants in as he had a goodly number and they scarcely ever heard preaching at all, and collect his family and I would try to preach to them. I felt impressed to preach. He complied rather reluctantly, as there were no neighbors in, however, he being a polite gentleman, all were seated. I took as a text Hebrew 2 verse 3, "How shall we escape if we neglect so great salvation." I had unusual liberty. His lady and a servant boy were deeply convicted. She spent the night in walking the floor and wringing her hands and praying.

Next day I was to preach at the close of the school hour as was my custom. She went to the appointment; a thing not common for her to do, as she was a fashionable lady and had few associates in that country. I preached from 1 Peter chapter 4 verse 18 "If the righteous scarcely be saved etc.". This was well adapted to her situation. I did not know how deeply her heart was broken up, but saw her greatly concerned. Her husband informed me that he thought her almost deranged. I on parting with her tried to comfort her with the promises of God, but when I returned I found her at the singing, soundly converted and the servant boy. Mr. Pareton was the most thankful man I have ever seen to be a wicked man. This terminated in the salvation of the entire family with a few exceptions.

I wrote a letter to my brother-in-law, Elisha King impressing him of my contemplated move to Georgia, and as he had no family, he came to see us in September with the intention of seeing his mother safe to our new home. He and my wife went the last round with me to my singings. He was not religious but much of a gentleman and appeared to be much interested in the closing exercises of the different schools, but not convicted as he had rather settled down on the Unitarian Doctrine and rather taken with Universalism, but was very prudent and careful not to say anything offensive to myself or his sister or his mother.

As soon as possible after our return we made arrangements to move to Habersham. My brother who had always been so friendly and with whom my interest was connected so long (Elisha) made an effort to keep me from moving in that he baffled me in taking my place as we had contracted but did at last take it when he found I was resolved in moving. We had some very bad weather and on getting to our place we had some difficulty as a man had settled below me and would not suffer me to go through. I made a call on my neighbors and they gathered in and we soon dug a way around the hills to his great astonishment.

Previous to my leaving North Carolina, I had promised Thomas Stringfield, my Presiding Elder, that I would go with him and make out a circuit on missionary ground. On Wednesday I landed and on Friday up rides Brother Moses E. Kerr, the man who was sent to travel our mission. We had no house but an Indian hut with part of our plunder laying out, but my wife and brother-in-law insisted that we should go out and form the mission.

We started on Saturday morning and during the next week we formed some 18 appointments, and he went back and commenced preaching and rest. It was some four miles to the nearest preaching place and that place belonged to the Georgia Conference. I was childish enough to have a preference for the Holston Conference and altho I had my membership in the Georgia Conference, my family all joined the class at home, and we had a good society raised at my house. The Holston preachers attended to Class Meeting regularly, and the society prospered and the appointments were largely attended. My wife and mother enjoyed the meetings much to their comfort.

Soon after we settled down, I visited Clarksville, the county site, sixteen miles from home. It was a village of not many years settlement, and as new places are generally dissapated, so it was. There was no society of any kind, but a few members in the place of the Methodists, Baptists, and Presbyterians.

The Baptist had a church one mile northwest of the village and on the road I travelled. I proposed to preach on the Sabbath of my first visit and form a respectable congregation. I then proposed to preach once a month provided the citizens would see that the groceries were closed and order preserved on the days when I attended. The citizens were to turn out and bring their children and when they ceased to do this, I was to quit. So we went on. Finely all denominations and classescame to church on my appointments. I had to preach in the courthouse as there was no church in the place.

In like manner I went to Clayton, the county site of Rabun county fifteen miles Northeast of my residence and I stipulated with them in the same manner and alternated my Sabbath appointments for two Sabbaths in each month. An application was made very soon that I should preach monthly at Nacoochy where there was a good society and old Brother Jesse Richardson as supernumery preacher and a citizen. This was a feast to attend as there were no societies at either of the other villages.

I then filled the other Sabbath at Soquee near where I lived. This filled up my time.

It was soon found out that I could teach school and I called the citizens together (at their request) and we entered into an agreement to have a school five months in every year embracing the winter and fall seasons, so I could make a crop in summer.

I employed my brother in law (Elisha King) to build me a good house, kitchen, smokehouse, and stable and I hired a young man to clear the land. I went into school the first monday in January 1827 two miles from home toward the meeting house so as to unite a part of three neighborhoods. They in a few days put up a good hewed log schoolhouse and we had a splendid school [with] some fifty scholars (some boarders) that winter. It was proposed to have a music school in the schoolhouse on Saturdays. This was largely attended and we raised a polemic [debating] society one night every week. This did extraordinarily well; we had some fine debates for a mountain county. We raised a sabbath school in the schoolhouse and with everything I was at that house every day.

My first reading school was only for three months as it was late in beginning, but our arrangement annually was to commence the first monday in October, which I did for many years. The noise of my schools soon got out and my manner pleased all the villages [so] that I could scarcely get to stay at home in the week for attending places where I was called upon for extreme cases.

Applications were made for music schools at Clarksville, Clayton, Nacoochy, and Mossey Creek [in the spring]. I commenced early in the month of May teaching and preaching as I formerly did in North Carolina. I went over to Tennessee Valley North Carolina and raised a school at Franklin and Clayton. This was one weeks work, and the other three schools was another weeks work and I also preached every other day at the close of school and filled all my sabbath appointments. After preaching a funeral at Franklin, I was exceedingly troubled about preaching funerals.

I hare stop to mention one occurrence, the school at Brittains. My old friend Humphrey Posey had moved to that neighborhood and his family was in school, also old Brother Stephen White a hard shell Baptist Minister had his family in school. One afternoon while singing the words of a tune newberg, there appeared some seriousness and I made some remarks concerning the verses we then repeated. While singing there was considerable weeping among the youth. I then gave a short exhortation and felt so much impressed that I proposed that if any desired that I should pray for them to manifest it by coming near me. The first was Jane White, the daughter of the old hard shell preacher. She made an attempt to come but fell prostrate on the floor and cried loudly for mercy. At least half the school came forward. I prayed and then another brother prayed, and we tried to restore the school to order but could not so we turned over school into a prayer meeting. Jane White struggled hard and at length rose shouting - happily converted. Our meeting lasted until sundown. Next day was my appointment to preach and it was like a campmeeting. The people ran together like those in Jerusalem in the day of Pentecost upon hearing of the conversion of Jane White. Here was my old brother Posey and old Brother White and two other preachers! The singing was shortened by request and I tried to preach from the text of 2 Corinthians 5:11 "Knowing the terror of the Lord we persuade men". I did not have liberty to preach but old Brother Posey being a great revivalist followed with a powerful exhortation and a great work commenced. Some dozen of my scholars were converted and many others; over fifty dated their convictions from that school, It was thought by many that I should wear myself out that year, but I held on and with one exception there were revivals in all my schools.

My business went on finely at home. My brother-in-law built me a splendid house and I made money enough to pay him and my cropper and to clothe myself decently and some to spare. On the 22nd of July my daughter Juliann E. Philips was born. She was more feeble and puny than any other of our children, but my wife was an excellent nurse and had the assistance of her mother and Ruth Starrett. Ruth made my house her home and was an excellent girl, but sickly.

My wife's brother was also a great help to her in my absence. I was very desirous that he should be religious and I was careful to always demean myself as a christian in his presence and had his entire confidence. He would go to church and was a great bible reader and critic. He saw how we all enjoyed ourselves and he commenced seeking Religion and being an eccentric man I could not tell how to approach him. He took a great liking to old Brother Richardson and I think by his preaching Elisha was conducted through the rocks and quicksand of Cameletism to the knowledge of atonement and sins forgiven.

I wound up all my schools in time to rest and get ready to commence my reading school on the first monday in October. My oldest daughter Clarinda [started] school that fall. I had a splendid school and we kept up sabbath singing and our weekly polemic. A goodly number of married men attended night school. The Soquee neighborhood was envied all over the country for their high privileges... My health was excellent and I could do a great deal at night in way of improvement. I may truly say that these were the days of my greatest enjoyment. I was able to teach a five month session without the loss of a day except christmas day and that day old Brother Richardson came up and we had a gracious meeting.

The winter of 1827/1828 was a mild winter. Reuben Philips raised a crop and taught schools in Northern Georgia. A typical house might be in a single room, twenty eight by twenty five feet in area with no ceiling as we know it, but open to the roof above. There was a large fireplace on one end and a door on each side --no windows at all. Two bedsteads, a spinning wheel, a packing case, which served as a bureau, a cupboard made of rough-hewn slabs, two or three deer-skin seated chairs, a connecticut clock, and a large poster of patent medicine, often constituted all the visible furniture either useful or ornamental in purpose.

Reverend Reuben. I closed my school on the last day of February 1828 and commenced for a crop. By the middle of April I had so many applications to teach music in [Hall, Franklin, and Jackson Counties] that I concluded to hire a man to make my crop and I turned out. I took a school at Shoal Creek, one at Gainesville, one at Hebron in Jackson, one at Ocona in the Presbyterian Church, [and] one at Borden Meeting House; Baptist. I was resisted by the church at first because I would preach to the youth, but a revival was commenced soon after my school was started and some thirty or forty were added to the Baptist Church at that place and a goodly number to other branches of the church. I went around to the fork in Hall County and to Couley's Meetinghouse, and to Mossy Creek. I had nine schools in operation all at once and only taught two days at each place once in three weeks and preached every other day, and filled my appointments at home all but one.

This was a great year for me in religious enjoyment. I may truly say that in all my schools there were revivals and the people flocked out by hundreds especially on the preaching day. In winding up my services that fall, there was a camp meeting appointed at a new place and I attended it. There were some 70 or 80 converted... The last night it was proposed to open the door of the church and I was appointed to do it and 68 joined the church that night and 53 of that number were my scholars! There were some complaints by other denominations that an undue advantage was taken in putting me forward as I was popular among my scholars.

This summer I earned enough money to pay up for my house and [for] clearing ten acres of good land. [I] wound up all my schools at the Presbyterian Meetinghouse, where I was succeeded by a campmeeting by the old Presbyterians. I remained and preached four times for them and trust [I] was instrumental in much good. This was the 20th of September.

I then went home and prepared to go to my annual school. I felt some worn out from the unusual labor I had done.

Our own neighborhood had erected a campground and arbor on Soquee at the church and our campmeeting began on the 25th so I barely got home in time to assist my family to move to the campground... Great good was done at this meeting and I was able to commence my school on the first monday in October.

My Brother in law, Elisha King, still lived with us and had joined the church and Ruth Starrett had long been a member so they concluded to form a matrimonial connection, and on the first of March 1829 they were married and settled within four miles of us near the campground and he became class leader.

I had closed up my winter school and prepared to make a crop myself. I only took two singing schools that I could go to on Saturday and return at night, but I had so many calls at a distance on funeral occasions and two day meetings that I had to back fires at night and hoe corn so as to keep my crop clean and gain saturday. I made a splendid crop that summer and preached a great deal.

We had rather a poor campmeeting that fall as there were many backslidings and some difficulty in the church. I had to hire some help to gather in my crop before I could commence school, and having small grain to sow it was an unfavorable fall. All my neighbors concluded to put off the school till later and to have only a three months session that winter. It was a very hard and cold winter so our school fell far short of doing the good that was usual.

Next year I commenced my crop and had leased some land to old brother William Daniel who had boys to help him and they cleared up some fifteen acres of good land. He lived with me three years and whenever he could see my light at night he would invariably come to me and would hoe as many rows as I did, saying that he could not preach, but could help me preach in that way. I worked hard, preached hard, and lived _well_. I owed no man anything, loved my neighbors and brethren and had a fine time to read. I attended meetings on sabbath [except] when I had to go off at a distance, and this was frequent. I made plenty of everything to live on, and had some money at interest.

About this time gold was discovered on Dickey Creek and the people were so aroused on the subject that many appeared to forget their religion and then only showed their unsound principles by being tempted to act mean. There were hundreds and I might say thousands flocked into the country of the wicked and low classes and our congregations changed in number and in quality so it appeared that all ministerial labor was lost. The sabbath was violated; groceries opened all through the country; gold hunters out all week and sabbath too. I became greatly disappointed with my situation. I however became more accustomed to the matter. I found it had been a means of drawing in many literary men and a goodly number of ministers, and in short time a discovery was made of gold in the Cherokee Nation and in Hall County, so the rabble soon left us and went in that direction and left us a better society.

I was called on in the fall of that year to go to Memphis, Tennessee to Collect some money that I had in suit for Dr. Askew by the foreclosure of the Equity of Redemption on a mortgage deed given by a man Hargess to said Askew for loaned money being now collected. I started on the 7th of December and was hindered by high waters and also by hunting up Alexander Starrett who lived near Troy in Obion County Western District. I had claims on him in behalf of his orphan sisters whose money he had got and used as kind brother while single but after marriage he left the country and wandered off, proved insolvent, and swindled his sisters out of their money. I found him and his family living in poverty and worse than all, no disposition to remunerate his sisters even if he had been able.

I remained one day and two nights with him and then made my way to Memphis, crossing the Obion Lake which had been made by the shaking of the earth in 1810. An eruption took place and threw up the earth across the mouth of the Obion River some 15 miles below where I crossed it. I could see the tops of the trees the water had backed over. Here I was greatly astonished at seeing the boatmen as they crossed the lake catching the flying fish by suspending a hook and line with a small bit of scarlet skimming the surface of the water. The fish would rise out of the water and take the hook; they caught numbers as we crossed. I crossed the Michigan Lake also. It was not so large. I saw a great many earth cracks occasioned by the shake above named, some so large that they had to be bridged where the road crossed them. It was strange to see the white sand thrown out on the black soil in so many places.

In travelling down the line of counties to Memphis I was so near the river I had to swim the bayous as the waters were very high. I rode all day on Christmas day being the wettest day I have ever witnessed. I however succeeded in getting to Memphis and got my money and started for home on the first day of January 1831. On my way home I came very near being drowned in Little River in the Cherokee Nation. I swam it after night and was washed below the ford but miraculously escaped. Before going into the water I tied all my money in my handkerchief and around my neck so that if I was drowned it might be found on my person. Through great mercy I got home safe, found all well, and though I lost my school that winter I made $150 by the trip and prepared for a crop.

On the same day I left Memphis for home, being the first day of January, 1831. My wife had a fine son born. We called his name <u>Lafayette</u>. This year I worked on my farm and made a fine crop, had everything in plenty, and time to read and go to meeting. I commenced school in October and my school was so large that I had to employ an assistant. I procured the services of Carter Jackson an old experienced teacher, and we taught a splendid school. My boarders came from the village. In the spring I quit teaching and left the school to him as many boys had to quit to go to work. I made a crop and improved my farm and enjoyed myself better than usual. I was still out of debt and lived quite happily. I taught a four months school with Carter Jackson during that winter and then abandoned the school and made a crop.

William Barker
to   Deed for part of lot No. 19 11th Dist.
Reuben Philips   6 acres

     Know all men by these presents that I William Barker of the County of Houston & State of Georgia for and in Consideration of the sum of twentyfive dollars to me in hand paid by Reuben Philips of the County of habersham & State aforesaid for a piece or parcel of land situate in the County of Habersham & State aforesaid being part of lot no.(19) twenty in sd district & No.(28) is sd district being sd Philips and Frederick Camps lands & running East to Camp's Hickory Station & to the creek thence a North direction with the Creek including the creek and with the foot of the hill parrellel with the road to a small Whiteoak Philips line thence a South West direction with the line of sd Philips to the beginning corner in the head of a swamp near Camp's fence containing six acres be the same more or less. I the sd Wm Barker Sen. my heirs executors & assigns do warrant and forever defend the above described piece or parcel of land with all its ways woods waters and minerals hereditaments & appurtances thereunto belonging or in any way appurtaining free from the lawful claim of any person or persons whatsoever unto him the sd Reuben Philips his heirs executors or assigns. I Witness thereunto set my hand & seal this the fifth day of February one thousand eight hundred and thirty two.

Signed Sealed & Delivered   Wm <u>his /y</u> Barker
in the presence of   mark
Eli Philips
Owen Haynes J.P.

I had in the month of August, 1832, been ordained deacon by Bishop Hedding in the city of Augusta. I was out of debt and had many friends and few enemies.

My Brother <u>Hiram B. Philips</u> visited me from North Carolina and persuaded me to unite with him in purchasing a store three miles below that had been carried on for some two years by Richard L. Powell, and Powell kept spirits to sell and did our community much evil. My brother expressed great desire to live near me and ... pledged himself to be a temperate man. I refused time after time, not wishing to engage in any speculation that would involve me with the world. He then commenced with my wife and so impressed her mind with the prosperity of my joining him and we could put down a grocery and do well. He was to manage the whole concern and not trouble me with it. I at length consented (a fatal day and deed for me) on the 19th day of December 1832.

Soon my brother proved treacherous, involving me greatly in debt and I was soon broken up and my religious enjoyments ruined. He became my enemy and continued to dissipate. At length he married a Miss Nancy Vaughn of Clarksville; threw the whole concern on my hands with heavy debts hanging over it and moved to Clarksville and commenced the practice of medicine. I purchased at a dear rate his interest and went behind the counter <u>myself</u>. My friends then came to my rescue; gave me their patronage until I sold out the entire stock, but before I could do this effectively I had to replenish with a few salable goods which caused me to create more debts, and the debts created before I took it into my possession amounted to something over four thousand dollars and [of] the debtors to the concern, large numbers were unable to pay money and many were insolvent. In winding up I found myself involved in an amount that I could not pay without selling lands. Although my land was of a superior quality, yet it lay in the mountains and so out of the way of trade that I could not sell to profit. I however managed to pay all but two thousand dollars and I knew I would have to sacrifice my farm to pay that.

During the winter of 1833 my mother visited me and spent the winter with me. Most of the time she remained with me at the store as my family was at the farm. While she remained on the 13th of November the day was exceedingly clear and calm and the sky was uncommonly dark and blue. The weather was a little cold as there was some snow still lying in places. About 3 O' clock in the morning I rose from my bed to attend to one of the little boys who was disturbed in sleep and on opening the door I saw an unusual appearance in the heavens, like stars shooting in every direction. I awoke my mother and children that were with me. We were much astonished at the wonderful sight and altho the meteors appeared to be within the atmosphere of the earth when they exploded or disappeared there was no noise to be heard. I remained up until daylight and the number greatly increased and also in magnitude. The whole canopy appeared in wild confusion and even after the sun had risen large meteors could be seen descending to the earth in a miraculous manner.

Many people came to see me before daylight and inquired of me what these things meant. I was myself at a loss to account for the unusual phenomena, but inasmuch as there was great uneasiness among all classes, I appointed to preach that night at our church and we had a truly exciting time. A great number came to the mourners bench that had never been concerned about religion before. Some continued to seek religion until they obtained it. Others as soon as the panic wore off returned to drinking, swearing, and to dancing again.

I remained at the store all the winter and in the month of March I moved my family down near the store, leaving young William Daniel to carry on my crop and take care of my house and what furniture we left.

[1834 was a severe winter. There was a spell of very cold weather in February and there was an early frost in September. It continued cold into January and February of 1835, with temperatures below zero.

On April 4, 1834 Virgil Philips was born to Reuben and Elizabeth Philips. Reuben took his mother Hannah home and never saw her again.]

This year was attended with some difficulty as I was absent from my farm and had a heavy crop of small grain and corn. While harvesting my small grain I superintended it myself and we had a great deal of grain exposed to heavy rain and I so exerted myself as to inflame my liver which brought on acute inflammation and I barely succeeded by powerful means to reduce the inflammation so as to live at all. The disease at length assumed a chronic form and continued threatening for two years.

In the late fall, I sold out all my goods that could be sold without replenishing. I sold the whole concern to R.S. Powell, received a credit on my note from him and I went home again to my farm. I hired four men to assist me in my next crop as I had a great deal of cleared land and my own boys [to work]. We made nearly three thousand bushels of corn and small grain. In proportion my stock greatly increased so that I sold in the fall and winter two hundred dollars worth of beef cattle, three hundred dollars worth of hogs, and some sheep. The whole amounted to nearly $1000.

My corn was greatly injured by an uncommon early and hard frost that came the 18th of September; killed vegetation, and so injured my late corn that I lost a great deal, but still had a quantity to sell as the frost had ruined the country [below] so much more than it did me as I lived high up in the mountains. I held up my corn until spring and learned that the Cherokee Indians were perishing for [want of] bread. I sent word to them and they came by hundreds and carried off my corn and paid me cash except for a few charity cases. This relieved me very much and I was enabled to pay a good deal of my debts.

I lived at home the ensuing year and made a crop, and in the fall of that year the Georgia annual conference proposed a rule that every county in the state should be a circuit, and that they would send a preacher to every county who should take charge of appointments and then add as many others as he could find suitable places to establish preaching. I was then recording steward, and urged our preacher, David Bauloo to go out and serve the Curry Lee Mountain people, but he refused. At the first quarterly meeting I entered a complaint and they handled him quite roughly, but he would not go out after any more work.

Brother Isaac Boring was then our presiding Elder and he was deeply impressed to have our preacher go among them. I told the conference that I had been among them the two years I taught music in the counties below and knew them to be approachable. After the meeting closed our Elder urged me with every consideration to take the county into my hands and that he would assist me all he could.

So we settled the matter and on Christmas Day, 1836 I commenced the work. I visited and preached at the different precincts of Habersham County and at the first quarter meeting I had formed twenty six new preaching places. My Elder was astonished to hear that none of those appointing were within seven miles of each other. I was measurably released from the old appointments for the next Quarter and the local preachers agreed to fill them. I preached every day and sometimes two or three times a day so as to go round every three weeks. After the second quarter meeting I went around once in four weeks. I still had no rest days but two and those I filled up in teaching two singing schools every round a day at each place. This injured my lungs as the youth of the country had never been taught music and parents and children all attended.

This quarter my congregation so increased as to make it necessary for me to preach the most of the time in the woods, as there were no churches but three in the bounds, two Baptist and one old Methodist church house long abandoned. I commenced reading the discipline and found the people of the area so much pleased to find our doctrine so different from what they had been told by the baptist and others. I also distributed gratuitous a number of disciplines and tracts so the prejudices of the people gave way to a great extent and I commenced opening the door of the church for old members where there were any and many joined, I now think about fifty that Quarter! While I went around and returned to the place appointed, I found great exertions had been made. They had built a very good house and I received into the church on probation that day seventeen members!

I had joined into church some hundred members by the third quarterly meeting and my Presiding Elder was so astonished at my success expressed a great desire to see that section of the country and the people. He instructed me to make known to my congregations that he would be with me on my last round before the fourth quarterly meeting which was to be in early september. During this time, my congregations increased so as to make it necessary for me to preach out in the woods at more than half the places.

The people also finding that I was the old music teacher that had taught below some years before pressed upon me to take up schools as there had never been any schools in that part of the country. I consented and on every round I sung two days one at each school and preached at the close of singing. This called out the people to an astonishing number and was the cause of may coming out to hear preaching that never would otherwise.

In 1837 there was a depression in those days called a

panic. Teachers might earn from twenty to fifty dollars in a three month term, but the pay was often in trade - meat, corn, oats, potatoes, homespun yarn, home woven rag carpet, furs, horse shoeing, tire setting, hauling, labor, clearing, plowing, hoeing, wood chopping, fence building, or other services.

There were as yet, no sawmills nearby, and sawed lumber was not available. The floor of the little church was made of split logs, hewed and finished with the broadaxe. Seats were backless benches. The pulpit board was split out with wedges and a heavy hammer and roughly dressed with a jack-plane.

Most likely there were two doors, one for the men and boys and one for the women and girls. Seats were also segregated, females on one side and males on the other with a gallery for the slaves. In winter it was cold, as no stove was allowed. No matter how bad the weather, the preacher would always come, even if he had to walk when his horse was sick.

Reverend Reuben. I now became anxious to know the results of my preaching. I read our doctrine and rules all round and commented on them and opened the door of the church at all the places advising all to wait until they were fully convinced and satisfied with our doctrines and discipline. I invariably opened the doors of the church every round and before my Presiding Elder came I joined some 200 members on probation.

The last round before the last quarterly meeting the Presiding Elder came and preached every day for two weeks with increased interest and we joined that round into the church thirty five members; he having to preach out of doors most of the time came near wearing himself out.

At length we reached Clarksville, the place for the last quarterly meeting. I preached four sermons during this meeting as it was protracted until Wednesday night. Old Colonel Brannon joined the church at this meeting and several other prominent citizens in the village. Brother Boring, My Elder and I became fast friends, which friendship lasted until his death.

I rode to Claytonville in Rabun County and preached at night. I was on my way to preach the funeral of Sister Polly Henly who was an old scholar of mine when a child and to whom I imparted the first knowledge of the alphabet and all she ever learned in the neighborhood of Newfound Creek. She was the youngest daughter of old brother and sister Silas and when grown up she married Brother John S. Henly a travelling preacher of the Holston Conference and had located and moved to Clayton and while there she died and all of her relatives lived in North Carolina. A stand was erected and seats prepared and such a congregation met as had never been seen in that part of the country.

The wind rose from the north west and it continued to get colder and the place selected was in a low gap of the Blue Ridge. I was somewhat worn out in my lungs from excessive preaching. I found it difficult to preach, but could not disappoint as many had come from a great distance. I proceeded to preach. I must confess I could scarcely go through. The wind blew so as to make me hoarse and I only preached one hour and was followed by a brother Roan. After dismissal I rode home 25 miles and was late in the night getting home; cold and sick. My expectoration was streaked with blood, but having to preach at Nauchoochy church that day I set up and preached to a fine congregation which turned out to be the last sermon I ever preached to them or at that place!

I rode next day to Dickeys Creek Church and preached and baptized some adults and children. This was wednesday and my lungs still pained me very much. I next day rode to Dalonaga and preached at night to a large congregation. I was accompanied next day to a camp-meeting near Knucklesville by two persons. I was called on to preach that night. I did so and called for mourners and both my travelling companions came forward. In the act of kneeling down, he professed religion. He was a physician, and he shouted and praised God and the people seeing him so happy they ran together in wild confusion and he exhorted his village companions and we prayed promiscuously. I must confess I never wanted physical strength more in all my life.

Next morning I was scarcely able to be up, having hot flashes followed by chills which threatened me with inflammation. I remained however during the meeting and did all I could. On thursday I left and took up my appointments. Having to preach two funerals that week, I found that I should sink under it as sabbath the sixth was quite wet and I exposed to the rain. I at night rested but little. My disease grew worse on monday. I tried to preach in an open house and did myself much harm. Tuesday I preached a funeral of a good sister in high standing and it was largely attended.

At night I rolled over and over with hot flashes and profuse sweating followed by cold chills and bloody expectoration. This was the trying moment with me. I found I must die or stop and my last appointments ahead of me were interesting,... but my friends told me to go home. This was the ninth of October, having preached on the eighth my last sermon. I turned my face for home and arrived at Clarksville that night, having rode 35 miles. I lodged with Judge Trippe that night and sent for Doctor Rusk. He came and after examining me pronounced it fatigue! Next day my old friend Dr. George D. Philips hearing of my situation called on me and pronounced me in a dangerous situation; sent for a carriage and took me to his residence, one mile from town. That night he bled me four times and covered my breast with ointment; tarter emetic. I remained there one week. My wife hearing of my condition came to see me and finding me so very sick was much troubled. The doctor told her that my lungs were inflamed, I had inflammatory bronchitis and only one chance in a hundred to live at all.

This alarmed my wife very much. I was not alarmed but with the assistance of the Doctor recounted my work from Christmas up to the eighth of October and found I preached 300 sermons, taught two singing schools and scarcely rested any. Using his own words: "My God this would kill any man!" I made my way home and carried with me medicine. I lived sixteen miles Northwest on Soquee River. I discontinued all operations and commenced battling with my disease and found it inveterate and almost unyielding, but counterirritants, blistering etc did me much good.

In the meantime my physicians advised me to go south. I exchanged my land with Brother John L. Richardson taking one thousand dollars worth of land in Alabama [on a claim from Doctor James Simmons]. I strove hard, sold off and gave away all my plunder, bought a wagon with four good oxen, filled in what I could of our most valuable furniture, and with two fine brood mares and one Indian pony, we started on the 12th of January 1838.

My oldest son Elisha was a good driver. I lay in the wagon most of the way and we on the 29th reached the <u>Hillabees</u> where I stopped a day or two and then proceeded to Doctor Simmons where I was to have land. The Doctor proposed to me his place including his buildings and 120 acres of land some 40 acres cleared. We agreed on the price at 800 dollars but I could not get possession until after another year. I was compelled to live in a hut a few hundred yards from the Doctors family. I got however land for my boys to tend and we made our bread.

The fatigue of travelling and the excitement so relapsed me that I was confined to my bed most of the time until August. Doctor Simmons kept me on a weak diet of rice. I was constantly expectorating and at length became so weak as to scarcely be able to stand alone. At one time I supposed the time of my departure was at hand. My ears were roaring and ringing and my pulse down to 30 to the minute. I felt cold on my hands and up to my knees. All thought I was dying. I felt resigned to death but I regretted having to leave my family among strangers.

Doctor Simmons was sent for and he pronounced me to be dying. I was in my senses perfectly and on seeing a string filled with pods of red peppers I advised my wife to boil it quickly and rub me with it. This she did and applied French brandy without and very soon a circulation wasrestored to the astonishment of all who saw me. I then determined to eat whatever I wanted as I had a good appetite and digestion and was hungry all the time.

I preached or lectured every sabbath when no other minister visited us, and our school increased. At the commencing of the new year 1839 we had sixty souls living on the campground. The church stood in the center and the families lived in their tents on the lines. We all met every night and morning in the church for prayers.

Cotton at Wetumpka was worth from 11 to 14 cents; bagging 22 to 24; hams 15 to 18 3/4; sides 14, shoulders 11; nails 9 to 10; butter 37 1/2; corn .75 to 1.00; coffee 16; molasses, 45 to 50; rice 8; sugar 9 to 10; whiskey 60 to 65.

In 1840 Reuben Philips taught school at Bethel in Alabama.

Reverend Reuben: This summer my boys and Franklin Stephens made a crop. Elisha appeared discontented having determined to be a scholar. Ewell was careless about school. In the month of November I went back to Habersham Georgia and found my brother in law Elisha King and [my son in law] A.S. Dorsey disposed to move. I made arrangements with them and brought them home with me. I settled A. S. Dorsey on 80 acres of land and rented the most of my farm to Elisha King for the coming year. He moved November 29, 1840. I also made arrangements for Mr. Diliach the Frenchman to move with me to my neighborhood. He married Elisha Kings Wife's Sister [Polly Starrett]. We all came on together and he settled near the schoolhouse on 40 acres of land where he continued until his death.

I opened my school early in the year of 1841. All my children went to school. Jane Simmons assisted me in the Grammar classes and we opened our sunday school. I preached a great deal that year and our church and school done well. We had some revival of religion and our church soon numbered sixty members.

On February 27, 1841 Reuben and Elizabeth's son Lafayette died.

Reverend Reuben: My long session closed the last of July. The people of Hatchet Creek came in the form of a committee to see whether I would come and teach one session for them again. The people of Hillabees consented and I went with part of my family and lived in my tent. I left my wife and brother in law and commenced August first at Mizion.

The following transcript was entered in a bible presented to Elisha Philips by his father Reverend Reuben Philips:

If men are to be punished in another world, God must be the punisher.
If God be the punisher, the punishment must be just
If the punishment be just, the punished must be guilty
If the punished are guilty, they could have done otherwise. They were free agents.
Therefore if men are liable to punishment in another world they must be free.   (logic)   R. P.

In 1842, Reuben was Postmaster at Hillabee, Alabama. His son Elisha went to school below Tuskega. Reuben was Ordained Elder in the Methodist Church this year.

It took a strong person to be a preacher in those days. Not only did the early day circuit riders make several appointments across the area, but sermons were often prolonged, lasting two to four hours, with other preachers often preaching another hour to fill in. The children were kept quiet, but the women often shouted.

The service would break for the noon meal in the early afternoon, and a big meal was prepared on the grounds of the church. Typical fare might include fried chicken, smoked or salt cured ham, fish soaked in brine, boiled eggs, steak, corn bread, biscuits, homemade bread, beans, peas, melon, and other fruits and vegetables with tarts, pies, and cakes for dessert. After the meal, the horses were fed with feed brought in the wagons.

After church, the boys would take the girls out in the buckboard courting. Holding hands and kissing was not encouraged, since it might lead to further intimacy.

Reverend Reuben: About the 15th of February 1842 ... Judge Tarrent [from Mardesville] rode up to my house [and] told me [he wanted me to go] to Mardesville to take the Female school. He remained all night and [we] concluded it would be best for me to go. [I] commenced school in the Presbyterian Church near the public square on the 28th day of March 1842 with 48 scholars. I had to have my son Ewell and daughter Julian to assist me. [by] the ...second month we had 68 in school and all did well.

I closed this scholastic year the 15th of November and had time to attend my Hillabee farm and all my business so as to open school on the 23rd of January 1843 in the Male Academy near Mardesville. We intended to have a male school but all wanted to send their daughters and I by general consent received all . I had 78 students and with Mrs Hardy in the sunday school we went on harmoniously and I preached a great deal that year.

Snow fell to the depth of several inches on the 23rd of March 1843, and it was cold for some time. This snow was extensive extending from Alabama into South Carolina.

In Alabama the newspaper Argus complained during part of this year about the scarcity of chickens, and the high price $2.50 per dozen. Turkeys both wild and tame were both plentiful and cheap ranging from 37 1/2 to 75 cents. Fish were abundant and cheap, the traps doing well.

Turkey traps were built in the following manner: Pens made of rails and covered with a hole under the bottom rail of one side from the outside reaching to the inside were built. The trench leading in was covered on the inside by something such as boards or heavy sticks for some distance in, and the pen was baited with corn or other grain, and so was the trench leading into it. The turkeys that entered could not get out and would travel around the pen rails and not see the escape trench which they were walking over.

Reuben and Elizabeth Philips' daughter Clarinda was married to Robert Hendrix in 1843.

Reverend Reuben: My son Elisha who had been going to school in Macon County came home and went to school to Mr. Finn. On the 4th sunday in October I preached at the campmeeting at Hatchet Creek and it was cold weather. While I was preaching I felt something break near my heart and I suffered great pain. There appeared to be a collection of water in the pericardium. I was only able to get home and was confined. Doctors Watkins, Poe, and McKenzie all advised me to stop all public exercises and I sent for Elisha to finish my term. [After] two weeks he took a school for himself. I took medicine and was fortunate to recover my health so as to ride about.

Hiram Philips found Reuben a teaching position in Jefferson County, Alabama in Jones Valley in 1844.

Reverend Reuben: We landed at Brother Greens the sixth and found no house to go into and the school not ready, but a meeting was called and the house put in order and I commenced teaching on the second day of February 1844. I sent an appointment to Elyton at Colonel McAdories request [on the 25th] of February. I preached to a large congregation. My school increased to 45 and we had regular reviews once in every five weeks.

Brothers Green and Burwell ... proposed that I should preach a sermon on temperance. I proposed ... offering a pledge that day, but was opposed by Brother Green. I persisted and preached a sermon [to] a large congregation and joined thirty to the pledge, but Brother Green never joined. We went on until most of the youth had joined. We succeeded in forming societies at Cahawly Church, Hagood, Ruhamy, Bethel and finally at Elyton. Many persons who formerly drank to excess were influenced to forsake it entirely.

About 1845-50: Advice to his son of leaving home. (By Reverend Reuben Philips):
I. My first advice to you is to save your soul and in order to do this.
    1. Read the scripture daily
    2. Be attentive to private prayer.
    3. Never neglect public worship first for your own good (2) as an example.
    4. Use all the means of Grace, and ordinances of Gods House, to promote the Health of the soul.
    5. Be faithful until death.
II. Your Temporal welfare.
    1. Be always employed, and industrious.
    2. Avoid going in debt, and in order to this buy nothing that your needs do not require and when you have anything that suits you, don't trade it, just to be Grading.
    3. Go no mans security under any circumstances.
    4. Be not extravagant in dress.
    5. Avoid the company of unchaste females and be polite to those who are virtuous.
    6. Reverence the aged, and be kind to orphan children.

7. Support the government and do public duty.
8. When in your power relieve the distress.
9. Keep a still tongue.
10. Drink no ardent spirits only as a medicine.

As I could not support my family I concluded to visit Blountsville and on doing so I made a good school in the village and returned to Elyton and bought John at sale for $515. My wife, Virgil, and myself started to Elisha Kings in Coosa County and I preached at Ruth King's funeral on the ninth of November and returned home and moved to Blountsville and opened school on the 29th of December 1845 in an old log house.

School houses were built to face south so the door could stand open in fair winter weather and let the sunlight in. In winter there would occasionally be a wood cutting bee for the school. Older children were sent after water with a bucket and when they returned, younger ones would pass around the dipper. If the lintel caught fire, water was thrown on it. The teacher often had to whittle pens for his pupils from goosefeathers.

My school so increased that at the close of the first session the people raised a subscription of $1100 and old Brother Hendrick undertook the building of a new academy and put my school in the Methodist Episcopal Church until the new house was finished.

Brother Thomas became my assistant and in three months we were put in possession of the new Academy. This was in the summer of 1846 and in the month of August my beloved wife was taken with Typhoid Fever and <u>died</u> August 26th. This event so affected me and disorganized my school that I dismissed the school to the care of my son Elisha for a time.

December the first 1847 I left, intending to spend the winter in South Florida, but on coming to Brother Greens, he and I in consultation concluded it best for me to call on the Widow [Caroline Owen] Sadler and propose a matrimonial connection. We were [married] on the 7th of December 1847.

In 1848, Reuben had a slave John who he sold to his wife and no longer personally owned slaves.

In 1853, Reuben Philips moved to Salem, Lee County, Alabama where he became Superintendent of the Female Academy.

In 1857, overseer John Fields was dismissed and Reuben

oversaw the hands which he continued doing on his wife's plantation in 1858. They had lost money in the Salem venture, but were still doing alright. In 1859, Reuben spent time in Jefferson County at Elyton where he conducted the service of Marriage for John M. Thomas and Margaret Emmaline Horton.

Reuben and Caroline employed Brother John Thompson as Overseer on the plantation in 1860. In 1861 Reuben visited his daughter Julian in Louisiana.

In 1862, Reuben made a trip to St. Andrews Bay to make salt, but could not make any because the yankees were there.

In 1865, Reuben Philips was living at Columbiana, Alabama and teaching school. The war had caused Reuben Philips to become poor. Yet, he had his farm, so he was not without food. He raised livestock, and likely hunted deer and wild hogs in the woods. It is likely that he raised bees. Watermelons were an important crop in Alabama, and Sweet Potatoes were soon profitable. Corn provided the most important food for man and beast.

At the close of the civil war the common cattle were Shorthorns and Devons. Ayershire and Jersey were being added. Hogs were Chester White, Berkshire, Jersey Red, Essex, and Irish Grazier(Now called Poland China).

In March 1866 Sweet Potatoes sold for $3 per bushel in Montgomery.

Reverend J.B. Stevenson, who was his presiding Elder wrote "I made the acquaintance of Reverend Reuben Philips in the winter of 1878-9. My first impression of him was that he was remarkably preserved in both body and mind, and that he was a man of intellectual culture far above an average for his day. I was impressed with his quick perception. He seemed to grasp a new idea or truth with the mental vigor of young manhood, and to take in these new truths and ideas in all their philosophical and moral bearings in nature and religion. He showed that he was a man of both reading and thought, that his reading and thinking had taken in a very comprehensive range for one sustaining the relationship to society that he did. To some he seemed dogmatical. This was almost an unavoidable consequence of his long continued service in the schoolroom, and not from any autocratic spirit in the man. There was a manly dignified courtesy about him that showed him to be a very high type of christian gentleman.

In 1871 Reuben Philips was preaching in and around Coosa

County, Alabama. The fire at Artesia caused William and Mollie Cannon to sell out.

Diary of Reverend Reuben Philips: Monday night 26th June [1871]. Arrived at Meridian 10 O clock at night. Arrived at Columbiana Wednesday 28th 2 O clock. Left Columbiana Thursday 29th. Met Jasper McAdory at Childersburg. June 30 we got to Jaspers at 2 O clock. We were quite weary. Sunday July 9th I superintended the Sabbath school. Monday 10th very warm. I am in unusual good health. Friday 14 heard Robert Nabors preach. I gave an exhortation and called for mourners. Sat. 15 I conducted the prayer meeting and preached at night. Sun. 23 I preached at Andrew Chapel with ease to myself. Sun 30 I rode 8 miles and preached at Sears Chapel.

August 1 I visited four families. Wed 2 went back to Sears Chapel preached one hour to a large congregation. Friday 4th I rode 8 miles on my way to Qr. meeting at Sylacogga. Sat 5 I arrived at Qr. Meeting. Heard the Elder Preach. I preached at night. Mn 7th I preached at 11 O clock. Heard Bro. Self at night. Tuesday 8th I preached at 11 O clock. I got home in afternoon. Rested well. Found all well but mother. She was again troubled with distressing symptoms in her esophagus. Thursday 10 I visited our community in preparing the Andrew Chapel church for our protracted meeting to commence. Friday night 11th I preached the first sermon . [he preached daily for about the next week] Sat. 19th I preached at 11 AM and baptized 5 persons ... and received 11 members into the fellowship of the church, our preacher being absent. Brother Stewart preached at night and we closed up the meeting. Sunday August 27 I preached at Andrews Chapel and baptized Dr. Hindmans wife by _immersion_ and two ladies by pouring and received 9 members into fellowship our preacher being absent.

Saturday September 2, 1871 - (at Rehobeth) preached and baptized Esquire Green and two young men and received them into the church. Sun 3rd I attended sabbath school; baptized one infant. I am still sick from a cold I suppose from going into the water. Saturday (9th) I rode across Hatchett Creek to an old church to assist Brother Archy Kelly in his protracted meeting. I preached at 11 AM and returned home. Sunday 10 I heard the bible class in sabbath school at Andrews Chapel and heard Brother Elbert Smith from Tuskega preach. Tuesday 12th I rode across the Coosa Hills 8 miles to assist Brother Rowland in his protracted Meeting. Took part in the exercises of the morning and night. Wednesday 13th I preached a long sermon and rode home in the rain. Sunday 17 I heard the bible class and also heard Brother Rowland preach a good sermon. Sunday 24 I attended sabbath school Heard Brother W.L. Smith preach. Friday 29 Jasper and Eliza, Mary Miles, Brother and Sister Garnett packed up and started in their wagons. I rode on a mule. Saturday 30 We arrived [at the campmeeting on Hillabee Creek]. I preached at 11 O clock to a large congregation.

Sunday October 1 I preached again at 11 O clock A.M. Monday 2 - We started home. We had only cloth tents and it looked like rain. Friday (6) Myself and mother started in a buggy to visit T.W. Sadler. Got 25 miles making coffee on the road for dinner. I got my hand badly burned so mother drove. We staid all night with Mrs. Lawson received kind treatment and no bill to pay. Sat. 7 we arrived at T. W. Sadlers at night. Rested Well. Sunday 8 I went to sabbath school to hear Brother Woodward preach, but preached myself at 11 O clock and heard Woodard at night. Saturday 14 Quarterly Meeting at Prattville. Sunday 15 - I went to Sabbath School. heard Dr. Mitchell preach and administer sacrament. Monday 16 I am at T.W. Sadlers all day and glad that they want family prayers attended to nearly all the time. Tuesday 17 - I wrote to Elisha Philips, P.J. McAdory, Flem(ing) Jordan & W.G. Cannon. Wed. 18 Our Mule ran away. Little Ollie followed it twenty miles but failed to get it. Friday 20th. I started after our mule. Went to Wetumka. Heard of him going up the river. I stayed all night at Billie Thomas. Sat. 21. I met a man riding my mule and he gave him up. Sunday 22 I preached at Prattville to a large congregation. Wed. 25. Brother Hazen furnished me with <u>Darwin's</u> book. I read it and disliked it very much. Sat 28th. I am at Toms all day reading Darwin's book.

Friday November 3, 1871 I am helping little Allie dig potatoes. Wed. 8 - wrote to Zac Hendrick, H. Jordan and Mollie. Friday 10th - I weighed cotton all day for Jasper. Sunday 12 Preached at Sears Chapel. Tuesday 16 I wrote to Penn Smith. Friday 17 White frost and ice. Saturday 18 I wrote to Ewell. Sunday 19 I preached to St. Andrew Chapel to 11 persons. Wed. 22 went and opened the mail. Sent letters to Brother Wetson, Bruce Harry, W.J. Cannon. Thursday 30 Brother Rowland and myself went to Thanksgiving. I preached and he gave a splendid lecture.

Monday December 4 This is my birthday. I enter into my 77th year. Wed. 7th Got letter informing us of W.G. Cannons great loss by fire. Sunday 10 A cold morning. I went to church and preached in Brother Stewards place as he failed to come. Women came to make preparations for a Christmas <u>tree</u>. Tuesday 19th. I was weighing cotton. A plank fell with a nail; struck my forehead; came near splitting my skull. Monday 25th We had a beautiful Christmas Tree. I addressed the people 40 minutes. Everybody pleased as the tree was in honor of our sabbath school. Wed. 27 I am trapping for rats, being much troubled with them. Sat 30 I caught 5 rats last night. Sunday 31 I rode to Flint Hill 8 miles and preached in the place of a new preacher who failed to come.

Saturday 6, 1872 I caught 4 rats last night and one large <u>mink.</u> Sunday 7 - Professor Walker here. Sunday 14 - I preached for Brother Stewart. He failed to come. Sunday 21 - Brother Patillo preached his first sermon; a good sermon. Monday 22 I am at the Vincent place teaching Willie and superintending the work. Thursday 30th. We are at the Vincent place part of the day but could not work.

March 1, 1872 I planted two acres in corn. Thursday 7th We planted Irish potatoes. Saturday 9th Pretty day. Mother came and we planted peas and other garden seed. Sunday 10 I organized Andrew Chapel Sabbath School and preached on that subject. Tuesday 12 - I made a Bee Bench at the Vincent place. Bought two stands at $2.50 each; put them up. Friday 15 - Hens are scratching up things. Sunday 17th Brother Bell preached and administered the sacrament. Tuesday 19 I am all day in bed;high fever. Sunday 24 - I ventured to go to the Sabbath School as superintendent, but had to return before preaching much to my mortification being the first time in my life that I can remember. Tuesday 26 we moved part of our things to the vincent place. Sunday 31 - I went to Sabbath School and gave a long lecture and gave directions for the teachers how to use the uniform lessons and magazine.

Tuesday April 2 - This is little Willie Curtis Cannon's birthday being two years old. He is having chills every third day. Wednesday 3rd - Mollie Cannon is very sick. Sunday 7 Jasper went for Dr. Baker for Mollie; failed to get him and Dr. Mathews arrived. At half past six O clock Mollie was delivered of a boy child all perfect. The child only lived five hours. Tuesday 9th I am going a-fishing in Hatchett Creek but caught nothing. Sunday 14 Eliza very sick. I bled her until she was sick. Monday 15 We sent for Dr. Baker. Mollies pulse sank down to 30 per minute. Tuesday 16 - Drew a blister on Mollie and she had never had a blister and could scarcely bear it. Sunday 21 - Eliza Worse, Mollie Better. Mother and I walked one mile to see Eliza. She is very sick. Monday 22 Eliza still very sick and Mollie also. Dr. Baker came to see Eliza and thinks she has measles. We all feel relieved. Sunday 28th. No preaching or Sabbath school.

The people fearing the measles. Eliza much improved.

Wednesday May first - I got into a buggy and went eight miles. Got a girl to come live with me to do any task and we are all so far well pleased.

In 1874, Reuben and Caroline lived with Jasper McAdory in Coosa County.

The physical features of Coosa County differ very much in different parts. Wetumpka lies on the floodplain of the Coosa River from which a high range of hills rises. These hills are rugged, nearly mountain-like, covered with trees and make a beautiful background for the town. This range of hills extends from Wetumpka to the Tallapoosa River though not so steep, and nowhere else so rocky. These hills have furnished a fine quantity of trees for lumber. The forests have been extensively logged and the logs floated across the Coosa to large sawmills. Pine was common in the eastern parts of the county with oak and hickory more abundant to the north. At Hanover, vegetation included long-needled pine, sweet gum, tuliptree, sumac, elderberry, sourwood, dogwood, and a variety of brambly berryvines.

To the north of this range of hills, and from a line nearly east and north of Wetumpka there is a gently rolling section of country, which at times is almost level. The soil here is light and sandy, with streaks of gravel. Some places it has a good loamy subsoil. All this was once covered with a fine pine forest. There is still a good deal of timber, but now it is second and third growth forest, overgrown with vines and bushes. There are many branches and small creeks of pretty clear water rippling over pebbly beds. Springs full of cattail abound along the streams, and their borders are rather marshy, heavily fringed with red bay, magnolia, laurel, gums, poplar, beech, water and post oaks, and with rich evergreen vines, passionvine, muscadine, and other creepers. In the spring many trees and shrubs are laden with blossoms that fill the air with fragrance, and are beautiful to look upon. In the dry seasons the water in the streams nearly dries up, leaving the bare sandy bottom open to lizards and snakes.

From this belt the surface becomes more broken, gradually the hills become steeper until in the northern part of the county and especially between Hatchett and Weogufka creeks they rise almost to the proportions of mountains. The soil is more varied in this portion, being generally more free from sand and of a darker gray color with a clay subsoil. There are streaks of red and brown soil, with occasional pieces of sandy pine land. This whole region has more or less rock, flint, granite, slate, and dark gray stones. The eastern part of the county is not so broken, and is more productive. Along the streams are some very rich bottoms and among the mountains are some very rich coves. The north sides of the steep hills are usually richer than the south sides. Streams are numerous and constant, fed by springs of water so cool that ice is not needed in summer to make them refreshing. The wells also of this section are likewise abundant in delightfully cold water.

Some of the rock is utilized in making fences, building chimneys, and sometimes houses, and is easily put into shape for use. These rocks render cultivation more difficult, and make the roads rougher, and more unpleasant in traveling. In this upper part of the country there was much very fine pine timber, but there was shortleaf pine in parts, and more oak of different varieties with hickory, poplar, beech, chestnut, walnut, and other varieties of hardwoods.

West of Hatchett Creek there is a country less broken, and the soil is good. Much of the soil is red and fine for apples and other fruits and grapes. Apples and peaches grew near Weogufka.

The cane which at first grew so profusely along the stream, and in many places on the uplands also, eventually died out, killed by the pigs and other livestock of the settlers. Up to the fifties, the settlers used to keep up the practice of burning off the woods in the spring... Keeping down the underbrush made it easy to ride through the woods and to see game or cattle at a distance.

Game was very abundant, both large and small, and the early settlers were able to keep their tables well supplied with the meat of bear, deer, and turkey. As late as in the fifties [1850s] deer were still right common and ever now and then, in the northwestern part, a hunter got a deer. Wild turkeys were sometimes common. Perhaps no part of the state had a better supply of fine timber both of the yellow pine and also hardwoods.

Letter, McKenzie Tennessee; August 30, 1875:

Dear Elisha and Julia,

Yours 17th inst came to hand two hours ago. Slow passage. I have heard nothing from you since we were here three years ago except a letter from Walter. I have sent some few letters to you and began to think all not right on your parts. We left here first January 1874 for Jasper McAdories Coosa County. Remained until June 9th following; arrived at Flem Jordans 11th remained there until 7th September and arrived at T.W. Sadlers 8th; remained there until November 5th. Then we went home. Spent the winter until April 15, 1875; left for Columbiana. [We] remained several days and then to Jefferson; arrived at Jordans 20th and remained until May 3rd 1875 and arrived at McKenzie the 4th; been here ever since.

Sometimes we have been very sick; Mother greatly afflicted with that stricture of the esophagus and always a distressing cough. I have never been clear of vertigo since I was at your house.

I have averaged about a sermon a week for every week for the last three years, but am preaching but little since here... Mother seldom goes to church on account of her cough. I go nearly all the time. W.J. Cannon is settled here for life [and] is now building a new brick schoolhouse. He professed religion two years ago and joined the Methodist Church; is now trustee and steward of the church a steady man. [they] have lost their two last children. Little Carrie lies near their room window; great affliction. We expect to leave for Coosa for winter quarters last of September.

At Flem Jordans in a few weeks I am called on to marry Carrie to John E. Ware of Columbiana on the 13th of October, then go on. We think of locating for want of ability and money to travel.

Virgil is now temporarily at Chattanooga; Ewell at Memphis, Julian at Greenville, Illinois and her family. Virgil left her some week ago, called on us to see us once more before we die. I am glad you preach the gospel. It is true it will not make you rich in this world, but may be instrumental in saving your own soul and that of your family and many others. You have a cousin who now ranks among the talented of the Holston Conference. Sewell Philips. His address is Eagle Furnace, Roane County, Tennessee. You may wish to open a correspondence. He weighs 300 pounds and is wealthy.
 If you don't write soon you had better direct to Hanover, Coosa County. Farewell now. Your affectionate Father,   Reuben Philips.

Letter; Montgomery, Ala; May 1, 1876

My Dear Brother (J.B. Stevenson)

I thought I would have had the opportunity to visit you all ere this time in person, but it has been ordered otherwise. The members of the Quarterly Conference and the church at Columbiana are no doubt getting weary of only hearing my annual report and not seeing more of me in person. I have always been reluctant to speak of myself by way of commendation. I very often retrospect my life, and sometimes survey it a year at a time, and find a great deal for which to reproach myself. But then again when I consider my opportunities, I am a wonder to myself.

If it would not be considered a vain thing by you, I would give a short synopsis of my life. My natural birth was December 4, 1795, and my spiritual birth was February 14, 1820. Between these periods I had changes that would almost satisfy me at least for a time, that my sins were pardoned. Never until the time above stated did I become fully satisfied that I was a new creature. In 1825 I received a license to preach the gospel - In 1831 ordained deacon and in 1842 ordained an elder. I have tried all the time so to demean myself as not to disgrace the Christian religion and especially the ministry. I do sometimes feel compunctions when I think how little good I have done. I am fully convinced that if I had joined the itinerancy at the call to the ministry that I might have done much more good... It never was any sacrifice for me to refrain from the evil habits of wicked men. I commenced teaching school in the year 1810 [and] being very young, I felt constrained to lead a moral life as an example to the youths committed to my care. I never drank any intoxicating liquor in my life only medicinally. I never swore a profane oath and never went to a dance or a theater in my life. [I] never went to the circus but once and that was by the advice of Brother Koger, my Presiding Elder. He advised me to take my school girls to see the animals and before we had gone round, the circus riding commenced and we could not conveniently get out until the clown made his speech. When he condescended to some dirty slang, I gave the signal and was followed by my pupils. I bid farewell to menageries forever.

I have never been sued for debt, nor called to serve as a juror in court, nor as a witness but to answer one question. If I owe any man a dollar, I do not know it. But how much owing to me! Myself and wife lost heavily by the results of the war, are now living with our children and are tenderly cared for. We have food, raiment, and friends, and are striving to be content therewith.

Since I came to this town I have heard eleven sermons from our Methodist ministers, two from the Presbyterians, and have preached four times myself: have attended the Young Men's Christian Association ten times, attended two class meetings, two love feasts, attended Sabbath school four times and made one Sabbath school lecture. [I] have been called on and have made twenty four public prayers. I attend to family prayers when I can. I have forgiven all my enemies, and love Jesus because he first loved me. And as soon as my passport is signed and sealed I trust I am ready to go home.
            R. Philips

Letter; Hanover, Coosa County, Alabama; January 13, 1879:

Dear Elisha and Julia

On reading over the preachers appointment in the Alabama Conference for 1879 I find that you are still in Mariana and I suppose you have not heard from us since I wrote last and may have felt some uneasiness about us while this yellow fever was raging in West Tennessee and knowing that we were in that region during the time it prevailed.

I conclude to give you a kind of synopsis of our whereabouts and how we did all the time. At present I am enjoying ordinary health. Mother is suffering more than usual from her cough and kidneys.

The time has come with us that we are <u>dependent</u>. We have suffered reverses and lapses so as to not be able to pay railroad charges and when we travel we have to do it at the expense of those whom we visit. Also we can scarcely bear up under the fatigue of travel. The cars make Mother so sick that she can scarcely live... We have a prayer at our table morning and night. Willie Cannon reads when I cant.
            Reuben

Reuben and Caroline were still living at the McAdory's home in Coosa County, Alabama in 1880.

Virgil Philips had served gallantly in the War of the Rebellion, but now, like many Vietnam veterans, he could no longer function well in society. At the time this condition was not known as an illness, and caused his father Reuben considerable grief.

Letter   Chattanooga Tenn
                    Feb. 27, 1880

Rev. Ruben Phillips

Dear Brother

I am pastor of the Whiteside St. Church Chattanooga and my pastoral charge includes the Vulcan Iron Works, and Bro. Boys sent me your letter and requested me to answer it.

I have taken some pains to learn some of the history and character of Virgil Philips, and will give you a true statement of the case as I learn it from reliable persons. I have only been here since the first of November, and I do not know him personally. But I learn he has been here about four years, he came here with a lady whom he said was his wife and she said he was her husband. The lady was said to be very much his senior in age. He explained his marriage to friends in this way; Said he was employed by a man of some wealth to keep grocery somewhere on the Mississippi river, and finely the gentleman died, and his business was in Virgil's hands, and he had requested him to take care of his widow and he married her. They soon spent the money and they were in great poverty when here and his wife did much work such as sewing and washing; he occasionally worked in the rolling mill. His wife died last october aged perhaps 74 years. Since her death he has not been keeping house. He has never been hurt seriously any way and is a stout hearty man. If he has any business I cannot find out what it is; He is boarding I believe with the man to whom he sent his furniture after the death of his wife. He spends his time I believe in town and it is said he indulges freely in dissipation. As I have not met him I am dependent entirely on the testimony of others. He is said to be a man of fine address and splendid mind and shows good cultivation and especially great familiarity with the scriptures. He told his friends his father and brother were ministers and that he had been a christian. He makes no predilections to be a christian now. He could not be an object of charity in his condition of health. It is painful for me to write such words to you concerning your son, but I have endeavored to give you a true statement as I have learned it from reliable persons. I intend to seek an interview with him and will do all I can to induce him to reform. I think it can hardly be that the continuous prayers of a father for his prodigal boy can go unanswered. Let us hope in Gods grace and trust he will help.

                                        unsigned

This Vietnam syndrome is treatable today, but it must have been much worse after such a terrible war as this had been, especially so since it was not known to be a psychological condition. We do not know the end of this story, nor what happened eventually to Virgil.

Letter; Hanover, Coosa County, Alabama; March 11, 1880:

Dear Ewell,

I only yesterday read a letter from Zac. written to Elisha in Florida in which he named that you are in Memphis. I have not heard a word from you since you wrote me that long letter after you left to do business for some man on the river and have enquired for you in every way. I thought that you might have been in Memphis last year in [the] time of the epidemic and fallen with others and not noticed. I wonder now why I receive no letter from you or your wife. I write these few lines to see if you will again correspond with us.

Mother has been now over a year sick; had symptoms of dropsy. Went to Prattville first of April and remained some two months and those symptoms disappeared. I took chills and had a hard time but got [well]. We then went to Jefferson and Mother was still sick and feeble. We left July 18th for this place and Mother took [to] her bed suffering from her esophagus and choking until she became helpless. For some three or four months she lay and suffered but ultimately she became able to sit in a chair and now for over a month she walks about the house and yard but has a bad cough all the time. I am in good health except vertigo that troubles me at times. I am preaching much as yet and am weighing more than I ever did in all my life. I am more than three months on my 85 year. Sight and hearing [have] failed very much. I must tell you that Jasper and Eliza have waited and attended on Mother beyond anything I ever witnessed in all my life, for which I feel grateful. She has proposed to be ready for her change all the time. We are cared for here every way, and I suppose will find our graves here.

Elisha is [presiding] Elder now in his fourth year on the Marianna District, has a good character, and said to be useful. Virgil is in Chatanooga but doing no good. T. W. Sadler is in Prattville and a successful lawyer. Allie Cooke also [is] living in Prattville; husband dead. Julia Jordan living near Birmingham; all OK.

When I learn your address I will be more voluminous.

We all join in love to you and your wife.

as ever your affectionate father,   Reuben Philips

In 1881, Reuben was still preaching occasionally, and was writing his autobiography for his daughter Mollie Cannon.

Letter; Hanover Coosa County Alabama; July 6th 1882:

Dear Elisha, Julia, and Boys. For a month now my eyes are more inflamed. I can however see to walk about though in great pain. I am thankful for even that much. I have no idea that I shall ever read any more. I closed up all public exercises Pulpit and Sabbath School last month. Was a year ago I preached my last sermon... I don't expect to ever try to preach again. I am now in my 87th year and must go soon. I feel ready...

Mother... gave me unwearied attention until she was taken down, now almost four months [ago]. She has been in her bed most of the time seemingly hopeless, but now she can walk a little. Jasper and Eliza in fine health only Eliza has spells of rheumatism that are awfully distressing, but they have given us kind treatment. W.J. Cannon and Mollie are here for over a year and her health is much recuperated. Has had a fine girl child born now over a year old and bids fair to live. Four others have died and their oldest is now twelve years old; a good boy. We don't know what they will do. They are not settled as yet where they will go but will go somewhere before cold weather.

Ewell was in the Peabody Hotel in Memphis when he wrote last. Julian E. Hendricks is now on a visit to her daughter in Kansas. Her oldest son Zack is dead and left a wife and two children. Allie the youngest is married to a man of property living at Elms Point in Illinois. Mary the oldest is there also. She has taught school four years in the same place and is one of the best christians of her sex. They are all doing well. Virgil I know nothing of him for over two years. He was in Chatanooga, Tennessee and rather dissipated. So we are scattered until called together by the Angel Gabriel. O may we all meet in Heaven. <u>Amen</u> and <u>Amen</u>.

My youngest sister Catherine Bell now lives in the house that you were born in. She is in her 80th year and my brother Elisha for whom you were named lives in the same place he first settled 68 years ago. He is nearly three years older than myself. His post office is Pigeon River in Haywood County.
Your affectionate Father R. Philips Mother C.M. Philips

Herbert Atkinson M. Bell was born September 16, 1882 son of George and Mattie Bell. He died August 18, 1883.

Elisha Philips; Pigeon River, N.C. Aug. 27, 1883;

Dear brother Rubin, This is in answer to a letter which I received last Saturday the 25th of August. I was glad to hear from you once more.

I am getting weak and feeble. I have very sick spells at times, at other times, I am able to walk about. I am at times almost blind in one of my eyes. My wife is not very stout, though she takes as much care of me as if I was a baby. My mother in law Sally Hall is yet alive though very old and feeble. She is living with us. We are all old and nearing eternity, and by the grace of God, we hope to meet in that temple not made with hands, eternal in the heavens.

I have one child living with me, my youngest child named Laura, an Idiot Girl. She is now about forty [years old]. I have six children dead and nine living. I have three boys living. Two of them are preachers. Harriet Rhinehart and Mahala Shook are both alive.

[letter to Rubin Philips] Park Ill]

Elms

Sept 1883

Dear Father
　　　　　Your Postal Recd. Was more than glad to hear from you once more. God grant you may live to write many more. This leaves us all moderately well. Alice has another daughter 6 weeks old. looks like Grand Pa Philips. I want it named Rubie for you. The hair is black and thick as a child 5 years of age. They have not decided just what to call it. Fannie & Vance are back from Kansas living in Greenville. He works in his fathers machine shop. Fannie will teach music. She has three children.

Mary teaches in the graded schools of Greenville. Stands high as a teacher. Has a permanent position if her health doesn't fail. She is very delicate. Mr Pauley thinks some of going west or rather Northwest to Nebraska. Thinks Alice would have better health. No wheat grown this year here. But fine corn. It is so dry now that stock can scarcely get water. Apples & Honey in abundance. Mr. Pauley has a cousin living near here that has raised 3000 Lbs of honey for sale this season from 40 stands. There is but little doing in the churches. Although we have a most excellent Minister. Br Gibson from Kentucky.

The Holiness Brethern seem more alive than any of the other sects. There are some real good people who belong to them but most of their membership are made up of low illiterate people and they all preach and say such foolish things it injures the cause with the better class - consequently they are ridiculed. There are a good many of them in this county. I took my letter from Greenville and put it in the Cumberland Church with Alice - so I attend that church with them and really I like them very much. If there had been a Methodist Church near I guess I would have put my letter in it. Will never feel altogether at home in any other church.

Is Br Elisha still in Florida? and do you know anything of Br Ewell or Virgil?
I do not know Mollies address. I have neglected to write to anyone for a long time. I know it is wrong to do so - but have gotten out of the way of writing but <u>I do love</u> to get letters. I sometimes think I will forget how to write. I don't do better. I hope you can read this & excuse.

My Grandchildren keep me busy have eight of them.
Write often and receive all our united love.   Your Daughter   Julia

Reuben's wife Caroline died February 14, 1884.

Letter; Hanover, Coosa County Alabama; March 10, 1885:

My Dear Grandson Shelton Philips

I am thankful to you for your letter of the fourth instant. Although I cant read it as I am nearly blind. My stepdaughter read it for me as she reads many things for me. Your father still writes to me but your mother has quit or else they never come. I have been now declining every way for several months so as not to live much longer. On Christmas I celebrate the birth of Christ in our church so as to call the young and old from desecrating that day by a sermon of an hour and a quarter long!! My voice has continued very good and my reason is good but my memory is failing greatly! I am thankful for so merciful a God. This christmas was my ninetieth (90). I gave the people the 149th Psalm as a text; it may be my last effort. I was licensed to preach September 30, 1825 and have averaged a sermon a week since that time.

My brother Elisha Philips has lived on the same place since 1815 and his first wife gave birth to 15 children and died and went to Jesus I have no doubt. Three of their sons are good industrious Methodist preachers, two of them itinerants in the Holston and North Carolina conferences, one with them at home. My brother is now in his 92nd year. I never knew my brother to go in debt in his married life nor go anybodies security!! His oldest daughter Aliff married Benjamin Robeson of Habersham County Georgia in my house is now a good citizen near Jonah Mountain Nachoocha Valley in Habersham County. Her sister Anna came to visit her awhile and was also married to his brother Andrew Robison [who] has been a noble itinerant preacher for years. [He] went to the Tennessee conference and I learned died a few months since and gone shouting to <u>Jesus</u>!!

All our stock are Methodists. My only living sister <u>Catherine Bell</u> a widow in her 84th year at Bell Post Office near Asheville N.C. raised one son and gave him a good education. The Episcopalians soon won him over and made him an Episcopalian Minister. I wrote to her to know what she had done. She answered Brother if there were only three Methodists in the U.S.A. I would be one of them.

My youngest daughter Julian E. Hendrix was sent with her family by my son Ewell P. Philips from Memphis in the time of the great epidemic to the Mississippi River to save life. They went up to St. Louis and then to Elms Point in Illinois and engaged in school. She is yet a widow. Her oldest son died not long since leaving a wife and two children. Her daughters are now in a high school in the capital of the State of Illinois. They are fine scholars. The eldest now taught five years in a high school and is in fine standing. You will find the youngest married and settled at Elms Point doing very well.

Please remember me to your father and mother and brothers. Poor old me. I could not see to read your letter at all. I am treated all <u>OK</u> by all my children. W.J. Cannon and my daughter Mary Betty (they call her Molly) [is] twelve miles from here doing well. I am at the will of God and I think nearly to go to Jesus in heaven. Still write to me occasionally. Give my love to all your brothers. I was very much pleased to hear your Pa preach. <u>Now Farewell</u> as ever I am your loving Grand P.   Reuben Philips

Reverend Reuben Philips died February 12, 1887 at Hanover, Coosa County, Alabama at age 91.

Alabama Christian Advocate; June 8, 1887:
... The subject of this memoir, Reverend Reuben Philips was born December 4, 1795; was converted and joined the M.E. Church, February 14, 1820; was licensed to preach the gospel at a conference held in the bounds of the Holston Conference, September 1825. His license was

signed by Reverend Jessee Cunningham, P.E. He was ordained a deacon by Bishop Heading in Augusta Georgia in 1831 and was ordained Elder by Bishop James O. Andrew in Talladega, Alabama in 1842. He was twice married - first to Miss Elizabeth King who died September 26, 1846. By this marriage he had six children, one of whom Reverend Elisha Philips died an honored member of the Alabama conference. He was married the second time to Mrs. C. M. Sadler, December 7, 1847. She was the mother of Honorable Thomas W. Sadler, now an exmember of congress from Alabama, Mrs. P.J. McAdory of Coosa County, and Mrs Flem Jordan of Birmingham. They had one child born to them, Mrs Mollie Philips Cannon of Sylacauga, Alabama.

To give a correct idea of the death of Brother Philips, I quote from the letter of Mrs Cannon written a few days after his death. " My dear friend, I write to inform you of the death of my dear father. I was summoned to his bedside on thursday the 10th and remained with him until he died Saturday morning February 12, 1887. I do not think he suffered much during his last illness. He was patient and resigned. His mind was clear and bright to the last moment of his life. Just fifteen minutes before he died, he spoke in a clear and distinct tone of voice, expressing a willingness to go, and said 'I am all right'. He died as he had lived, in the full assurance of faith in Christ...".

I scarcely know where to begin to write of my dear and now glorified friend. In the year 1865 I was sent to the Jacksonville District as Presiding Elder. I found Brother Philips living at Columbiana, Alabama and engaged in teaching school. This was my first personal acquaintance with him, and I was impressed at once that he was no ordinary man, and that his influence for good in the community and especially his school was wonderful. In april of this same year we commenced a meeting in the Methodist church of the town which resulted in the conversion of eighty souls, in which glorious work he was one of the principal factors. The lamented Nabors was one of the converts of the meeting, and a fast friend of Brother Philips to the day of his death. Brother Philips watched the developing greatness of young Nabors with a fatherly solicitude to the day of his seemingly premature death.

The manner in which, by his influence, he swayed old and young was wonderful. I have been very much amused with what ease and readiness he could quiet a whole pew of Sunday-school urchins with one flash of his bright and piercing eye. He was a born commander, a man of positive character and strong convictions, and courage to speak and act them out.

I quote from the letter of Brother J.B. Stevenson, who was his presiding Elder after me, "I made the acquaintance of Reverend Reuben Philips in the winter of 1878-9. My first impression of him was that he was remarkably preserved in both body and mind, and that he was a man of intellectual culture far above an average for his day. I was impressed with his quick perception. He seemed to grasp a new idea or truth with the mental vigor of young manhood, and to take in these new truths and ideas in all their philosophical and moral bearings in nature and religion. He showed that he was a man of both reading and thought, that his reading and thinking had taken in a very comprehensive range for one sustaining the relationship to society that he did. To some he seemed dogmatical. This was almost an unavoidable consequence of his long continued service in the schoolroom, and not from any autocratic spirit in the man. There was a manly dignified courtesy about him that showed him to be a very high type of christian gentleman."

7-4-1 Clarinda b. 9 Sept. 1821 d. March 29, 1864 m. A.S. Dorsey.

In the Month of September on the 9th day we were blessed with the birth of our first child, a daughter. We called her name Clarinda, and as we had not as yet joined any church, I felt it my duty to dedicate our babe to god in the ordinance of baptism. I accordingly went as soon as my wife was able to a small church east up the Bull Mountain and gave myself and child to the Methodist Episcopal Church and my heart to God.

My oldest daughter Clarinda started school [in the fall of 1827.]

Reuben and Elizabeth Philips' daughter Clarinda was married to Robert Hendrix in 1843.

Clarinda Dorsey died March 29, 1864.

7-4-2 Elisha b. 8 Mar. 1823 m. July 17, 1856 Julia A. Smith(b.July 25, 1834 d. March 28, 1899).

On March 8, 1823 Elisha Philips was born to Reuben and Elizabeth Philips.

Reuben: I strove hard, sold off and gave away all my plunder, bought a wagon with four good oxen, filled in what I could of our most valuable furniture, and with two fine brood mares and one Indian pony , we started on the 12th of January 1838. My oldest son Elisha was a good driver. I lay in the wagon most of the way and we on the 29th reached the <u>Hillabees</u> where I stopped a day or two and then proceeded to Doctor Simmons where I was to have land.

Reuben Philips 1840 - This summer my boys and Franklin Stephens made a crop. Elisha appeared discontented having determined to be a scholar.

The following transcript was entered in a bible presented to Elisha Philips by his father Reverend Reuben Philips:

If men are to be punished in another world, God must be the punisher.
If God be the punisher, the punishment must be just
If the punishment be just, the punished must be guilty
If the punished are guilty, they could have done otherwise. They were free agents.
Therefore if men are liable to punishment in another

world they must be free.   (logic)   R. P.

In 1842, Reuben was Postmaster at Hillabee, Alabama. His son Elisha went to school below Tuskega.

Reverend Reuben 1843: My son Elisha who had been going to school in Macon County came home and went to school to Mr. Finn. I sent for Elisha to finish my term. [After] two weeks he took a school for himself.

Reverend Reuben: In the summer of 1846 and in the month of August my beloved wife was taken with Typhoid Fever and died August 26th. This event so affected me and disorganized my school that I dismissed the school to the care of my son Elisha for a time.

Elisha Married Julia Smith, a teacher from Connecticut in July 25, 1856

Walter Howard, the son of Elisha and Julia(Smith) Philips was born in Alabama March 4, 1860.

The Reverend Elisha Philips served at Greenwood Church in Marianna District from 1876 to 1880.

March 11, 1880 Elisha is [presiding] Elder now in his fourth year on the Marianna District, has a good character, and said to be useful.

MINUTES
The Second Quarterly Conference for the current year, 1885 Seale & Huntsboro Charge. Montgomery District, Alabama, Conference, was held at Huntsboro April 18th, 1885, _____, P.E., in the Chair.
After religious service conducted by Rev.J. M. Mason P.E.
The roll was called and the following members were present:
Rev Elisha Phillips P.C.
WT Davis, E N Brown J B Banks W H Banks & E H Glenn
E H Glenn was elected Secretary
Question 12. What is doing for the cause of Missions? Ans PC has visited Hatchae remaining there 24 hours some church members, Methodist & other Churches & he intends having service there on 5th Sunday.

Question 13 What is doing for the cause of Education? [2.] Ans Children generally in School in Seale & Huntsboro

Question 25. Is there any miscellaneous business? Ans.

Election of delegates to District Conference by nomination E H Glenn W T Davis J McBrannon E N Brown P A Green J B Banks. Alternates Shamas S Davis J B Henry Charles Owens

Question 26 Where shall next quarterly conference be held? Ans Seale

The minutes were read and approved, and Conference adjourned.

                 J M. Mason , Presiding Elder
E H Glenn , Secretary
P A Green , Recording Steward

Supplement A.
The Sunday Schools are in good working condition exhibiting interest & improvement. I think some little change in one or two items might be profitable to both schools.
1st Some classes are too large to access personal development both in the knowledge of the word of God and individually in faith and obedience to the gospel of the son of God.
2nd I fear that whatever irregularities in attendance the Sunday School comes more of indifference than season or weather.

I am trying at all times to talk to the children about serving their blessed Savior, and conform to his instructions for their souls salvation.
There has been raised for SS purposes Seale 13.05 Huntsboro $15.15 this quarter.
                 E Phillips, P.C.
                 Huntsboro April 18, 1885

letter to : Mr Shelton Philips; Bronson, Levy Co. Florida
       J. M. DeLacy, Proprietor
       Meriwether County. Ga., July 25, 1885

Dear Son,
         Yours of the 20 came to hand the 22 instant. I was very glad to hear from you and of your prospects. My health is improving, but very slow from about 14th of April last til about the first of July it was a very grave question in my mind whether I should live through the year but God's mercies prevailed in my behalf and I began to [improve]. [Everyone] here encourages me on my improvement so ought to get well from this attack as so much has been gained over the main points dyspepsia, indigestion, and constipation if other points can be gained the strengthening my nervous system and there is great improvement in this. When I left home, I could not

read five minutes or write a note. I could walk about 100 yards, now I can read half an hour, write letters, and on good days walk from one to two miles, yet I am weak as compared to last year. I have not been in a church since the fourth sabbath in April. The congregations of Seale and Huntsboro made up a purse for my present expense... I have been here since the last day of June; will stay till next Thursday. My third quarterly conference convenes at Seale. I want to be there. I can leave here at 7 AM and arrive at Seale by Noon the second day. I shall send your letter to you in the mornings mail. I should like to write more but I must close...

            Your Father
            E Philips

MINUTES
The __3rd__ Quarterly Conference for the current year, 1885 __Seale & Huntsboro__ Charge, __Montgomery__ District, __Alabama__ Conference, was held at __Seale Aug 8th__, 1885, __Rev J. M. Mason__, P. E., in the Chair.

After religious service conducted by __Rev J M Mason__, P.E.

The roll was called, and the following members were present:
Rev E Phillips PC
J B Banks W.H. Banks HB Perry PA Green JM Brannon W H Washington Ben Jennings and E H Glenn
EH Glenn was elected Secretary.

Question 4. Is there a written report from the preacher in charge on the general state of the Church? Ans. __None PC has been sick during this quarter__.

Question 8. What amount has been raised the present quarter for the support of the ministry, and how has it been applied? Ans. Seale $65.25 Huntsboro $69.50 $134.25 Pd P. E. $21,50 P.C. $112.75

Question 12. What is doing for the cause of Missions? Ans. __Some missionary work is being done by Huntsboro Sunday School__

Question 14. Have the General Rules been read? [3] Ans __They have not__

Question 15. Is there a Church Register and a Record of Church Conferences, and have they been faithfully kept? [3.] Ans __There is and it has been kept the Book is not__ before the Conference but will be at the 4th Quarterly Conference

The Minutes were read and approved, and Conference adjourned.

       J M Mason, Presiding Elder.
E H Glenn, Secretary
P A Green, Recording Steward

Elisha Philips died November 29, 1885 at Seale, Alabama where he was employed. He was the son of Reverend Reuben Philips and his wife Elizabeth King, and was born March 8, 1823 on Whitson Creek, Buncombe County, North Carolina, just East of Asheville.

When only twenty years of age, Elisha began a career as a school teacher, teaching between Mardisville and Talladega in Alabama. He was admitted on trial as a preacher in 1850 and soon proved to be a valuable minister. In 1855 he was ordained elder at Mariana, Florida. He moved to Centreville Alabama, and from there to Green County Alabama where he was superintendent at the Trinity and Boligee Colored Mission in 1858 and 1859. He then spent a year at Forkland, two at Livingston, three at Belmont, a year at Suggsville, two at Orrville, one at Havana and one at Fort Deposit.

In the year 1872, Elisha moved back to Mariana where he was Presiding Elder of the Mariana District. He remained in Mariana until 1880, serving as Presiding Elder and/or Principal of the Mariana District High School. In 1881 he was at Henry in the Eufala District and then spent two years in the Montgomery District.

He was married to Miss Julia Smith of Connecticut. Their children were Walter Howard b. March 4, 1860, Sheldon, Julian, and Albert. (newspaper clipping, March 1899) On Tuesday morning the 28th inst. at the house of her brother in law Albert W. Locklin, this much beloved christian woman breathed her last. Mrs Phillips was born in New Haven Conn. in 1835. Her parents, Mr. and Mrs. Howard Smith, had four children, three daughters and a son. The subject of this sketch went to Alabama as a music teacher and in 1857 became the wife of Rev. Elisha Phillips, a member of the Alabama conference, in which he has served as presiding elder. Four sons were born to them, two living in the south, one in Oneida N. Y. and the fourth in this city (Gloversville, N.Y.). These last two sons are well known here. On Mr. Phillips death, his wife and two younger sons came to this city arriving in 1886 taking up her residence with her sister. Her health failed last October and by slow degrees sapped her vital energies. Tenderness and skill exhausted their resources. Her patience and resignation were wonderful and her faith and hope never failed her...

Obituary
Elisha Philips was born in Buncombe County, North Carolina March 8, 1823. He joined the Alabama conference in his 27th year and at once took rank as one among our best men and ablest preachers. He was a student the whole of his ministreal life andbecame a man of varied and general information. No wonder that his company was sought by wise and thoughtful men and women, nor that his preaching was entertaining, instructive and beneficial. For 33 years he went in and out among the people giving to all the example of a blameless and godly life. On the district, on the circuit, on the station he was hailed as an eloquent, zealous, successful minister of the gospel of Christ. After our last conference his health failed rapidly insomuch that he preached his last sermon on the 25th of April, 1885 from which time he was a patient sufferer until the master took him to the place where men suffer and die no more. "I am on the downgrade," he whispered to the friend at his side the day before he died. "No, you will get well." said his friend. Speechless he lifted his hand and pointed his attenuated finger upward.

He leaves a wife and four sons behind him. We all know where to find Elisha Philips. Let us follow and find him.

In the Minutes for Seale and Huntsboro January 30, 1886 there appears the following statement by D C Crook PC: the church sustained a serious loss & sore affliction in the death of their beloved Pastor E Phillips last year. He was so afflicted as to render them but little service.

The following record of Births, deaths and marriages were entered in the bible of Elisha Philips by Julia A. Philips, wife of Elisha Philips [and by others not named]:
Adam Philips was born December 29, 1751
Hannah Philips his wife was born 1755
Reuben Philips was born Dec. 4, 1795 Son of Adam and
 Hanna Philips
Elizabeth, his wife was born June 18, 1792
Clarinda Philips was born Sept. 9, 1821. Daughter of
 Reuben and Elizabeth Philips
Elisha Philips was born March 8, 1823. Son of Reuben and
 Elizabeth Philips.
Ewell P. Philips was born Jan. 3, 1825. Son of Reuben and

Elizabeth Philips

Julia A. Philips was born July 22, 1827. Daughter of Reuben & Elizabeth Philips.

Lafayett Philips was born Jan. 1, 1831. Son of Reuben & Elizabeth Philips.

Virgil Philips was born _____ 1831 son of Reuben & Elizabeth Philips.

Mary E. Philips was born _____ 1849 Daughter of Reuben & Elizabeth{should read Caroline} Philips.

Julia A. Smith, wife of Elisha Philips was born July 25, 1834.

Walter H. Philips was born March 4, 1860. Son of Elisha and Julia A. Philips.

Shelton Philips was born Feb. 18, 1864. Son of Elisha and Julia A. Philips.

Julian Philips was born March 29, 1866. Son of Elisha and Julia A. Philips.

Charles Albert Reuben Philips was born April 6, 1873. Son of Elisha and Julia A. Philips.

Albert Roux, son of Shelton and Ida Philips was born June 20, 1890.

Russell, son of Shelton and Ida Philips was born Feb. 7, 1894.

Mildred, daughter of Shelton and Ida Philips, was born Feb. 7, 1894.

Ruth, daughter of Shelton and Ida Philips, was born Dec. 1, 1896.

DEATHS

Adam Philips died Dec. 27, 1859.

Hannah, his wife, died in the year, 1850, having lived together 73 years,

Elizabeth, wife of Reuben Philips, died Sept. 26, 1846.

Clarinda Dorsey died March 29, 1864.

Lafayett Philips died Feb. 27, 1841.

Elisha Philips, son of Reuben Philips died Nov. 29, 1885.

Walter H. Son of Julia A. and Elisha died _____

Julian died Sept. 26, 1925 at 6:00 A.M.

Albert Roux Philips, son of Shelton and Ida died July 28, 1925; Automobile Accident.

MARRIAGES

Reuben Philips was married the second time to Mrs. C. M. Sadler, December 7, 1847.

Elisha Philips was married to Julia A. Smith July 17, 1856

Clarinda Philips was married to Dorsey

Mary E. Philips was married to Capt. William Cannon.

Shelton Philips was married to Ida D. Helvenston March 14, 1889

7-4-2-1 Walter b. March 4, 1860

>Yellow Pine Camp, no. 12, W.O.W.
>office of the clerk
>W.H. Philips, Clerk
>Whitfield, Walton Co. Fla. April 2, 1899

Dear Shellie

Your letter came last night. I had received one from J.(Julian) telling of Mothers death and it shocked me more than I imagined it would as I had been expecting it for so long and had fully made up my mind that she was dead to you & me and as it had been twenty years since I saw her. I can remember her as if it was yesterday. I wrote to A.(Albert) to night to find out what it would cost to have a photo of her enlarged from one he has & I would send him the money as I have none of her except one taken with Aunt J. and L. and of Fathers. I have none of him... J. wrote to me to know if I would help to fix up Fathers grave & I told him I would do all I could. It depends on the time I make this season. One cant save much on $25.00 per month and feed & clothe the crowd I have. Still if I can make any ways like [extra] time I can help some say 15 or $20.00.

Well if there is any truth in the Bible our parents are reunited again after a long separation and are happy in their everlasting home. How many of their sons will join them rests with each one of us. I am not of a religious turn and have no one to blame but myself. But my companions for the last eighteen years have been those of the worst characters. I am a great believer in Churches and so were there any one in this country towards churches & SS. The Preachers always make our house headquarters & many a tiff we have. I wrote to the company you said but twas a stamp wasted as it does very little good to write for work as there is nearly always someone around a big mill to fill any vacancy. I am A-1 in my speciality marking and inspecting & can get the best of references from a dozen mill men and shippers. I thoroughly understand the Interior and Continental classification of lumber in all grades. If I was able to knock off & hunt work I might get better wages than I am here. Well I will close. Ella sends her love to Ida & the children.

>Lovingly,
>Walter

Walter Henry Philips was born March 4, 1860, in Coffee County, Alabama and when a young boy came to Florida with his parents. Having an eagerness to make some use of his intellect, he attended college for four years after growing to manhood, and completing his studies in school, taught school for nine years. While engaged in the teaching profession he fell in love with one of his girl pupils and later married her. To this union there were born six children, the youngest son passing away after reaching manhood; the five still living being Mrs Sheffield and Ross Philips, residing in Millville; Mrs. J.S. Gray of Bay Harbor; John S. of Jacksonville, and Harry of Houston, Texas.

On March 11, 1922 his companion passed away, leaving life very lonely; but he found great consolation in the knowledge that he would soon go away to join his dear wife and baby boy who had preceeded him to that "City not made by hands."

The past four years "Dad" Philips as he was known by all, had made his home with his daughter, Mrs Sheffield, who has tenderly administered to his every wish. He has surviving him besides his two children, two brothers, Sheldon at Williston, Florida and Albert at Gloversville, New York: a brother Julian having passed beyond two years ago.

At the time of his death, Mr. Philips was clerk for the supply department at the round house for the company here. Just the evening before his death, he was downtown chatting with his son and some friends, apparently in his usual health but about midnight or a little later he called his family and was suffering considerably. Everything possible was done to relieve his condition, but it was not to be; and he passed away shortly before daybreak the following morning.

Many people who knew of his love for reading and his extensive knowledge of various subjects have come to him for information and advice. He was also a lover of good music and the radio in his home afforded him many hours of entertainment.

Funeral services were held at the cemetery here (Panama City?), and every walk of life seemed gathered to pay a last tribute, each order with which he was associated taking part in obsequies --Masonic, Klan, Church, Woodmen, every step to the shrine being represented--and each bowing with regret that so worthy a man should be called from our midst. As the body was placed by loving friends into its last resting place and returned to "The God who gave it," a favorite song, both his and his wife's was rendered, "Abide With Me".

In his funeral arrangements every detail was executed as

he had requested. He had carefully laid away some choice lumber some time ago to be used for his casket and box; but when his dear mate was called home, some lumber was taken out—to be used for her purpose, and more lumber replaced, with the remark to his fellow workmen that he expressly designed this material to be used for his burial, and so it was to be as he wished. The entire community have the happy memories of enjoying his friendship, and sincerely grieve with the loved ones at his early passing, June 4, 1926.

Undertaker J.B. had charge of the preparation for burial.

7-4-2-1-1 Julia Ella b. December 21, 1888 Point Washington, Choctawhatach Bay, Florida. d. Feb. 3, 1955. m. Joseph Sylvester Gray. The Gray family was to play a big part in the business and political life of the Panama City and Bay County area came from the Wiregrass area of South Alabama to Santa Rosa County, Florida in 1892. John Clark Gray was the head of this family. After living on a farm near Baker Florida in the Blackman Community, John C. Gray and family left and traveled by wagon to St, Andrew BAy, taking six days to travel and arrived in Millville on Sunday April 30, 1899.

7-4-2-1-1-1 Mary b. Oct 28, 1907 m. John Henry Minge, Jr. November 30, 1940.

7-4-2-1-1-1-1 Mary Tonita b. July 27, 1944

7-4-2-1-1-1-2 Jeanie Gray b. April 15, 1944

7-4-2-1-1-1-3 Malcolm Gray b. April 22, 1946

7-4-2-1-1-2 Corine Gray b. January 24, 1910 m. William Zeba Lindley July 8, 1940

7-4-2-1-1-2-1 Mary Juliet Gray b. April 15, 1944

7-4-2-1-1-2-2 Jeanie Gray b. April 15, 1944

7-4-2-1-1-2-3 Malcolm Gray b. April 22, 1946

7-4-2-1-1-3 James Shelton Gray b. March 11, 1913 m. Irma Askew April 9, 1942

7-4-2-1-1-3-1 Jack Shelton b. April 18, 1947

7-4-2-1-1-3-2 James Kent Gray b. September 16, 1947

7-4-2-1-1-4 Philip Gray b.

January 9, 1916 m. Esther Nance June 15, 1940

    7-4-2-1-1-4-1 Daniel Philip Gray b. July 16, 1941

    7-4-2-1-1-4-2 Ellen Louise Gray b. February 2, 1943

    7-4-2-1-1-4-3 James Robert Gray b. May 14, 1946

    7-4-2-1-1-4-4 Neda Mae Gray b. August 29, 1951

    7-4-2-1-1-4-5 Julia Nance Gray b. October 2, 1953

7-4-2-1-1-5 Nelda Gray b. October 23, 1919 m. Dr. William Joseph Furey September 4, 1943

    7-4-2-1-1-5-1 Eileen b. June 16, 1944

    7-4-2-1-1-5-2 Madeline b. September 13, 1945

    7-4-2-1-1-5-3 Cecilia b. June 2, 1950

    7-4-2-1-1-5-4 Theresa Lorraine b. April 2, 1959

    7-4-2-1-1-5-5 Megan Loretta Gray b. October 11, 1960

7-4-2-1-1-6 John Clark Gray b. January 11, 1922 m. Ruth Bryan June 29, 1946

    7-4-2-1-1-6-1 Michael Clark Gray b. August 8, 1949

    7-4-2-1-1-6-2 Thomas Critchen Gray b. March 12, 1952

7-4-2-1-1-7 Lois Gray b. December 17, 1924 m. Dr. Raymond Henschen September 4, 1948

    7-4-2-1-1-7-1 Martha Louisa Henschen b. November 14, 1951

    7-4-2-1-1-7-2 Joseph Gray Henschen b. February 24, 1954

7-4-2-1-2 Grace Phillips m. Thomas Sheffield. Children were Neal who became a Catholic Priest, James who died young, and Hilda.

7-4-2-1-3 Harry Phillips m. Eva L. York May 8, 1918 Georgiana, Alabama.
    7-4-2-1-3-1 Malcolm Howard b. March 28, 1920 Millville, Florida. d. October 19, 1992. m. Kathly Antionette McDonald August 27, 1940
        7-4-2-1-3-1-1 Nancy Antionette b. July 20, 1941
        7-4-2-1-3-1-2 Malcolm Howard Jr. b. September 20, 1945
        7-4-2-1-3-1-3 Diane Lee b. June 9, 1959
    7-4-2-1-3-2 Julian Harry Phillips b. March 13, 1922 Millville, Florida m. Ruby C. Kirk October 21, 1941

Resume of Julian H. Philips

Born 13 March 1922 - Millville, Florida
Schooling: Franklin Elementary School/ Thomas Edison Junior High/Charles H. Milby Sr. High (Grad June 1940)

Military: Joined Co. "G", 143rd Infantry, 36th Division - 7 July 1938
36th Division Mobilized - 25 November 1940
Enlisted service 25 November 1940 - 4 November 1942
Graduated O.C. S. Ft. Benning GA. 5 November 1942

Married Ruby C. Kirk - 21 November 1941

Officer Rank: 5 November 1942 2ndLt., Ft. Benning, Ga.
26 February 1944 1st Lt. Southern Italy
10 May 1946, Capt., Anchorage, Alaska
29 August 1951, Major, Sasabo, Japan
21 June 1960, Lt. Col. Coeppengin, Germany

Retired 1 August 1961 - Presidio of San Francisco, Calif. (23 & 1/2 yrs service)

Awards: Combat Infantry bdge
Presidential unit Citation (15 Mar. '45 - 17 Mar. 45)
Silver Star
Bronze Star with two clusters
Purple Heart with Clusters
Division Commendation (San Pietro)
European Theater Ribbon with
    1 bronze Arrowhead (Southrn France)
        7 Bronze Campaign Stars (Battle Campaigns in Italy,

France, and Germany)
Military Schooling:
   Infantry officer Candidate School, Ft. Benning, Ga. 1942   Special Service School, Ft. Monmouth, N.J. 1948
Nov - Dec 1943 - 1944 Platoon Leader Co. G., 143rd. Inf.
March 1944 Executive Officer.
June 1944 Commanding Officer Co. F. , 143rd Inf.
June 1944 - Oct 1944 Special Platoon 1st. Bn., 143rd Inf.

Dec 1944 - 13 Mar 1945 Home for Christmas
13 Mar '45 Commanding Officer Co. A 143rd Inf.

Sports record
Camp Bowie and Camp Blanding 1940- 1942 Excelled in Boxing and on the division Basketball team where he also excelled

1946 - 1948 Fort Richardson, Alaska excelled in Football, Basketball, Baseball, Badminton, and Volleyball taking the Alaskan Championship in each sport.
1948 Excelled in the "Long Branch Sea Howks Football team, Long Branch, N.J.
1948 - 1950 Ft. Jackson, S.C. All Army team two years in Basketball two years 3rd Army team
1949 Outstanding player, Southeastern AAU Tournament Atlantic, Georgia. Football, baseball, volleyball, and badminton and excelled in each.
1950 - 3rd Army sports officer.
1951 - 1953 Japan Tour
BAsketball - Runner up far east championship - Volleyball and Badminton - Far east Championship.
1954 - 1957 Camp Gordon, Georgia - Excelled Badminton
1957 - 1960 European Tour - Officer in Charge of Division Teams of Boxing, Basketball, Football, Volleyball, Squash, Baseball, and Golf. Played and excelled at Squash.

"TINY FINDS A LOADER"

By Julian "Duney" Philips

When I joined Co. G. 143rd infantry in the Spring of 1938, I was 16 years old. I had asked my parents to let me follow my older brother, Malcolm, who had joined Co. G. that March to go to summer camp. Camp Bullis, Texas was there the 36th Division was to hold it's Annual Summer Encampment.

I stood 6'1" and weighed 140 pounds and because of my height I was placed in the 1st platoon where most companies put their tall men. It was commanded by 1st lt. Andrew Y. Austin and was an exceptionally good group of men. One of the men was outstanding in many ways. Cleveland "Tiny" Thompson stood 6" and weighed at least 265 pounds. He was light on his feet - had been a good athlete from San Jacinto High School in Houston where he played football. One outstanding feature of Tiny's was his smile. One very seldom saw him when he wasn't smiling.

Soldiering was new to me but I had accepted it and was determined to do the very best I could.

We had only been at Camp Bullis for two days when Sgt.

Edwin Temple stopped me in the company street and said, "Private Philips the company will go on Guard Duty tomorrow and Co. F. hasn't sent over the Spurs to mount the guard. Would you run over to Co. F. and get them from the supply Sgt.?" Trying to satisfy all the Sgts. plus everyone with one stripe and above, I answered, I answered "Yes Sir" and was off running on one of my first lessons as a soldier.

As I arrived at the C.P. in the Company F. area, I asked to speak to the 1st Sgt. I was ushered inside and there was 1st Sgt. Jack D. Prentice, who spoke as I tried to introduce myself. "Soldier, can I help you?" I answered, "Sgt. Prentice Company G is going on guard duty tomorrow and Sgt. Temple sent me over to get the Spurs to mount the guard." Without a smile the Sgt. answered, "soldier the spurs are kept in the supply tent. Run down to our supply tent and get them from the supply Sgt. He will have you sign for them." I answered, "thank you Sir," and was off running.

As I entered the supply tent I asked to speak to the supply Sgt. A middle aged Sgt. sitting behind a field desk looked up and gruffly said, "I'm the supply Sgt., can I help you? I answered, Sgt., I'm from Co. G. and we go on guard duty to morrow and Sgt. Temple sent me over to get the Spurs to mount the guard." Without blinking the Sgt. said, "Damn it, I should have known someone from Co. G. would be sent over to pick them up. I've just had our artificer take them to Battalion Headquarters supply room so Co. G. would have them in time to mount the guard." He turned and yelled the artificers name, then added, "did you take the Spurs to Battalion Headquarters?" I heard the answer loud and clear. "Yes Sir Sgt." The supply Sgt. turned back to me and said, "the spurs are at Battalion Headquarters; Company supply tent. Soldier run up there and pick them up." I answered, "thank you Sgt." and was off running.

When I got to the Battalion Headquarters supply tent I got the same answer, the Spurs had been sent to the Regimental Headquarters Company supply Sgt. The Sgt. said, "soldier run up there and get the spurs." As I stepped outside, Tiny was just coming out of the Aid-station and when he saw me he asked what I was doing at Battalion. I answered, "Tiny, Sgt. Temple sent me over to Co. F. for the Spurs to mount the guard tomorrow." I told him every place I had been and the answers I had gotten and would up by saying I was on my way to Regimental Headquarters Co. to get the damn Spurs. Tiny put his hand on my shoulder and said, "Duney, hasn't Malcolm told you what to look for here at Camp? There aren't any spurs in this damn division. This is an infantry outfit and that spur crap to mount the guard is as old as the army! They take a young soldier and send him running to get the spurs to mount the guard and everyone gets a big laugh as the kid leaves. Come on back to the company with me and tell Sgt. Temple to go to Hell." As we walked back to the company area, Tiny told me he was allergic to Poison Ivy, so when he arrived in camp each year he found a poison ivy vine to infect himself with. He would then be placed on light duty, no marching and no maneuvers. He would lay up in his tent and swab the infected area with calamine lotion for the next ten to twelve days. As I recall this was also Tiny's way out of our famous twenty five mile marches.

From that day on, Tiny took it upon himself to mother me until I became Army wise enough to take care of myself.

After we were mustered into federal service on 25 November 1940, Tiny and myself were still in the same squad in first platoon and were still as close as ever. My older brother was with us but he was more interested in making the Army a part of his life. He wanted to be the best drill Sgt. in the division.

Company G. 143rd Infantry was rated as one of the best companies in the division and from time to time we would receive an officer just commissioned a Second Lieutenant, or we would receive one transferred from other units. The army was expanding and our older officers who mobilized with us were moving into higher and better jobs.

During the year 1941, Co. G. received two outstanding young officers, Second Lieutenant Henry T. Waskow and Second Lieutenant William G. Buster. Both men fit right in the company training program, getting their platoons ready to live up to the company's past record.

No one knew in the fall of 1941 what to expect from the Japanese and Germans. Then orders came from the War Department that the National Guard Divisions that were on active duty would have their enlistments extended indefinitely. Then we got word over the radio on Sunday December 7, 1941 that the Japanese had attacked Pearl Harbor - the United States was at war. (Congress declared war on both Japan and Germany.) From December 8, 1941 our training took on a different light. Roosevelt had finally gotten what he wanted, the U. S. standing with the Allies to fight the Axis Powers; we were at war.

In 1942 Company G. saw men and officers come and go at an unbelievable rate. The army was expanding, so the men were being pushed up the ladder of rank so the company could meet its quotas to training schools and cadres to form new divisions. Some transferred to the Army Air Corp., some went off to O. C. S. and then there were quotas sent down for officers service schools at Ft. Benning, Georgia. The division had to fill quotas for Ft. Sill, Oklahoma, others went to Ft. Knox for armored school All branches of service had their schools and were looking for young bright Sgts. to pass and move into their branch of service.

When Sgt. M. H. Philips was picked to go to Ft. Benning for Officers Candidate School in early summer of 1942, Capt. Milton H. Steffin, from Huntsville, Texas put me in charge of the 1st platoon. By this time we had moved from Camp _____ Bowie, Texas to Camp Blanding, Fla. and we were all working hard to get ready for the North Carolina maneuvers.

Capt. Steffin and Company G. came through with flying colors, but G. Company wasn't the same. The Company had seen Lt. George La Bounty from Lampasses, Texas transfer to the Army Air Corp. along with S/Sgt. Robert E. Lee of Houston, Texas and Sgt. Ezra Patton of Addicks, Texas. Cadres to form new divisions had seen Corp. Harrold Hooper of Houston, Texas leave with many others who had come in as recruits in 1941. Lt. Waskow and Lt. Buster had received promotions and had moved to other companies in the Regiment.

When the North Carolina maneuvers ended in 1942 I was told to get ready for the train going south to Ft. Benning, Georgia for O.C.S. The school of the 90 day wonders.

When I said my good-byes I was surprised to hear that many of the men wanted to leave too. I had recommended that Sgt. Mitchell Woods of Houston, Texas take the 1st Platoon and capt. Steffin went along with my recommendation. Sgt. Donald Appfell, from Houston, Texas moved in as platoon guide. The day I left Company G. for O.C. S., I left with tears in my eyes. This had become my home and I loved it.

I was into my second week of O.C.S. when I received a letter from Tiny telling me he and Phil Strom had transferred to Cannon Company. Will DuRant of Houston, Texas transferred to Co. F., 142nd Infantry. J.D. Vickers had put in his papers for the Paratroopers while John Lewis was leaving for the 1st Ranger Battalion. My heart was heavy because Capt. Steffin had asked me to try to get back to the division after receiving my commission and I knew with all these men gone Co. G. would never be the same.

The division moved to Camp Edwards, Massachusetts, where they continued to train. Capt. Steffin tested his company against F. Co., commanded by Capt. Carl R. Bayne of Yoakum, Texas. Then it was off to Africa where the training intensified. The men could smell combat and were eager to be tested. Capt. Wiley Stem from Waco, Texas had worked his company night and day going through every phase of training, always trying to get his men psyched up for combat.

The 36th Division wasn't used in the fighting in Sicily, so they kept training, knowing full well it wouldn't be long before they would be tested. That time soon came when the division was loaded on ships for the invasion of Salerno at Paestum, Italy. When the loud speakers on the Navy ships sounded, "Now hear this - now hear this - prepare to debark", Tiny's heart skipped a beat. He had trained six years with the 36th Division for this moment and it suddenly hit him. Here it was 9 September 1943 and before the sun went down that day he might have to kill or be killed. He always boasted that this would give him no problem but it was a problem that every soldier on the line had to face at one time or another.

Tiny's mind was a million miles away as he felt the Navy craft come to a stop on the soft sands in the Bay of Salerno. He soon came back to reality as he heard, "Now hear this - now hear this - start your engines and prepare to debark."

Tiny and his crew had been hearing artillery fire for some time - long before the craft touched the sands, but now he could smell death. It was burned sulphur from shells that had exploded on the beach.

As Tiny maneuvered his vehicle down the ramp, he saw the body of an American lying on the sand. It was Lt. Anthony Haulk from F. Company, 143rd who had been killed as he stepped on the sandy Italian beach earlier that morning. Tiny realized this was the final test for the division after years of training. He also knew Cannon Company was ready.

As Captain Wiley Stem's platoons rolled ashore, there were plenty of missions for them to fire. Regimental headquarters of 143rd Infantry had all types of targets for Cannon Company to fire on; machine gun nests, tanks of the 16th Panzer Division, and just plain defensive fire.

Captain Stem had to be proud of his officers and men. In just six days he had seen elements of the 16th and 26th Panzer, along with the 29th Panzer Grenadier Divisions attack again and again. Each time they had been on target but Cannon Company was able to turn the Germans back.

By the 14th of September 1943, Tiny and the Cannon Company could be called veterans, but their job was a long way from being over. German tanks were still in the area and Cannon Company platoons were scattered. They were trying to cover the area and give support to the troops that were trying to hold the front.

Tiny and his crew were on the way to the Calore River area when they topped the crest of an Italian hill and saw a German Mark IV tank down in the valley below. The tank was hunting targets but had its gun pointed away from them. After a quick discussion the decision was made to knock out the Germans. They knew they must hit the tank before the Germans could turn the turret 180 degrees and get off a round. Tiny's crew fired and he couldn't believe it. When he saw the projectile slam into the Italian soil on the other side of the tank, he knew he had fired long. His eyes had never left the German tank. He saw the long gun swing around the 180 degrees and come to a stop pointing right at him. Then he saw a puff of smoke leave the barrel. At the end of the barrel there was a dot of fire about the size of a pin head. The ball of fire grew to the size of a marble as it came toward the Self Propel. Then it was the size of a golf ball, then a baseball still on target, coming straight toward him. Tiny couldn't move - he stared at the projectile and by now it was the size of a basketball. The fireball was still on course heading straight toward him. Tiny pushed back in the seat to let the ball of fire in the window. He froze as the projectile exploded above and to his right. He felt his life slipping away for he knew the shrapnel would be tearing through his body any second. As the shrapnel whizzed over his head he realized he hadn't been hit. His ears were ringing but he knew he had been lucky this time. He pulled himself out of the driver's seat and stared at the spot where the 50 caliber machine bun had been. When the projectile exploded it knocked the machine gun off as smooth as if it had been done with a cutting torch. As Tiny stood up he could see the turret on the German tank turning as they looked for other targets, thinking they had knocked out the American Self

Propel. Then Tiny thought about his crew. There were no injured or wounded in the body of the Self Propel, so he eased over the rear expecting to see a dead or wounded member of his gun crew lying on the ground. But when he couldn't find a single member of his crew, it dawned on him that he was alone. There wasn't an American in the area, so he ducked down and crawled back over the crest of the hill, out of sight of the German tank.

He took out on foot heading back to the company area to report what had happened to his M-7 and see if he could find his crew. He had covered about 700 yards when he came upon 1st Lieutenant William G. Buster of Dallas, Texas. Lt. Buster was with Company F. and Tiny had known him when he was in G Company in 1941. He asked Tiny what had happened. Tiny went over every detail and as he finished his story, he asked Lt. Buster if he had seen his gun crew. Buster told him he hadn't seen them and asked Tiny to show him the German tank. Tiny said, "You are nuts, that German doesn't miss and I realize now just how lucky I am. I want no more of that tank."

Lieutenant Buster came right back with, "Tiny come on back up the hill with me and show me the German's position. You said there was only one German tank, come on and show me."

Tiny answered, "Hell no, I don't want no more of those Germans and neither do you. He is one hell of a shot." Lt. Buster took Tiny by the shoulders and with his voice nearly pleading he said, "Tiny I want to go up the hill and see the tank and I want you to go with me."

Tiny said, "Lieutenant Buster, you are as crazy as hell and I know I am, but lets go."

As they topped the crest, Tiny pointed to the tank in the valley below and said, "There's the bastard; now are you satisfied?"

The tanks turret was turning in a 360 degree circle hunting a target. The German commander was still sitting half out of the turret looking through his field glasses for anything he could fire on. As Tiny and Lt. Buster lay on the ground watching the tank turret turning round and round, Tiny spoke. "The bastard is still hunting meat; let's get the hell out of here." Lt. Buster didn't move, just lowered his voice as he said, "Tiny let's knock out that German tank."

Tiny couldn't believe what he was hearing and answered, "Are you crazy? I'm not sure our gun will still fire and if it does we need time to get two rounds off before it could turn to fire on us. It's fast plus he's good. Have you ever fired one of these guns?"

The lieutenant just moved to the rear of the Cannon Company vehicle and as he started to pull himself up he said, "Tiny let's see if this gun will fire."

As Tiny pulled himself up on the M-7 he asked again, "Lt. Buster have you ever fired or loaded one of these?"

"Tiny, I have never fired or loaded one of these guns but I know you can knock out the German tank and I will load for you."

Tiny came right back with "Lt. Buster, have you ever loaded one of these before?"

Buster said, "No, Tiny, I have never fired or loaded one of these guns but I have faith in you. I know you can knock out that tank, so let's get started."

Tiny was already checking the piece. He opened the breech and then slammed it shut. "Stay low and out of sight because if the German sees you, he just might do a better job than he did last time." He told the Lieutenant.

He cranked the muzzle down and then back up, then from side to side until he was sure the gun was operational. He turned to Lt. Buster and said, "We will start here."

It wasn't easy trying to show a man the mechanics on inserting one shell then throwing it out to get ready for a second round, knowing a mistake could cost them their lives. Tiny went through the dry run routine time and again, until he was sure Lt. Buster was ready.
He turned to the Lieutenant and said, "You know you are crazy and I'm crazier than you for even trying this. You are as ready as you will ever be, so lets get the show on the road."

Lt. Buster put his hand on Tiny's shoulder and said, "Tiny I know you will knock him out - just have faith."

Tiny said, " Keep low and if I miss the first round, get ready fast. Let's get on with this show."

Tiny adjusted the piece until the cross hairs were centered on the German tank and he was sure that he was right. He didn't fire until he went over his movements, centering those cross hairs time and again. Tiny came to himself as he heard Lt. Buster say. "Tiny, I'm ready."

Tiny looked at the German tank through the sights. The tank commander was still sitting half out of the turret with his back toward them. He was looking away from Tiny's Self Propel in the direction his gun was facing. Tiny checked his sights once again and when he was sure he was on target, he fired.

His eyes never left the projectile as it headed toward the German tank. Lt. Buster was already ejecting the spent round and was inserting a good round into the breech, as he heard Tiny yell, "I hit him! We have knocked him out!"

Lt. Buster stood up in the Self Propel and turned toward the valley as the German tank burst into flames. By now, Tiny and Lt. Buster were jumping for joy with Buster saying, "Tiny, I knew you could do it." Tiny came right back with, "I couldn't have done it without a 'loader' who had faith in me."

As Tiny and Lt. Buster calmed down, Tiny moved to the driver's seat and said, "Well, loader, lets see if this damn thing will start so we can get it back to the rear and have a new 50 caliber machine gun put in place."

Tiny turned the switch, the engine started, and he backed it over the crest of the hill. They had travelled about 400 yards when the lieutenant said, "Drop me off here. Company F is just down the hill and to the right."

They came to a stop and Tiny climbed out of the driver's seat. They faced each other and Buster spoke, "Tiny, you are one hell of a soldier and today your courage proved it. Tiny came right back with, "I couldn't have done it without your faith in me."

Lt. Buster eased out the rear of the vehicle and said, " Tiny, take care of yourself."

By this time, Tiny was back in the driver's seat, had put the M-7 in gear and was off to the company. As Tiny pulled into the Cannon Company area, men came from all directions saying, " Tiny, you are supposed to be dead and this tank destroyed!"

"Yeah, I know, but that damn gun crew didn't even stop to check my pulse to see if I was dead. I didn't even get a scratch. We just need a new machine gun and this M-7 will be as good as new."

From that day, on, Lt. Buster was given the nick-name **"LOADER"**. He accepted the title as it was given with the pride and satisfaction that he and Tiny Thompson had done a job they had trained for.

Lt. William G. Buster was killed on November 16th, 1943 on the forward slopes of Mount Rotondo as the Commanding Officer of Company F, 143rd Infantry. He lies in Section C - Row 13 - Grave #20 in the American Cemetery at Natturno, Italy just a short piece from Anzio. Each time we visit the cemetery we place a red carnation on his grave and I find myself saying, "Thanks, **"LOADER"** for a job well done.

> 7-4-2-1-3-2-1 Julie Ann b.November 27, 1943
> 7-4-2-1-3-2-2 Randy Wayne b. August 15, 1947
>
> 7-4-2-1-3-3 John Norman Phillips b. May 7, 1928 m. Bonnie Joy Link April 1, 1949
>> 7-4-2-1-3-3-1 John Stephen
>> 7-4-2-1-3-3-2 Michael Lee

7-4-2-1-2 Grace b. January 12, 1891 d. August 3, 1955 Houston, Texas

7-4-2-1-3 Harry b. December 12, 1892 died 1977 Houston, Texas

7-4-2-1-4 Ross William b. Feb. 14, 1895 d. April 14, 1965 Panama City, Florida. m. Martha Jane (Mattie) Silcox April 3, 1918 Jacksonville, Florida.

> 7-4-2-1-4-1 Claude b.January 15, 1919
> 7-4-2-1-4-2 Billie Oliver Phillips b. September 14, 1932 Panama City, Florida. m. (1.) Florence Whalen August 24, 1957 Columbus, Ohio
>> 7-4-2-1-4-2-1 Kala Sue b. July 25, 1961 Columbus, Ohio m. Matthew Martin July 10, 1982
>>> 7-4-2-1-4-2-1-1 Meghan Martin b. September 22, 1987
>>> 7-4-2-1-4-2-1-2 Matthew Martin Jr. b. July 7, 1990
>
> When Florence died October 24, 1972, Billie remarried to Helen Annabel Grover.

7-4-2-1-4-2 David Allen b. January 24, 1983 Columbus, Ohio

7-4-2-1-5 John Garrett b. January 31, 1897 d. December 9, 1962 Panama City, Florida Choctawhatche Bay, Florida. m. Gussie _____
    7-4-2-1-5-1 Russell Phillips
    7-4-2-1-5-2 Elizabeth Phillips
7-4-2-1-6 James Albert b. February 3, 1903 Millville (Panama City) Florida. d. August 9, 1962 Panama City, Florida. When James, a schoolboy, was about fifteen years old, he had a bad tooth pulled, and they could not stop the bleeding. He bled to death.
7-4-2-2 Shelton b. February 18, 1864 m. Ida Helvenston on March 14, 1889.

    S. Philips, Supt.
  Bronson Fla. 4 - 29-1890

Dear Albert;
    Some time since received quite a long and interesting letter from you. I regret very much not having answered it before this but my time has been very closely occupied since the reception... I had to make a trip to Ocala, to attend the State Teachers Association and after my return I had to keep going to and fro a distance of 6 miles to superintend the improving of...

I moved as soon thereafter as things were made habitable. We are now domiciled in our new home. I have a boy with me and we are at work from early morn to late eve. I have changed quite materially the appearance of things now in a little over two weeks. In two or three years I hope to have a nice place - and one too of some revenue to me. I have over 50 orange trees over half of which are bearing trees. I shall get this year only enough to eat and give away -- I may get one thousand and probably less. I want ten thousand next year. I have not paid for my place yet, 80 acres and a house to live in with 80 or 90 different trees for $800 and five years in which to pay for it. I can save some out of my salary and then the trees will help next year. The cold coming so late this spring killed all the young growth that would have put out the bloom and beside the bloom that had put out on them was very considerable all in Fla ruined. The most disastrous freeze in 20 years or more. I am glad you have a good situation and a fair salary now. You are getting as much as I. You all must come down and see me

now since I have a shanty of my own. I want Mother to come and stay with me, --live with us. Write to me often. I shall do better from now on. Give my love to all. Albert, I want your photo;--I have none. Have one taken for me. All send love.
I am your loving Brother. (Shelton)

Bronson Fla. May 12, 1898

Dear Mother:
I have neglected you too long already, and I see there is no such thing as finding time for my family correspondence so I write you now, by stopping all else to do so. I am secretary of so many associations that my time for several weeks has been almost altogether occupied. I have sent you my last work in the way of getting up our State Teachers Association Constitution and By-laws. We have been busy going of late to see the soldiers pass by. The ... Plant System 7 is carrying the troops and some material. Some days 25 trains will pass enroute to Tampa. I have seen soldiers, coal, horses, cannon, ambulances, etc. until I would begin the movement of 50 thousand men and as a large part of them will be on the Plant Line, I guess we shall see all the war outfit pretty soon. We see several negro companies: they ought to all be made to go and to go right to the front. Tampa is only four hours run from Williston. We do not feel at all uneasy for we do not fear an invasion of our territory. I do not put much dependence in the Cubans either. These who work in our cigar factories look treacherous. Our proximity to the seat of war does not offer to us any better facilities for hearing news.

Many a fine fellow whom we see pass to the seat of war reminds us that the hot scorching sun, together with disease close his chances of ever seeing home again. It is sad to think of such, but such is war. Perhaps God is in this war. I believe Providence directs the general results of crises and hence I believe He will rid the Island of Cuba of those miserable Spaniards. Iva and the babies are well. Our four children are healthy and bright. Ruth is the pet of the family. Mother Mc will be to see us tomorrow. All send love. I'll write soon.
Lovingly, Shelton

Letter addressed to Mrs. Julia A. Philips
Gloversville, N.Y.

The father and grandfather of Shelton Philips were Methodist ministers and both were teachers of prominence; the latter established a female seminary near Talladega, and his son was president of the District High School established in 1875 at Mariana, Florida by the Methodist District Conference.

Shelton attended this high school for four years afterward pursuing his studies at the Chipola Academy at Greenwood, Florida and the Abbeville (Alabama) High School from which he graduated in 1882. He chose teaching as his life work, true to his ancestors and taught for two years in the institution from which he graduated. In 1884, he returned to and after teaching one year in Jackson County, joined the force of Levy County. Three years later he was elected to the office of county superintendent, and the success and popularity is attested by the fact that he has been continuously retained in that responsible position to the present time.

Although only 24 years old when first elected he began at once to work with and influence the teachers of the county. Realizing the great necessity for good teaching and professional work Supt. Philips after overcoming all opposition on part of school board employed Prof. J.M. Guilliams (his first work of the kind in the state) to conduce one month's normal school at Bronson and secured the attendance of teachers by using a resolution to the effect that those who attended would be given preference in the appointment of teachers.

As was to be expected, some few who would not attend put this resolution of school board to test by refusing to be lowered in rank or salary and in this they had the backing of their communities. So hotly were the cases fought that the good offices of State Superintendent Russell were invoked by the dissatisfied teachers. To have yielded would have been to lose all power of position. No compromise would be accepted and ever after when there was a call for an institute teachers who were not privileged came.

Early in his administration the matter of grading the schools was undertaken. Levy County was among the first in the state to adopt rules regulations and courses of study.

The task of systematizing the work was vigorously prosecuted from the first and within three years it could have been truthfully said that the schools of Levy County, both town and country, white and colored were graded.

Supt Philips has been a strong advocate of local and county institutes, and has been prominent in the councils of teachers at such gatherings. He has the unbounded confidence of his teachers who respect and love him for his loyalty and fellow-feeling. His people regard him as a man of sterling worth and fine executive ability. It has been said that in fourteen years he has never failed in a single instance to effect a compromise between contending parties on any school question.

When chairman of the executive committee of the state association last year his business ability was manifested by his securing... the special rate of one and one half cents per mile to the Ocala meeting. This had been persistently refused for several years preceding. He was largely the means of securing the same rates again this year...

Newspaper Clipping(undated) From the Ocala Star
Shelton Philips was born in Livingstone, Ala February 1864. His father was a Methodist minister of the Alabama conference and for many years served as presiding elder. The Rev. Elisha Philips was a man of rare and striking ability. He was also noted for his erudition and qualities as a teacher, he having founded district high schools in different portions of the country, including that of Mariana in 1875.

Reuben Philips, the Grandfather too was a teacher and preacher of exceptional qualities and started the first female seminary in Alabama. This man was known for his uncompromising speech against evil and wrongdoers... Reuben Philips was a remarkable man and one of the best organizers he had ever known. It so happens that the proclivities for educational work found in the subject of this sketch come to him thru a long line of ministers and teachers, and it is no wonder that when Shelton Philips was elected to office of county Superintendent of Schools, he applied himself to the work of organizing the schools of that county upon a basis that his made him and his remarkable words...

Superintendent Philips has placed the schools of Levy County upon an enduring basis...

Shelton Philips
(Journal of American Vocational Association, February 1938, T. H. Quigley)
December 16 (1937) at his home in the village of Williston, Levy County, Florida, where he had lived for half a century, in the seventy third year of his age there passed to the great beyond my friend Shelton Philips, formerly State Director of Vocational Education in Florida.

As an early progressive superintendent of schools and State Rural School Supervisor Mr Philips was known and loved in almost every schoolhouse in Florida. He served many terms in the legislature, working always for better schools, especially civic and political adding interesting variety to a busy and useful life.

Mr. Philips, I often thought, had the ability, had he wished to use it, to attain to and creditably acquit himself in almost any situation in life. But despite travels far and wide and the beckoning of fame and fortune, he cared not to remain long away from his beloved family circle, home and friends in the back-woods of Levy County. And his younger associates and circle and in the hospitality of that home would be the last to question that wisdom of his choice.

His friendships were lifelong. In youth he enlisted under the banner of W.N. Sheats, father of the public school system in Florida. A generation later Mr. Philips sat in a hotel room in Jacksonville holding Doctor Sheats hand as that old warrior of education breathed his last.

Mr. Philips was one of the most gracious gentlemen I have ever known. A man of few books, he knew and lived those to a degree that seems to be disappearing with Mr. Philips generation. Whatever he learned — and he learned rapidly, especially people — soon became much knowledge. This with his quick logic that could penetrate to the meat of the matter, his instant command of drawing-room or Florida Cracker English,, his histrionic ability, especially as a mimic, the flash of his gentle humor and his disarming smile, make him one of those rare people who teach effectively by precept. As long as I live I shall catch myself re-thinking and re-saying with him the ready analyses of men and events by which he would arrive at his rules of behavior or evolve them into his common sense philosophy. Younger associates of such men as Mr. Philips owe to them unconscious debts that seem to be repaid only by the sincere tribute of unconscious imitation.

7-4-2-2-1 Albert Roux b. June 20, 1890 d. July 28, 1925 (Automobile Accident)

7-4-2-2-2 Russell b. Feb. 11, 1892 m. Myrtle Grainger

Newspaper Clipping: Russell Philips:

Funeral Services for Russell Philips 68 of McIntosh who died August 16 in Rome Italy have been set for tuesday afternoon at 3:30 in the McIntosh Methodist Church, of which the deceased was a member and lay leader. Mr. Philips and his wife Myrtle Grainger Philips were on a European Tour when he was stricken and died of a stroke in a Rome hotel room.

A native of Williston, he was the son of the late Shelton and Ida Helveston Philips. He was educated in Williston schools and began his almost half century of service with the Seabord Airline Railroad in January 1911. At the time of his death, Mr. Philips was engineer on the Silver

Meteor.

He is survived by his widow, Myrtle G. Philips, McIntosh; one son Russell Jr., Jacksonville; and two sisters Mrs. W.H. Morton and Mrs H.A. Peacock, Gainesville.

Mr. Philips was a devoted church worker and a man who loved people. He was a member of McIntosh Lions Club, and a master Mason of Waldo Lodge No.10. He belonged to Morocco Temple, Pilgrim Comandry No. 7, Knights Templar, Gainesville; Grand Chapter of the Royal Arch Masons, Gainesville; and Wildwood Division 836, Brotherhood of Locomotive Engineers.

He would have retired as Seaboard Engineer in February, 1962.

   7-4-2-2-3 Mildred b. Feb. 7, 1894
   7-4-2-2-4 Ruth b. Dec. 1, 1896
7-4-2-3 Julian b. March 29, 1866 d. Sept. 26, 1925 at 6:00 A.M.
7-4-2-4 Charles Albert Reuben b. April 6, 1873. Newspaper Clipping (undated) Albert C. Philips Funeral services for Albert C. Philips were held at 3:30 this afternoon at the family home at 77 First Avenue. Rev. George H. Phelps of the First Presbyterian Church officiated. The Board of Directors of the Gloversville Savings and Loan Association attended the funeral in a body. Burial was made in Prospect Hill cemetery.
7-4-3 Ewell Petty b. 3 Jan. 1825
7-4-4 Juliann b. 22 July 1827 m. Robert Hendricks

On July 22, 1827 Juliann E. Philips was born to Reuben and Elizabeth Philips.

I commenced school in the Presbyterian Church near the public square on the 28th day of March 1842 with 48 scholars. I had to have my son Ewell and daughter Julian to assist me. [by] the ...second month we had 68 in school and all did well.

In 1861 Reuben visited his daughter Julian in Louisiana.

July 6, 1882 (from Reverend Reuben) Julian E. Hendricks is now on a visit to her daughter in Kansas. Her oldest son Zack is dead and left a wife and two children. Allie the youngest is married to a man of property living at Elms Point in Illinois. Mary the oldest is there also. She has taught school four years in the same place and is one of the best christians of her sex.

[letter to Rubin Philips]
Park [Ill]

Elms

Sept 1883

Dear Father

Your Postal Recd. Was more than glad to hear from you once more. God grant you may live to write many more. This leaves us all moderately well. Alice has another daughter 6 weeks old. looks like Grand Pa Philips. I want it named Rubie for you. The hair is black and thick as a child 5 years of age. They have not decided just what to call it. Fannie & Vance are back from Kansas living in Greenville. He works in his fathers machine shop. Fannie will teach music. She has three children.

Mary teaches in the graded schools of Greenville. Stands high as a teacher. Has a permanent position if her health doesn't fail. She is very delicate. Mr Pauley thinks some of going west or rather Northwest to Nebraska. Thinks Alice would have better health. No wheat grown this year here. But fine corn. It is so dry now that stock can scarcely get water. Apples & Honey in abundance. Mr. Pauley has a cousin living near here that has raised 3000 Lbs of honey for sale this season from 40 stands. There is but little doing in the churches. Although we have a most excellent Minister. Br Gibson from Kentucky.

The Holiness Brethern seem more alive than any of the other sects. There are some real good people who belong to them but most of their membership are made up of low illiterate people and they all preach and say such foolish things it injures the cause with the better class - consequently they are ridiculed. There are a good many of them in this county. I took my letter from Greenville and put it in the Cumberland Church with Alice - so I attend that church with them and really I like them very much. If there had been a Methodist Church near I guess I would have put my letter in it. Will never feel altogether at home in any other church.

Is Br Elisha still in Florida? and do you know anything of Br Ewell or Virgil?

I do not know Mollies address. I have neglected to write to anyone for a long time. I know it is wrong to do so - but have gotten out of the way of writing but <u>I do love</u> to get letters. I sometimes think I will forget how to write. I dont do better. I hope you can read this & excuse.

My Grandchildren keep me busy have eight of them.

Write often and receive all our

united love.   Your Daughter   Julia

March 10, 1885 from Rev. Reuben. My youngest daughter Julian E. Hendrix was sent with her family by my son Ewell P. Philips from Memphis in the time of the great epidemic to the Mississippi River to save life. They went up to St. Louis and then to Elms Point in Illinois and engaged in school. She is yet a widow. Her oldest son died not long since leaving a wife and two children. Her daughters are now in a high school in the capital of the State of Illinois. They are fine scholars. The eldest now taught five years in a high school and is in fine standing. You will find the youngest married and settled at Elms Point doing very well.

      7-4-5 Lafayette b. 1 Jan. 1831 d. 27 Feb. 1841
      7-4-6 Virgil b. 4 April 1834

On April 4, 1834 Virgil Philips was born to Reuben and Elizabeth Philips.

Reverend Reuben: My wife, Virgil, and myself started to Elisha Kings in Coosa County and I preached at Ruth King's funeral on the ninth of November and returned home and moved to Blountsville and opened school on the 29th of December 1845 in an old log house.

On May 14, 1861 Virgil Philips enrolled at Randolph Tennessee and was placed in George Mellersh's company (later Company E.). He was wounded at Murphreesboro on December 31, 1862. On January 4, 1864 he was elected and promoted to second lieutenant Company H. 28th regiment Alabama. From September 13, 1864 he was in Ocmulgee Hospital, Macon, Georgia.

August 30, 1875 - Virgil is now temporarily at Chattanooga; Ewell at Memphis, Julian at Greenville, Illinois and her family. Virgil left her some week ago, called on us to see us once more before we die.

Virgil Philips had served gallantly in the War of the Rebellion, but now, like many Vietnam veterans, he could no longer function well in society. At the time this condition was not known as an illness, and caused his father Reuben considerable grief.

Letter   Chattanooga Tenn
                                                       Feb. 27, 1880

Rev. Ruben Phillips
    Dear Brother
        I am pastor of the Whiteside St. Church

Chattanooga and my pastoral charge includes the Vulcan Iron Works, and Bro. Boys sent me your letter and requested me to answer it.

I have taken some pains to learn some of the history and character of Virgil Philips, and will give you a true statement of the case as I learn it from reliable persons. I have only been here since the first of November, and I do not know him personaly. But I learn he has been here about four years, he came here with a lady whom he said was his wife and she said he was her husband. The lady was said to be very much his senior in age. He explained his marriage to friends in this way; Said he was employed by a man of some wealth to keep grocery somewhere on the Mississippi river, and finely the gentleman died, and his business was in Virgil's hands, and he had requested him to take care of his widow and he married her. They soon spent the money and they were in great poverty when here and his wife did much work such as sewing and washing; he occasionally worked in the rolling mill. His wife died last october aged perhaps 74 years. Since her death he has not been keeping house. He has never been hurt seriously any way and is a stout hearty man. If he has any business I cannot find out what it is; He is boarding I believe with the man to whom he sent his furniture after the death of his wife. He spends his time I believe in town and it is said he indulges freely in dissipation. As I have not met him I am dependent entirely on the testimony of others. He is said to be a man of fine address and splendid mind and shows good cultivation and especially great familiarity with the scriptures. He told his friends his father and brother were ministers and that he had been a christian. He makes no predilections to be a christian now. He could not be an object of charity in his condition of health. It is painful for me to write such words to you concerning your son, but I have endeavored to give you a true statement as I have learned it from reliable persons. I intend to seek an interview with him and will do all I can to induce him to reform. I think it can hardly be that the continuous prayers of a father for his prodigal boy can go unanswered. Let us hope in Gods grace and trust he will help.
unsigned

This Vietnam syndrome is treatable today, but it must have been much worse after such a terrible war as this had been, especially so since it was not known to be a psychological condition. We do not know the end of this story, nor what happened eventually to Virgil.

7-4-7 Mary Ann Elizabeth (Mollie) (Eliza) b.

ca. 1849 m. Capt. William J. Cannon

7-5 Mary Ann Philips b. April 21, 1798 d. after 1860 m. Joseph Wilson Pharr 16 Nov. 1818

The Reverend Joseph Wilson Pharr died November 16, 1858 in Cherokee County, Georgia. He was born September 14th 1796 in Lincoln County, North Carolina where his parents Samuel and Elizabeth(Bailey) Pharr were living at the time. They moved to Abbeville District South Carolina where he was raised. In 1818, he went to Buncombe County North Carolina where he met and married Mary Ann (Allie) Philips daughter of Adam and Hannah (Bailey) Philips on November 16, 1818 They settled in Haywood County North Carolina where he joined the Methodist Church and became a preacher. He moved first to Habersham County, Georgia and later to Cherokee County.

7-5-1 Juliette Pharr b. 5 Sept 1819
7-5-2 Elizabeth Pharr b. 27 Dec. 1821 m. William Samuel Brown. m. 1845 Cherokee Co. GA.

7-5-2-1 Alexander Melvin Brown b. 22 April 1846 Cherokee Co. GA. m. Susannah Armilda Ervin Nov. 25, 1866. Entered the Confederate Service in October 1863 at age 17 Company C Cavalry - Phillips Legion. Which was organized in Cherokee County Georgia June 1, 1861. This Legion joined Young's Brigade and was engaged in the battle of the Wilderness and also at the Spotsylvania Battle. Dr. Brown surrendered at Appomattox. M.D. Georgia Eclectic College Atlanta 1878. He practiced medicine in Pickens County Georgia until 1887 when he moved to Alabama where he was licensed to practice in 1888. He practiced at Round Mountain. Died in 1919. Susannah died in 1902 and he remarried to Lilla Jane Jennings in 1903.

7-5-2-1-1 Jacob Wiley Majaland (Jendy) Brown 1867. Graduataed fraom the Georgia Eclectic College of Physicians and Surgeons 1891 with a Doctor of Medicine Degree.
7-5-2-1-2 James W. L. Brown 1869
7-5-2-1-3 Rosalie Brown b. 1874
7-5-2-1-4 Alexander Melvin (Pete) Brown 1878.

7-5-2-2 Louisa
7-5-2-3 Mary Josephine
7-5-2-4 Roxannah
7-5-2-5 Armanillia

7-5-2-6 Samantha
7-2-5-7 Irene
7-2-5-8 William Olen
7-2-5-9 Samuel Jefferson Brown
7-2-5-10 Ira Lewis Brown
7-2-5-11 Goldie Jennings Brown
7-2-5-12 Irley (died age 3)

7-5-3 Adam Dowling Pharr b. 22 Dec. 1823
7-5-4 unnamed daughter b. 18 Jan. 1826 d. inf.
7-5-5 Martha Pharr b. 10 Feb. 1827
7-5-6 Moses Summerfield Pharr b. 29 Mar 1829 m. Elvira _____ in 1850. Died November 8, 1896

7-5-6-1 Joseph Turner Pharr b. July 25, 1853 m. Lincey Collins d. December 11, 1905

7-5-6-1-1 Nancy Elvira Pharr b. January 3, 1875 m. William Fowler Burgess. d. Oct. 25, 1938

7-5-6-1-2 Eric Dotson Pharr b. August 25, 1876 m. Laura Mae Fowler d. May 26, 1942

7-5-6-1-2-1 Mattie Florence Pharr b. 1898

7-5-6-1-2-2 Jasper Turner Pharr b. 1899

7-5-6-1-2-3 Early Earnest Pharr b. 1903

7-5-6-1-2-4 James Arthur Pharr b. April 26, 1905 m. Ruby May Wiley

2-4-1 Donald Eugene 1932
2-4-2 Franklin D 1934
2-4-3 James Harold 1936
2-4-4 John Paul 1938
2-4-5 Jack Reuben 1941
2-4-6 Betty Jane 1946
2-4-7 Mary Elizabeth 1949

7-5-6-1-2-5 Clara Pharr b. 1907

7-5-6-1-2-6 William Pharr b. 1909

7-5-6-1-2-7 Lucy Elizaabeth Pharr b. 1915

7-5-6-1-3 James Arthur Pharr b. August 20, 1879 d. November 20, 1894

7-5-6-1-4 William Thomas Allen Pharr b. April 6, 1883

7-5-6-1-5 Chester Lee Pharr b. July 30, 1885 m. Alma _____

7-5-6-1-6 James Oscar Pharr b. November 12, 1887 m. Ann _____

7-5-6-1-7 Annie Jane Pharr b.

September 2, 1889 d. January 31, 1948

7-5-6-1-8 Lewis Sylvester Pharr b. December 12, 1891

7-5-6-1-9 Carter Lester Pharr b. December 18, 1893 m. Bonny Mullins

7-5-6-1-10 Fannie Elizaabeth Pharr b. September 11, 1896 m. Clifford Moore

7-5-6-1-11 b. June 9, 1899 m. Martha Lucinda _____ d. June 5, 1961

7-5-6-2 Adolphus Pharr b. January 30, 1855

7-5-6-3 Richard Wesley Pharr b. Februaray 9, 1857 d. May 9, 1922

7-5-6-4 Marshall T. Pharr b. July 27, 1860

7-5-6-5 George E. Pharr b. Oct. 19, 1862 d. Mar. 28, 1940

7-5-6-6 Walter Thomas Pharr b. Feb. 14, 1865 m. Amanda _____

7-5-6-7 Mary Jane Pharr b. July 16, 1867 d. January 11, 1944

7-5-6-8 John Grover Pharr b. April 4, 1872 d. January 13, 1922

7-5-6-9 Julie Pharr b. October 12, 1875 m. John D. Reynolds d. March 19, 1947

7-5-7 Theodore Atkin Pharr b. 22 Sept 1831

7-5-8 Mary Pharr b. 26 Dec. 1833

7-5-9 Arminus Emory Pharr b. 23 Feb. 1836

7-5-10 Julia Pharr b. 23 November 1838

7-5-11 Antonie Olin Pharr b. 26 Feb. 1841

7-5-12 dau b. 27 Jan 1845 d. inf.

7-6 Catherine b. ca. November 15, 1800 d. March 24, 1892 m. 1. _____ Parks 2. James F. Bell

7-6-1 George Hamilton Bell b. 21 August 1845 d. 24 Jan 1923 m. 1) Martha Gregg 1 Mar 1865 2) Helen Ozane 3) Penelope Neill White

George Hamilton Bell died January 24th 1923 and is buried at Haw Creek Cemetery, Bethel Methodist Church in Asheville North Carolina. He was the only son of James and Catherine (Philips) Bell and was born August 21, 1845 near Haw Creek in Buncombe County, North Carolina. His mother was a well known teacher in and around Asheville. George also became a teacher in the local schools, but as so many of his relatives had done, he eventually became a minister. He was ordained deacon in the Episcopal Church in 1873, and in 1883 he became a priest. He was married three times; first to Martha Gregg March 1, 1865, second to Helen Ozane, and third to Mrs. Penelope White Neill widow of G. Robert Neill. His children, all by his first wife, included May who married Robert Carter,

Minnie born September 6, 1870 and died 1949 who married William Henry Clark; Lawrence M. who married Mattie Roberts, Ida Bell born 1869 who married W.F. Lindsey December 27, 1893, Alma Leona born March 22, 1876 who married George Marion Pressley, and James Edward born April 21, 1878 who married Kelly M. Capps.

GEORGE HAMILTON BELL

George Hamilton Bell, the son of James and Catherine Bell was born in Buncombe County where he spent most of his life. He received his education in the Asheville Public Schools, becoming known for his very remarkable memory, as well as his insatiable love for books. He became an instructor in the schools. However, his really deep desire for his lifetime was to become a minister. His belief was that all men are equally entitled to a full and free exercise of religion.

The beginnings of the church at Haw Creek are closely associated with Rev. George H. Bell and his family. Mr. Bell was evidently preparing for the ministry when he and others decided to build a chapel on the Bell estate. This consisted of fifty acres, and his mother as I am told gave a piece of land for a Chapel, which was built in 1870 as far as I can learn. It was a small Chapel, which was appointed for the Church's worship. There were some eleven communicants at the time. The Bishop, Bishop Atkinson, visited the Chapel in July 1871, confirming three additional ones. It was of a Sunday afternoon after the bishop's visit to Trinity Church, Asheville in the morning whose rector, Dr. Buxton was in charge of the Chapel, hence its name, Trinity. This is the earliest record of a Church at Haw Creek in the Diocesan Journals. The place was called Bell in those days, and lies in the Swannanoa Valley, some five miles from Asheville. Mr. George Bell was ordained a deacon in 1873, continuing as such for ten years, when he became a priest. He was thrice married, and I have visited his son, George, who and his wife lived in Biltmore. He has recently died. George was retired after long years of service on the Biltmore estate, the last thirty five years of which were spent as Gatekeeper to the Estate. There were daughters of Mr. Bell's last wife, before their marriage, she being a widow, one of whom married J. Bergin Reese. Mr. Reese's family were early members of Trinity Chapel. Also of early members were the families of Langmoid, Coxe, Lane, and Rabb. Mr. Bell, the first priest, taught school, both of public and private nature. After there was need for a larger building for the congregation, the present structure which had been built for the Methodists was bought from them. The old Chapel was used by Mr. Bell for school, day-school, purposes. There was a Sunday School conducted from the beginning of the Mission, and Dr. Buxton visited for services twice a month, soon once a month, Mr. Bell assisting in the work. Also I read that Mr. William Rice was Superintendent of the Sunday School, who later was to enter the ministry.

Dr. Buxton reports baptisms for 1876, and for several years after. From reports of the other mission churches in the Asheville area we know how Mr. Bell and Mr. Rice, the latter after ordination, as belonging to the Ravenscroft Associate Mission of Asheville, were continually ministering at them. From 1877 and for several years, however, Mr. Bell was appointed in charge of Missions in Watauga County.

Bishop Atkinson's visit 1877:
(July 14, 1877) at Ore Knob in Ashe County, and on the 15th at Jefferson in the same county, Rev. R.W. Barber read prayers and I preached. July 17th at Doffin Station in Watauga County, Rev. Mr. Bell said morning prayers, and I preached and confirmed one person. July 19th at Boone, I preached and administered the Lord's Supper assisted by the Rev. Mr. Bell.

"Chunn's Cove lies beyond the mountain east of Asheville thru which the Beaucatcher tunnel now takes the traffic in and out of Asheville. Fifty years ago, the days of which we are writing, one needed to go over the mountain, as Doctor Buxton needed to do by horseback; and Mr. Rice coming from the east to the cove, came by horseback as also by buggy. He came from a settlement named for his family, Riceville. Rev. George H. Bell also ministered at St. Lukes, and was from a native family, the settlement of Haw Creek having been previously named Bell. Both Mr. Rice and Mr Bell received their preparation for the ministry under Dr. Buell and Mr. Stubbs."

During the summer of 1885, Rev. Geo. H. Bell began to officiate at Hot Springs, having been transferred by the Bishop from the Ashe and Watauga county field... He was ordained to the priest hood at Trinity Church, Asheville, July 1883.

Dr. Buxton was visiting Trinity Chapel Mission once a month, reporting in 1885 that the Sunday School was "flourishing." Mr. Rice continued regularly to come for services, and by 1890 Mr. Bell began again to have charge.

Asheville, N. C. November 3, 1897

To the Right Rev. Joseph B. Cheshire,
    bishop in charge of the Missionary Jurisdiction of Asheville.

As provided by Chapter IV, Cannon 1, Section 1, of the Constitution and Cannons of the Protestant Episcopal Church of the Diocese of North Carolina, which are also in force in this Jurisdiction, The undersigned, male communicants, of full age, residents of said jurisdiction, do make the following Presentment, to-wit;

First;
That one George H. Bell, a Priest of said Church within said Jurisdiction, has been guilty of disorderly conduct.

Specification;
In this that during the past two years he has utterly neglected all religious duty, and has so acted as to injure his own reputation as a gentleman and a clergyman, and to bring disgrace upon his Church.

Second;
That George H. Bell, a Priest of said Church, within said Missionary Jurisdiction, has been, to-wit, on or about the 15 day of June 1897 and subsequent to that date, guilty of conduct unbecoming a Clergyman, and a gentleman,

Specification;
is this that on or about the said 15 day of June 1897, he, the said George H. Bell, in company with a woman, whose name is known to your presentors, did drink liquor, and did become drunk, and with said woman sat in a scandalous and disgraceful manner, in a public place, and to such an extent that the said woman, being a member of the Methodist Episcopal Church, was brought to trial by the duly constituted authorities of said Church and expelled therefrom.

Specification;
Is this that said George H. Bell has subsequently to said 15 day of June 1897, with said woman acted in such manner as to give rise throughout the community to serious charges of immorality between them.

Your Presentors farther state that they do not make these presentments on account of any ill will or malice towards the said George H. Bell, nor upon mere rumor, but that upon hearing such rumor, and knowing it to be current in the community, they have investigated the same as fully as time and opportunity did permit, and have statements from parties whom they believe to be honorable and reliable, which fully sustain said presentments and specifications.

T. W. Patton
Haywood Parker
Henry Redwood

April 14, 1898 in Trinity Church, Asheville, in the presence of the Rev. Alfred H. Stubbs and the Rev. McNeely Dubose, Presbyters, I deposed from the ministry George Hamilton Bell, some time Priest of this Jurisdiction, in accordance with the findings and sentence of the court ecclesiastical by which he had been tried.

Thirty six communicants were reported for Trinity Chapel in 1903. In 1908, there were 87 reported in the Sunday School, and 86 in the Mission School. A priest came from Asheville only once a month. Mr Bell again assuming charge, continuing until he retired in 1918 from his active ministry, services were held more frequently, twenty seven communicants were reported in 1912, and continued about the same number during Mr. Bell's Time.

Reverend Bell spent his last days in leisure, enjoying his beloved collection of fine books as well as his children and grandchildren. He died where his family had lived for three generations.

The Reverend George Hamilton Bell died January 24, 1923 in Asheville, North Carolina and is buried at Haw Creek Cemetery, Bethesda Methodist Church.

    7-6-1-1 May Etaline Bell b. Dec. 9, 1868.
    7-6-1-2 Minnie Agnes Bell b. Sept. 6, 1870
    7-6-1-3 Lawrence Murdock Bell b. Oct. 16, 1872
    d. March 10, 1906
    7-6-1-4 Ida Evangeline Bell b. June 9, 1874
    d. Jan 16, 1904
    7-6-1-5 Alma Leona Bell b. March 22, 1876
    7-6-1-6 James Edward Bell b. April 21, 1878
    7-6-1-7 George Folk Bell b. Oct. 25, 1880
    7-6-1-8 Herbert Atkinson M. Bell b. Sept 16, 1882
    d. Aug 18, 1883
    7-6-1-9 Lillias Gertrude Bell b. March 6, 1886

7-7 Hiram b. May 7, 1803 m. 1833 Nancy Vaughn
On April 9, 1832 Hiram B. Philips received permission from the county court in Haywood County N.C. to open a store and to sell "ardent spirits". He was evidently renewing a previous license, since he is shown on another list as being a store owner in 1831. On July 12th Hiram B. Philips was appointed patroller in Haywood County.

Cherokee County Georgia Land Records has the following record: Book A Page 470 - Deed dated Habersham County 25 Oct 1833, Recorded 07 June 1834 from Charles J. Thompson of Habersham County and Benjamin Vaughn of Habersham County to Hiram B. Philips. In consideration of the sum of $20 conveys all that tract of land known as Land Lot 109 3rd District, 2nd Section. Signed Charles J. Thompson and B. Vaughn. Witness: Joseph Hughes and Isaac Black J.P.

Reverend Reuben Philips writes: My Brother <u>Hiram B. Philips</u> visited me from North Carolina and persuaded me to unite with him in purchasing a store three miles below that had been carried on for some two years by Richard L. Powell, and Powell kept spirits to sell and did our community much evil. My brother expressed great desire to live near me and ... pledged himself to be a temperate man. I refused time after time, not wishing to engage in any speculation that would involve me with the world. He then commenced with my wife and so impressed her mind with the prosperity of my joining him and we could put down a grocery and do well. He was to manage the whole concern and not trouble me with it. I at length consented (a fatal day and deed for me). Soon my brother proved treacherous, involving me greatly in debt and I was soon broken up and my religious enjoyments ruined. He became my enemy and continued to dissipate. At length [he] married a Miss Nancy Vaughn of Clarksville; threw the whole concern on my hands with heavy debts hanging over it and moved to Clarksville and commenced the practice of medicine.

Know all men by these presents that I Reuben Philips of the County of Habersham and State of Georgia for and in consideration of the sum of one hundred dollars to me in hand paid by Hiram B. Philips of the same county and state for one undivided third of lot no. Eighteen in the eleventh district of the above named county & state including minerals as far as the above named one third may claim in undivided state I the sd Reuben Philips for myself my heirs my administraters and assigns hereby warrant & forever defend the described interest (one third) with all its ways woods waters and minerals & lawful appurtanances in fee simple from the lawful claim of any person or persons whatsoever unto him the sd Hiram B. Philips his heirs executors and assigns.

In witness I hereunto set my hand and seal this 31 day of January (1834) one thousand eight hundred and thirty four
Signed Sealed and delivered in the presence of
NR Bradshaw   Reuben Philips (seal)
S.A. Wales Not. Pub.
                        Recorded 29th October 1834
                                J. T. Carter clk.

The earliest record of the Philips family in Cherokee County Georgia is associated with Hiram.

Cherokee County Records Book A P. 470. Deed dated Habersham Co. 25 Oct, 1833 recorded June 7, 1834 from Charles J. Thompson and Benjamin Vaughn to Hiram B. Philips for $20 lot 109 3rd District, 2nd section.

   Hiram Philips found Reuben a teaching position in Jefferson County, Alabama in Jones Valley in 1844.

8. ?Catherine Phillips b.? Fredrick Co. MD married Joseph Long   Rowan Co. NC 13 June 1793.
9. Elizabeth Phillips b. 4 July 1768 Fredrick Co. MD. m. ?William Hughey 3 July 1791 Rowan Co. NC
10? John Phillips (No data)

Phillips Family Bibliography

Brawley, James S. _Rowan County ... a Brief History_ N.C. Dept. of Cultural Resources 1977.

Brewer, George E. _History of Coosa County, Alabama_, Alabama Historical Quarterly Vol. 4 Nos 1 and 2 Spring and Summer Issue 1942. Reprint 1990.

Clark, Elmer T. _Methodism in Western North Carolina_ Historical Society 1966.

Earle, Swepson. _Maryland's Colonial Eastern Shore_ Weathervane Books, New York. 1916 (1976 Reprint)

Hall, Clayton Coleman. _Narratives of Early Maryland 1633 - 1684_ Charles Scribner's Sons 1910 (Reprint 1988)

Hilton, Suzanne. _The World of Young Andrew Jackson_ Walker and Company; New York, 1988.

Jones, Elias. _New Revised History of Dorchester County Maryland_. Tidewater Publishers, Cambridge Maryland 1966.

Lawrence, Harold. _Methodist Preachers in Georgia 1783 - 1900_ Harold Lawrence, Lawrenceville, Georgia 1984

Medford, W. Clark. _The Middle History of Haywood County (NC)_ Miller Printing Company, Asheville, NC 1968.

Petrucelli, Katherine Sanford. _The Heritage of Rowan County North Carolina Volume I, 1991_. Genealogical Society of Rowan County.

Phillips, John Wesley. _Phillips Family Papers_ John Wesley Phillips 1981.

Phillips, John Wesley (ed.) _Johnny The Autobiography of John Richard Phillips_. Privately Printed 1986.

Ray, Worth S. _The Mecklenburg Signers and Their Neighbors_ Genealogical Publishing Company, Baltimore. 1975.

Rice, Millard Milburn. _New Facts and Old Families from the Records of Frederick County, Maryland._ Genealogical Publishing Company INC, Baltimore 1984.

Rice, Millard Milburn. _This Was The Life Excerpts from the Judgement Records of Frederick County Maryland 1748 - 1765_. Genealogical Publishing Company INC.

Baltimore 1984

Ward, Doris Cline. *The Heritage of Old Buncombe County Volume 1 -- 1981* Hunter Publishing Company 1981

Williams, T.J.C. and Folger McKinsey. *History of Frederick County Maryland.* Regional Publishing Company, Baltimore 1979.

Winchester, George T. *A Story of Union County and the History of Pleasant Grove Camp Ground* Mineral Springs NC 1937.

Index

Abbeville, Alabama - 363
Abbeville District, SC - 371
Abeline, Texas - 191
Academy, Asheville - 294-296
Academy, Chipola - 363
Academy, Mardisville - 318,320
Academy, Salem - 320
Adobe Walls Indian Dancers - 229
Ajo, Arizona - 192
Alabama - 20,29,97,98,99,100, 193,195,269,270,288,292,293, 315-322,329,331,332,334-336, 339,341-343,345,347,349,363, 364,368,371,380
Alamo Canyon - 194
Albuquerque, New Mexico - 211, 213,215,220,227
Alexander County, NC - 55
Alexanders - 293,294
Algonquin Indians - 5
Alibates Dolomite - 210
Alibates Flint - 210
Alibates Flint Quarries National Monument - 209,210, 218,225,227-230
Alibates Ruin - 218
Alpine, Texas - 192
Amarillo College - 227,231,
Amarillo, Texas - 215,218,220, 223,224,227,231,233,239
Andersonville Prison site - 209
Andrew Chapel - 322,323,324
Andrews Bay, Alabama -
Animal life - (see also birds, reptiles, fish, mammals, etc) - 1,11,67,120,122,123,206,224, 228,
Annapolis - 13
Anson County, NC - 21,60
Appomattox Courthouse National Historical Park - 194,198
Arbuckle Mountains - 187
Ardmore, Oklahoma - 187
Arizona Sonora Desert Museum - 217
Arthur Wright Creek - 5
Asbury Campground - 274
Ashe Co. N.C. - 376
Asheville, NC - 62,63,68,82,90, 91,92,257,263,264,272,273,281, 282,283,287,294,296,335,342, 373,375,376,378
Athens, Alabama - 97,98
Athens Female College - 273
Athens Tennessee - 273
Atlanta, Georgia - 209,261,371
Augusta, Georgia - 309,336
Austin Elementary School - 147, 148,172,173,179
Austin, Texas - 146,147,227, 229, 232
Bacon's Rebellion - 5
Baldy Mountain - 178
Ballinger, Texas - 110,112-114, 116,118,123-125,138,141,142, 146,148,151,171,192
Baltimore County, Maryland - 10,12
Barrel Making - 2,5
Barwise Elememtary School - 147,172
Battle of Alamance - 15
Battle of Cowan's Ford - 58,68, 77
Bay St. Louis, Mississippi - 193
Beatrice, Nebraska - 204
Beatties Ford - 58,68
Beaucatcher Tunnel - 376
Beaver Creek - 210
Bees - 1,4,59,321
Belmont, Alabama - 342
Belton, Texas - 112
Berries - 1,2,139,140,189,261, 325
Bert Bean Coffee Company - 145
Bethel - 316,319
Bethel Methodist Church - 373
Bethel Presbyterian Church - 6
Big Bend, Texas - 192,193
Big Ivey - 294,297
Big Springs, Texas - 104
Big Thicket, Texas - 193
Biltmore Estate - 375
Birds - 1,11,16,91,122,152, 154,173,184,186,191-194,196, 200,202,203,206,211,224,229
Birmingham, Alabama - 331,336,

Blackwater Creek - 5
Blair's Mill - 61
Blount County, Alabama - 97
Blount County, Tennessee - 21, 22,26
Blountsville, Alabama - 320,368
Blountsville, Tennessee - 55, 56
Blue Ridge - 10,300,314
Blue Ridge Parkway - 198
Boats - 1,8,129,202,206,207,307
Borden Meeting House - 305
Borger Nursing Center -
Borger, Texas - 213,216,223, 224,228,233, 234,243
Bradshaw Mountains - 221
Brea, California - 197
Bronson, Florida - 340,361, 362,363
Brownwood, Texas - 100-102, 123,151
Buffalo Creek - 37
Bull Creek - 93
Bull Mountain - 294
Buncombe Co. NC -17,61,62,64-66,68,70-72,76-78,80,82,92, 93,95,254-257,259,260,262,263, 270,279,285,287,293,297,300, 342,343,371,373,375
Burbank, California - 198
Burke Co. NC - 55
Cabarrus County, NC - 21,60,61,
Cahawly Church - 319
Cahawly Valley - 292
Calico Cloth - 5,111,137
California - 28,33,34,36,101, 105,107-109,145,146,149,161, 168,171,179,182,197,198,244, 349,
Camargo, Mexico - 96
Camargo, Oklahoma - 226
Cambrian System rocks - 187
Camino, California - 146
Campbell Farm - 174
Camp Blanding - 351
Camp Bowie - 351
Camp Bullis - 351
Camp Call - 96
Camp Edwards - 355
Camp Gordon - 351
Camp Juda P. Benjamin - 100
Campmeeting - 59,286,303,305, 306,314,316,318,323
Camp Lonesome - 206
Camp Merritt - 126
Camp M.K. Brown - 229
Camp Travis - 126
Camp's Hickory Station - 308
Canadian River - 210
Cancyachuga Manor - 11
Canton, Georgia - 96,97,210, 252,253
Canton, N.C. - 272,275
Cape Sable - 202
Capulin Mountian National Monument - 225
Carlsbad Caverns - 217
Carroll County Arkansas - 28
Carroll County, Georgia - 37,38
Catalina Island - 171
Catawba River - 58,68
Cathey's Meeting House - 60
Cecil Co. MD - 2,4,6,7,9,11,12, 15,19,21,26,37,39,52,54
Cecil County Militia - 7
Cedar Creek - 60
Centre Church - 58
Centreville, Alabama - 342
Charlotte, NC - 15,21,58-60,278
Charleston, South Carolina - 200,235
Chatahoochi River - 93,299
Chatanooga, Tennessee - 101, 110,257,331,332
Cherokee County, Georgia - 93-97,110,111,210,252,371,379,380
Cherokee Indians - 21,27,48, 292,311
Cherokee Nation - 22,27,48,307, 308
Chesapeake Bay - 1-3
Chicago, Illinois - 197
Chickasaw Recreation Area - 217,232
Childersburg, Alabama - 322
Chisos Mountains - 193
Chokoloslee Island - 207,209
Choptank Indians - 5
Choptank River - 2,4,5
Christian Point - 200,202-204
Christiana Presbyterian Church - 6
Christmas - 120,121,129,132, 134,143,165,166,179-181,197,

211,215,223,227,234,243,282, 283,285,287,296,304,307,311, 315,323,324,334,350
Christmas Bird Count - 194
Chunn's Cove - 376
Clarendon, Texas - 220
Clarksville, Georgia - 302,303, 309,313,315
Class Leader - 280,289,306
Clayton, Georgia - 302,303,314
Claytonville, Georgia - 299, 313,
Clear Creek, Tennessee - 298
Cleburn, Texas - 123
Clothes - 1,3,7,10,61,63,91, 96,130,143,147,148,182,235, 304,345
Collier County Historical Commission - 209
Colonial National Historical Park - 199
Colonial Parkway - 199
Columbiana, Alabama - 321,322, 327,328,336
Committee of Safety - 16
Compton, California - 198
Confederate Army - 56,262,371,
Confederate Congress - 56
Confederate Veterans - 100
Connecticut - 275,292,305,339, 342
Cooking - 3,120,128,152,177,
Cookware - 3
Cooper's trade - 5
Coosa County, Alabama - 269, 320,321,325,327,329,331,332, 334-336,368
Coosa Hills - 322
Coosa River - 325
Copperas Cove, Texas - 193
Corinth, Mississippi - 110-112
Cornwall College, - 292
Corona Del Mar, California - 198
Coquerricus Field - 5
Couley's Meeting Mouse - 305
Cowan's Ford - 58,68,77
Crane Creek - 17,39,54
Cream Bakery - 126,133-137,141
Cretaceous period -185,188
Criner Hills - 187
Crooked Creek - 16,58-61,278

Crops - 1,2,10,13,35,59,66,68, 90,91,111,122,124-126,149,159, 266,272,282,294,295,297,302, 304-306,308,310,311,316,321, 338,
Cubans - 362
Cumberland Church - 289,334
Curry Lee Mountain - 311
Dalhart, Texas - 229
Dallas, Texas - 98-101,103,105, 120,151,197,226,357
Darwin, Oklahoma - 188
Davidson's River - 297
Decatur, Alabama - 104
Decatur, Illinois - 126
Decatur, Tennessee - 257
Delaware - 5
Delaware Indians - 5
Delmarva Peninsula - 1
Denison, Texas - 188
Devonian Age formations - 187
DeWitt, Nebraska - 204,212
Dickey Creek - 306
Dorchester County, Maryland - 3-5,7-9
Dry Creek - 177
Duane's Military Tactics - 282
Dublin, Texas - 185
Dust Storm - 142
Dutch Buffalo Creek - 54
Dutch (German) Language - 279
Dutchman's Creek - 16
Dutch Second Creek - 19,21,52, 53,58,60
Eagles - 191,196,203,211,227
Eagle Furnace, Tennessee - 273
Eagle Pass, Texas - 104
Eagle Press - 227
Eastern Shore - 1
Eddleman's Sawmill Branch - 39
Ellis County, Texas - 112,123
Elms Point, Illinois - 332,333, 335,366,367,368
El Paso, Texas - 142
Elyton, Alabama - 284,288,291, 319-321
Ennis, Texas - 123
Erath County, Texas - 123
Eufala, Alabama - 342
Everglades Chamber of Commerce - 207
Everglades City, Florida - 200,

202,203,206,208,209
Everglades Lions Club - 207
Everglades National Park - 199-210
Everglades Welcome Station - 206,208
Fall Branch, Tennessee - 55,56
Fall Branch Seminary - 55
Farming - 1,2,3,10,13,33-35,52,59, 66-68,90,91,95,96, 111,121-126,149,159,174-178, 188-190,262,266,272,282,274, 294,295,297,302,304-306,308, 310,311,316,321,338,
Fifer's Mill - 38
Fish - 1,2,16,111,115,134,163, 189,201,206,211,229,307,317, 318,
Fish dam - 58
Fisher cat - 1
Fishing - 3,16,33,63,104,113, 114,115,209,307,324
Fish Traps - 16,318
Flags - 199,221
Flagstaff, Arizona - 106
Flamingo, Florida - 200,202,203
Flax - 4,10,35,59,61,91,266, 279
Flooding - 10,60,63,217,262
Floodplain - 325
Flora - 1,2,11,13,91,184,189, 191,193,202,203
Florida - 101,151,200,201,204, 214,263,320,331,334,340,342, 345,346,347,349,360,361,363, 364,365,367
Florida Bass - 201
Florida Bay - 200,202
Florida War - 96
Fodder - 111,122
Foods - 2,11,91,111,127,182, 185,321,
Forkland, Alabama - 342
Forrest - 6
Forsyth Co. GA. - 109
Fort Deposit, Alabama - 342
Fort Worth, Texas - 106,216,226
Fort Pitt (Pittsburg) - 13
Fountain City, Tennessee - 257
Franklin Co. Georgia - 305
Franklin, North Carolina - 303
Frank Phillips College - 216, 231,234
Frederick County, Maryland - 7, 9,10,11,12,13,14,15
Fredericktown - 11,13
French Broad Circuit - 297
French Broad River - 261,262, 283,300
Fritch Museum - 222,229
Fritch, Texas - 209-219,222, 224-230,232,233,243,244
Frog Level, Alabama - 289,291
Fruit - 1,2,4,10,152,158/9, 261,317,326
Furniture - 2,3,305,310,315, 330,
Gainesville, Florida - 366
Gainesville, Georgia - 305
Gallup, New Mexico - 217
Gardening - 4,10,14,59,91,94, 104,158,324
Georgia - 15,17-19,24,26,28,29, 37,38,40-42,59,67,93-96,98,111, 210,214,242,243,247,252-254, 261,267,270,273,276,299,301, 302,304,308,311,316,335,336, 351,354,368,371,379,380
Germans - 10,11,127-129,164, 239,279,353,356-359
Germany - 33,105,106,164,165, 209,349,350,353
Giles County, Tennessee - 97
Glass - 4,187
Glouster, NC - 300
Gloversville, New York - 342, 346,362,366
Gold - 141-143,145,148,149,154, 156,182,306,307
Gold Dust, New Mexico - 142,145
Goliad, Texas - 227
Goose Creek - 61
Granbury, Texas - 123
Grand Canyon, Arizona - 182, 194,198,202,213,221
Grassy Branch - 62,64,65,93
Grassy Creek - 54
Grayson Co. Texas - 125
Gray's Prairie, Texas - 139
Great Britain - 1,3
Great Choptank River - 2
Great Snowstorm - 6
Green County, Alabama - 342
Green County, Tennessee -56,

287,298
Greensboro, NC - 275,276
Greenspring Plantation - 196
Greenville, Illinois - 327,333, 334,367,368
Greenville, S.C. - 45
Greenville, TX - 100,105
Greenwood Church - 339
Greenwood, Florida - 363
Grovelling Plantation - 4
Guadelupe Mountains National Park - 217
Guilford County, NC - 15
Gulf of Mexico - 193,202,206
Gulf Port, Mississippi - 193
Gumbo Limbo Trail - 201,202
Gunter, Texas - 125
Habersham Co. GA - 93,254,267, 270,273,276,299,301,308,311, 316,335,371,379,380
Hagood Church - 319
Hall County, GA. - 305,307
Hanging Rock, NC - 38
Hanover, Alabama - 269,325,327, 329,331,332,334,335
Harper's Ferry, West Virginia - 196,205
Hatchet Creek - 317,318,322, 324-326
Havana, Alabama - 342
Haw Creek(See also Whitson Creek) -
Hay - 1,35,66,67,90,176,177,
Haywood Co, NC - 266-268,270 - 273,275,284,285,297,332,371,378
Head of Elk - 6
Hebron, Georgia - 305
Henrietta, Texas - 131,162
Henry, Alabama - 342
Hens - 324
Herbaceous powders - 124
Herbs - 2,11,16,261
Hico, Texas - 163,167,183,192, 193,197,204,208,209,214
Hillabees, Alabama - 315,317, 318,323,338,339
Hillsboro, New Mexico - 144, 145,148,165,174
Hiway, Tennessee - 21,22,27
Hogg Creek - 4
Holbrook, Arizona - 191
Holiday Creamery - 131

Holiness Brethren - 333
Holston Conference - 257, 269,273, 297,302,314,327
Hominey Creek - 279,284,285, 297,
Homestead, Florida - 200,205, 244
Horse Racing - 54,291
Hot Springs, New Mexico - 142, 148,173
Hot Springs, North Carolina - 261,262,264,376
Houses - 1,3,59,60,63,68,91, 110,114,125,141,146,147,148, 171,172,175,181,182,185,188, 191,206,216,217,218,231,233, 269,286,293,301,302,304,361
Houston, Texas - 100,103,104, 151,225,346,351,354,360
Hudson Creek - 5
Hunting Lott - 13
Huntsboro, Alabama - 339-341, 343
Hurricane - 3
Hutchinson Co. TX - 244
Hutchinson County, Texas Genealogy Society - 215
Indiana - 283
Indian Pony - 338
Indian Pottery - 4
Indian Quarter - 10
Indians - 5-7,10,11,15,16,22, 27,28,48,93,210,220,227,229, 231,261,262,288,292,299,301, 311
Iroquoian Indians - 6
Isaac's Field - 3
Jackson Chapel - 118
Jackson County Alabama - 29,363
Jackson County, Georgia - 19, 305
Jackson County, Tenn. - 27,
Jacksonville District - 336
Jacksonville, Florida - 204, 214,360,365,366
Jacksonville, Texas - 346
James River - 195
Jamestown Festival Park - 196
Jamestown, Virginia - 195,196, 198,199
Jefferson Co. Alabama - 319, 321,327,331,380

Jefferson, NC - 376
Jennings, Louisiana - 104
Jonah Mountain - 270
Jonesboro, Tennessee - 274
Jones Valley, Alabama -288
Kaufman Co. Texas - 98-100,104-108,112,115,120-122,138-140, 160,216,226,245-247,250,252
Kentucky - 56,67,165,272,333
King Creek - 121
Lafayette, Georgia - 254
LaFollette, Tennessee - 254-257
Lake Fryer, Texas - 222,225
Lake Mead, Arizona - 194
Lake Meredith Aquatic and Wildlife Museum - 212,224/5
Lake Meredith Marina - 229,241
Lake Meredith National Recreation Area, Texas - 209, 219,226
Lake Tahoe, California - 146
La Porte, Texas - 147,188
Laredo, Texas - 117,118,192,
Laugh and be Fatt -12
Laurel Branch - 65
Lawrence City, Alabama - 97
Lawton, Oklahoma - 213
Layton, Utah - 230
Lee County, Alabama - 320
Levy County, Florida - 340,363-365
Liberty Academy - 58
License to Exhort - 254,298
Limestone County, Alabama - 97
Lincoln Co. NC - 55
Little Choptank River - 5
Little River - 54
Little Troublesome Creek - 37
Livestock - 2,6,10,13,61,62, 66-68,90,91,96,122,262,266, 272,281,282,311,321,326,333, 367
Livingstone, Alabama - 342,364
Locust Old Field - 285-287
Long Beach, California -
Longstreet's Corps -
Los Angeles -
Louisiana -
Louisville, Kentucky -
Louisville Medical School -
Lubbock, Texas - 131,166,179, 191,195,213,231
Luling, Texas - 112
Luray Caverns, Virginia - 197
Macon County, Alabama - 288, 318,339
Macon Georgia - 98,368
Madison County, Arkansas - 28-32
Madison Co. N.C. - 259,261-264
Mardisville, Alabama - 318,342
Mariana District, Florida/Alabama - 342,363,364
Marquette, Michigan - 224
Marshall County, Mississippi - 221
Maryland - 1-7,9-14,16,26,37, 45,
Masons - 112,113,117,118,272, 278,346,366
McCowan's Bluff - 288
McIntosh, Florida - 365,366
McKenzie, Tennessee -326,327
Measles - 295,324,325
Mecklenburg County, NC - 15-18, 21,26,38,58-61,77,278
Memphis, Tennessee - 307,308, 327,331,332,335,368
Meridian, Alabama - 322
Methodist Church - 7,23,62,92, 149,161,172,178,213,215,219, 222,230,243,254,256,257,261, 264,269,273,275,278,279,285-289,294,295,299,302,312,317, 320,327,329,334-336,338,339, 362-365,367,371,373,375,377,378
Mexican War - 96,97
Miami, Florida - 207,208
Miami, Texas - 243
Midwestern University - 147, 172,186,187
Mill Creek - 5
Mills River - 281
Mineral Wells, Texas - 163,183
Mirey Branch - 17,52
Missouri - 67,99,126,284
Mississippi - 101,102,110,112, 117,193,221,245,247,250
Mississippian sediments - 187
Mississippi River - 126,330, 335,368,369
Mizion Church - 317
Mobeetie, Texas -212,229

Monacacy River - 10
Money - 7,32,104,132,141,145, 146,266,268,273,289,291,300, 304,305,307-309
Montgomery Alabama - 321,327, 339,341
Montgomery District - 342
Montgomery Co. NC - 39
Moore House Kitchen - 197
Morgan Mill, Texas - 183
Mossy Creek - 305
Mules - 17,34,54,61,67,90,91, 96,121-123,323
Murphreesboro, Tennessee - 368,
Murphy, NC - 91
Nachoocha Valley, Georgia - 93, 278,299
Nacoochy - 302,303,335
Nanticoke Indians - 5,6
Naples, Florida - 244
National Park Service - 181, 191,192,194,196,199,231,233
Newfound - 283,285,286,288,297, 314
New Jersey - 4,5
New Mexico - 142,144,145,147- 150,165,173,179,191,195,211, 215,217,221,223,231
New York - 67,109,116,126,127, 130,131,346
Norfolk, Virginia - 197
Norman, Oklahoma - 223,224,227, 229,231,233,243
North Carolina - 15-18,21-23, 26-29,52,54,55,58-68,70-73,75, 76,79,82,88,90,92,95,97,195, 212,240,254-257,260,261,267- 270,272,273,275,276,278,292, 293,301,303,309,314,334,342, 343,354,371,373,377-379
Northwards Creek - 19
Nottingham, Maryland - 6
Ocala, Florida - 361,364
Ocmulgee Hospital - 368
Ocona, Georgia - 305
Ogallala Formation (Miocene) - 210
Ogden, Utah - 205
Oglethorpe Co. Georgia - 19
Ordovician sediments - 187
Ordway, Colorado - 211,216, 220,221,230

Ore Knob - 376
Organ Church - 15
Organ Pipe Cactus National Monument - 192,194
Orrville, Alabama - 342
Outbuildings - 3,52,59,63,175, 188,282,302,315
Overton Co. Tenn. - 21,22,26, 27,30,31
Paint Rock, NC - 261,262
Paint Rock, Texas - 124
Paleozoic rocks - 187,194
Palm Springs, California - 198
Palo Duro Canyon - 225,229
Panama City, Florida - 346,347, 360,361
Panhandle Plains Historical Museum - 226,229,231
Parliament - 3
Patauxant River - 10
Patent Medicines - 63,305
Peabody Hotel - 332
Peede, Texas - 112,120-122,216, 245,
Pendleton District, SC - 39,48
Pennsylvania - 5,6,212
Pennsylvanian age rocks - 187
Permian sediments - 188,194,210
Petersburg National Battlefield - 198
Petrified Forest, Arizona - 182,191
Petrolia, Texas - 126
Philadelphia - 10
Phillips Bottom - 7
Phillips Creek -5
Phillips Range - 2
Phoenix, Arizona - 146,194,197, 198,206,213,215,217
Pickens County, Georgia - 371
Pickens District(County), SC - 17,39,42,48
Piedmont Section - 10
Pigeon River - 269,270,282,332
Pigeon Valley -272
Piney Point Plantation - 5
Pipe Creek - 12
Pipe Springs, National Monument - 195
Placer Mining - 141,142,182
Placerville, California - 146
Plains Village Indians - 225

Plantation - 2-4,48,59,60,63,67,113,196,199,282,321
Plant life - 1,2,11,13,91,184,189, 191,193,202,203
Polemic Society - 303
Pontiac's Conspiracy - 13
Population - 21,27,60,125,147,170,171,172,
Postal Service - 95,97,184
Poultry - 2
Prattville, Alabama - 323,331
Prescott, Arizona - 194
Prescriptions - 124
Prince George County, Maryland - 7,10
Queen's College - 15
Quemado, New Mexico - 195
Rabbits - 1,11,120,191,196,199,211,219,220,
Rabun Co. Georgia - 40-42,48,299, 302, 313
Rachoon Range - 6
Rackoon Range - 9
Railroads - 110,121,124,125,127,131,136,182,262,289,329,453,362,365
Randolph, Tennessee - 368
Rangers, Stock - 6
Reagan Jr. High - 147,179
Rehobeth Church - 322
Reeves and Riper Store - 56
Regulator Movement - 15,21
Reptiles - 11,91,113,190, 193,196,199,200,201,211, 225,228,229,230,279,325
Resurvey on Walnut Bottom - 11
Revolutionary War - 16,22,26,37,,38,58,68,71-74,76,77,82,85,90,92,205,212,243,260,263,296
Rims Creek - 297
Ringfield Plantation - 199
Rio Grande - 253
Rita Blanca Lake - 229
Roane County, Tennessee - 273,274,327
Rock Creek - 10
Rockdale, Texas - 218
Rock Presbyterian Church - 6
Rocks - 177,182,183,185,188,189,190,194,282,326
Rock Springs Church - 27
Rocky Ford, Colorado - 220

Rocky Mountain National Park - 230
Rod and Gun Club - 206
Rogers, Arkansas - 208
Rosses Range - 5
Rowan County, NC - 15-17,19,21,22,26,27,37-39,52,54,55,58,92,380
Rowan House - 15
Royal Palm Area - 200-203,205
Ruhama Church - 290,319
Ruidosa, New Mexico - 221
Runnels County, Texas - 110,114,118,124,125
Russell Cave, Alabama - 195
St. John's Church - 15
St. Louis, Missouri - 123,126,204,335
St. Mary Anne Parish - 7,11,12,37
St. Mary's Episcopal Church - 8
St. Peter's Lutheran Church - 14
Salem, Alabama - 320,321
Salisbury Academy -
Salisbury, NC - 15,16,58-60,68,77
San Angelo, Texas - 103,104,106,112-114,123,142
San Antonio, New Mexico -
San Antonio, Texas - 103,116,123,126,150
Sandymush Creek - 285-287,294,300
Sandymush Mountain - 267
Santa Fe, New Mexico - 217,230
Santa Fe Railroad - 124
Santa Rosa, California - 146
Scaffold Branch - 60,61
Schools - 12,36,46,55,56,59,61,62,107,111,112,120,124,125,139,143,147,148,164,172,178-183,188,191,192,214,216,218,221-225,228,230,232,255-257,273,274,278,279,281-298,300-306,308,312,315-321,327,328,333,335-337,339,342,346,349,351,363-366,373,375
Scottsdale, Arizona - 198
Scurry, Texas - 112,116,123,139
Sea Food - 1,2
Seale, Alabama -339-343

Sears Chapel - 322,323
Seminole War(Florida War) - 96
Shawnee Indians - 7
Shenandoah National Park - 196
Shepard Air Force Base - 172
Shoal Creek - 305
Shoemaking trade - 52,58,62
Sierra Blanca - 142
Silurian age formations - 187
Singing Schools - 286,287,290-293,296,297,300,301,303,304,306,312,315
Skellytown, Texas - 233,234,240
Slaughter Creek - 5
Slave Rebellion - 7
Slaves - 18,37,58,59,90,91,298,313,320
Slavery - 3
Small Grains - 1,10,13,59,67,68,91,126,159,306,310,311,318
Smallpox - 6,69,88
Snakes - 11,91,113,190,196,199,201,211,225,229,230,279,325
Soils - 1,13,27,66,91,159,191,242,307,325,326
South Canadian River - 210
South Carolina - 17,41,62,67,93,200,235,318,371
South Carolina Conference - 299
South Dakota - 106
South Mountain - 10
South Ridge Village Site - 218
South Turkey Creek - 62
Southern Christian Advocate - 94
Spanish American War - 362
Spanish Pottery - 4
Stamp Act - 13
Stevenville, Texas - 226
Stinnett, Texas - 229
Suggsville, Alabama - 342
Sullivan Co. Tennessee - 56
Sulphur Springs, N.C. - 254,255
Sunset, Utah - 218,244
Surry County, NC - 15
Surveying - 2,4,5,6,10,11,39,60,219,226,282
Susquehannock Indians - 6
Swannanoa River - 63,65,282,293,
Sylacogga, Alabama - 322
Talbot County, Maryland - 2,3
Talladega, Alabama - 336,342,362
Tallapoosa River - 325
Tampa, Florida - 362
Taylorsville, North Carolina - 55
Tennessee - 17,21,22,23,26-31,53,55,67,90,97,101,110,195,212,254,256,257,261,263,264,273,274,287,295,298,307,326,327,329,332,368
Tennessee Conference - 270,335
Tennessee Valley, NC - 303
Terrell, Texas - 98-100,106,118,
Texas - 97-109,112-114,116-118,120,122,123,125,131,133,136,137,144,146,147,161,170,172,179,182,191,192,205,209,210-212,214,216-218,222,223,224,226,228,243,245-247,250,252,346,351,354,355,357,360
Texas A&M University - 227
Texas Archaeological Society Field School - 222
Texas Historical Commission - 231
Texas Retired Teacher's Association - 243
Texas Society of Geology Clubs - 187
Texas Panhandle - 131,210,216,217,221,227
Texas Tech Clinic - 227
Texas Technological College - 104,179,191
Texas University - 243
Third Creek Presbyterian Church - 21
Thompson's Fish Dam - 58
Thyateria Church - 60
Tides - 2
Tobacco - 1,3
Tools - 2,3,209
Trapping - 16,122,123,318,324
Trees - 1,2,10,11,13,16,62,66,91,120,139,146,149,155,157,159,162,177,178,181,183,187,191,192, 196,200,201,210,224,228,242,

280,282,307,323-325,361
Trinity and Boligee Colored Mission - 342
Trinity Chapel - 375
Trinity River - 123
Tucson, Arizona - 211,215-217, 221,244
Turkey Creek - 61,62,175,177, 255,279,299
Tuscaloosa, Alabama - 288
Tuskega, Alabama - 317,322,339
Union County, NC - 21,58,60
Union Lutheran Pine Church - 15
University of Texas - 243
Valera, Texas - 123
Valley Towns - 22,27
Vernon, Texas - 131,223
Village Creek - 288
Vincent Place - 324
Virginia - 4,5,66,102,195-199,254,260,274,287,293
Vulcan Iron Works - 330
Wachovia Bank and Trust - 272
Waco, Texas - 126,355
Walnut bottom - 11
Walton Co. Florida - 345
War of 1812 - 93
Washington, D. C. - 73,74,76, 80,82,86,88,95,197,198,205, 252,263,272
Washington State - 171
Watauga Co. N.C. - 376
Waxahatchie, Texas - 123
Waynesville, North Carolina - 286
Wetumpka, Alabama - 316,325
Whiskey Making - 266
Whiskeytown National Recreation Area - 198
Whiteside St. Church - 330
Whitfield, Florida - 345
Whitson's Creek (now Haw Creek) - 65,267,342
Wichita County, Texas - 147,172
Wichita Falls High School - 179,181
Wichita Falls, Texas - 125,126, 131-134,136-138,144-147,159, 166,167,171,172,180,182,183, 186,187,190-193,195-198,204, 208-220,222,225,226,228,230, 231,233,243

Wichita Indians - 220
Wichita Mountains - 181
Wickenburg, Arizona - 146,168, 194,195,197,208,209,211,214, 217,221
Wilber, Nebraska - 204,212
Wild Horse Mountains - 142
Wildlife - 1,192,199-202,210, 212,225
Wilkes County, Georgia - 17,18, 26,37,59
Wilkes County, NC - 17,21,54-56,64
Williamsburg, Virginia - 196,198
William's Good Will - 5
Wills Creek, Alabama - 288
Williston, Florida - 346,362
Wilmington, California - 145
Wooden Implements - 2,3,5,62
Woodsboro, Maryland -14
World War I - 126-131
World War II - 351-360
Wythe County, Va - 254
Wytheville, Virginia - 274
Yadkin River - 68
Yellow Fever Epidemic - 329
Yellow Pine Camp; W.O.W. 345
York Co. SC - 39
York River - 195
Yorktown Battlefield - 195
Yorktown Day - 197
Yorktown Tour Road - 198
Yorktown, Virginia - 195-199
Zion Lutheran Church - 15
Zion National Park - 195
Zwonecek and Aksamit Mill - 204

Abbott, Mr. - 124
Abbott, Dick - 139
Acord family - 34
Adams, Bobby Neel - 276
Adams, Evelyn Russell - 276
Adams, Kent Russell - 276
Adams, Mack Neel - 276
Adams, Thomas Turner - 276
Alexander, Althea - 277
Alexander, Elizabeth - 125
Alexander, James Washington - 270
Alexander, William - 267,277
Allen, Bennet - 13
Allen, Rufus - 125
Anderson, JoAnn - 106
Anderson, Mr. - 44
Anderson, Rochelle - 44
Anderson, William - 18,37
Andrew, Bishop James O. - 336
Anthony, Ophelia - 248
Apprell, Donald - 354
Arch, John - 292
Archer, Lucy N. - 100
Arnett, Abe - 138,146
Arthur, Trevor - 195
Arve, Guss - 41
Arve, Rachel - 41
Arve, Roxie - 41
Asbury, Daniel - 62,280
Atkinson, Bishop - 375
Austin, Andrew - 351
Bailey, Hannah - 58
Baines, Bill - 145
Baker, Dr. - 324
Ball, Elizabeth Brown - 56
Ballard, Jim - 191
Balser, Kathy - 225,226
Baltimore, Lord -
Banks, J. B. - 339-341
Banks, W. H. - 339,341
Barber, Reverend R. W. - 376
Barger, Mary - 219
Barker, Frank - 139
Barker, Joel - 48
Barker, Mattie - 136
Barker, Minnie Belle - 48
Barker, Nellie M. - 48
Barker, William - 308
Barlow, Jon - 192
Barnes, Elizabeth - 6
Barnes, John - 6

Barnes, Solomon - 54
Barnett, Roy - 45
Barr, Reverend David - 60
Bass, Annie - 272
Bass, Ralph - 272
Bauloo, David - 311
Bayard, James - 11
Bean, Bert - 145
Bean, Roy - 193
Beatty, Thomas Jr. - 14
Bell, Alma Leona - 374,378
Bell, Catherine Philips Parks - 92,269,332,335,373
Bell, George Folk - 375
Bell, George Hamilton - 373, 375-378
Bell, Helen Ozane - 373
Bell, Herbert Atkinson - 378
Bell, Ida Evangeline - 374,378
Bell, James Edward - 374,378
Bell, James F. - 373
Bell, Kelly Capps - 374
Bell, Lawrence Murdock - 374,378
Bell, Lillias Gertrude - 378
Bell, Mattie Gregg - 373
Bell, Mattie Roberts - 374
Bell, May Etaline - 373,378
Bell, Minnie Agnes - 373,378
Bell, Penelope White Neill - 373
Bell, Robert - 287
Bellah, Moses - 39
Bellough, Elizabeth - 19
Bender, Diane Clark - 108
Bender, Mr. - 108
Bennett, Professor - 55
Benson, Eloise - 215,217
Benz, Ed - 229
Berringer, Captain - 26
Berry, W. G. - 283
Best, Samuel - 263
Betz, Beverly - 275
Beyer, Arthur - 186
Bird, Captain Daniel - 96
Black, Edward - 21
Black, Isaac - 379
Black, John - 60
Black, Rebecca - 21
Black, Samuel - 60
Black, William - 16
Blackford, Allen Herklee - 26

Blackford, Blanche Honiker - 26
Blackford, Cynthia Phillips - 26,32
Blackford, Jefferson Sylvester - 26,32
Blackford, Lonnie - 26
Blackford, Mallie - 26
Blackford, Mary Smith - 26
Blackford, May Brown - 26
Blackford, Mazie Gyer - 26
Blackford, Ozzie - 26
Blackmon, John Homer Jr. - 99
Blackmon, John Homer III - 99
Blackmon, Sharon Ann - 99
Blair, E. L. - 260
Blake, Elizabeth C. - 98
Blake, Mary Lavinia - 98
Blazer, Emma L. - 263
Blazer, W. Howard - 197
Blew, Malcham - 52
Booth, Julia Ann - 20
Boring, Isaac - 311,313
Bounty, George - 354
Bowen, Doug - 207
Bowen, Leah - 206
Braddock, General - 12
Bradshaw, Andrew - 111,221
Bradshaw, Catherine Hefley - 111
Bradshaw, Cynthia Catherine - 110,211
Bradshaw, Dorcas Prigmore - 212
Bradshaw, John - 212
Bradshaw, Nancy Ann(Clendennin) - 212
Bradshaw, N. R. - 380
Bradshaw, Samuel - 212
Bradshaw, Susannah - 97
Bragg, Mrs. J.L. - 257
Brannon, Captain - 37
Brannon, Colonel - 313
Brannon, J.M. - 341
Breazeale, Gambrell - 39
Breazeale, Kennon - 39
Bridges, Evelyn - 99
Brier, Eddie - 204
Brier, Irene McJunkin - 204
Brittain, William - 64
Broadaway, Mr. - 2
Brown, Alexander Melvin - 371
Brown, Armanillia - 371
Brown, Mrs. Barry - 162

Brown, Bob - 219,220
Brown, E. N. - 339,340
Brown, Goldie Jennings - 372
Brown, Ira Lewis- 372
Brown, Irene - 372
Brown, Irley - 372
Brown, Jacob Wiley - 371
Brown, James W. L. - 371
Brown, John - 259,290
Brown, Lester - 164
Brown, Louisa - 371
Brown, Mrs. Lily - 198
Brown, Mary Josephine - 371
Brown, May - 26
Brown, Nancy - 208
Brown, Rachel - 266
Brown, Rosalie - 371
Brown, Roxannah - 371
Brown, Roxie - 208
Brown, Samantha - 372
Brown, Samuel Jefferson - 372
Brown, Slim - 145
Brown, Stanley - 207
Brown, Timothy - 37
Brown, William Olen - 372
Brown, William Samuel - 371
Bruner, James G. - 55
Bruner, Roy Lee - 106
Bruner, Tracey Lynn - 106
Bryan, Amelia Suzanne - 106
Bryan, George Edward - 106
Bryan, JoAnn Vincent - 106
Bryan, Margaret Sumner - 106
Bryson, Bernice - 45
Bryson, Doyle Columbus - 45
Bryson, Eva Belle - 45
Bryson, Eva Leola - 45
Bryson, Lois - 45
Bryson, Luther Columbus - 45
Bucar, Helen - 34
Buell, Dr. - 376
Bumgardner, Amon - 55
Buono, Frank - 206
Burcher, Har. - 52
Burd, Instill - 79
Burgess, Mallie - 24
Burgess, William Fowler - 372
Burk, Etta - 24
Burkes, Polly - 25,32,
Burnett, Clyde - 126,141
Burtz, Joshua - 109,216,
Burtz, Nancy - 109

Burtz, Samuel P. - 210
Burtz, Susan - 109
Burwell, Brother - 319
Buster, William G. - 349
Buxton, Dr. - 375
Byers, Parson - 286,288
Cabe, J. M. - 270
Cain, Donald - 107
Cain, Theresa Jean - 107
Caler, Jacob - 288
Call, Peter - 52
Camp, Frederick - 308
Campbell, Alexander - 28
Campbell, Claude - 153,167,<u>174-178</u>,182,211,213,220
Campbell, Irma - 153,167,<u>174-178</u>,182,211,213,216,220,230
Campbell. James - 54
Campbell, Lula Mae - 211
Campbell, Pat - 220
Campbell, Ross - 167,213
Cannon - Abel - 40
Cannon, Carrie - 327
Cannon, Elizabeth - 40
Cannon, Henry - 40
Cannon, Ida A. - 40
Cannon, Julia A. - 40
Cannon, Melissa - 40
Cannon, Mollie Philips - 322,324,331,332,335,336
Cannon, Russell H. - 40
Cannon, Willie Curtis - 324
Cannon, Captain William J.(W.G.) - 322,323,327,332,335,344
Canupp, Clifford - 51
Capps, Kelly -
Carsont, Billy - 247
Carithers, Dan - 131
Carr, James Drew - 250
Carr, James Larry - 250
Carr, Marion Mills - 250
Carr, Phillip Allen - 250
Carr, Yvonne -250
Carter, Fred - 194,197
Carter, Jan Laidley - 194
Carter, Patsy - 103
Cathey, Will - 58
Chabb, Tina - 204
Chambers, Arene - 50
Chappel - 45
Chase, Samuel - 13

Chastain, Eli E. -
Cheakley, John - 260
Cheek, A. C. - 251
Cheek, Albert - 251
Cheek, Barney James - 251
Cheek, Elbert J. - 251
Cheek, Minnie McKee - 251
Cheek, Noel Douglas - 251
Cheshire, Rev. Joseph - 376
Childs, Francis Mills - 248
Childs, Martha Jo - 248
Childs, Milton David - 248
Chockley, Bessie - 263
Chockley, Eugenia - 263
Chockley, John - 263
Chockley, Stella - 263
Christopher, Joseph - 272
Church, Catherine - 258
Clark, Chuck - 223
Clark, Dana A. - 108
Clark, Dana O. - 108
Clark, Diane - 108
Clark, "Dude" - 34,35
Clark, Elizabeth - 267
Clark, Ellen Dareen - 108
Clark, Ellen Amanda - 267,268
Clark, J. R. - 267
Clark, Jane - 298
Clark, Maxine - 33,34, 35
Clark, Nannie - 259
Clark, O. A. - 34
Clark, Oren Lee - 108
Clark, Peggy - 35
Clark, Rufus - 35
Clark, Theresa Dawn - 108
Clark, William - 270
Clark, William Henry -
Clarke, Richard H. - 73,74,75,76,
Clarke, William J. - 85
Claypool, Jeanne - 219
Claypool, Miss - 179
Claypool, Patricia Nell(Pat) - 214
Claypool, Ralph Jr. - 219
Claypool, Ruth Hall - 147,155,162,171,188,189,212,214-219
Clemens, John M. - 27
Clemens, Samuel - 27
Clendennin Family - 212
Click, Nannie - 263
Clingman, Thomas L. - 78,80,

Clober, William Charles - 117
Clontz, William - 258
Cockran, John - 60
Coffin, Dr. - 287
Coker, Margaret Snider - 45
Cole, James - 48
Coles, William Temple - 52
Collett, Jaimie - 225,228
Collier, Glenn - 187
Collins, Vida - 274
Conant, Roger - 193
Condon, Clara Jane - 103
Condon, Marise Anne - 103
Condon, Michelle - 103
Condon, Robert C. - 103
Connelly, Milo - 136,141
Conway, Beulah - 25
Cooke, Allie - 331
Cooksy, Dollie
Cooper, Amelia - 106
Cooper, Coleman - 247
Cooper, Dana Christina - 248
Cooper, David Clayton - 248
Cooper, Donald Coleman - 248
Cooper, Ethel Mills - 247
Cooper, Horace C. - 247,248
Cooper, Linda Cornelius - 247
Cooper, Michael Anthony - 248
Cooper, Stephen Philip - 248
Correll, Jacob - 52
Correll, John - 52
Cornwallis, General -
Corson, Hugh - 52
Coulter, John J. - 29
Couzzouart, Jim - 225
Crawford, Narvel - 276
Crawford, Narvel James - 276
Crawford, Tymah Phillips - 276
Crockett, David - 27
Crosland, Pat - 208
Crouch, Jonathan - 55
Crowley, Doc - 160
Cummings, David B. - 297,298
Cunningham, Annie Williams - 100
Cunningham, Audrey Avelina - 100
Cunningham, Cherrie Isabell - 100
Cunningham, Clara Creighton - 102
Cunningham, Dick - 192
Cunningham, Frances Carlotta - 102
Cunningham, George - 65
Cunningham, Humphrey - 62
Cunningham, James Calvin - 100
Cunningham, Jesse - 336
Cunningham, Jesse Leonard - 100
Cunningham, Minnie - 115
Cunningham, Richard Devon - 100
Cunningham, Thomas - 29
Cutlip, Jerry - 206
Dalquist, Walter - 186
Daniel, William - 306
Darwin, Charles - 323
Davidson, William - 58,62,68, 77,
Davis, Mrs. Opal -
Davis, Shamas S. - 340
Davis, W.T. - 339,340
Day, Edwin Arthur - 210,215, 216, 219,225,228,
Day, Paula Reigel - 216
Day, William T. -
Delacy, J. M. - 340
Delaney, Christopher C. - 103
Delaney, Clara C. - 103
Delaney, Clara Jane - 103
Delaney, Jack W. - 103
Delaney, John Thomas - 103
Delaney, Joseph Patrick - 103
Delaney, Patsy - 103
Delaney, Robert James - 103
Delaney, Susan Anne - 103
Dennis, Jesse J. - 98
Deaton, Charles Quinton - 47
Denton, Isaac T. - 28
Denzer, Sherman - 33
Digges, John - 12
Diliach, Mr. - 316
Dion, Elisha - 277
Dixon, Clarence
Dobbins, Alex - 52
Donaldson, John - 59,60
Donaldson, Elizabeth - 59
Dorsey, A.S. - 316
Dorsey, Clarinda Philips - 338
Dotson, Matilda Catherine - 23
Dotson, Melissa Emma - 23
Dow, Lorenzo - 284
Dragging Canoe - 27
Dryman, Clerinda - 47
Dryman, Edd - 47

Dubose, McNeely - 378
Dugard, Herman - 247
Duncan, Roda Essie - 42
Durant, Will - 354
Dutton, Hub - 198
Dyer, Bill - 217
Dykes, Margaret L. - 56
Easterling, Hosea - 24
Eaton, William - 284
Edmondson, John - 5
Edney, B.M. - 79,80,81,84,87,89,90
Edwards, J.L. - 73,74,76,78,80,
Edwards, J.S. - 75
Eikren, Jacobina - 105
Elder, Durward P. - 100
Eller, O. S. - 145
Elliot, Mary Francis - 23
Elonworth, Mr. - 2
Elston, Steve - 233
Ervin, Susannah Armilda - 371
Etchieson, Meeks - 218,219,225,
Evans, Bill - 32
Evans, Clarissa - 266,272,273,275
Evans, Francis - 268
Evans, James Jackson - 24
Evans, Jim - 32
Fain, Andrew J. - 267
Farr, Mr. - 43
Farris, Samuel - 299
Faulkner, Shannon - 45
Fay, Dorothy - 104
Ferguson, Elizabeth Phillips - 6
Ferguson, Janet - 231
Few, Joan - 225
Fields, John - 320
Finn, Mr. - 318
Finson(Phinson, Vincent), George - 52,58,60
Fisher, Dick - 192
Fisher, Elizabeth - 24,31,248
Fitzpatrick, Tommie - 118
Forster, Brother - 298
Forester, Charles - 54
Forrester, Thomas - 284
Foster, Eleanor McJunkin Safarik - 215,216,217,223,227,231,234,243
Foster, Huber - 215,216,217,223,232
Foster, Thomas - 93
Fowler, Fern - 179
Francis, Kathleen - 125
Freeman, Moses - 284
Furey, Cecilia - 348
Furey, Eileen - 348
Furey, Loretta - 348
Furey, Megan - 348
Furey, Nelda Gray - 348
Furey, Theresa Lorraine - 348
Furey, William Joseph - 348
Gall, Duane - 230
Gallup, George -
Galt, Catherine - 109
Galvin, John - 206
Gambold, Father - 292
Gant, Allan - 219
Gant, Amber - 219
Gant, Anna - 219
Gant, Bob - 160,167,214
Gant, David - 219
Gant, Jeanne Claypool - 167,214,218
Garcia, Al - 204
Gardner, Charles M. - 263
Gardiner(Gardner), David H. - 260,263
Gardner, Frank - 264
Gardner, Hiram - 264
Gardner, Hugh - 364
Gardner, John L. - 264
Gardner, Leslie - 264
Gardner, Mary - 264
Gardner, Maurice - 264
Gardner, Ruth - 264
Gardner, Wells - 264
Gardner, William Marshall - 264
Garnet. Samantha - 40
Garnett Family - 323
Garrison, N. J. -95
Gasaway, Mahala - 41
Gassaway, Elizabeth Minerva - 50
Gazaway, Reverend - 279
Geiger, Helen - 34
Gents, George - 54
Gibson, Brother - 333
Giddes, John - 39
Giddings, Roger - 196
Gilbert, Henry - 141,142,145

Gill?, Sarah - 93,95
Gillaspie, Harry - 115
Gillespie, Ada A. - 273,274
Gillespie, Hannah - 274
Gillespie, R. A. - 274
Glance, Mary - 262
Glasgow, J. - 60
Glenn, E. Hundan - 339-342
Gordon, Faye - 43
Gordon, Mr. - 43
Gordon, Paul - 200
Grady, E. E. - 109
Graham Family - 150
Graham, Aunt Belle - 136,143, 160
Graham, Johnny -187,210,232,
Graham, Norman -120
Graham, Olin -
Graham, Ophelia - 136
Graham, Paul - 137
Graham, Uncle Sam - 139
Graham, Stella -120,153
Gramling, Captain - 96
Gray, Corine - 347
Gray, Daniel Philip - 347
Gray, Ellen Louise - 347
Gray, Esther Nance - 347
Gray, Irma Askew - 347
Gray, James Kent - 347
Gray, James Robert - 347
Gray, Jack Shelton - 347
Gray, James Shelton - 347
Gray, John Clark - 347,348
Gray, Joseph Sylvester - 346, 347
Gray, Julia Ella - 347
Gray, Julia Nance - 347
Gray, Lois - 348
Gray, Mary - 347
Gray, Michael - 348
Gray, Neda - 348
Gray, Nelda - 348
Gray, Philip - 347
Gray, Ruth Bryan - 348
Gray, thomas C. - 348
Gregory, Harry - 193
Gregory, Mrs - 148,173
Green, Benjamin - 68
Green, Brother - 319
Green, Duff - 74,84
Green, Esquire - 322
Green, General Nathaniel - 77,

Green, P.A. - 340-342
Green, Silas - 283
Green, Wilson - 263
Gribble, Thomas - 61
Grimes, Dovey R. - 25
Grimes, Peter - 8
Grimes, William K. - 25
Griminger, Fredk - 52
Guardipee, Gunnar - 198
Gudger, James - 284
Gudger, Samuel B. - 256
Gudger, William -295
Guilliams, J. M. - 363
Gunn, David Cooper - 107
Gunn, Horace Lindsay - 107
Gunn, John Winston - 107
Gunn, Marjorie Phillips - 107, 226
Gunn, Mark Leslie - 107
Gurly, Faraby - 39
Guthrie, Mr. - 120
Gyer, Mazie M. - 26
Hall, Ada - 119,146,160,
Hall, [Amos Harley] - 150
Hall, E. - 269
Hall, George - 270
Hall, Hazel - 165,219
Hall, Henry - 160,219,221,227
Hall, James - 38
Hall, John - 269,270
Hall, John Henry - 119,164,
Hall, Lydia - 119
Hall, Salley - 269,333
Hall, Velma - 160
Hamil, Andrew - 299
Hamilton, Ollie - 23
Hamilton, Robert - 64
Hamilton, Sammy - 206,207
Hammons, Abraham - 25,33
Hammons, Ada Phillips - 25,33
Hammons, Cora Phillips - 25,33
Hammons, Elizabeth - 22
Hammons, Joe - 25,33
Hampton, Raby - 157
Harden, Marthena - 42
Harden, Mr. - 43
Hardin, J. J. -94
Harmon, Lillie Phillips - 25
Harmon, Slias - 25
Harriott, Maude - 202
Harris, Louisa J. - 24
Harrison, Colemore - 38

Harrison, Hastus - 299
Harrison, Nathan - 286
Harry, Bruce - 323
Hart, Tom - 145,146
Hatch, Charles -
Haupt, Barbara Jean - 248
Haupt, Billie Carol - 248
Haupt, Billy Glenn - 248
Haupt, Michael Glenn - 248
Haver, Stanley - 118
Hawkins, Dallas - 125
Hawkins, Gene - 107
Hawkins, Hershall - 107
Hawkins, Horace - 125
Hawkins, John - 72
Hawkins, Michael - 108
Hawkins, Sandra Lee - 108
Hawkins, Susan Meyer - 108
Hawkins, Walter - 107
Hawkins, William - 29
Haworth, Florence - 260
Hayes, Joseph - 37
Hayes, Rutherford B. -
Haynes, Ann Mills - 249
Haynes, H. P. - 270
Haynes, Lewis Patrick - 249, 250,
Haynes, Owen - 309
Haynes, Tracy Renee - 249
Hazen, Brother - 323
Hearn, Ebenezer - 289
Hedding, Bishop - 309
Hefley Family - 150
Heikola, Heidi - 211
Helm, Gladys - 107
Helms, Ruth - 249
Helvenston, Ida D. - 344,361
Hempy, dorothy - 100
Henderson, John - 19
Henderson, Larry - 191,194, 198,
Hendricks?, Alice - 333,334
Hendricks, Allie - 332
Hendrick, Brother - 320
Hendricks(Hendrix), Julian E. - 318,332,335
Hendricks, Mary - 333
Hendrix, Robert - 318
Hendrick, Zac - 323,331
Hendricks, Zack - 332
Henry, J. B. - 340
Henry, Nellie - 42

Henly, John - 314
Henly, Polly - 313
Henschen, Joseph - 348
Henschen, Lois - 348
Henschen, Martha - 348
Henschen, Raymond - 348
Herd, Thomas -
Hereford, Henry - 54
Herren, Duncan - 277
Herren, Elizabeth - 275
Herring, Stephan - 16
Herron, Katherine Elizabeth - 100
Hicks - 22,27
Hicks, Anna - 254
Hicks, Hannah - 254
HIcks, Lawrence - 254
Hicks, Robertson - 254
Hicks, William - 273
Higgins, John - 217,230
Hill, Abraham - 52
Hill, E. G. - 105
Hindman, Dr. - 322
Hipps, Anna - 254
Hipps, Hannah - 254
Hipps, Lawrence - 254
Hipps, Nathan R. - 254
Hodges, Buster - 224
Hoffman, Addie - 100
Hogan, Ruth - 25
Holcombe, Hosea - 289
Holland, Amelia - 25,33
Holland, Jean - 33
Hollifield, L. C. - 272
Hollingsworth, Zebulon - 10
Holman, Mr. - 124,125
Holmes, Bee - 233
Holt, Ora B. - 25
Holtshouser, Andrew - 21,51
Honea, Caroline - 252
Honiker, Blanch - 26
Hood, John - 60
Hooper, Mattie - 44
Hooper, Harrold - 354
Hooper, Mr. - 44
Hornbager, Valentine - 52
Horton, Margaret Emmaline - 321
Houston(Huston) family - 212
Houston, John - 216
Houston, David - 10
Houston, Samuel - 7
Howard, Lucy Ann - 100

Howard, Richard - 227
Hoy, Bill - 192
Hundpeth Family - 150
Huffman, Lydia - 99
Huggins, Susan - 256
Hughes, Eula - 44
Hughes, Joseph - 379
Hughes, Mr. - 44
Hughey, William - 380
Hunt, Avellina - 99
Hunt, Cedric - 99
Hunt, Don Edward - 250
Hunt, Dorothy - 100
Hunt, Isaac - 99
Hunt, Joseph Samuel - 100
Hunt, Joseph Samuel Jr. - 100
Hunt, Lydia -99
Hunt, Mabelle Thomas - 100
Hunt, Mardell - 99
Hunt, Marie - 100
Hunt, Nadine Allen - 100
Hunt, Patsy Ruth - 100
Hunt, Sammy - 151
Hunt, Thomas Isaac - 99
Hunt, Vincent Ford - 100
Hunt, Virgie Marie - 100
Hunt, Wayne Roy - 100
Hunt, Yvonne Carr - 250
Hupper, Henry - 8
Hurd, Betty Russell - 275
Hurd, Beverly Betz - 275
Hurd, Caitlin Elisabeth - 276
Hurd, Gary Russell - 276
Hurd, Jane - 276
Hurd, Leslie Jean - 275
Hurd, Louis Charles - 275
Hurd, Nathaniel - 276
Hurd, Phillip Charles - 275,276
Hutchins, Kathy Merle - 248
Hutchins, Kelley Eugene - 248
Hutchins, Lisa - 248
Hutchins, Martha Childs - 248
Hutsell, Eli K. - 254
Hutsell, Harry - 257,258
Hutsell, Julia E. - 256
Hutsell, Lucile Seabolt - 257
Hutsell, Mary Ann - 256
Hutsell, Mary Ann Wells - 254
Hutsell, Pearl - 257,258
Hutsell, Robert A. - 255,256, 257
Hutsell, Robert K. - 257

Inman, Alonzo Berry - 24
Inman, Arlie - 24
Inman, Bert - 23
Inman, Daisy - 24
Inman, Flora Ellen - 24
Inman, John Henry - 23
Inman, Mary Jane - 202,203
Inman, Thursa Mae - 23
Inman, Tilda Catherine - 23
Ivester, Mr. - 49
Jackson, Carter - 308
Jackson, Vic - 192
Jacobson, Mr. - 35
James, Ralph - 140
Jennings, Lilla Jane - 371
Jensen, H. Lee - 108
Jeter, Annie - 103
Jeter, G.A. - 104
Jeter, J.M. - 104
Jennings, Ben - 341
Jewell, Clara - 204,212
Jewell (McJunkin), Bertha - 212
Johnson, Calvin - 249
Johnson, Donald Alfred - 106
Johnson, Gregory Scott - 149
Johnson, Greta Carol - 149
Johnson, Helen R. - 274
Johnson, Henry - 269
Johnson, Juliette - 252
Johnson, Sarah - 25,31/32, 32,
Jones family - 155
Jones, Catron - 10
Jones, Clell - 24
Jones, Densmore - 23
Jones, Eli - 24
Jones, Forrest - 147,171,188
Jones, Glendall - 158
Jones, Henny - 164,193
Jones, James Alvin - 101
Jones, John - 10
Jones, Karmen Anita - 101
Jones, Kathleen - 125
Jones, Kathy - 219
Jones, Kerry Nelson - 101
Jones, Logan - 24
Jones, Mr. - 154
Jones, Morgan - 124
Jones, Robert - 10
Jones, Robert(Bobby) - 164
Jones, Rose - 101
Jones, Velma Hall - 147,171, 188,

Jones, Will - 139
Jordan, Carrie - 327
Jordan, Fleming - 323,327,
Jordan, H. - 323
Jordan, James - 94
Jordan, Julia - 336
Judd, Frank - 192
Karpinski, Maija - 107
Kay, Dorothy - 246
Keith, J. L. - 94
Kelly, Archy - 322
Kelly, J. P. - 97
Kelley, Laura Dawn - 101
Kelley, Rachel Star - 101
Kelley, Robert Earl - 101
Kincannon, Dorthula - 25
King, Amy - 66,[295],
King, Elisha - 295,301,302,304, 306,316,320,
King, Elizabeth - 65,278,287, 292,320,336,342,368
King, Henry - 6,29
King, Oscar - 44
King, Ruth Starret - 284, 306,320,368
Kinsland, J.O. - 272
Kirby, Kathy - 197
Kirk, Ruby - 349
Knox, "Bub" - 108
Knox, Christine LeEllen - 108
Knox, David - 108
Knox, Dorothy - 108
Knox, Florence - 107
Knox, Ila Joe - 108
Knox, Janice - 108
Knox, Judith Ann - 108
Knox, Kathy Lunsford - 108
Knox, Martha RAe - 108
Knox, Mary Alice - 107
Knox, Walter L. - 107
Koger, Brother - 328
Kreis, Cheryl Lee - 102
Kreis, Dena Katherine - 102
Kreis, Donald Joseph - 102
Kreis, James L. Michael - 102
Kreis, Kristopher Alan - 102
Kreis, Pamela Dawn - 102
Lakin, Elizabeth Ann - 106
Lakin, Mary Lynn - 106
Lakin, Thomas Edward - 106
Lantiss, Henry - 14
Larson, Linda - 276

LaRue, Claudia Elizabeth - 265
LaRue, Joseph Lafayette - 260, 264
LaRue, Mary - 265
LaRue, Paul - 265
LaRue, Ruby - 264
LaRue, Ruth Dexter - 264
Larrum, LLoyd - 146
Laster, J. B. - 34
Laughlin, Henry A. - 105
Lawrence, Bonnie Mae - 125
Lawson, Mrs. - 323
Lawson, Sanford - 251
Lawyer, Grace - 6
Lawyer, William - 6
Lay, Bill - 126
Lear, Christopher Kyle - 246
Lear, Mary Lois - 246
Lear, Micky Ann - 246
Lear, Ted Norman - 246
Lear, Tom - 246
Ledbetter, Ethel - 24
Lederer Family - 198
Ledford, Mr. - 44
Lee, Bob - 224
Lee, Delphia - 50
Lee, James C. - 50
Lee, Jesse -
Lee, Nancy H. - 50
Lee, Rachel - 50
Lee, robert E. - 354
Leimer, Virgil - 195,198
Leopard, Dora - 44
Leopard, Walter - 44
Lewis, John - 354
Lewis, Selma - 125
Lianzi, Theresa - 205
Liddon, John - 39
Lindley, Corine - 347
Lindley, Jeanie Gray - 347
Lindley, Malcolm Gray - 347
Lindley, Mary Juliet - 347
Lindley, William Zeba - 347
Lindsey, Ida E. - 374
Lindsey, Mr. W. F. - 374
Ling, Mr. - 142
Linkletter, Art - 220
Lintz, Christopher - 221
Little, Thomas - 68
Locke, Barbara Jean - 248
Locke, Francis - 21,26
Locke, Thomas Houston - 248

Locke, Vivian Clyde - 248
Locklin, Albert W. - 342
Logan, J. C. - 260
Logan, James - 263
Long, C.D. - 120
Long, Ema - 274
Long, Emmett - 125
Long, Joseph - 380
Long, Mollie LeeAnn - 251
Lovelace, Mr. - 188
Lowrey, James - 285
Lowrey, Lucille - 143
Lowrey, Mary - 143
Lunsford, Kathy - 108
Lusk, Samuel - 65
Luttrell, James Van - 99
Lynne, Mr. - 132
Mackeel, Cornelia Ross Phillips - 6
Marcum, Eddie - 232
Marlow, Frank - 34
Marshall, Andrew David - 99
Marshall, Annie Corley - 99
Marshall, Charles James - 98
Marshall, Charles N. - 98
Marshall, Demetra - 98
Marshall, Elizabeth C. - 98
Marshall, Ernest - 98
Marshall, Ethel - 98
Marshall, Eugene - 99
Marshall, Everette A. - 99
Marshall, Fredna Jackson - 99
Marshall, Gertrude Eva - 99
Marshall, Hubert W. - 98
Marshall, James N. - 98
Marshall, Katie - 98
Marshall, Leonard Stroud - 98
Marshall, Lonnie Mack - 99
Marshall, Mary Francis - 99
Marshall, Mary Sue - 90
Marshall, Ollie - 99
Marshall, Omera - 98
Marshall, Sarah Beth Axe - 99
Marshall, Sarah Phillips - 98
Marshall, Susan - 99
Marshall, William R. - 98
Marshall, Willie - 99
Martin, Maggie Mae - 25
Martin, Matthew - 360
Martin, Megan - 360
Mason, J.M. - 339,341,342
Mason, Mr. - 288
Matheson, Eloise - 43
Mathews, Dr. - 324
Mathus, Adda - 260
May, Betty - 229,232
Maxwell, Frances - 102/103
Maxwell, Jack Richard - 103
Maxwell, James - 60
Maxwell, Jott - 103
McAdory, Colonel - 319
McAdory, Eliza Philips - 323, 331,332,336
McAdory, Jasper - 322,323,325, 327,331,332
McAdory, P. J. - 323,336
McAuly, Lowell V. - 106
McBrannon, J. - 340
McCallum, Percy Eugene - 99
McCaule, Thomas - 58
McClellan, Joyce - 49
McClellan, R. Lake - 49
McClellan, Virginia - 49
McCormick, Mr. - 120
McDougal, Professor - 120
McEntire, Bevil - 258
McGowan - 251
McHenry, Bruce - 192,196, 208
McHenry, Brucie - 196
McHenry, Dolly - 196
McHenry, Keith - 196
McHenry, Martha - 196
McIntosh, Monica - 223,228
McJunkin, Bertha (Jewell) - 168,212
McKenzie, Dr. - 319
McKee, Annie Belle - 246
McKee, Arthur Benton - 246
McKee, Barney Eugene - 251
McKee, Bennie - 245
McKee, Betty Ruth - 251
McKee, Billy W. - 246
McKee, Clifton - 246
McKee, Clovis - 246
McKee, David Paul - 246
McKee, Debra Sue - 247
McKee, Earl Webster - 246
McKee, Eugenia LaVern - 251
McKee, George - 246
McKee, Harold Ray - 251
McKee, Hassel Eugene - 251
McKee, Hershall Edward - 250
McKee, James L. - 250
McKee, James Madison - 245

McKee, James U. - 246
McKee, Jane Callie(Aunt Callie) - 143,245
McKee, Jay Durwood - 247
McKee, Jean Lee - 247
McKee, Jerry Wayne - 246
McKee, Jewell Owen - 251
McKee, Lela - 245,247
McKee, Linda - 247
McKee, Lloyd - 250
McKee, Lola - 246
McKee, Lottie - 246
McKee, Louise - 246
McKee, Mary Hamm - 247
McKee, Minnie Boyd - 251
McKee, Mural Dean - 251
McKee, Ola - 246
McKee, Ollie - 251
McKee, Otis - 246
McKee, Ralph - 245
McKee, Reatha Alma - 250
McKee, Robert Leon - 250
McKee, Roland J. - 250
McKee, Ruby Estelle - 246
McKee, Silas - 251
McKee, Walter Deen - 245
McKee, Walter Jr. - 246
McKee, William Felton - 246
McKee, William Harvey - 245,246
McKee, Winifred - 246
McKinzie, Zoe Isabella - 98
McMahon, Brother - 298
McMinn, Cynthia - 247
McMinn, Denese - 247
McMinn, Leon - 247
McMinn, Leticia - 247
McMinn, Phyllis - 247
McMinn, Ronald - 247
McMinn, Reba Mills - 247
McPherson, Malcolm - 294
McRae, R.M. - 90
Meade, William - 24
Mellersh, George - 368
Metcalf, George W. - 105
Metcalf, Richard Chilton - 105
Metcalf, Robert Lance - 105
Metcalf, Susan A. - 105
Middaugh, Captain John - 12
Middleton, James - 198
Miles, Mary - 323
Millard, Rebecca C. - 56
Miller, Betty - 125
Miller, Captain - 52
Miller, Elizabeth - 259,262
Miller, Henry - 263
Miller, John - 65
Miller, Margaret - 198
Miller, Mary Glance - 262
Miller, Mrs. - 147
Miller, Wendle - 21
Miller, Windle - 52
Miller, William - 262
Millikin, Chuck - 208
Mills, Allen Wayne - 247
Mills, Annis Quebelle - 247
Mills, Ann LaRue - 249
Mills, Ann Loyd - 249
Mills, Betty Jo - 247
Mills, Callie Mae - 250
Mills, David - 249
Mills, Debra Lynn - 249
Mills, Donald Wayne - 249
Mills, Douglas Eugene - 248
Mills, Edward - 8
Mills, Elmer Leslie - 247
Mills, Ethel Ross - 247
Mills, Felix - 247
Mills, Felix Webster - 249
Mills, Francis McKee - 248
Mills, Gloria Sue - 249
Mills, Herron Don - 249
Mills, James Drew - 249
Mills, James Ronald - 249
Mills, Jeffrey Owen - 248
Mills, John Michael - 249
Mills, Lela Mae - 247
Mills, Leslie Scott - 247
Mills, Leslie Wayne - 247
Mills, Marilyn Linda - 249
Mills, Marion Swan - 249
Mills, Mary Fisher - 248
Mills, Michael Douglas - 249
Mills, Nancy Griffin - 247
Mills, Noel Douglas - 248
Mills, Ophelia - 248
Mills, Patsy Nell - 247
Mills, Peggy Louise - 249
Mills, Reba Jay - 247
Mills, Samuel - 280
Mills, Thelma Doris - 247
Mills, Vivian Clyde - 248
Mills, William Terrel - 249
Minge, Jeanie Gray - 347
Minge, John Henry - 347

Minge, Malcolm Gray - 347
Minge, Mary Philips - 347
Minge, Mary Tonita - 347
Mitchell, Dr. - 323
Mitchell, Robert M. - 95
Mize, Elizabeth - 45
Moffitt, J. R. -276
Moffitt, Tinna E. - 276
Mohrs, Bob - 219
Mohrs, Elisha - 219
Mohrs, Jennifer - 219
Mohrs, Lynn Gant - 219
Montgomery, Charles - 275
Montgomery, Elizabeth - 30
Montgomery, Mary Anne - 275
Montgomery, William - 30
Moor, Andrew - 59
Moore, Alvin Henry - 45
Moore, Annie E. - 45
Moore, Betty Caroline - 47
Moore, Dorothy Christian - 46
Moore, Edward David - 46
Moore, Elnora Christine - 47
Moore, Evertie Edward - 45
Moore, Francis Olivia - 47
Moore, Frank - 125
Moore, Fred William - 46
Moore, Genevive - 47
Moore, George Daniel - 45
Moore, Gerald Fred - 47
Moore, Green - 270
Moore, Harold Cleveland -47
Moore, Heywood Cleveland - 47
Moore, Ida Chapell - 45
Moore, James - 45
Moore, James Daniel - 45
Moore, Levine Henry - 47
Moore, Linda Gayle - 47
Moore, Lula Geneva - 47
Moore, Mary Ruth - 47
Moore, Rachel Esterline - 47
Moore, Sandra Lee - 47
Moore, Sarah P. - 271
Moore, Shirley Sue - 47
Morrill, James Thomas - 107
Morris, Thomas A. - 254
Moses, Bertha - 272
Moses, Samuel - 272
Norton, Grissel - 8
Morton, Mrs. W.H. - 366
Mosley, Celia - 44
Mosley, Francis - 44
Mosley, James - 44
Mosley, John - 43
Mosley, lela Mae - 106
Mosley, Margaret Mahala - 44
Mosley, Martha - 44
Mosley, Presley - 39,43
Mosley, Sallie - 40,43
Mosley, Sarah - 44
Mowrer, Frederick - 52
Mulkey, John Newton - 28
Mullenix, Ellen Hall - 55
Murphy, Mr. - 50
Murry, A. J. - 268,272
Murry, William - 8
Nabors, Robert - 322,336
Neely, John I - 82,85
Neill, G. Robert - 373
Neill, Penelope White - 373
Nelson, General - 96
Nelson, Jennie - 25
Nelson, Thelma Doris - 247
Newell, Norine - 36
Nicholson, Evan A. - 43
Nickle, Elizabeth - 264
Nielson, Larry - 210,213,214,
Niles, Samuel B. - 95
Nix, Charles - 292
Noble, Mary Lou - 103
Norman, Jay - 162
Ogletree, Roy - 164,165,167, 188-190,193,208,216,218-220
Ogletree, Velma Hall Jones - 164,167,188-190,193,208,216, 218,232
Oliver, Newton Commodore - 45
Ostertag, J. A. - 117
Otto, Donna - 225,226
Overton, Francis - 2
Overton, Mary - 2
Owen, Caroline - 320
Owen, Lawrence - 12
Owen, Parson Thomas - 289,292
Owen, William - 289
Owens, Charles - 340
Owens, James - 44
Page, Wilda - 223
Pageton (Pareton) family - 300, 301
Paine, Robert - 274
Patillo, Brother - 324
Patton, Brannon - 296
Patton, Elizabeth - 270

Patton, Ezra - 354
Patton, James - 270
Patton, James W. - 71,72
Pauley, Mr. - 333
Peacock, Mrs. H. A. - 366
Peede, Mrs - 120
Peede, Ambrose - 139
Peede, Hulda - 139
Pence, David - 56
Pence, Susan - 265
Pendergraft, Don - 107
Pendry, James - 93,254
Pendry, Matilda - 93,254
Penland, John - 79
Penland, P. A. - 270
Perry, Jim - 25
Peterson Family - 145
Peterson, Loraine - 108
Pettaway, Joseph - 16
Pharr, Adam Dowling - 372
Pharr, Adolphus - 372
Pharr, Alma - 372
Pharr, Amanda - 373
Pharr, Ann - 372
Pharr, Annie Jane - 372
Pharr, Antonie Olin - 373
Pharr, Arminus - 373
Pharr, Betty Jane - 372
Pharr, Bonny - 373
Pharr, Carter Lester - 372
Pharr, Carter Lester - 373
Pharr, Chester Lee - 372
Pharr, Clara - 372
Pharr, Donald Eugene - 372
Pharr, Early Earnest - 372
Pharr, Elizabeth - 371
Pharr, Elizabeth Bailey - 371
Pharr, Elvira - 372
Pharr, Eric Dotson - 372
Pharr, Fanny Elizabeth - 373
Pharr, Franklin - 372
Pharr, George E. - 373
Pharr, Jack Reuben - 372
Pharr, James Arthur - 372
Pharr, James Harold - 372
Pharr, James Oscar - 372
Pharr, Jasper Turner - 372
Pharr, John D. - 373
Pharr, John Grover - 373
Pharr, John Paul - 372
Pharr, John W. - 116
Pharr, Joseph Wilson - 110, 266,297,371
Pharr, Julia - 373
Pharr, Julie - 373
Pharr, Juliette - 371
Pharr, Laura Fowler - 372
Pharr, Lewis Sylvester - 373
Pharr, Lucy Elizabeth - 372
Pharr, Marshall T. - 373
Pharr, Martha - 372
Pharr, Martha Lucinda - 373
Pharr, Mary - 373
Pharr, Mary Ann Philips - 371
Pharr, Mary Elizabeth - 372
Pharr, Mary Jane - 373
Pharr, Mattie Florence - 372
Pharr, Moses Summerfield - 372
Pharr, Nancy Elvira - 372
Pharr, Richard Wesley - 372
Pharr, Ruby Wiley - 372
Pharr, Samuel - 371
Pharr, Theodore Atkin - 373
Pharr, Walter - 373
Pharr, William - 372
Pharr, William Thomas - 372
Phelps, George - 366
Phelps, Mr. and Mrs. - 139
Phillips, A. R. - 50
Phillips, Aaron - 56
Phillips, Ada - 25,33,273,
Phillips, Ada J. - 25
Phillips, Ada L. - 275
Phillips, Ada Maria - 119,214, 217,222,225,243
Phillips, Adam - 12,15,17,18, 19,21,22,24,28-32,52,58-92, 205,343,344,371
Phillips, Adam David - 218, 220,244
Phillips, Adam N. - 30
Phillips, Adam Wesley - 24
Phillips, Addie - 43
Phillips, Ader - 51
Philips, Albert - 342,346
Philips, Albert Roux - 344
Phillips, Alexander Joshua - 110,
Phillips, Alexander P. - 42
Phillips, Alfretta - 22,28
Phillips, Aliff - 268
Phillips, Alissa - 267,272
Phillips, Allen Newton - 25, 31,33,

Phillips, Allie - 41,277
Phillips, Allie May - 24,33
Phillips, Althea - 267,268,277
Phillips, Alvin Lloyd - 33
Phillips, Amanda - 43,
Phillips, Amanda E. - 23
Phillips, Amanda Isabella - 48
Phillips, Amanda M. - 20
Phillips, Ambry - 118
Phillips, Amelia Cooper - 106
Phillips, Amelia Marjorie - 106
Phillips, Amos Richardson - 23
Phillips, Anah - 49
Phillips, Anderson - 39,41
Phillips, Angeline - 118
Phillips, Anna - 24,40,269
Phillips, Anna Lee - 117,118
Phillips, Anne - 6
Phillips, Annie - 49
Phillips, Annie Lee Jeter - 103
Phillips, Andrew - 23,110
Phillips, Andrew J. - 56
Phillips, Angeline Ada - 50
Phillips, Anor(Anna) - 40
Phillips, Ara - 49
Phillips, Arah Adeline - 44
Phillips, Archie - 25
Phillips, Ardis Ellen - 107
Phillips, Arthur - 48
Phillips, Arthur Blaisdell - 118,148,171,174,183,193,214,
Phillips, Artie J. - 25
Phillips, Ary - 42
Phillips, Avellina - 99
Phillips, "Babe" - 32
Phillips, Barbara Dean - 107
Phillips, Basil - 48
Phillips, Beatrice - 43
Phillips, Beatrice Smith - 50
Phillips, Beaty - 21,22
Phillips, Benony - 6
Phillips, Berdie E. - 41
Phillips, Berta Barbosa - 117
Phillips, Bertha Lee - 117,140
Phillips, Betsy - 30
Phillips, Beulah - 25
Phillips, Beunice - 41
Phillips, Bieman - 49
Philips, Billie - 360
Phillips, Bonnie - 251

Philips, Bonnie Link - 360
Phillips, Bry - 42
Phillips, Burl M. - 25
Phillips, Bynum - 267,268,269, 272,275
Phillips, Byron - 252
Phillips, Canzada - 48
Phillips, Carlton - 41
Phillips, Caroline Honea - 252
Philips, Caroline Owen Sadler - 278,320,329,344
Phillips, Carrie J. - 50
Phillips, Catherine - 2,7,9,11,12,14,15,18,19,26, 37,38,50,55,59,61,64,92,268, 274,275
Phillips, Catherine Bradshaw (Kate) - 110,146,211
Phillips, Catherine C. - 50
Phillips, Catherine M. - 274
Phillips, Catherine Ramsey - 44
Phillips, Catherine Galt - 109
Phillips, Celia Ann D. - 49
Phillips, Charles (Charley - ect) - 29,30,33, 42,43,50,
Philips, Charles Albert Reuben - 344,366
Phillips, Charles Alexander - 107
Phillips, Charles Frank - 25, 33
Phillips, Charles Terry - 107
Phillips, Charles W. - 31
Phillips, Charlotta - 39,41, 42,51
Phillips, Charlotte - 41,48
Phillips, Charlotte Jeter -
Phillips, Charlotte Stubblefield - 49
Phillips, Christenberry - 93, 252,268,270-272
Phillips, Christine - 47
Phillips, Cicero - 254
Phillips, Cinthia - 32
Phillips, Clara - 51
Phillips, Clarence B. - 50,51
Philips, Clarinda - 294,304, 318,338,343,344
Phillips, Clarissa Evans - 267,273,275,276
Phillips, Claud - 43

Philips, Claud - 360
Phillips, Claudelle - 48
Phillips, Clayton J. - 41
Phillips, Clem - 43
Phillips, Cleo - 51
Phillips, Clerinda - 47
Phillips, Clinton - 43
Phillips, Clifton - 49
Phillips, Coates L. - 51
Phillips, Cora M. - 25,33
Philips, Corinne - 214
Phillips, Cornelia - 5
Phillips, Corrie - 49
Phillips Cynthia Heidi (Cindy) - 211,244
Phillips, Cynthia Louisa Jane - 25
Phillips, Danie - 43
Phillips, David - 29,42,152
Phillips, David Allen - 361
Phillips, David Crockett - 98
Phillips, David Gardiner - 289
Phillips, David Michael - 36
Phillips, Deborah Ann - 109
Phillips, Delia - 30
Phillips, Della - 44
Phillips, Delphia Lee - 50
Phillips, Desta Louanna - 24
Phillips, Dick - 104
Phillips, Donald Ray - 43
Phillips, Donald Richard - 109
Phillips, Dora - 42,49
Phillips, Doris Kay - 51
Phillips, Dorothy - 2,6, 104, 105
Phillips, Dorothy Ann - 105
Phillips, Dover - 41
Phillips, Dovey - 25
Phillips, Dr. Doyle Vivian - 104,105
Phillips, Drucie - 41
Phillips, Drury - 23,30
Philips, Duney - 351
Phillips, Edward - 47,49,274,
Phillips, Edward B. - 274
Phillips, Edward S. - 25
Phillips, Edwin - 51
Phillips, Edith - 51
Phillips, Edith Evelyn - 275
Phillips, Effie C. - 49
Phillips, Eleanor - 15
Phillips, Eli - 252

Phillips, Eli A. - 62,64,65, 93,94,109,309
Phillips, Eli E. - 252
Phillips, Elijah - 41,55
Phillips, Eliner - 7,8
Philips, Elisha - 295,297, 315-318,320,323,326,329,331, 332,336,338-345,364
Phillips, Elisha - 60,266, 267-270,271,272,275,276,284, 288,297,300,301,332
Philips, Elizabeth(King) - 60,65,254,278,287,292,293,310, 317, 318, 336,338,342-344, 366,368
Phillips, Elizabeth - 2,14,15, 19,20,22-25,31,32,48,50,52,53, 55,56,60,64,98,100,254,260, 262,268,270,277,361,380
Phillips, Elizabaeth Brown Ball - 56
Phillips, Elizabeth Cope - 56
Phillips, Elizabeth Ella - 25
Phillips, Elizabeth (Herron) - 100,
Phillips, Elizabeth Louella - 98
Phillips, Ella - 44
Phillips, Elmer - see Lucius Elmer
Phillips, Elmer Jackson - 24
Phillips, Elore Catherine - 10
Phillips, Eloise - 43
Phillips, Elsie Gertrud - 33
Phillips, Elvira - 25
Phillips, Ema D. - 274
Phillips, Emily - 268,277
Phillips, Emily C. - 275
Phillips, Emily Waddil - 252
Phillips, Emma - 48,51
Phillips, Essie - 42,49
Phillips, Ethel B. - 51
Phillips, Ethel Belle - 118
Phillips, Etta - 43
Phillips, Eunice Jane - 118, 120,146,191
Phillips, Eva Lucille - 98
Philips, Eva York - 349
Phillips, Evan - 39,40,42,43,
Phillips, Evva Leona - 276
Philips, Ewell Petty - 298, 316,318,331,332,335,344,366,

Phillips, Ezekiel - 43
Phillips, Fanny A. - 50
Phillips, Faraby - 40,
Phillips, Faraby Adeline - 42
Phillips, Faye - 43
Phillips, Feriba - 22,23,28
Phillips, Fleeta - 49
Phillips, Fleta - 41
Philips, Florence - 360
Phillips, Forrest - 26,34
Phillips, Frances J. - 49
Phillips, Francis - 20,28,
Phillips, "Frank" - 28,33, 34
Phillips, Franklin - 251
Phillips, Fred D. - 41
Phillips, Frieba - 28
Phillips, Furman - 48
Phillips, Gena - 49
Phillips, Gene - 193
Phillips, George - 43,113,244,
Philips, Dr. George D. - 315
Phillips, George J. - 49
Phillips, George Paul - 45
Phillips, George Richard - 104,113
Phillips, George W. - 31,44
Phillips, Gladys Ellen - 107
Phillips, Glenn Edward - 43
Philips,Grace - 360
Phillips, Grace - 14,51,348
Phillips, Green Berry - 24
Phillips, Gregory Dean - 36
Phillips, Greta - 41
Phillips, Grover - 47
Phillips, Gus - 41
Phillips, Gussie - 50
Phillips, H. H. -
Phillips, Hallie - 49
Phillips, Hannah - 42,55,64, 266-268,272
Phillips, Hannah Bailey - 58, 68,93,310,343,344,371
Phillips, Hannah Elizabeth - 23
Phillips, Hannah Malois - 49
Phillips, Harbin Portman - 45
Phillips, Harlie W. - 49
Phillips, Harmon - 49
Phillips, Harold N. - 49
Philips, Harry - 346,349,360
Phillips, Harve E. - 25
Phillips, Hattie - 49

Phillips, Helen - 274
Philips, Helen Grover - 360
Phillips, Henry - 19,20,26,39-43,49,98
Phillips, Henry Bryant - 33
Phillips, Henry Dean - 98
Phillips, Henry Gaston -103 103,104,113-116 (H.G.)
Phillips, Henry P. - 41
Phillips, Hettie - 49
Philips, Hiram B. - 61,93, 309,319,378-379
Phillips, Horace - 51
Phillips, Hoyle - 252
Phillips, Icie - 51
Phillips, Ida - 41,48,274,344
Philips, Ida Helvenston - 361
Phillips, Ida L. - 48
Phillips, Ida M. - 51
Phillips, Ida Mae - 98
Phillips, Ila - 49
Phillips, Ira - 43
Phillips, Ira Lorenzo - 254
Phillips, Irene - 268
Phillips, Irenia - 267,272
Phillips, Isaac - 41
Phillips, Iva - 362
Phillips, J. M. - 98
Phillips, J. V. - 51
Phillips, Jacob - 55,56,57, 64,
Phillips, Jake - 51
Phillips, James - 20,29,42, 277
Philips, James Albert - 361
Phillips, James Allen - 25
Phillips, James B. - 50
James C. - 50
Phillips, James Crate -51
Phillips, James Donald - 118, 146,163,183,191,193,209,226, 234
Phillips, James Ervin - 25
Phillips, James J. - 50
Phillips, James O. - 62,93,<u>96-109</u>
Phillips, James Richard - 146-148,151,154,157,161,165,167, 172-174,179,180,182-190,196, 197,205,206,209,211,213-220, 222-228,230,232,233,243,244,
Phillips, James Virgil - 47

Phillips, James W. - 20
Phillips, James Wayne - 33
Phillips, Jane - 48
Phillips, Jane Callie Brilla - 245
Phillips, Jeffrey Andrew - 109
Phillips, Jennie - 48
Phillips, Jesse - 17,18,21,<u>52-53</u>,54-56,58,60,64
Phillips, Jesse A. - 47
Phillips, Jessie - 41
Phillips, JoAnn - 106
Phillips, Joel - 48,49
Phillips, John - 2,6,7,11,12,14,15,22,29,56,58,60,104,274,380
Phillips, John B. - 42
Phillips, John David - 33
Phillips, John E. - 44
Phillips, John Edgar - 164,166,207,209,211,213,215,217-227,230,232,234-244
Phillips, John Edward - 117,118,171
Phillips, John Franklin - 44
Philips, John Garrett - 361
Phillips, John Gus - 51
Phillips, John Henry - 120,252
Phillips, John L. - 47
Phillips, John M. - 20,41,274,
Phillips, John Newton -
Philips, John Norman - 360
Phillips, John P. - 43
Phillips, John Richard - <u>119-167</u>,186,193,196,209,212,213,
Philips, John S. - 346
Phillips, John Sloan - 50
Philips, John Steven - 360
Philips, John Walter - 50
Phillips, John Wesley - 146, <u>168-244</u>
Phillips, John William - 98
Phillips, Jonas - 17,18,<u>39-51</u>,
Phillips, Jonas Jr. - 39,41,48,
Phillips, Jonas B. - 49
Phillips, Jonas E. - 50
Phillips, Jonas J. - 49
Phillips, Jonathan L. - 48
Phillips, Jones N. - 41
Phillips, Jordan - 118

Phillips, Joseph - 48
Phillips, Josie - 24
Phillips, Judge -103
Phillips, Judith - 54,55,64
Philips, Julia Ann - 360
Phillips, Julia Ann - 20
Phillips, Juliette Johnson - 252
Philips, Julian - 342,344,346,366
Philips, Julian Harry - 349
Philips, Juliann E. - 304,366
Philips, Julia Smith - 318,326,329,344
Phillips, Julius - 50
Phillips, June - 118
Philips, Kala Sue - 360
Phillips, Karen - 43
Phillips, Katie Belle - 117,118,192
Phillips, Katherine Herron -
Phillips, Kathryn - 105
Philips, Lafayette - 317,343,344
Phillips, Lala Genova - 47
Phillips, Lassie - 47
Phillips, Laura - 268,269,277,333
Phillips, Lawrence - 41
Phillips, Leander J. - 45
Phillips, Leasy - 43
Phillips, Ledbetter - 49
Phillips, Lela - 49,106
Phillips, Lester - 252
Phillips, Levi - 10,17,18,19,20,21,30,<u>37-38</u>,52,54,
Phillips, Lewis - 48,49
Phillips, Lex Vance - 51
Phillips, Lijah - 49
Phillips, Lila - 43
Phillips, Lillie - 41,45
Phillips, Lillie Maud - 25
Phillips, Lilly - 43
Phillips, Linda - 118
Phillips, Linda Francis - 34,36
Phillips, Linda Kaye Porter - 205,206,209,211,213,215-218,227,244
Phillips, Logan - 42,43
Phillips, Lorenzo - 94

Phillips, Louis Edwin - 105
Phillips, Louisa - 20,25
Phillips, Louisa Harris - 24
Phillips, Louisa Herron - 99
Phillips, Louise - 41
Phillips, Louise E. - 105
Phillips, Louise Mussman - 118,183
Phillips, Lucinda - 42,267, 268,276
Phillips, Lucinda Smith - 94
Phillips, Lucius Elmer - 115, 117,122
Phillips, Lucius Elmer Jr. - 117,118
Phillips, Lucy - 43
Phillips, Lucy Ann Howard - 100
Phillips, Lula - 50
Phillips, Lula Belle - 45
Phillips, Lula Mae - 49
Phillips, Luther - 41
Phillips, Maggie Yarbrough - 25
Phillips, Mahala - 40,41,42, 48,
Phillips, Mahala B. - 51
Philips, Malcolm Howard - 349, 351
Phillips, Malissa - 45,99
Phillips, Malissa C. - 41
Phillips, Manerva Elveda - 24
Phillips, Manerva J. - 57
Phillips, Margaret - 23,40,45, 48,
Phillips, Margaret Dykes - 56
Phillips, Margaret Louvenia - 47
Phillips, Marie - 251
Phillips, Marjorie - 107
Phillips, Marshal - 50
Phillips, Martha - 20,23,30, 254
Phillips, Martha A. - 41
Phillips, Martha Eliza - 25
Phillips, Martha Elizabeth - 24
Phillips, Martha Ellen - 23
Phillips, Martha J. - 44
Philips, Martha Jane - 360
Phillips, Martha Lucy - 106
Phillips, Martha Lula - 50

Phillips, Martha Mize - 47
Phillips, Martha S. - 42
Phillips, Martha W. - 57
Phillips, Martha Yates - 25
Phillips, Martin - 42,49
Phillips, Mary - 5,7,43,45,56,
Phillips, Mary A. - 42,274
Phillips, Mary Ann - 41,50, 267,268,276
Phillips, Mary Ann (Allie) - 60,371
Philips, Mary Ann Elizabeth (Mollie) - 344
Phillips, Mary Anne - 275
Phillips, Mary C. - 40,44
Phillips, Mary Esther - 120, 125,146
Phillips, Mary Francis - 23
Phillips, Mary Katherine - 105
Phillips, Mary M. - 50
Phillips, Mary Marie - 105
Phillips, Mary Overton - 2
Phillips, Mary Susannah - 20
Phillips, Matilda - 254
Phillips, "Matt" - 32
Phillips, Matty - 51
Phillips, Maude C. - 47
Phillips, Maurice Sheppard - 252
Phillips, Max Lee - 112,118, 122,123
Phillips, Maxine - 31
Phillips, May - 41,251
Phillips, McKane - 25,32
Phillips, Melissa - 43
Philips, Michael - 360
Phillips, Micheal - 55
Phillips, Mildred - 344,366
Phillips, Miles - 49
Phillips, Miles Leroy - 48
Phillips, Milton - 47
Phillips, Minerva - 32
(see Manerva p.24)
Phillips, Minnie - 24,42,43,
Phillips, Minnie Bell - 100
Phillips, Monroe - 99,100
Phillips, Moses - 21,
Phillips, Moses J. - 50
Phillips, Myra - 41
Philips, Myrtle Grainger - 366
Phillips, Nancy - 23,41,44,

Phillips, Nancy A. M. - 48
Phillips, Nancy Addie - 47
Phillips, Nancy Alice - 47
Phillips, Nancy Ann Manerva - 41
Phillips, Nancy Ann Spencer - 57
Phillips, Nancy Burtz - 109, 110
Phillips, Nancy Butts - 50
Phillips, Nancy H. - 50
Phillips, Nathan - 37,48
Phillips, Nathaniel - 39,40, 41,42,48,55,64
Phillips, Nathaniel Joshua - 216,244
Phillips, Nathaniel W. - 48
Phillips, Nell - 50
Phillips, Nellie - 40
Phillips, Nellie F. - 44
Phillips, Nellie M. - 48
Phillips, Newton - 49
Phillips, Noah J. - 55
Phillips, Nora - 51
Phillips, Norman - 49,245,
Phillips, Norman Sylvester - 98
Phillips, Oda Stella - 25
Phillips, Ollie - 41
Phillips, Olive - 49
Phillips, Omer Green - 33
Phillips, Opal - 104
Phillips, Parks Pharr - 252
Phillips, Patton A. - 48
Phillips, Patton K. - 41
Phillips, Patty - 118
Phillips, Pearl - 42,49
Phillips, Peggy - 42
Phillips, Perry L. - 47
Phillips, Pete - 51
Phillips, Peter - 39,42,45
Phillips, Phebe - 48
Phillips, Philetus Benson - 275
Phillips, Polly - 54
Phillips, Priscilla - 98
Phillips, Prudence E. - 50
Phillips, Prudence Elizabeth - 51
Phillips, R. A. - 40,42
Phillips, R. J. - 50
Phillips, Rachel - 14,42,50,

Phillips, Rachel A. - 50
Phillips, Rachel C. - 48
Phillips, Rachel Canada - 41
Phillips, Rachel Whisenant -
Phillips, Ralph - 51
Phillips, Rance - 41
Philips, Randy Wayne - 360
Phillips, Ray Ezekiel - 43
Phillips, Raymond - 43
Phillips, Raymond Andrew - 108
Phillips, Raymond Ayers - 108
Phillips, Reecie - 49
Phillips, Rubin(Reuben) - 1,6, 7,9-15,17-19,21,22,23, 25,26,28, 29-32,37- 39,43,52,54,59,214
Phillips, Reuben Jr. - 54,64
Philips, Rev. Reuben - 60-62, 65,93,266,267,269,273,<u>278 - 337</u>, 343,344,364,379
Phillips, Ruben Edward - 57
Phillips, Reuben Frank - 93, 94,109,111
Phillips, Reuben J. - 43
Phillips,Reuben L. - 23
Phillips, Reuben Matthew - 25,32
Phillips, Reuben W. - 48
Phillips, Richard Alexander - 100,104
Phillips, Richard Forrest - 105
Phillips, Rity - 50
Phillips, Robert - 274
Phillips, Robert Asbury - 42
Phillips, Roberta Safarik - 168,192,194,196,197,207,208, 209,224,229
Phillips, Rosa Belle - 24
Phillips, Rose - 47
Phillips, Roseanna S. - 49
Philips, Ross - 346,360
Phillips, Roy - 41
Philips, Ruby Kirk - 349
Phillips, Rupert - 106
Phillips, Rupert Hicks - 106
Philips, Russell - 344,361, 365,
Philips, Russell Jr. - 366
Philips, Ruth - 366
Phillips, Ruth - 14,25,344
Phillips, Ruth C. - 44

Phillips, Sally B. - 51
Phillips, Samuel - 7,22
Phillips, Sarah A. - 57
Phillips, Sarah - 14,25,42,43,64
Phillips, Sarah C. - 252
Phillips, Sarah Etta - 49
Phillips, Sarah (Gills) - 62, 93,94,109
Phillips, Sarah M. - 50
Phillips, Sarah Nancy - 48
Phillips, Sewell - 255,267, 268,273,327
Philips, Shelton - 269,334, 340,342,344,346,361
Phillips, Simeon - 20
Phillips, Stella - 44
Phillips, Sue Rivers - 98
Phillips, Susan - 25
Phillips, Susan Allie - 105
Phillips, Susanna - 254
Phillips, Susannah A. - 44
Phillips, Susannah Bradshaw - 97
Phillips, Tempy -
Phillips, Theodosia -
Phillips, Theresa Ann - 163, 205,207,211,212,218-220,224, 225,230,231,232,234
Phillips, Thomas - 2,3,4,5,6, 17,18,19-20,21,22,38,43
Phillips, Thomas Jr. - 2,5,6
Phillips, Thomas (III) - 6,7,8, 9,15,
Phillips, Thomas Jefferson - 24,31
Phillips, Thomas R. - 42
Phillips, Tinna E. - 276
Phillips, "Tommy" - 32,33
Phillips, Tymah - 276
Phillips, Verlin Thomas - 33
Phillips, Vianna - 40,42
Phillips, Vida - 274
Philips, Virgil - 310,320, 327,329,330,332,344
Phillips, Virginia - 34,36
Phillips, W. S. - 100
Phillips, Wade P - 51
Phillips, Wallace Stanley - 107
Phillips, Walter E. - 25
Philips, Walter Henry - 345
Philips, Walter Howard - 339, 342,344,345
Phillips, Wayne - 118
Phillips, Wesley - 33
Phillips, Wesley Allen - 33
Phillips, Wesley Pharr - 110-117,120,123,209
Phillips, William - 2,6,26,42, 274
Phillips, William Eugene - 275
Phillips, William F. -
Phillips, William H. - 47,49
Phillips, William Henry - 25, 32
Phillips, William Jonah - 45
Phillips, William Jasper(Jap) - 24
Phillips, William L. - 48
Phillips, William Lafayette - 43
Phillips, William Lee - 23,24
Philliam, William S. - 50
Phillips, William Thomas - 25
Phillips, Willis - 23,31
Phillips, Wymer - 41
Phillips, "Zeke" - 43
Phillips, Zelia - 51
Phillips, Zelia T. - 51
Phinson(Finson,Vincent), George - 52,58,60
Pickens, Andrew - 298
Pierce, Jonathan - 232
Pierce, Mr. - 125
Pierce, Temperance - 19
Pierce, William - 55
Pitts, Andrew Ramsey - 41
Pitts, Beunice - 41
Pitts, Edwin Grant - 41
Pitts, Roxie - 41
Plemmons, A. J. - 256
Plemmons, Jack - 265
Plinxton, Thos. - 52
Poe, Dr. - 319
Poling, LaNelle -
Polk, Thomas - 16
Pool, David - 52
Poole, Kimberly - 219
Pooler, Alice Jo - 107
Pooler, Patricia Ann - 107
Pooler, Theresa Jean - 107
Pooler, Woodrow W. - 107
Porter, Rev. Francis K. - 287,

292,294,296
Porter, Linda Kaye - 205,244
Porter, S. M. -
Posey, Humphrey - 285,286,292, 303,304
Powell, Richard L.(S.) - 309, 311
Powers, Bradley - 66
Prentice, Jack - 352
Presley, Alma Bell - 374
Presley, George Marion - 374
Price, Dolphus Bradley - 101
Price, Randall Scott - 101
Price, Robert Bradley - 101
Prude, Sister - 290
Putnam, W. M. - 95
Qualls, Ada Phillips - 25
Qualls, Effie Mae - 25
Qualls, Eldon - 25
Quarles, David - 39
Quarles(Qualls), Delilah - 24, 30
Quarles, Hubbard - 39
Quarles, Nancy Addie - 47
Quigley, T. H. - 364
Rademacher, Frank - 215
Rader, Betty - 153
Rader, Billy - 211
Rader, Francis - 211,220
Rader, Jewell - 211
Rader, John - 152
Rader, Larry - 165
Rader, Linda - 153
Rader, Lula Mae Campbell - 211,220
Radford, Mr. - 44
Radford, Reta - 44
Ramey, Amanda - 43
Ramey, Ella - 43
Ramey, Frank - 43
Ramey, Henry L. - 43
Ramey, John T. - 43
Ramey, Logan - 43
Ramey, Mary - 42
Ramey, Mr. - 42
Ramey, Nelson - 43
Ramey, Savannah - 43
Ramey, Sibbie - 43
Ramey, Simon - 43
Ramsey, Catherine E. - 44
Rasbury, Sarah - 198
Rasbury, Mrs. Sherry - 198

Ray, John - 195
Reban, Alicia - 228
Redwood, Henry - 377
Reed, Frank - 198
Reese, J. Bergin - 375
Reeves, Elizabeth Ann - 106
Reeves, Martha Nell - 106
Reeves, Mary Kathryn - 106
Reeves, Richard Hiram - 106
Reeves, Robyn Renee - 106
Reeves, Virgie - 106
Reeves, William Felton - 105, 106
Rennoc, Reverend - 289
Reynolds, H. C. - 43
Reynolds, John - 63,72,92
Rhinehart, Harriet - 269,333
Rhodes, Donna M. - 33
Richardson, Jesse - 62,280, 302,304
Richardson, John L. - 315
Rice, William - 375,376
Ridge, John - 292
Ridge, Major - 292
Rinefield, Ethel - 155
Rinehart, Harritt - 269
Roan, Brother - 314
Roberson, William P. - 270
Roberts, Charles Andrew - 275
Roberts, James - 60
Roberts, James Michael - 275
Roberts, Leslie - 275
Roberts, Mattie - 374
Robertson, A. E. - 273
Robertson, Benjamin - 267,273
Robertson, S. S. - 273
Robertson, V. L. - 273
Robertson, W.J. B. - 273
Robeson, Alissa - 267,272,335
Robeson, Andrew - 267,276
Robeson, Benjamin - 267,269, 272,335
Robeson, C. E. - 276
Robeson, C. P. - 276
Robeson, Lucinda - 267276
Robeson, J. R. - 276
Robeson, J. W. - 276
Robeson, Jackson - 276
Robeson, R. K. - 276
Robin, Anne - 260
Robins, Abel - 40
Robins, Eli - 109

Robins, M.P. - 109
Robinson, Andrew - 267
Robinson, Lavisey - 272
Robinson, Mrs. - 179
Robinson, William M. - 270
Robison, Andrew -269,335
Robison, Anna - 335
Robison, Rachel A. - 262,263
Robson, Mary Phillips - 6
Rochester, Mr. - 45
Rogers, Bennie - 106
Rogers, J. W. -30
Ross, A. E. - 253
Ross, Cornelia - 6
Ross, Edwin - 5
Ross, Ethel - 247
Ross, Francis - 17
Ross, Hall - 34,36
Ross, John - 5,292
Ross, Mabel - 5
Rossi, Arthur - 118
Rossi, Ashley Ann - 118
Rossi, Bertha Phillips - 118
Rossi, Nadine - 118
Rowland, Brother - 322,323
Rowley, Erastus - 273
Runge, John - 219
Runge, Pat Claypool - 160,167, 214, 219,225
Rupe, Jesse - 115
Rusk, Doctor - 315
Russell, Annie - 272
Russell, Archibald - 267,270-272
Russell, Archibald G. - 272
Russell, Bertha - 272
Russell, Betty Lee - 275
Russell, Billy Martin - 275
Russell, Clovis Claypool - 156,214,218,225,226,230-233
Russell, Daisy - 272
Russell, Dale - 219
Russell, Dora - 272
Russell, Emily - 272
Russell, Evelyn Jean - 276
Russell, Fred - 272
Russell, Garland - 214,218
Russell, Grover - 272
Russell, Hannah Phillips - 272
Russell, James Frank - 276
Russell, Jesse Milton - 272
Russell, Joseph Faine - 272

Russell, Joseph Hascue - 272
Russell, Robert Phillips - 275
Russell, Susan - 214
Russell, Tina Smathers - 272
Rutherford, Griffith - 16,21
Sadler, Caroline Owen - 278, 320,344
Sadler, Catherine Mims -
Sadler, Thomas W. - 288,323, 327,331
Safarik, Carl - 208
Safarik, Edgar - 155,157,168, 192,197,208,209,232
Safarik, Eleanor - 151,155, 157,168,192,208,209,211,212, 213,232
Safarik, Jack - 198,223,227, 229,231,233,234
Safarik, Louise - 208
Safarik, Margaret(Mrs. Robert) - 208
Safarik, Monica - 208
Safarik, Nancy - 198,208
Safarik, Otto - 198,208
Safarik, Paula Jean - 197
Safarik, Robert(Bob) - 197, 208
Safarik, Roberta - 168,194, 195,196,197
Safarik, Sharon - 223,229, 234,
Sale, Cornelius - 282
Samuels, Vernon H. - 99
Sanders, Ronnie - 149,179,180, 197
Sandersen, Janna - 231
Sanford, Thomas - 39
Sarpaulius, Bill - 229
Sartain, Alan - 192
Savage, Midge - 222,224,226, 228,229,230
Savage, William - 230
Sawyer, Isaac B. - 68,70,75, 77,78,82,84,92
Scalon, Clara - 247
Schmidt, Beverley - 218
Schmidt, Harriett Edith - 105
Schmidt, John - 198
Schumate, Steve - 225,226,
Scott, April - 101
Scott, Cherrie - 100
Scott, Cherry Catherine - 101,

151
Scott, Churchill - 100
Scott, Churchill LaSalle - 102
Scott, Claudia Lucille - 102
Scott, Irvin Devon - 102
Scott, James Frederick - 102
Scott, John - 54
Scott, John Frederick - 102
Scott, Sylvia Madill - 101
Scott, Verna Katherine - 102
Scott, Vernon Mack - 101,102,
Scott, William - 267
Scroggins, M. D. - 117
Seabolt, Lucile - 257
Self, Brother - 322
Shaad, David - 269
Shamlen, William - 54
Sharp, Silas - 256
Shaw, George W. - 118
Shay, Clarence - 191
Sheats, W. N. - 365
Sheffield, Grace - 348
Sheffield, Hilda - 348
Sheffield, James - 348
Sheffield, Mrs - 346
Sheffield, Neal - 348
Sheffield, Thomas - 348
Shelby, Evan - 13
Sherman, General - 261
Shoap, overseer - 93
Shook, Jacob - 286,287
Shook, Mahala - 269,333
Shuster, M.I. - 24
Silas, Brother - 299,314
Siler, Thomas - 288
Simmons, Billie - 219
Simmons, Doctor James - 315, 316
Simmons, Jane - 317
Simpson, Jennie - 120
Simpson, William - 4
Sire, Glenn - 204
Sire, Viola McJunkin - 204
Skinner, E. G. - 263
Skinner, Selma Wells - 262, 263,
Sluder, Francis - 282
Small, Ruthann - 247
Smallwood, E. M. - 202
Smathers, Jesse - 270
Smathers, Tina - 272
Smith, Avis Pauline - 250

Smith, Billie Ruth - 250
Smith, Claud - 25
Smith, Coleman - 250
Smith, Colonel(Captain)(Major) James - 71,296
Smith, Edith - 264
Smith, Eleanor - 50
Smith, Elbert - 322
Smith, Howard - 342
Smith, J. - 109
Smith, James C. - 250
Smith, Reverend James S. -
Smith, Racoon John - 28
Smith, Joseph E. - 97
Smith, Julia - 339,342,344
Smith, Leroy - 50
Smith, Linda Joyce - 251
Smith, Lucinda -
Smith, M. B. - 50
Smith, M.J. - 260,263
Smith, Maurine - 246
Smith, Mary - 26
Smith, Norine - 34,36
Smith, Penn - 323
Smith, Reverend - 132
Smith, Sammy Sue - 250/251
Smith, W.L. - 323
Smouce, John - 14
Snelson, Thomas - 283
Snider, Annie Moore - 45
Snider, Barbara Louise - 46
Snider, Eula - 44
Snider, "Frank" - 44
Snider, Grover - 44
Snider, Hazel - 44
Snider, Henry Edward - 44
Snider, James Leroy - 46
Snider, James "Roy" - 44
Snider, Jane - 45
Snider, Lavina - 44
Snider, Mamie - 44
Snider, Margaret Marie - 45
Snider, Mattie - 44
Snider, Maude - 44
Snider, Novie - 44
Snider, Retta - 44
Snider, Rochelle - 44
Snider, Ronnie - 44
Snider, Rosie Lee - 44
Snider, Roy - 44
Snider, Ruby - 44
Snider, Samuel - 44

Snider, Sarah - 44
Snow, Bernice - 23
Sohart, William - 269
Sorley, Gene - 195
Sorley, Imogene - 195
Sparks, Joseph - 291
Spears, Florence - 245
Spencer, Nancy Ann - 57
Spinhirne, Mrs. Joe - 212
Squires, Daddy - 130
Squires, W.A. - 131
Stamfli, Vic - 126
Stamps family - 35
Stamps, Anna - 33
Stanfill, John - 153
Stanfill, Stella - 153
Stansell, Sarah - 48
Stanton, Linda - 197
Starret, Alexander - 284
Starret, Polly - 284,316
Starret, Ruth - 284,298,304
Steadman, Lillie - 120
Steele, Clarence Herbert - 23
Steffin, Milton - 354
Stem, Captain - 355.356
Stevens, Franklin -
Stevens, Squire - 60,61
Stevenson, Henry - 4
Stevenson, J.B. - 321,327, 337
Stevenson, Thomas - 4
Stewart(Steward), Brother - 322,323,324
Stewart, Matthew - 60
Stillwell, Colonel - 124
Stilwell, Elijah - 59
Stone, Mary Phillips -
Stoner, Janie - 260,263
Stringfield, Thomas - 302
Strom, Phil - 354
Strother, John - 64
Stroud, James - 30
Stubblefield, Charlotte - 49
Stubbs, Mr. - 378
Suits, Bill - 34
Sullivan, Eloise - 198
Suttles, Mary Jane - 25,31
Swain, David Lowrey -
Tabor, Sarah C. -31
Tarrent, Judge - 318
Tassey, Elizabeth Phillips - 25
Tassey, Robert H. - 25

Taylor, Arthur - 2
Taylor, Dorothy Phillips - 6
Taylor, Ewing - 125
Taylor, Jimmy - 194
Taylor, John - 2,3
Taylor John Jr. - 2
Taylor, Keith - 225
Taylor, Lela - 49
Taylor, Mary - 2
Taylor, Robert -2
Taylor, Sandy - 194
Tedder, Charles Richard - 264
Tedder, Claudia - 264
Tedder, Edith - 264
Tedder, Elizabeth - 264
Tedder, Jodie - 264
Tedder, Kenneth Allen - 264
Tedder, Robert Wells - 264
Tedder, Ruth - 264
Tedder, Ruth Ellen - 264
Temple, Edwin - 352
Temple, Nathaniel - 216
Thomas, Billie - 323
Thomas, Brother - 320
Thomas, John - 321
Thomas, Margaret Horton - 321
Thomas, William - 8
Thomason, M. D. - 289
Thompson, Charles J. - 379
Thompson, Cleveland(Tiny) - 351-360
Thompson family - 160
Thompson, John - 321
Thompson, Lydia Ellen - 119
Thompson, Nell - 159
Thompson, William Edgar - 99
Thrift, Grace Pauline - 51
Thrift, William H. - 39
Tidwell, Annis Mills - 247
Tidwell, Burnie - 247
Tidwell, Charles - 247
Tidwell, Doris Kelley - 247
Tiner, Boley - 24
Tipps, Miss - 179
Tregoe, John - 6
Triplett, Letha - 164
Triplett, Randy - 164
Trippe, Judge - 315
Trosper, Nicholas - 19
Truesdale, Bill - 202
Tucker, G.A.R. - 253
Tucker, Lizzie - 24

Tully, Dr. - 205
Turner, Allen - 287
Turner, Gordon - 28
Turner, Merwin - 243
Turner, Reverend - 288
Underwood, Mr and Mrs - 146
Vance, Robert B. - 70,76,82
Van Curen, Faith Helen - 108
Van Note, Barbara Dean - 107
Van Note, Carol Deane - 107
Van Note, Marvin Omer - 107
Van Note, Roger Dale - 107
Van Note, Stephen Phillips - 107
Vaughn, Benjamin - 379
Vaughn, Nancy - 379
Vaun, Betty - 8
Vickers, J. D. - 354
Vincent(Phinson, Finson), George - 52,58,60
Voelkel, Idie - 125
Waddil, Emily - 252
Wadsworth, Diane Rosalie - 34, 36
Wafford, General - 299
Waggoner, Kenneth - 182
Wakeley, Mrs. - 142
Walker, Foy - 125
Walker, Henry - 52
Walker, M. G. - 116
Walker, Professor - 324
Wall, Rebecca - 8
Wallace family - 145
Ward, Benjamin - 20
Ward, Nicea - 20
Ward, Rachel - 20
Ware, John E. - 327
Ware, Matt - 162,234
Washington, George - 60
Washington, W. H. - 341
Waskow, Henry T. - 353
Waterhouse, Catherine - 274
Waterhouse, Euclid - 274
Watkins, Dr. - 186,319
Watkins, Jackie Lloyd - 186
Watson, Jane - 276
Wauer, Roland - 193
Wear, Thomas - 287
Weaver, Jacob - 298
Webb, Hazel - 44
Webb, Larry - 231
Webb, Mr. - 44

Webb, Ruby - 44
Weeks, Barry Len - 250
Weeks, Callie Mae - 250
Weeks, Jesse Glen - 250
Weeks, Timothy - 250
Welch, Mrs - 286
Wells, Andrew Decater - 259,261, 262,263
Wells, Bessie A. - 259-263
Wells, Carrie Shields - 259,260,262,264
Wells, Decater - 260,261,265
Wells, Elisha K. - 259,260, 262
Wells, Elizabeth Miller - 259,260
Wells, Elizabeth Phillips - 254,260
Wells, Francis Marion - 259, 260-262
Wells, George Franklin - 259, 260,261,262,263
Wells, H. F. - 260
Wells, Hannah - 254
Wells, Harriett J. - 259,260,
Wells, Henry S. - 260
Wells, Henry - 71,81
Wells, Hiram Jefferson - 259,260,263
Wells, Hiram Phillip - 265
Wells, Jefferson - 261,262
Wells, John Vaney - 260,265
Wells, John Phillips - 259-263
Wells, Joseph R. - 259,263
Wells, Laura Alice - 259-263
Wells, Lucretia - 254
Wells, Maria Elizabeth - 258
Wells, Mary - 261,262
Wells, Mary Ann - 254,255, 260
Wells, Mary J. - 259
Wells, Raymond - 263
Wells, Robert H. - 259-263
Wells, Rufus - 260,265
Wells, Selma - 259,262,263
Wells, Tilitha Cami - 260,265
Wells, W. Henry - 259,260, 263,
West, Jeremiah - 282
Westall, Thomas - 65
Wetson, Brother - 323
White, Carl - 246
White, Jane - 303,304

White, Mickey Ann - 246
White, Moses - 285
White, Penelope -
White, Stephen - 288,303,304
Whitfield, George - 7
Whitlock, Edward Lee - 47
Whitlock, James - 47
Whitlock, Rachel Esterline - 47
Wicks, Loren D. - 186
Wilbanks, Jabe - 50
Wilbanks, Tabitha - 48
Wilcox, Elvira Phillips - 25
Wilcox, George W. - 25
Wilcox, Susan - 25
Wilder, Louise Phillips - 47
Wilder, Robert - 47
Wilder, Tony - 47
Willard, Vernon - 215
Williams, Abel - 39,42
Williams, Albert - 44
Williams, Allen - 40
Williams, Amanda - 44
Williams, Annie - 100
Williams, Charlie - 229
Williams, Charley M. - 44
Williams, Charlotta - 40
Williams, Clarissa - 41
Williams, Elisha Berryman - 40
Williams, Elizabeth Nancy - 40
Williams, Ephraim - 44
Williams, Fanny - 40
Williams, Feriba - 39,40
Williams, Henry James - 40
Williams, John - 40
Williams, Julius H. - 44
Williams, Margaret - 44
Williams, Martha - 40
Williams, Martha D. - 44
Williams, Mary - 40,
Williams, Mary G. - 40
Williams, Mary S. - 44
Williams, Melissa Jane - 40
Williams, Samantha - 40
Williams, Sarah - 40,48,56,
Williams, Sarah E. - 45
Williams, Surreptha - 40
Williams, Warren - 44
Williams, William - 40
Williamson, Ann Loyd - 249
Willis, Wendell - 148,179,180
Wilson, Betty Jo - 247

Wilson, David - 58
Wilson, Donald - 247
Wilson, Jimmy - 247
Wilson, Larry - 247
Wilson, Michael - 247
Wilson, Randy - 247
Wilson, Ricky - 247
Winchester, Evangeline - 47
Winchester, Geneva - 47
Winchester, Joseph - 47
Winchester, Joseph Daniel - 47
Winchester Lawrence - 47
Winchester, Leona - 47
Winchester, Louise - 47
Winchester, Margaret L. - 47
Winchester, Marvin - 47
Winchester, Stella - 47
Winchester, Vinela - 47
Winkler, Edith - 125
Wise, Annie R. - 260,263
Wiser, Avis Brilla - 250
Wiser, Charles D. - 251
Wiser, Connie D. - 250
Wiser, Connie McKee - 251
Wiser, Forrest Young - 251
Wiser, Francis McKee - 251
Wiser, John - 251
Wiser, Nolan Douglas - 251
Wiser, Velma Scottie - 251
Withrow, Richard - 29
Witt, Daniel - 287
Wood, James - 31
Wood, Randy - 34
Woodard, Brother - 323
Woodruff, Sarah - 56
Woods, Mr. - 44
Wynn, Doris - 125
Yarbrough, Clementine - 25
Yarbrough, Elisha - 24
Yarbrough, Maggie - 25
Yates, Fonzo - 34
Yates, Martha Eliza - 25,32
Yingst, Lincoln Hallie - 23
Yingst, Scott - 23
Younger, Ashley Dawn - 244
Younger, Jeffrey Lowell - 224, 226-228,230-234,244
Younger, Theresa Phillips - 233,234,244
Zeman, Danielle Jean - 105
Zeman, John - 105
Zeman, Susan A. - 105

Zenith, John - 34
Zwonecek, Faye - 204
Zwonecek, John - 204
Zwonecek, Mae - 204

www.ingramcontent.com/pod-product-compliance
Ingram Content Group UK Ltd.
Pitfield, Milton Keynes, MK11 3LW, UK
UKHW051301180426
11947UKWH00020B/1838